A Triple

Helen Huntley

Volume 2 of my Family Memoirs

Part Sequel to
World War 1 and Workhouse Hill

Perfect
ublishers Ltd

ISBN: 978-0-9928533-8-9

Cover Design by Duncan Bamford
http://www.insightillustration.co.uk

Edited by Jan Andersen
http://www.creativecopywriter.org

PERFECT PUBLISHERS LTD
23 Maitland Avenue
Cambridge
CB4 1TA
England
http://www.perfectpublishers.co.uk

September 2016

Dear Sarah,

Your interest in your paternal family history is so rewarding for me. Thank you.

This book will give you an insight into your Grandad's young life and you'll also discover some of your Great Aunt's secrets. It is all based on facts, including Alan's life.

I do so hope you enjoy the read.

Special love from

Pauline x

alias: Helen Huntley.

Dedication

I dedicate this book to my children, Michael James
Hunt and his wife Christina, my daughter Patricia
Fricker and my granddaughter Hannah Maria
Fricker.

Acknowledgements

ANN AYLIN-WHITE, for sending me the John Bull newspaper cutting, which gave me the PREFACE FOR ANNABELLE information. Ann is the granddaughter of Freddie Cox, authentic name, who lived at 47 Newbury Road, Enham. He was the character Geoffrey Knox in *WORLD WAR 1 and WORKHOUSE HILL* where I used fictitious names. The cutting was found in his belongings on his demise. Mr Cotton, who is mentioned in the cutting, was a lodger in Mr Cox's home in Enham during his Enham life. Also thanks to Ann for providing some of the photographs in this book.

JOHN BULL MAGAZINE, 10th August, 1929. Public Domain.

MONA CLARKE (nee Guest) for much information, which has helped to make this book a more conclusive record.

JULIE CLATWORTHY, posthumously. For everything she did. Always my loyal and helpful friend.

JADE DICKSON, a carer here, for fixing my printer when it misbehaved.

JEAN HARDWICK for keeping my flat clean so I had more time to write.

BARBARA LARGE, MBE, my Adult Education Writing Tutor for always being there for me.

PETER MARCHI, my brother, posthumously. For providing me with information.

GRAEME ROBINS, a carer in the Extra-Care Home where I live, for research conducted in helping me locate the Will Hay sketch.

My great niece, SARAH CHANNELL, for scanning photos for the book.

HOME COOKING DELIVERED, a Family Business owned by Dennis and Allyson Smith, and their staff, for keeping me fed with hot dinners whilst writing.

FRIENDS, FOR THEIR CONSTANT ENTHUSIASM AND ENCOURAGEMENT: Joanna Gosling, Hilary Holt, Stella Joyce, Hilary and Steve Paige, Vic and Gwen Papai, Jeannette Rastrick, Jacques and Nicole Roinac and June Taylor.

DESCENDANTS OF WW1 SETTLERS IN ENHAM ALAMEIN, for helping me with information for Volume 2.

Doug Saunders, Freddie Hall, Hazel Wood, Olive Cronin, Joe Geoghegan, Les Brant, Maureen and Terry Roll, Molly Lowman and Rita Rose, who emigrated to Australia from Enham in 1969. Thanks to the Internet, she has still been able to provide me with information. Those underlined have been my particular man/girl Fridays. (Maiden names used for females).

LAST BUT NOT LEAST, to anyone I may have omitted to mention, I apologise most sincerely here and now.

Contents

Foreword

Two years later than hoped, I have completed Volume 2 of my family memoirs.

I am now 85 years old and wish to thank many people for helping to keep me in a state of health such that I could continue writing. I don't particularly like lists, but I feel on this occasion it is necessary. Those people, or establishments are listed hereunder:

1. Sharon Banks for saving my life with her medical knowledge.
2. Dental Department, Royal South Hants Hospital.
3. Hedge End Medical Centre.
4. Home Cooking Delivered.
5. Laburnum House Carers.
6. Southampton General Hospital; various departments.
7. South East Hants Ambulance Service.

Without all the above help, I doubt my second volume would ever have been completed.

In this Foreword I want to include the ENHAM BABES. That is the name the authorities in Enham Alamein call us oldies, who are the children of the WW1 settlers. I'd like to include the names of those of us that I know are still living at the time of editing. Original birth names are given, with married names in brackets.

Leslie Brant (male)
Clive Broughton

Geoffrey Crabbe
Jacqueline Crabbe (Atkinson)
Olive Cronin (Golton)
Susie Ewers (Foord)
Janet Ewers (Keeble)
Joe Geoghegan
Terry Geoghegan
Mona Guest (Clarke)
Fred Hall
Molly Lowman
James MacCallum
Pauline Marchi (Hunt)
John Moody
Terry Roll
Rita Rose
Doug Saunders
Pat Shears (Barton)
Ann Spratt (Griffiths)
Brenda Tomlin (Mole)
Angela Tomlin (Hannon)
Hazel Wood (Aldridge)

My appreciation goes out to one and all, and if you have read Volume 1, I hope you'll enjoy Volume 2.

Sincerely,
Pauline...alias Helen Huntley

Preface 1 for Annabelle's Story

Of interest only to those who have read my first book.

The Scandal of Enham Village Centre 1929

This book, entitled *A TRIPLE AFFAIR* is Volume 2 of my family memoirs and is a part sequel to my first book, *WORLD WAR 1 & WORKHOUSE HILL*. That story, in the main, is a factual account of my father Alberto's life from being wounded in Flanders in 1917 until he found his utopia in Enham Village Centre in 1928.

This part sequel covers the years 1935 to 1955. However, an occurrence that took place in 1929, between the two books, is very relevant and MUST BE TOLD. I gained this knowledge from a newspaper cutting, passed to me by Ann, the granddaughter of Mr Freddie Cox, one of the WW1 Enham settlers, which was taken from The John Bull magazine, dated 10th August 1929.

For your information, in Enham Village Centre on Tuesday, 29th June 1926, H.R.H. the Prince of Wales opened the new, larger social centre, donated by Mr & Mrs Landale Wilson. (See Chapter 17 of my first book). On that occasion, Sir Henry Cavendish-Bentinck appealed to the British nation by radio broadcast for funds required to keep this magnificent, unique, village centre (Charity No. 211235, which is still in existence today) thriving and enlarging, to train, settle and accommodate many more wounded men. The British people responded generously.

I detail below the John Bull article. PLEASE NOTE: Three asterisks *** within the text denote unreadable areas within the aged folds of the paper cutting.

(QUOTE)

The disabled ex-service men's centre at Enham, near Andover, has recently been the scene of some extra-ordinary incidents, and relations between the men and the management there are strained near to breaking-point

The Enham Village Centre was opened in 1919 for the training of men with a high rate of disability from wounds. All the buildings and Estate were purchased by private subscription and it is administered by The Village Centres Council, of which Lord Plumer is President.

In the years following its foundation hundreds of men were trained in various crafts and passed on to jobs in many industries. Over one hundred men who had reached a high standard of skill became permanent settlers.

Cabinet-making, upholstery and furniture workshops turned out splendid work. Four farms were established, including a home farm of 240 acres, where cattle were raised, which secured numerous prizes at famous shows.

The men were content and working busily.

Then, some two years ago, the Village Centres Council, on which the Enham men are not represented, decided on a change of management at Enham. "Pep" was needed and punch - and business organisation.

The Council at once installed a staff of new managers. These arrived *** control the hundred settlers and other men undergoing training.

The heavy hand of bureaucracy descended on Enham.

SKILLED MEN'S PLIGHT. One by one the various industries disappeared. The farms were let; the home farm went to an outside farmer. The furniture-making industry was transferred to another place. The market gardens were abandoned

Two simple crafts remain - basket-making and knocking nails into rabbit hutches and poultry-houses.

The stream of unalloyed discontent gradually rose. Then a few weeks ago, on the formation of a branch of the British Legion in the Centre, it culminated into a final outbreak.

Finally, a Legion poster advertising a branch meeting was torn down from the workshop notice-board on the manager's instruction.

A branch meeting was held, attended by 75% of the Centre, and the Secretary, Mr C.H. Spicer sent a letter to Mr Tallyn, the manager, asking why the poster had been torn down.

Spicer was summoned to the manager's office and immediately dismissed from his job for "challenging the management's authority."

He was escorted to his room by two clerks, and was watched over while he packed. Then he was taken to the railway station and handed a ticket to his home in Wales.

At Salisbury he was intercepted by a car from the village containing two of his workmates, who asked him to return. *** who had ceased work on hearing of his dismissal.

They asked for Spicer's reinstatement. It was refused. From then on events moved speedily, and for callous tactlessness the subsequent action of the management would be hard to beat.

A lock-out was declared and the next day, whilst a representative from the British Legion Headquarters was conducting negotiations, the management descended on the hostel and turned all the men out into the road with their beds and belongings.

At 6pm, the hostel was locked and the men were left to fend for themselves.

Some were without legs or arms, and were carried into the streets by their comrades. Others were neurasthenics, and the homes of most of them lay in remote parts of the country. The nearest railway station was three miles away.

Through the hospitality of the Enham cottagers, they were taken into various homes and kept for the night and some ensuing days. Had this not been done it is impossible to tell what grave hardships might have been undergone or the disastrous consequences of this mad action.

About the subsequent events the least said the better, but ultimately the men apologised for ceasing work and were taken back. Though their own supervisors had treated them as strikers, an independent Ministry of Labour committee at Southampton decided, after hearing the case, that they were not strikers, and issued unemployment pay during the interval they were out of work.

In the case of four men – Spicer, Woolgar, Cotton and Moore, all officials of the British Legion branch – the management were immovable, and they were finally dismissed on the grounds that they were "temperamentally unfit for village life."

MONSTER PETITION. A petition voluntarily signed by practically the entire community and addressed to The Village Centres Council protesting against the injustices inflicted on them by the management met with no reply.

A visit was paid by the Chairman, Lord Henry Cavendish-Bentinck, and the men were asked to let bygones be bygones, but after he left the dismissal of the four men was confirmed.

One of them has been there ten years and has a cottage and a family, another seven years and another six.

Thus what was once a contented community, living close to the ideals of its founders, is now a hive of discontent and seething disquiet.

In the interest of the public, who have given vast sums of money that the rest of these men's broken lives should be serene and useful, we suggest that Lord Henry Cavendish-Bentinck should take immediate steps to remove the existing grievances.

(UNQUOTE)

After being made aware of the above article, Lord Henry Cavendish-Bentinck lost no time in arranging for new management to be put in place and soon returned Enham Village Centre to its former glory as a domain of peace, tranquillity and contentment for its war torn settlers, including the four who had been considered temperamentally unfit for village life.

Thus, Volume 2 of my Family Memoirs can continue in the same Utopian environment in which Volume I ended.

Preface 2 for Andre's Story

"When are you going to get off your butt and look after this miserable kid properly?"

"If I hear him say those words once more, I swear I'll kill him," Amy groaned to herself about her husband.

"My poor little Cockney boy," she whispered lovingly as she stroked the baby's tiny cheek while he was lying helpless in her arms. Finding a smile for the baby, she said, "This is all your fault you know," nodding her head. "It took much more out of me pushing you out than it did producing your sister."

The baby was not amused and started to whimper. Afraid to let him cry again for fear of her husband's temper, she put the baby to her breast once more in an attempt to settle him down. This time, thankfully, it worked.

With babe safely tucked in his crib, Amy made her way to the scullery at the back of the house to deal with the bucket of nappies that had been soaking during the night.

"I must get these clean now, in case I feel worse tomorrow," she said to herself.

Amy was having such a struggle to get over the birth. Baby was two weeks old, but Amy had no life in her; just miserable and tearful all the time. Perhaps the District Nurse would be able to help her the following day when she visited. Her sister Rosie would call in soon and get some shopping for her. Amy would ask her to bring in some beef, so she could make some beef tea; that's a good pick-me-up. She would ask her to fetch some eggs too, because she had to be able to nourish her baby.

With a concerted effort Amy found the strength to make a macaroni cheese for dinner, to keep them fed.

Chapter 1

Annabelle Alessandro
Daughter of Alberto and Alice Alessandro

THE GUARDIAN ANGEL (TGA) SETS THE SCENE: *(She is screaming on the back doorstep. I want to comfort this fretful child, but physically that is impossible. Thankfully, Auntie Dottie, the next-door neighbour, is running to help.)*

"Is it your mummy, little missie?"

The little one nods her head and wipes tears away with scrunched up hands as the two of them disappear inside the door.

"Cooeee! Are you all right Alice?"

"Yes, I am now, thank you Dottie. I dropped my knitting needle under the chair and before I could find it Annabelle ran to the door, as usual, screaming 'blue, blue'."

Looking down at the little one, Dottie said quietly, "No need to cry any more, little one. We'll wipe those tears away and Auntie Dolly will lift you onto Mummy's lap."

Cuddling her up closely and kissing her cheek as she lifted her, Auntie Dolly said, "Ooh, you're a lovely little bundle. That's better. You're safe with Mummy now and that's a nice little smile for us, too, bless you. You know Alice, you've got to stop this bending over business. It upsets this little mite every time. Why didn't you ask her to pick the needle up for you?"

1

Rubbing her brow, she replied, "I don't know Dottie. It's not as easy as you think. Bending over to pick something up is such a natural thing to do and I always forget. Trouble is, the old ticker never does; the damaged valves just can't send the blood back up. I know I've got to try harder to stop myself from doing it. It's not good for either of the children. The lack of oxygen soon shows in my face and I know only too well that it's serious."

"Look, my dear, try to remember that it's no trouble at all for me to help out. I'm nearly always indoors and if I'm going out I'll tell you. I'm sure Annabelle will be happy to run round any time. My Phil often has a laugh because Annabelle calls me Auntie Dolly, instead of Dottie, as though I'm one of her toys."

"I know, Dottie. It's lovely the way she calls you that. It seems to us, too, as though she thinks you're her playmate. She'll be wanting to put you in her dollies' pram next!"

Dottie gave her ready laugh, as she replied, "Well I'd have to shrink a bit to fit into that, that's for sure. Now tell me, what about the knitting needle; did you find it?"

"No, I didn't."

"Well, what a waste of time. Come on Annabelle, you can find Mummy's knitting needle for her, can't you?"

Annabelle was under the chair like a shot. She looked a picture in her pink lacy dress that had been crocheted by her mother. Her white blonde hair hung in ringlets, which were tied in bunches either side of her head with ribbon to match her dress and her rosy cheeks glowed as she proudly handed the knitting needle to her mother.

"Would you like to stay for a cup of tea with us Dottie? At least that's something I can do without going blue, thank goodness."

With a nudge, Dottie laughed back. "That's right Alice; just make sure you keep your pecker up and everything will be perfect." They had another laugh together as she continued, "I'd love to have a cup of tea my dear, but I can't stay right now. I've got a couple of bets to put on the gee-gees for Phil."

Annabelle put her little hand into Dottie's.

"Annabelle come too?"

"Not this time my darlin'. Auntie Dolly's busy today. You come to see me another day."

After their cup of tea, Alice looked out of the scullery window to see if the cows were in the farmer's field. They were there, so Alice, who was nervous of cows, knew she could safely take Annabelle to pick some wild flowers from the meadow.

As they walked home, they heard the factory hooter telling them that it was 5pm and the factory was closing for the day. Annabelle rushed ahead along the pavement and into their garden gate, because the men would all be trudging down the road. Immediately, she was standing on the bottom rung of the white picket fence at the bottom of the lawn, waiting for her daddy. As usual, Mr Baker was the first one down the road and he always stopped and said the same thing, "Hello my little peaches and cream," as he touched her lovely silky ringlets before continuing his way.

As soon as she saw her daddy approaching, Annabelle waved frantically until he waved back. Alberto ignored the garden gate and continued on a few paces until he was stood on the pavement opposite Annabelle. She then gave him a big cheeky grin as she eagerly started to tap out a rhythm on the spikes of the fence. Using both hands, she tapped out the rhythm he had previously taught her: Bang tiddy-bang-bang, bang, bang.

"Your turn, Daddy,"

On the pavement, Alberto Aless (everybody in the village shortened the family surname) tapped the same rhythm with his feet.

"Come out on the pavement with me, Annabelle. It's your turn to tap your feet now."

For about fifteen minutes, they were having a good time together, with feet tapping various rhythms, but that had to come to an end when Alice opened the window and called them in for tea. Annabelle looked a picture of happiness as her daddy bent down so she could put her arms round his neck and be carried indoors.

TGA: *(Following Annabelle's stressful time earlier in the afternoon when her mummy's face went blue, it is cheering for me to see her looking so happy at this end of the day.)*

Alberto carried his daughter up the two white-washed doorsteps with the long flight of stairs facing them. They turned immediately left and Annabelle tried to kiss her daddy's reflection in the mirror that hung on the left wall, just inside the door.

4

"Keep your head still, Daddy. I'm trying to kiss you," she implored, with infectious giggles.

They were in the living room. It was a bright room with the front window on the left, next to the mirror. Beneath the window was a large seat that fitted just below the window ledge. The seat, which was covered in gold fabric, was Alberto's substantial-sized tool box, which had been awarded to him by the Ministry of Pensions after he had completed a Carpentry Training Course in Roehampton Hospital, following the loss of his arm in the Great War. An exact replica of the window was at the opposite end of the room, overlooking the back garden. Both windows were draped with golden curtains in the same fabric as the window seat.

Heading for the sink at the far end of the scullery to wash their hands, they passed the laid-up tea table on their right and turned right through the door at the back end of the room into the scullery.

Hand washing was interrupted by Al C, who had dashed in through the back door.

"What's for tea Mum? I'm hungry."

"There's no tea at all for you young man, until you scrub both those hands and knees."

Al C pulled a face, but did as he was told. Very soon he was scrubbed up and sitting at the back of the table, with Annabelle on his right, swinging his own legs and trying to kick Annabelle's. As his sister was getting a bit older, he was becoming a big tease. Alberto was next to sit at the table, opposite Al C, with his false arm removed and his shirt sleeves rolled up. Alice put boiled eggs and egg cups on the table with bread and butter soldiers. Soon the children were banging their eggs with teaspoons to remove the top shell, before dipping in 'soldiers' and tucking in hungrily.

Alice, who was last to sit down opposite Annabelle, helped Alberto with his egg, because he was finding the job difficult with only one hand. Alice and Alberto's backs were to the cooking range, which was unlit as the weather was quite warm.

"What did you do at school today, Al C?"

"Scripture," he replied, pulling a face. "I hate that, Dad. Every bloomin' morning, it's the same. It's okay when they tell us parable stories, but when we have to pray they **don't** pray for things we **need**."

"So what sort of things do you need?"

"Well, to start with, we could do with some swings in the playground, and more than that, we really do need some new lavvies. The one's we've got are disgusting." He pulled as ugly a face as his neat features would allow.

Alice and Alberto laughed and told him he should pay attention to his scripture lessons, because he had a lot to learn.

Al C was just six years old. Before he started school, he was known as Alberto Jr. After starting school, things changed. He came rushing in from school one day, telling his parents he was learning the alphabet, and pleaded urgently with them to call him Al C.

"Why do you want us to call you that?" asked Alice.

"Well, the men all call dad Al B, (Alby) so I want to be Al C. It is the next letter in the alphabet."

From that day on, he became known as Al C.

"And what about you, Annabelle; what have you been up to today?"

Annabelle, who was four years old, told her daddy, "I picked those flowers for you in the meadow, daddy. And I picked up Mummy's knitting needle."

"So," looking at his wife, "am I right in thinking that you didn't bend over to pick the needle up, Alice?"

"Alberto, I wish I could say I didn't, but I did. I forgot. I bent down for it and Annabelle was frightened. She screamed at the door and Dottie dashed round."

"Alice, my lovely Alice, what are we going to do with you?"

"When we're naughty, we get our bums smacked," said Al C, widening his eyes hopefully.

"That's a very good idea, Al C. Did you hear that, Alice? One more time and that's what we'll all do," Alberto grinned.

Annabelle started clapping her hands, joining in the fun, as Alice told them, "I'm definitely not going to give any of you that pleasure. I shall try to be very strong with myself."

After tea, Al C asked if he could call for Kenny Woods, his friend next-door but one. Alice told him he could go out to play for a little while, but to be sure to come home when it was starting to get dark. She then started clearing the tea table while Alberto took Annabelle out into the back garden.

Annabelle loved working out there with him, because he often sang songs as he worked. She had her own set of little gardening tools and was busily digging the earth beside him.

Alice seized the opportunity to do a bit of ironing before calling Annabelle in for bed. At that, Annabelle was unhappy.

"I'm helping Daddy," she cried.

"I know all about that, little one," she replied, as she gave Annabelle a sea-side bucket and brush to clean her gardening tools. "You can help Daddy again tomorrow. It's time now for you to get to bed so you can be fresh to help me make some little cakes in the morning."

"Ooh, can I push some chocolate buttons in and see them melt?"

"Of course you can, sweetheart. Say bye-bye to Daddy now. He'll tuck you up later."

When she was in her nightdress ready for bed, Annabelle called out to her daddy in the garden from the landing window. "I'm ready for you to tuck me in, Daddy."

Alberto came in to the scullery, took off his garden shoes, rinsed his hand under the tap and went upstairs.

"Say night-night to Mummy now, Annabelle."

No sooner had the words been spoken than she was standing on the bed giving her mummy a big hug and lots of kisses on each cheek. Poignantly, she then clung to her mother and whispered, "I wish you could tuck me in sometimes, Mummy."

"I know, sweetheart, and so do I, but you know what happens when I bend over. I'll leave you with Daddy now and not too much giggling mind."

Annabelle, looking angelic in her pretty pink nightie, stayed on the bed, jumping up and down, hoping to play with her father.

"Come along, young lady. That's enough; time to settle down. Pull the covers back and then we'll have a little dance to calm you down."

Soon she was clinging round her daddy's neck as he started softly singing:

"Wee Willie Winkie, runs through the town,
Upstairs and downstairs, in his nightgown.
Tapping at the window, crying through the lock,
Are the children in their beds, it's past eight o'clock".

As he gently danced round with her, they peered through the drawn curtain to see if Willie Winkie was tapping at their window. No. He wasn't there. Next Annabelle wanted to peer through the door lock, but he wasn't there either.

"Come on then," said Alberto, "jump into bed before he gets here."

Annabelle lay on her side facing her daddy who proceeded to tuck the blankets in around her body, pushing hard with his hand, first to the front of her and then to the back, which made her giggle.

"There's a cold patch by my neck, Daddy."

"Righty-ho, Moosh. I'll soon fix that."

Another strong push brought more giggles.

"Now there's one by my tummy."

Alberto leaned over and kissed her pink cheek.

"I think my Annabelle is turning into a little monkey."

"No I'm not, Daddy. I'm still me."

"I'll only believe that, you little monkey, if you can hum a tune with me, like my Annabelle does. Are you ready?

Twinkle, twinkle, little star, how I wonder what you are.
Up above the world so high, like a diamond in the sky.
Twinkle, twinkle, little star, how I wonder what you are."

Two renditions later, Annabelle was fast asleep.

Through the summer, Alice and Mrs Shears, a neighbour from further up the road, took turns in looking after each other's daughters so they could play together. Annabelle and Pat were good playmates, but that was brought to an end late in July when Pat had to start school. Although the girls were of similar age, Annabelle's birthday was not until Christmas Eve, way past the August cut-off date for admission to school that year. That meant that she had to wait a whole year before she could start school, by which time she would be getting on for six years old. Annabelle cried her heart out. Not only had she lost her playmate, she was desperate to start school and learn to read and write, just like Al C.

Through the autumn months, Alice did well by her daughter. On rainy days Annabelle would sit on her mummy's lap with her small collection of books and learn to read. She knew that when her daddy came home from work he would want her to read something to him. That way, she made steady progress.

In parallel, Annabelle found another friend. One day a lady knocked the door. She introduced herself as Ella, daughter of Mrs Piggin, who lived in one of the houses up the crescent. She was holding the hand of a little girl, Pam Angel, her niece.

"Hello, Mrs Aless. I hope you don't mind me calling. My sister has come home from London for a few days with her daughter Pam, here. She is very lonely with all us grown-ups, so I'm wondering if she could play with Annabelle for a few hours."

"I think Annabelle would like that very much. Do come in, Ella."

"Hello little Pam. That's a pretty yellow dress you're wearing. Come in and say 'hello' to Annabelle."

The two girls smiled at each other, but both were shy.

"Why don't you show Pam your dollies, Annabelle? She might like to play with them with you."

It didn't take long. The two little girls became besotted with each other and didn't want to part company when Ella came to take Pam home to tea.

"No tears now, from either of you," said Alice. "Pam can come to play again tomorrow. She can stay all day and have dinner with us."

Those words cheered the girls and they gave each other little kisses before Pam skipped off down the garden path with her Auntie Ella.

Over the tea table that night, Annabelle told her daddy she'd got an angel for a friend.

"Don't be so stupid," chipped in Al C. "Angels are up in heaven. They work for God. You'll soon find out when you come to school."

"Now, now, Al C. Let Annabelle tell us how it is that she's got an angel for a friend."

Annabelle told him all the events of the day and said, "It is true, Daddy. It is true, honest. She is an angel. I don't care what Al C says. Her name is Pam Angel. You ask Mummy." She was almost in tears.

"Don't get upset sweetheart. Yes, of course you are right; her name is Pam Angel, but you must forgive Al C, because he was right too."

"Well that's that one sorted nicely. You're both right for a change," smiled Alberto.

Pam came to play every day for three days, before she had to go back to London with her mummy. Whilst together, Pam helped to do jobs for Alice, along with Annabelle, and was quite comfortable calling Alice, 'Auntie'.

Annabelle was a bit lost for a while after Pam had gone home, but soon knuckled down to her full-time domesticity, especially with the days getting more and more wintry. When the coke fire in the range needed re-fuelling, Alice would lift the iron ring top off the fire so Annabelle could get small shovels full of coke from the brass coal scuttle by the hearth and put them onto the fire. Alice would then replace the lid and Annabelle would sweep up any mess with the small shovel and brush from the companion set.

With her daughter's constant help, Alice got better at remembering not to bend over. Annabelle became her right hand, doing all the low level jobs. Together they made a good team. On dry days, they would go to the woods to collect sticks, fir cones and anything burnable for Alberto to light the copper, which was positioned next to the sink. That was his job on Monday mornings before going off to work, so Alice could get hot water to do the washing. Annabelle became adept at opening the furnace door at the bottom of the copper and feeding the fire with all the rubbish. If the fire went out and had to be re-lit, she had to run for Auntie Dolly, because she was frightened to strike the Swan Vesta match. Auntie Dolly was apprehensive about Annabelle dealing with the fire, but Alice reassured her that Annabelle had her wits about her and was quite safe doing the stoking.

When the washing was done, Alice mangled it in the second hand mangle that was kept under the draining board behind a curtain and the surplus water from the clothes fell into the white enamel bucket. She then topped up the bucket with a jug of nice soapy water from the boiler and carried it to one of the two outside drains. At the same time, Annabelle got the Dettol and the long-handled brush from under the sink and went outside to clean the two drains, together with their respective grilles, while her mummy was pegging up the washing.

TGA: *(I watched this little four-year-old child, working like an adult. It was not right. She should*

13

have been playing with toys and dolls; certainly not stoking fires and cleaning drains.)

Over the autumn period, although she didn't realise it, Annabelle was receiving quite a varied education at home. It had started at the beginning of August when Auntie Dolly (who was a country girl, born and bred) came into their kitchen to teach Alice (formerly a Londoner who had moved to the country when she married) how to salt down the plentiful supply of runner beans that Alberto had grown in the garden, to preserve them for the winter. Annabelle was stood on a stool at the sink washing out the big jars in which the runner beans were to be preserved. She was also busily blowing bubbles by making a film with the very soapy water in the hole made by her finger and thumb.

"Look, Mummy. There's a bubble coming to you."

"That's so pretty, Annabelle. Look at all the lovely colours. Oh dear! It's crashed onto the ceiling."

"Doesn't matter. Here's another one for Auntie Dolly."

Actually, Annabelle was putting off drying the jars. They were a bit heavy for her to handle and she was really glad when Auntie Dolly said she would dry them.

As soon as Auntie Dolly took over that job, Annabelle wanted to help her mummy. Suspecting that would happen, Alice fixed her up at the table with a small knife and showed her how to top and tail the beans, which Annabelle mastered easily.

When the beans were all sliced, they then had to be layered in the jars with salt. Auntie Dolly showed Alice what to do and when the first layer of runner beans was in the jar, Annabelle had the job of putting in a layer of salt. Her little hand and arm fitted easily into the jar to press the salt down, making a firm bed for the next layer of runner beans.

Finally, they stacked the jars on the stone floor under the big shelf in the larder, before saying a hasty goodbye to Auntie Dolly. She had to hurry home because the lunchtime hooter had just gone and the men were coming home for their dinner.

Later that day, Al C was bought home by Kenny, because he'd hurt his knee. He and Ken had gone up to the North Park to play football with many of the other village boys.

"It really hurts, Mum," said Al C with a whimper.

"How did you hurt it so badly, then? Did someone kick you?"

"No, they didn't, Mrs Aless," Kenny answered. "Al C saved a goal."

"I did, Mum. I was copying Sagar of Everton's save, just like I saw in Dad's paper last Sunday."

"Golly gosh. So you were the hero of the day, no doubt?"

"That's right, Mrs Aless," replied Ken, "Al C threw himself forward and landed on both knees, with the ball. He stopped them getting a goal, so we won the match."

"Well, thank goodness he got some reward for hurting his knee. Come along, Al C, take off your boots and socks and sit up here."

As she spoke she laid a towel on the wooden draining board and boiled a kettle on the primus stove in the scullery.

Putting his feet into the warm water in the sink, Al C grinned and said, "That's lovely, Mum. Can we do this every night?"

He soon changed his tune when his mother dabbed his grazed knee with the iodine.

"Ouch! That stings!"

Well, it serves you right for showing off. Next time you play football, think about your own knees before you think of Sagar of Everton."

Autumn was passing by all too quickly at the Alessandro household; the daily routines facilitated that. Monday was always a very busy day; it was washing day, so an easy dinner of cold meat left over from Sunday's joint, served with nice hot fried bubble and squeak was the regular main meal. Tuesday was usually the day for ironing as well as buying meat from the butcher's delivery van to last for three days, up to and including, Thursday. Alice always cooked fish and chips for dinner on Fridays as she was able to buy fresh fish from the fishmonger's van earlier in the day. The butcher's van came round again on Saturday mornings when Alice would regularly buy chipolatas for Saturday dinner and a big joint of meat for Sunday.

The above weekly routine was like a pendulum rapidly ticking the weeks away towards Christmas. One dry day in September, Alice and Annabelle went to see Mr Ewers, the village farmer, about purchasing some eating apples to store for Christmas. He gave them a couple of wooden slatted trays and took them to the orchard to pick their own apples. He showed them the best trees to pick from for storing and told them to leave the full trays on the ground, which he would deliver and charge for later in the day. Alice picked an apple off the tree carefully and gave it to Annabelle to place gently into a tray.

"You must be very careful with the apples, Annabelle," she said. "We mustn't bruise any of them. If we do, they will go bad and won't keep until Christmas."

Another autumn day was spent making Christmas puddings. Before he had left for work in the morning, Alberto had got the big china mixing bowl from out of the low cupboard and left it on the scullery table along with three pudding basins. Alice was able to gather all the ingredients from the top cupboards and she and Annabelle took turns at putting a little bit of this and a little bit of that into the mixing bowl. When all the dry goods were in the bowl, Alice cracked an egg into the mix and gave Annabelle, who was patiently waiting with wooden spoon in hand, the OK to start mixing.

"This is too hard for me, Mummy. It won't mix."

"I'm sure you're right, Annabelle," Alice laughed. "Hold on a minute and I'll put some milk in, as well as another egg. That should help. Now try again."

Annabelle still struggled.

"You do it, Mummy. It's too hard for me."

Later Annabelle asked, "Shall I break another egg in for you?"

"I think that's a good idea, Annabelle, but you'd better break it into a cup first. We don't want to get any eggshell in our pudding, do we? I think Al C would have something to say about that."

Annabelle's first attempt at breaking an egg was a disaster. After cracking it on the side of the cup, the white of the egg oozed out, made the shell slippery and in trying to keep hold of it she crushed it in her hands and the whole thing dropped into the cup, the eggshell in smithereens.

Alice quickly got a wet cloth and wiped Annabelle's hands.

"Never mind, sweetheart, you practise again when we have scrambled eggs for tea. I've only got two eggs left, so we can't risk another accident."

Later, when Alice was happy with the consistency of the mix, she separated it into three pudding basins and gave Annabelle the more manageable task of putting a silver three-penny piece into each of the mixes, which she did with the end of a teaspoon. Next, Alice used string to tie greaseproof paper over the top of the basins, before tying on their 'cotton hats', the ends of which were tied to each other forming handles above the basins with which to lift them into the big pot of boiling water that was on the range.

The dark evenings on the run-up to Christmas were all passed busily in various ways for the family. Often Alberto would unroll his tap dancing mat on the scullery floor and do a bit of practice with Al C. Sometimes Annabelle would try to dance with them, but she was learning how to knit and she liked to sit by the warmth of the range and do that.

"What are you knitting, Annabelle?" asked Al C.

"I'm knitting myself a scarf to wear to school next year."

"It's jolly lucky you don't need it till next August. It'll take you a long, long time to get that done," replied Al C with brotherly sarcasm.

TGA: *(Mr and Mrs Aless keep a very happy household for their children. Through the winter the range gives warmth and the wireless is always on, so the family can sing along to the music. It is gratifying for me that Annabelle has such a good happy home to grow up in. However, that gratification is quashed because I can see she is heading for the role of a real life Cinderella).*

When Alberto wasn't tap dancing, he was busy with his woodwork, making photo frames for Christmas presents. He'd conjured up his own design, which resembled a fan-like effect from a narrow base, opening out a bit towards the top. Two pieces of glass would fit into a rebated slot on the inner side of each of the fan frames, which were joined along the bottom. Different processes took place on different evenings, until reaching the final process – painting the frames. A selection of different colours was chosen. Alberto chose natural wood to be varnished, Alice chose gold, Al C chose brown and Annabelle chose green. On the evening that Alice and Annabelle were wrapping them up as presents, Annabelle said, "I like mine the best; it's the prettiest."

"You're so stupid, Annabelle. Of course you like your own the best," blurted Al C. "I like mine the best, so there."

"Now, now, Al C. She's only a little girl. You should look after her, not squabble. She doesn't deserve that. Come on, my little sweetheart. It's time for bed now. Are you ready Alberto?"

"Of course I'm ready. Come along little one. Shall we go and look for Wee Willie Winkie?"

Three days before Christmas, on Sunday 22nd December 1935, Annabelle was very excited. Her Granny Howitz was coming to stay for the holiday. Al C was not so keen for his granny to visit. It meant he had to move into Annabelle's small bedroom at the back of the house so that Annabelle could sleep with her granny in Al C's double bed in the bigger room at the front.

On that morning, Alberto and Al C walked to Andover Junction Station to meet Granny Howitz from the train. She had a struggle to get down the two steps with her suitcase, but Alberto and the guard were soon there to assist.

Alberto gave her a welcome kiss and Al C shuddered as he courteously did the same. Granny Howitz had difficulty in holding her back up straight, undoubtedly because, in her lifetime, she had given birth to 23 babies. As Al C followed his father and granny out of the station, he was grinning to himself and trying hard not to laugh out loud. For him, the back view of his Granny was mostly bum, due to her bent stance and his short height. Because she had sat on the train for a long time, her fawn coat was badly creased horizontally, which had the effect of shortening it, and with her short, plump, fawn stocking clad legs dangling beneath, it conjured up the rear image of a tortoise for him.

It was too much for Granny Howitz to walk home, so they caught a bus to the Andover bus station and from there they caught another bus to Enham.

A delicious smell of roast beef welcomed them as they arrived home in time for dinner.

Alice greeted her mother excitedly. It was the first time they had met in about seven years.

"Mother, it's wonderful to see you again. How are you?"

"Better for seeing you, dear, and this must be your lovely little Annabelle."

Annabelle blushed as she stood before the elderly lady. Alberto picked her up and said, "Say 'hello' to Granny Howitz, Annabelle."

Annabelle was shy and leaned her head onto her father's shoulder.

Patting her knees, Granny said, "Come along Annabelle; come and sit on my lap, so I can cuddle you."

Alberto leaned forward and Granny took the little girl.

"Who's looking after the shop while you're away, Mother?"

"Oh, Daisy's running it. She's 22 now, of course. She hates opening at 6am and working till midnight, but I told her that's got to happen. I've got to look after the elderly who use the workhouse. They still leave their little bits of jewellery or other treasures with me before going to the workhouse for a night's shelter, and know

21

they can pick them up again at 6 in the morning, when they're chucked out. I've looked after them all the years I've been in that shop and I will do so until I die. Anyway, that's enough about us. Now you can tell me the truth about you. How is your health? You never answer that question in your letters."

Alice explained that she usually felt quite well, but was frustrated at not being able to bend over.

"Annabelle helps me a lot with the bending down jobs, which is a Godsend, but I don't know what will happen next year when she starts school."

Easy chatting continued until Annabelle, who looked quite comfy curled up on her granny's lap, piped up, "Granny, I'm going to sleep with you tonight."

"Are you, my lovely? Then Granny will sing you some songs."

Eventually, all the family sat round the table for a late Sunday dinner. The roast beef with horseradish sauce was delicious. It was served with roast potatoes, Yorkshire puddings and runner beans from the garden that Alice and Annabelle had salted down. For the special occasion, Alice had baked an apple pie and made custard for a pudding.

At the table, Al C asked his granny what songs she was going to sing in bed.

"I'm not sure, Al. It all depends what songs come into my head, but there'll probably be a few sea shanties. If there's room in the bed, you can come in with us if you like, and then you'll find out."

TGA: *(As I watched this homely scene, I detected that Al C was cringing at the thought.)*

The only reply Granny received was, "I'm not Al. I'm Al **C**."

Granny's visit made the days pass quickly and before anyone could blink, Christmas Eve 1935 was upon them. It was Annabelle's fifth birthday. She received another doll to fit in her dollies' pram and a knitting set with two short, thick yellow knitting needles with black knobs and six small balls of multi-coloured wool in different shades, all neatly displayed in a box. Annabelle wanted to start knitting straight away, but there were other things to be done.

Alice hurried to the village stores to buy last minute goodies for the following night's party as well as some stout for her mother. At home she always had a glass of stout before going to bed. While Alice was out, Granny busied herself at the sink preparing potatoes, parsnips and Brussel sprouts for Christmas dinner the next day and singing a little ditty at the same time for Annabelle, who was playing with her new doll.

My little dolly is very sick. Run for the doctor, quick, quick-quick.
Doctor came with a rat-a-tat-tat; gave me his stick and he gave me his hat.
Looked at dolly, shook his head; said mother dear, put her to bed,
Keep her warm and very still, and I'll call tomorrow morning.

Christmas morning's weather was mild, but the day started with a flurry. Annabelle and Al C were awake at dawn. The Christmas tree, that was positioned on the front window ledge above the window seat, was not too big but nicely decorated with lots of different coloured little woollen pom-poms, as well as small Christmas Crackers (created with spent matchsticks and shiny toffee wrappers) that had all been made by Alice in the autumn. At the top of the tree was a delightful little fairy that, unbeknownst to the children, had also been made by Alice. At the bottom, colourful parcels tied with red ribbons were lined up along the window ledge, as well as on the window seat below.

When Alberto entered the room he found the children prodding and poking the parcels, their eyes sparkling with wonderment and delight.

"Look at all these parcels, Daddy. Can we open some?"

"Not yet, you little imps. You should still be fast asleep. And don't forget, there are presents for Granny, Mummy and me, as well as you."

After a subdued second, in unison they said, "Let's go and wake Granny."

"Ah well, it is Christmas," Alberto said to himself as he started to light a fire in the range.

The children had a wonderful day. Annabelle had lots of lovely hand knitted dolls' clothes and a pencil case filled with coloured pencils, which she'd asked for in her letter that went up the chimney to Santa Claus. Al C was thrilled with his brand new Cubs' uniform, which he had been wanting since he joined the cubs in September. He was also excited to find he'd got some roller skates and couldn't wait to go out and try them.

As the day was quite mild, the family decided to walk off their big Christmas Dinner and take Granny out to see something of the village. They had to walk slowly with her, of course, which suited Al C. He was getting used to his roller skates and kept skating away from everybody before speeding back to them. At the same time, Alberto was proud to show off The Landale Wilson Institute, the new social centre where he gives tap dancing lessons and puts on shows.

"Goodness me, Alberto, you fell on your feet good and proper when you found this village, didn't you? That lovely building is right on your doorstep."

"I certainly did, Ma, and I hope you agree it is the perfect place for Alice, too. She loves it here and makes stage costumes for my troupe of dancers."

"You don't have to tell me, Alberto. I can tell she is very happy here."

After their walk, the family returned home so that Alice and her mother could start laying out a spread for later. They were expecting their friends, Jane and Joe Geoghegan and their five children, to come for a Christmas Party evening. Jane's elderly mother would also be with them, so she would be nice company for Granny.

At about 10pm, the party was going with a swing. Beers and egg nogs were going down a treat; jolly singing was the order of the day and these two families were enjoying a typical family Christmas together.

While that was going on, Annabelle was fast asleep in the double bed, but not all alone. She was cuddled up with her new baby doll, dressed in pink. Granny was not yet to bed and would have to sing to Annabelle another night.

TGA: *(I was delighted with Annabelle's Christmas Day. Her Grandmother was there to help Alice, which meant that Annabelle, for Christmas at least, was not slaving the day away as if she were an adult.)*

Chapter 2

Andre Kliskey

Mrs McKenzie was seething. Eugene Kliskey had dumped a baby on her; a horrendous thing to happen. She was outraged at having to cope with his newborn baby. She'd had her eye on Eugene in the local vicinity for a long time. Usually, he was either hopping on a bus, or hopping off one. Always he looked smart and stood out in the crowd. That crowd was in a busy street on the posh side of Norwood, London. Mrs McKenzie knew none of his business, nor where he lived, but she was very aware of his presence.

Basically, she was a woman who kept herself to herself and looked after her sons well. Ron was 15 and growing fast. Daniel was only 5, so not as costly. To them she was a good mother, but she was not a good wife. In her household, arguments ensued day after day after day. When her 'old man' could take it no more, he cleared off and she rejoiced.

From that point in time, she determined to pursue a new, better-class, breadwinner; with a bit of luck, someone with a ready-made home for her and her sons to move into. Paying her own rent as well as bringing up children was a bit of a pinch. She knew exactly where to look for her new man. With a plan in mind, she made it her business to improve her appearance. Her figure, which was nowhere near matronly, was her priority.

Immediately, she put herself on a strict diet. While Ron was at college and Daniel at school, she sported the money to make regular trips to the hairdresser, seeking a new stylish hairdo and grudgingly faced up to lower-heeled footwear. Because the man she had set her sights on was not overly tall, she decided it would be a good idea to look for stylish, low-heeled shoes.

During that period, whenever their paths crossed, she earnestly studied her quarry's movements. It was her intention to put herself in his way good and proper one day, supposedly quite by accident! She had observed that on Friday afternoons he didn't hop off the bus and disappear into the throng as quickly as usual. Instead, he held back and helped an elderly lady to get off.

She had decided that that would be a good time to pounce and was excited when Friday came around. In accordance with her plan, she set the time five minutes ahead on the broken watch that she held in her hand. Her heart skipped a beat when the bus came into view. It skipped a few more beats when she saw her potential beau about to hop off. The elderly lady was not there!

Her attempt had been foiled, but her quick-thinking saved the day. She gave the impression of scurrying forwards to catch the departing bus, crashed into him in her rush and let the broken watch slip from her fingers as she was trying to hurry on by.

It worked. Within seconds a posh voice said, "I'm so sorry. Looks as though I've made you miss your bus madam, but I believe you dropped this watch."

First she looked at the watch and then her wrist. "Oh my goodness; I couldn't have done it up properly. Yes, it is mine. Thank you so much." She gave him a sweet, innocent smile.

"No need to thank me. I'm glad you dropped it. I've had my eye on you here in Norwood for some time. Thanks to our collision we've now made 'contact', if you'll excuse the pun."

"How nice," she replied somewhat gushingly, working the revelation to the maximum. "I feel quite flattered."

"How's the watch? Is it still working?"

She checked. The dial still said 4.15pm.

"Oh dear! Apparently not." Taking her time before looking into his eyes, she continued, "Such a pity; I've had it for a long time and it is sentimentally valuable to me."

"Perhaps I can help. I dabble in repairing clocks, big clocks. You know; Grandfather clocks and the like. Maybe I could try my hand at a delicate ladies' watch?"

Her gaze on him lingered. Was he referring to the watch, or to her, when he said those last few words?

"Would you? I'd like that."

"Well, I can't promise I'll be able to fix it, but I'll see what I can do. How can I contact you to return it?"

"I think a telephone arrangement would be best. I'll give you my number."

His phone call came sooner than expected; in fact, on the Monday evening after the weekend.

"Hello." His voice was unmistakable. Her spine tingled. "You'll be pleased to know I've fixed your watch."

"Really? That's wonderful news. Thank you."

"You're welcome. Now I need to know how to return it to you."

"Oh dear. I'm a bit embarrassed about that. I can't invite you to my home and I don't want to be seen with another man in Norwood, or anywhere else, come to that. It's complicated."

"What about up in town? Or, should I post it to you?"

With indecent haste, "Oh no, please don't do that. I'll match your honesty and tell you that I really do want us to meet again."

"Look, I sing in the choir in St. Paul's Cathedral, so I'm up there for rehearsal twice a week. We could have an arrangement somewhere nearby. How does that sound?"

"Could we meet before your rehearsal? I don't want to be up in town later in the evening."

"Of course. I can manage that. My rehearsals are Tuesdays and Fridays. Take your pick."

For Mrs McKenzie it was a fortuitous coincidence that Daniel, her five-year-old had received an invitation to go to a party quite soon, on a Friday after school. She could make a special arrangement to pick him up a bit late after the party, following her appointment. That way she'd have no worries about his safety. Ron, who was older, would not be a problem; he often spent nights away from home staying with different friends. Yes, Daniel's party day would be the ideal date. Lady Luck had smiled on her. She had come down two dress sizes, felt good about herself and was ready and waiting for her rendezvous.

"Let's say Friday week then. I need a bit of time to arrange things."

"OK. How about meeting at Mansion House Tube Station between 5.45 and 6pm? We can get a cup of tea somewhere and have a chat."

"Yes, that's a good place to meet. I'll be there."

"Good. No need to wear a red rose in your lapel. I'd recognise you anywhere."

She had to sit down. Her legs were trembling.

"Looks like I'm chasing the already ensnared," she thought to herself, feeling thrilled.

He was waiting at Mansion House Tube Station when she arrived. He looked awesome in a smart, well-fitting black suit, crisp white shirt and a bright, distinctive orange, light grey and black striped tie.

"Enough to make any woman weak at the knees," she thought.

"Hello there. You've made it, then. I'm so glad to see you."

She was not only bowled over by his appearance, but by his powerful voice. Leading her by the elbow, he guided her through the throng and out into the street.

"I know a quiet café just round the corner from here. Pretty remote; I don't think you need to worry about being seen."

Even so, he led her to an empty table right at the back of the café, away from the big front window.

Alone, with a pot of tea for two and some toasted tea cakes in front of them, they felt free to talk.

"Here's your watch, all repaired and ticking away nicely and here's to us." He grinned seductively as he raised his cup.

"To us?" she countered questioningly. "So how long have you been singing in St. Paul's Choir?" she asked, for want of something better to say to this knight in shining armour.

"Forever, it seems. I used to sing in St. Paul's Boys' Choir and graduated when I was old enough."

"Does that mean you're religious?"

"Not necessarily; it just goes with the job. Why, are you?"

"No; I'm afraid I'm not."

"No need to be afraid. Look, let's not beat about the bush like this. We don't have enough time to be wasting it. "The reason I am here is because, whenever I see you, I can't take my eyes off you, and that was the case even before you slimmed down a bit!" Expectantly he awaited her reply.

That last remark took the wind out of her sails. She felt herself blushing as she replied, "I'm both flattered, and..." looking directly up into his eyes, "relieved. Thank you."

"Now what's that supposed to mean?"

"It means I'm relieved to know that you have some feeling for me. Such a coincidence. I've been dreaming about you ever since my husband cleared off; and before he cleared off, too."

"Amazing. That is a coincidence indeed. Almost as though your dropping the watch was an act of God."

She glossed over that last remark, trying hard not to blush again with, "Trouble is I'm not free to see you. That's the complication. At the moment I'm going through a divorce."

"So for you it's only a matter of time?"

She nodded.

"OK, so now I'll put my cards on the table. Blatant truth is, I'm stuck. Stuck in a bad marriage and my wife is very ill with child at the moment, so it's not a good time to file for divorce."

Ignoring the blatant truth in favour of the earlier revelation, she gave him a radiant smile and said, "I think it's high time I introduced myself. I'm Kit McKenzie and I'm delighted to meet you." She held out her hand across the table.

"I'm Eugene Kliskey and very glad to meet you too," he said positively, as he slowly enunciated his last three words, "at long last."

This man was a charmer and Mrs McKenzie began to wilt in his presence. He knew how to pull a woman and she wanted more. She could not stop herself.

He squeezed her hand tightly as he said, "Kit McKenzie, today you've made me a happy man and I sincerely hope this meeting is the start of something extra-special between us."

She felt seventeen years of age all over again.

That magic spell was broken when he reminded her that their time was nearly up. They agreed to meet at a different tube station in two weeks' time and left the tea shop separately.

33

Many clandestine meetings followed at different locations in London. Eugene Kliskey finally got his wish to spend a night in a London hotel with Kit when her divorce was made absolute.

Bearing in mind that Eugene still had a wife, their meetings became as regular as caution would allow. They couldn't get enough of one another. His lovemaking was sublime; out of this world sublime. Kit McKenzie had to have him, whatever the cost.

The cost was another child. His wife had died giving birth.

Being the beneficiary, Eugene Kliskey dealt with his wife's affairs remarkably quickly and with indecent haste arranged for his new woman to move in. There being no grief to overcome, he was as happy as the day was long.

For Kit it was another story; she had got what she had wished for. Her new man could accommodate her and her boys, but she was horrified by the slum property on the poor side of Norwood in which she now found herself and her boys living. How could he live in such a dump? He always looked so smart and well-off. The terraced property was a damp, dark and smelly hovel, the ground floor being in the basement.

Their dining room was small and bleak as it looked out upon a rough and dirty concrete wall, which was about three feet from the window. Looking up to ground level, you could see black painted iron railings, which protected pedestrians on the pavement above from falling down into the pit on top of the coal that was always delivered over the railings.

Kit McKenzie began to wonder if this was a fair swop for the bed mate of her dreams.

That was all five years ago.

Things worsened for her when Ron, now 20, got fed up with sharing a small room with his 10-year-old brother, as well as watching the way his mother was treating her stepson. She was abominably unfair to him in comparison to her own son, Daniel. His patience finally broke as one day he angrily let rip, "Mother, you can't expect me to go on living in this hell-hole any longer, and even worse than this is the unfairness between the two boys that I have to witness daily. I find your behaviour towards Andre despicable and I can't stand another day of it. GOODBYE, AND I WON'T BE BACK. EVER," he shouted as he stormed out of the house.

Ron's departure coincided with the start of a new school year at the end of July 1935 and Andre Kliskey, now five years old, a child far too small for his age, was in that catchment. Daniel, his ten-year-old step-brother, was supposed to take him to school, but Andre couldn't keep up with him. It was difficult walking with shoes that were far too big for him. Andre had the sneaking thought that he wouldn't be missed if he spent the day playing in the pond instead, but the threat of more trouble at home deterred him, so he followed other children into the school gate and stood by the reception teacher in the playground, who was trying to take care of a lot of nervous new children.

She was asking the parents of luckier children to leave quickly.

"They will soon settle down once you are out of sight," she called out loudly.

When the classroom door closed, the lady introduced herself as Miss Rees, the infants' teacher, and told the children she would be their teacher for their first year at school. She then explained that she was going to call the register, which was a record of who was attending school on that day and who was absent.

"Present, Miss!" Andre responded clearly.

The classroom was full of small desks with small chairs to match. Andre liked it. At home, the chairs and the table were all too big for him to fit comfortably.

After the register, Miss Rees took them to the big hall for assembly. It was the place where the whole school and all the teachers met for prayers and general announcements. Andre had never said prayers before in his life, so he shut his eyes and thought about the newts swimming in the pond. Prayers over, they then had to sing a hymn. Andre liked the hymn. It had nice words:

Glad that I live am I;
That the sky is blue;
Glad for the country lanes,
And the fall of dew.

After the sun, the rain,
After the rain the sun;
This is the way of life,
Till the work be done.

All that we need to do,
Be we low or high,
Is to see that we grow,
Nearer to God on high.

Assembly over, everybody formed long queues and were led back to their respective classrooms by their teachers.

Miss Rees told her infants that their first lesson would be arithmetic.

"What's arithmetic?" asked one bold child.

Andre put his arm up. "I know, Miss."

"Alright, Andre. Go ahead."

"Arithmetic is learning how to add up numbers."

"Very good, Andre. That is part of the answer. How do you know about arithmetic?"

"I know because my stepmother helps my stepbrother Daniel, and I listen."

"Well, I hope you'll be interested to know that I can teach you to do other things with numbers besides adding them up."

Andre's first day at school passed by too quickly for him. He wished he could stay there all night with Miss Rees, but she told him he must go home to sleep and then come back the following morning.

As soon as he was outside the school gate, he kicked off his shoes that were far too big for him. His feet were hurting where he'd clenched his toes all day long, trying to keep the shoes on. Walking home in his stockinged feet was a luxury; a soon to be forgotten one.

When his father came home from work he found Andre sitting all alone in the corner of the dark dining room.

"So what are you being punished for today, son?"

"Because I walked home in my socks. Ma says I've got to mend them after dinner, because I've made holes in them."

"Well, it was a bit stupid to take your shoes off to walk home, wasn't it?"

"No, it wasn't STUPID," shouted Andre defiantly. "The shoes are too big for me. They were Daniel's."

"Don't you shout at me, my son. You're lucky to have a pair of shoes. At the dinner table tonight I want to hear you tell your mother you are sorry for ruining your socks. They all cost money you know." That said, Eugene Kliskey cleared off upstairs to fiddle with his clocks.

Andre remained on the chair and thought about nice Miss Rees. He was humming the school hymn, *Glad that I live am I*, to himself when his stepmother started to lay the table. After that he remained silent.

When dinner was ready, Andre was allowed to interrupt his darning and sit in his place at the table opposite Daniel.

No one asked Andre how he got on at school. He felt crushed. He knew they all hated him, but didn't know why. He so missed his older brother Ron. He would have asked how he got on. He was a good friend and had once told him so.

"Andre, I'm your best friend. Don't you ever forget that. Whatever happens, I'll always keep in touch with you. I know you're treated badly here."

As it was, the only words that were spoken to him were his father's prompting, to which Andre responded, "I'm sorry I wore holes in my socks today Ma."

After dinner he was left alone on the chair in the corner with a needle and thread, trying to darn his socks. His stepmother had shown him what to do and he was trying his best. He didn't want to get into more trouble.

Andre was up and ready for school early the next day. He'd shuffled along the pavement in his big shoes and knew that some of the other children were poking fun at him. As soon as he saw Miss Rees in the playground, he went and stood by her. His second day at school was similar to his first day, except they didn't have assembly. He liked discovering about numbers and sums and enjoyed the English lesson, where he was learning his ABC. The last part of the English lesson was an introduction to poetry, which Andre enjoyed. They were given a simple eight-line poem to learn by heart and he kept repeating it over and over in his head, to help him remember it for the next lesson.

Unlike all the other children, Andre was again sad when the bell rang for home time. He still wished he could stay at school with nice Miss Rees, but he knew she had to go home, so he had to go home too. With no other option open to him, Andre dawdled home on his bare feet, with his socks tucked safely in his pocket.

For dinner that night, Andre could smell the stench of the over-cooked yellow greens, so he knew he would be gagging on them again. The same applied when cauliflower or swede chunks were put on his plate. To him they stank. He knew she didn't like him and often thought his stepmother was trying to poison him. Did she put poison on his portions which made them taste worse than the rest of the family's dinners? More often than not, he had to sit at the table until he'd cleared his plate. He preferred to sit there all night rather than be poisoned. Sometimes he would fall asleep and would be found with his head in the plate and would get a good spanking. Other times, he would try to avoid that happening again and looked around him, studying that dark gloomy room. He hated every inch of it; it was imprinted on his memory.

The room was small, dark and overcrowded. The rectangular table was in the centre with dark wooden chairs around it. At meal times, Mr Kliskey always sat on the short side with his back to the tall narrow window, which didn't let in much light due to the close proximity of the houses the other side of the road that shadowed it. Mrs Kliskey had often threatened to put a thick net curtain up to stop the 'buggers' looking down. Andre would not dare to disagree with her, but he knew that when he looked down from the railings, the window just reflected blackness. He couldn't see inside the room at all. To darken the room even more, a big sideboard stood in front of the window with a green bushy plant in a blue and white pot in the centre. At each end of the sideboard stood figures of big black horses rearing up on their hind legs. Their stances were the same, but reversed, as if about to charge at each other over the thick 'hedge' between them.

Mrs Kliskey sat opposite her husband. Daniel sat at one long side of the table, on his own now that Ron had gone. Behind him was a big, dark wooden, imposing Welsh dresser with a gigantic blue and white oval plate on a central shelf and lots of round plates of different sizes, as well as some saucers, displayed on surrounding shelves. There were also matching cups hanging from hooks on the edge of the shelves. Every item of furniture was made of dark wood, including the bookcase on the wall behind Mrs Kliskey. Andre's place was opposite Daniel on the other long side. There was only just enough room for everyone to squeeze in round the polished table, which was protected by a fawn coloured tablecloth with a dark green and deep red design and tassels hanging all around the bottom. Mrs Kliskey had more space behind her chair to get seated, as she was bigger than Mr Kliskey or either of the boys. For mealtimes, the fawn cloth would be covered with a black and white-squared oilcloth and they were all instructed daily not to dirty it with scraps of food or gravy.

It must be said that Kit Kliskey provided reasonably nutritious meals for her family, usually consisting of meat and two different vegetables, and coped well with providing them in the pokey little scullery she'd inherited. Andre was so undernourished because he avoided the foods he thought were being poisoned. A good boost for his nourishment always came on Fridays when they regularly had fried fish and chips from the chip shop. Once a week, at least, he was able to tuck in with relish.

School days had improved Andre's life immensely, but those happier days were rudely interrupted when half-term came around. He hated it for two reasons. Firstly because he had no escape from home, accentuated by the fact that he could not spend the day with Miss Rees. The other reason was the chores he had to do at home. He didn't mind doing them; he liked helping because he hoped, every day, to please his ma, but basically he was not strong enough to do the chores asked of him. His stepmother had made him aware that during half-terms it was his responsibility to empty the chamber pots first thing every morning. Actually, it was necessary to do two, sometimes three trips downstairs to the outside lavatory with the slop bucket, because he couldn't carry it if it was too full. Another, more manageable job, was to tidy the hearth and leave the fire laid ready for lighting later in the day, but carrying the coal scuttle indoors after he'd filled it from the pit was impossible. That job fell to Daniel, after he'd completed his job of doing the shopping at the local stores, for which he was given a bit of money to buy sweets.

Glad to get back to school, Andre hobbled there in a different pair of shoes. Daniel had a new pair, so his old ones had been passed down. Later that week, Andre was given a letter to take home to his parents. It prompted a hullabaloo at home.

Dear Mr & Mrs Kliskey,

I wish to make you aware that Andre's feet are becoming crippled by clenching his toes to keep shoes on his feet that are too big for him. I recommend that you buy a pair of shoes, preferably from Scholl's, to fit his feet properly.

Yours faithfully,
School Nurse

All hell was let loose when Mr Kliskey arrived home from work. Andre, who knew his stepmother was angry, was in the living room, which was a little brighter than the dining room. The stone wall was about six feet away from the window, but when his father entered, a bitter, icy atmosphere filled the room. Mrs Kliskey showed him the letter.

"How dare they tell us what to do?" She was furious. "I control the purse strings here. Do they think we're made of money?"

"Calm down, Kit. They could be right." Raising his well-articulated voice a notch, he asked, "Have you thought of that?"

Mrs Kliskey was thrown. It was unusual for her hen-pecked husband to stand up to her.

"You can't be thinking of spending on a **new** pair of shoes for him?" she retorted, with venom in her voice.

"Yes I am. I don't want the School Board on my back. God knows where that would lead us. Imagine the local paper headlines: 'Couple too mean to buy their son a pair of shoes to fit his feet'." He looked at her imploringly.

She exploded. Now red with rage, she spat, "I can't believe what I'm hearing. You know as well as I do that we can't afford new clothes for both of them. "One day there'll be murder done in this house, Eugene Kliskey. You mark my words."

Mrs Kliskey was at the end of her tether. The old adage, *Out of the frying pan, into the fire,* came into her mind, but more realistically she had to cope with the embarrassment of plummeting from dignity to indignity for the sake of lust. In her heart she knew that the lust was still strong and holding her and Eugene together, but having his last child to cope with was almost too big a price to pay.

Andre tossed and turned all night. Her words, "One day there'll be murder done in this house, Eugene Kliskey," kept going over and over in his mind. He felt feverish with the reality of it all. He knew he was her victim. Brutal thoughts were filling his mind. "Well, she certainly wouldn't kill Daniel, and I've never seen her get cross with my father before. No. It's got to be me," he thought. From that day, uppermost in his mind was a plan of action for his escape.

Thoughts of escape were disturbed on the night of 30 Nov-1 Dec 1936, when Andre became alarmed as he lay in his bed. Lots of voices, including his stepmother's, had awakened him. Curiosity, strengthened by defiance, gave him the courage to dare to find out what was going on. His bedroom door, along with all the other bedroom doors, was on the ground floor above the living accommodation. From there, along the passage, he could see the family all dressed in night attire, standing on the pavement outside the front door.

They were stood as still as stone statues, all looking up to the sky in the same direction. His curiosity drove him on. He crept to the front door, confident that if he didn't make a sound, no one would notice him. What he saw was a huge red glow in the sky that looked to him as though the sun had made a mistake and come out at night. With that vision imprinted on his memory, he tip-toed back to bed unnoticed.

The next day, it seemed everyone in the world was talking about the burning down of The Crystal Palace in London.

After that event, at long last the day came when his father took him to the shoe shop to buy a new pair of shoes. Andre felt as though he was walking on air the first day he wore them to school. He walked very carefully so he didn't scratch them; he wanted them to stay new forever. Miss Rees noticed and asked, "Are your feet more comfortable in those new shoes, Andre?"

His face lit up. "Yes thank you, Miss. It didn't take me so long to walk here today."

What he didn't tell her was the misery he had gone through at home because of them. All his life he'd been able to slip his feet into big second hand shoes with laces already tied. Consequently, he had never learned to tie laces. Mr Kliskey did not have the patience or understanding to help his son master the art. Instead, he would get angry and wrap him over the knuckles with a cane. That only served to magnify the boy's difficulty, with painfully sore fingers. On one such occasion, Mr Kliskey stormed out of the room in a rage, shouting, "You keep practising, Andre, and if you can't tie them by the end of the week I'm going to take you to the police station."

TGA: *(I despaired for the boy, but Miss Rees saved the day. She taught Andre to tie his shoe laces, which enabled him to keep peace with his father. By now, I am sure you have guessed that Andre Kliskey is the other child I am watching over. As you have seen, the poor boy really does need a Guardian Angel.)*

Chapter 3

Annabelle Goes to School

It was a Monday morning in late August 1935. Annabelle looked smart in her dark green gym slip, which accentuated her lovely blonde ringlets, white ankle socks, black patent leather shoes and nice crisp white blouse, ready for school. She was sitting on her mother's lap in the living room. The smell of fried bacon filled the air and the morning sunshine streamed through the front window.

"I don't want to leave you, Mummy. I'm afraid you'll bend over."

The child's tortured face brought tears to her mother's eyes. She cuddled Annabelle tightly and said, "I promise you, Annabelle, I won't do that. I'll remember to call Auntie Dolly, your special friend." Nodding in confirmation as she spoke, she continued, "You know she'll help me."

"Then **please** remember to do it?" Annabelle pleaded, with heart-rending emotion.

For Alice, the despondency of the child's plea left her bereft of words. Choked up, she cuddled her daughter more closely and slowly nodded her head.

"So promise me again, Mummy, that you won't ever forget. I'm frightened. I don't want you to die."

TGA: *(The image of that child's worried face looking searchingly into her mother's eyes, truly reflected her deep feeling. It was not only tragic, but hauntingly memorable.)*

Sitting together in her mother's armchair by the side of the unlit range, Alice said, "I won't forget, my little sweetheart. I mustn't. I do promise. Try to believe me."

For a while they were locked seriously into each other's eyes. Alice broke the spell with, "Now **you**, young lady," pointing her finger at Annabelle as she crossed her eyes to aid her request, "give me a nice little smile, so I don't have to worry about you worrying about **me**." This time she pointed a finger at herself as she continued, "Worrying about you worrying about me worrying about you," and so on, until laughter took over.

Annabelle's spirits were lifted by the fun; it was turning into a good game. They gained speed with each repetition, fingers pointing everywhere in haste and tongues getting tied, until giggles got the better of them. Uncontrollably writhing with laughter, they missed Mary's first knock on the door. When they finally heard a knock, they hurried to the front door.

"Is Annabelle ready for school, Mrs Aless?" asked Mary, who was dressed exactly the same as Annabelle, apart from brand new, patent leather shoes.

"Yes, she is, Mary. You'll take extra care of her for me, won't you dear? She's been a bit upset this morning."

Mary, who was eight years old, nodded. She was the youngest daughter of Joe and Jane Geoghegan and she was going to walk Annabelle to school and look after her until she became familiar with the routine and made friends with children of her own age. It was the village ritual for the older children to look after the younger ones.

Alice waved them off as the girls started their two-and-a-half-mile journey to Smannell C of E school, via Anton Lane, the cinder track and the hamlet of Woodhouse.

Mary held Annabelle's hand all the way until, inside the school gate, Miss Roberton, the teacher on reception duty said, "OK Mary, you can run along. I'll look after Annabelle now.

Mary gave Annabelle a kiss on the cheek and said, "Wait for me after school Annabelle and I will take you home."

Annabelle felt nervous as Miss Roberton, the juniors' teacher, gathered together the new starters. At 8.50am, she led them through the front porch of the brick and flint building into the big school room for senior pupils. There were two doors leading from that room. One on the right led into the juniors' classroom, and one at the back led into the infants' room. That room ran across the entire width of both the other rooms. All three classrooms accommodated two consecutive school year intakes, and the three teachers each taught their two separate school year classes simultaneously.

In the infants' room, Annabelle met the teacher, Miss Wells, who was standing with her back to a strongly guarded, low level, coke fire, facing the desks. She was a plumpish, motherly-looking lady of about 28 years old, wearing a colourfully designed floral dress that brightened up the room.

The warm, wide, rectangular shaped room was furnished with five wide rows of small chairs and desks; each desk fitted with a sunken inkwell. The five rows were separated by an aisle half way along. Last year's intake were all seated on the left of the aisle. At the back of the room, opposite to Miss Wells, were two wide windows, both overlooking the school playing field and another one on the far left, which overlooked the house of Miss Kyles, the headmistress. To Miss Wells' left, practically central to the room so both classes could see it, was a big blackboard with chalks and a chalk rubber on its lower ledge, resting on a wooden easel. To her right, butting the side wall, was a long table, laden with books and also a door that led into the concrete-floored cloakroom. The cloakroom was equipped with rows of pegs at varying heights and low wooden form seating along three walls. To the left of the fourth wall was a square porcelain sink, with one cold water tap and a roller towel fitted on the wall by its side. On the same wall, further along, was an outer door from the cloakroom, which led to the lavatories, as well as the playground and the playing field.

"Good morning, children," said Miss Wells brightly. "Welcome to your schooldays and I hope we can make them enjoyable for you. The first thing we have to do is allocate a chair to each of you, seating the taller pupils at the back so everyone can see the blackboard."

When all the new children were seated, Miss Wells asked them to put their hand up if they couldn't see the blackboard. After a bit of re-shuffling, she asked them to look around to see which row they were in and who was sitting next to them.

To the second year pupils on the left side of the room, she said, "While I am busy getting the new children settled, I want you to sit quietly studying the fifth chapter in your reading books. Concentrate well on the story because I shall be asking questions about it later, as well as expecting you to read out loud individually."

Addressing the new intake again, she said, "Right, now I'm going to test you on finding your correct chair. Please all leave your seats now and stand at the edges of the rows."

The comparative silence in the room was swallowed up by a thunderous racket as the numerous wooden chair legs were scuffed along the floorboards. When silence returned, she quietly said, "Very good. Now, when I blow my whistle I want you all to return to your seats as quietly and courteously as possible. Remember, there are others trying to work in this room. No pushing or shoving, please. It is important that you consider the others. I also want you to remember that in school, where you don't have your mums around, I am your friend as well as your teacher." She blew the whistle.

"Good. You did that very well for a first attempt. I shall expect you to be quicker and quieter as time goes on."

"Next, I have to tell you about an essential school rule that must be understood and obeyed. When I ask you questions, you must not shout answers back all at once. What you have to do is hold your hand up and wait patiently. You will all

51

get your turn to speak, one at a time, so everyone can hear what you have to say. Another thing; if you want to go to the lavatory, just put your hand up and say, 'Please Miss, may I be excused'.

"Today, being Monday, we start with a prayer and the school hymn, as indeed we do every Monday morning."

Walking to the left side of the room, she said, "Class 2 will join us for this. Today, we will say *The Lord's Prayer,* which I hope will be familiar to you. You may remain seated, put your hands together, close your eyes and say after me, "Our Father, who art in heaven...

"Well done. Most of you knew that prayer. Next I want you to stand while we sing our school hymn. We sing the same one every week and you will soon learn it."

Glad that I live am I;
That the sky is blue;
Glad for the country lanes,
And the fall of dew.

After the sun, the rain,
After the rain the sun;
This is the way of life,
Till the work be done.

All that we need to do,
Be we low or high,
Is to see that we grow,
Nearer to God on high.

Miss Wells then proceeded with the business of the day. She instructed the children to open their desks where they would find pencils to use, rather than pen and ink, for the first term. She then asked if anyone had already learned to write their own name. Lots of voices answered at once. She quickly put her hands to her ears and pulled a painful face as she said, "My goodness me, I can't possibly hear what each of you is saying. What is it you have to do when I ask a question?"

So many hands went up.

"That's much better, but I see I have to rephrase the question. Is there anyone here who doesn't know how to write their own name?"

No hands appeared.

"Well, well, well. This is a wonderful start."

On that happy note, she held up a book for them to see, which she said would help them to learn to read.

"I have one of these books for each of you."

With all eyes fixed upon her, she took a stack of books and placed a pile at the end of each of the five rows of desks.

"Take one for yourself and pass the rest along. What I want you to do now is write your name on the first page inside the book." She showed them the place with her own book.

Continuing, she went to the table again and picked up a blue covered book.

"Now, these are called exercise books, in which you will do written work as you learn."

Again she placed a pile of books at each end desk and told them to take one and pass the rest along. The first one was entitled *READING,* the second, *WRITING* and the third, *ARITHMETIC.*

While the children were busy, Miss Wells looked up at the clock on the wall above the fireplace and then left the room to collect the milk. On returning, she checked that each child had the correct number of books before telling them to place them inside their desks.

"Well done, children. Now you can reward yourselves with a nice drink of milk."

Holding up the small, third of a pint bottle, that had a two-inch-thick layer of cream on the top, she showed them how to hold it firmly and push their finger into the perforated centre of the card lid, curl the finger under and pull the top off. She smiled.

"There now, I'm sure you'll all be able to manage that. If not, sit quietly, put your hand up and I will come to help you. When you've finished your drink, **carefully** place your empty bottle in the crate on the table here; we don't want any broken bottles, do we? As soon as you've put your empty bottle in the crate you may go out to play. Don't forget to use the lavatory if you need to. When I blow the whistle, I want you to queue up at the cloakroom door, so we can re-enter the classroom in an orderly fashion."

While drinking her milk with a drinking straw, Annabelle plucked up enough courage to look across to the older children and had a pleasant surprise. There she saw her friend Pat. They waved. Outside Annabelle said, "Quick Pat, I want to go to the lavvy."

"Come on then; they're just over here."

When she came out, Annabelle, looking somewhat distraught, said, "I don't like those lavatories. It's too dark in there and I couldn't see if the seat was clean. Al C said they were disgusting."

Understandingly, as she held her friend's hand, Pat said, "I know; we all hate them, but it's better to use them than wet your knickers."

Playtime over, the infants had the first reading lesson of their school life. Annabelle was deeply absorbed in her work, which helped lunchtime to come round quickly. Miss Wells then instructed the children to place all books in their desks and collect lunches from their satchels in the cloakroom. Annabelle remained seated and put her hand up tentatively.

"Yes, Annabelle, what is it?"

"Please Miss Wells, may I run home to see if my mum's alright? I do know the way, Miss. Mary showed me this morning."

Going to Annabelle's desk, Miss Wells asked sympathetically, "Why are you so worried about your mummy, Annabelle?"

Annabelle blushed scarlet as she replied, "Because the doctor says she mustn't bend over…" A pensive pause, then, "…but she forgets." She raised the tone of the last few words and opened her eyes wide in frightened desperation. "It could make her die, just like our cat did. That means you can never see them again."

The emotional depth and urgency of her next plea; "You will let me go, won't you Miss?" alarmed Miss Wells.

"Annabelle, I'm sorry to hear about this. Look, you eat your sandwiches while I go and talk to the headmistress."

On her return to the classroom, Miss Wells was happy to share the decision.

"Annabelle, when you've finished your lunch, I'm going to take you home on my bicycle so you can check on your mummy. You can sit on the seat at the back of my bike and hold on to me."

Seeing tears of relief running down the little girl's cheeks prompted some of her own, which she struggled to choke back.

Alice and Alberto, who was home for dinner, were shocked to see their daughter in the middle of the day. Standing on the doormat at the top of the doorsteps, Alice stooped down to hug Annabelle.

"Whatever's the matter with my precious little one?"

Miss Wells introduced herself and explained about Annabelle's anxiety.

"Do come in for five minutes, Miss Wells, so I can tell you about my heart condition."

"I'm so very sorry to hear what you are up against, Mr and Mrs Alessandro. I sincerely hope you will be able to cope without Annabelle. Her schooling is very important. Perhaps, as the days and weeks pass, she will become more confident at having to leave you. Thank you for the information. If you don't mind, we will make a note of the circumstances on Annabelle's record for future reference."

"Are you happy to go back to school now, Annabelle?"

"Yes please. I want to go back."

In the afternoon, Annabelle blushed yet again. She was engrossed in her arithmetic lesson, learning to add up, when it was interrupted by Miss Wells.

"I think someone has made a bad smell in this room."

Grinning like a Cheshire cat and obviously pleased as punch with himself for having something to say, a new boy named Freddie Cox put up his hand.

"Yes Freddie?"

"Please Miss, my mum always says, 'First smeller, first stinker'."

While the rest of the class were struggling to restrain giggles, Miss Wells said, "Thank you for that, Freddie. Now I will tell the class what I have to say. If you feel the need to break wind, you should put your hand up and ask to be excused. It is far preferable to let it go in the fresh air."

The rest of the afternoon passed by busily with lessons and when it was time to go home the infants all had to wait for their older partners to escort them. Annabelle was delighted to see Mary and wanted to run all the way home.

Alice was waiting patiently on the front doorstep. At the sight of her, Annabelle ran up the garden path into her mother's arms. Without bending down, but holding her daughter close to her tummy as she smoothed her head, Alice said, "Hello my little Annabelle. I'm so glad to have you back at home and thank you, Mary, for looking after her. You're a very good girl."

"That's alright, Mrs Aless." Starting to leave, she called out, "I'll come again tomorrow morning."

"Hey, wait a minute Mary. I've got something for you."

Alice quickly collected a white paper bag from the living room table and gave it to Mary.

"I made some toffee apples earlier today, so there's one in the bag for you and one for your older sister Lucy."

"Ooh, scrummy, Mrs Aless. Thank you."

Al C almost knocked Mary over as he swept up the garden path like a tornado.

"Where were you at dinnertime Annabelle? I looked everywhere and couldn't find you. Honestly, Mum, she wasn't there and when I found her in the playground in the afternoon she wouldn't tell me where she was."

"Because you were angry with me," retorted Annabelle. Anyway, Mummy knows where I was, so it's alright."

"Try to calm down, Al C. Would you like a toffee apple?"

"No. I want to know where **she** was," he demanded, his gaze fixed on Annabelle.

"Of course you do Al C. She came home to see if I was alright."

"On her own?"

"No she came on the back of Miss Wells' bike."

"Jammy thing. Trust you. Goody-goody."

"That's not nice, Al C. There'll be no toffee apple for you unless you tell your sister you're sorry."

"I don't want one."

"Alright, that's up to you, but I shall tell your father. You should try to be kind to your sister. She helps me a lot at home."

Later, when Annabelle was washing her sticky fingers, Al C joined her at the sink and quickly said, "Sorry."

Alice overheard and said, "That's better Al C. Now you can choose a toffee apple."

At the tea table, with the late afternoon sunshine streaming through the back window, the family were discussing Annabelle's dinnertime check on her mummy. Alberto gave her a well-deserved hug and promised her a treat. He became choked as he said, "So my precious little girl looked after my lovely Alice, even from school."

"Yeah, and she was jammy enough to get a ride on Miss Wells' bike to do it," chipped in Al C.

"Well, that should make you very proud of your sister. What treat would you like, Annabelle?"

"Easy-peasy, Daddy," she replied, her face glowing. "Before my tap dancing lesson tonight, can you to take me for a walk up the road on your feet? I like doing that."

"OK, Moosh," he agreed, using one of his buddy-buddy names normally reserved for his London mates, which he now bestowed lavishly, quite out of context, on his beautiful blonde, fairy-like daughter. "Your wish is my command. I'll just lay the tap dancing mat on the scullery floor for Al C and keep my false arm on, so you can hold on to the hook."

Outside of the gate, Annabelle faced her father, held his right hand with her left and the hook of his bent, artificial arm with her right. Then she stood on his feet.

"How far are we going, Daddy?"

"I'm going to take you all the way to the other end of the village."

"Goody-goody; that's a nice long way."

Alberto began to think Annabelle might well fall off his feet during their long journey, as she became more and more weak with the giggles. Passers-by were making jovial remarks, but Annabelle was begging, "Please don't stop, Daddy. This is good."

As Mr Baker passed, he said, "Well, well, is that my little peaches and cream walking backwards to Christmas?"

Lucy and Mary were playing on their front lawn as they approached and ran up the road to meet them.

"Where are you going, Mr Aless?"

"I am going to No. 81 Newbury Road; the last but one house in the village. Do you know where that is?"

"That's ours. We live there."

"As if I didn't know," teased Alberto, with a boyish grin. "Annabelle's having a 'walk-on-my-feet-treat' for being a good girl at school today."

"Coo you're lucky, Annabelle. Our dad doesn't give us treats like that," said ten-year-old Lucy.

Mary bent down and said, "I hope you enjoy your trip back home, Annabelle. I'll call for you again tomorrow morning."

Indoors, they found Al C doing his tap dancing practice to his mother's singing accompaniment.

Getting into her nightie ready for bed that night, Annabelle told her mother that something else had happened at school that day.

"Oh, and what was that Annabelle?"

An embarrassed Annabelle blushed. "It's very rude, Mummy. Come nearer so I can whisper. Miss Wells said someone had made a bad smell in class and then a boy called Freddie Cox put his hand up and said, 'Please, Miss, my mum says, *First smeller, first stinker*'. Mummy, it was terrible. He said that to the teacher!" By now, her pink blushes had deepened into crimson.

Alice burst into laughter, which aroused Alberto and Al C's curiosity. Gradually, Alice blurted out the story.

"Cor blimey. Good one, Freddie," chortled Al C.

The humour of the moment soon spread to Annabelle, who quickly joined in, releasing the earlier embarrassment and stress.

Annabelle loved school and very soon was walking there with Pat and other children from her class, but a cloud marred her horizons when she began to be troubled by headaches. After tea, she would nestle on her father's lap and he would keep turning a cold wet flannel on her hot forehead. While lying there, she twiddled her fingers around the shirt covered arm stump.

"Where's your arm, Daddy?"

"It's a long way away in another country."

"What were you doing there?"

"I had some dangerous work to do and had an accident. The doctors couldn't fix it, so they made me an artificial arm."

"I wish the doctors could have helped you, Daddy. Did it hurt?"

Quickly diverting the subject, Alice said, "I'm hoping the doctors will help a certain young lady tomorrow."

"Not me, Mummy. I'm going to school."

"I know that Annabelle, but if this goes on you won't be able to do your work properly. We'll go to the surgery tomorrow morning and see what the doctor says."

In his very clinical white surgery, with a big window at the back that overlooked the flowered part of his walled garden, Dr MacCallum asked Alice if she was having school milk.

Annabelle nodded.

"Did she ever drink milk at home?"

"No, she never does, although she does get milk in puddings and other things."

"Well, it could be that the school milk is too rich for her. Otherwise, I'm wondering about her eyesight."

Simultaneously, he lifted the eye chart from the wall and placed it in a lower position on his desk, leaning against the back wall.

"Now, Annabelle, I want you to sit in my chair." He pulled it further away from the desk. "I want you to tell me how many letters you have learned at school."

Quickly, Annabelle rolled off the tongue, "A, B, C, D, E, F, G."

"My goodness me. You are doing well. And can you see the blackboard alright at school?"

She nodded.

"Reading the chart from top to bottom, can you tell me every line that has an A in it?" He pointed to the top line, working downwards.

"Well, she doesn't appear to have any problems there," he said to Alice.

"Let's try the letter C now."

"Thank you Annabelle. You deserve a big tick for that. I think your eyesight is perfect."

Looking at Alice, he said, "I think the way forward is to stop the milk for a few weeks. If the headaches don't stop, come back to see me again."

The next morning Annabelle took a note to Miss Wells from her mummy, asking if she could be excused from drinking milk for two weeks. At the end of the day, Annabelle took a note home from Miss Wells to her mummy saying that they would need the doctor to write to them with the necessary instruction.

From the time Annabelle was finally excused from drinking school milk, the Alessandro household were willing her headaches to stop. She had begun to love her cuddles with Daddy after tea, gently rubbing the stump of his arm to comfort him.

That particular evening, Alberto was wearing his artificial arm and Annabelle looked snug, laying back, contentedly playing with the swivel hook to open and close the 'arm'.

"That's enough now Annabelle; you'll wear my arm out."

"Can I can play with it again tomorrow night?"

"Not tomorrow sweetheart. I'll be teaching tap dancing at the Institute."

"Look, how about me telling you a story about a man who lived a long time ago, before I take you up the wooden hill?"

"Oooh, yes please. Is he Old Father Time?"

"No, but that's a very clever guess, Annabelle. No, his name was Henry Work and he wrote a song about his grandfather's clock."

"Was it a clock like the big black one in your bedroom?"

"No, it was what they called a longcase clock. It stood on the floor and was a lot taller than Mr Work."

"Taller than you?"

"If you can be quiet long enough, Miss Muffett, I'll sing you the song he wrote."

My grandfather's clock was too big for the shelf,
So it stood ninety years on the floor.
It was taller by half than the old man himself,
Though it weighed not a pennyweight more.
It was born on the morn of the day that he was born,
And was always his treasure and pride;
But it stopp'd, short - never to go again -
When the old man died.

Chorus
Ninety years without slumbering
Ti-ick tock, ti-ick tock.
His life seconds numbering,
Ti-ick tock, ti-ick tock.
It stopp'd, short - never to go again -
When the old man died.

"Thank goodness when your black clock stopped, you didn't die, Daddy."

"Of course I didn't die; that was just how Mr Work finished the song. Anyway, the happy ending to this story is that all longcase clocks were renamed grandfather clocks when his song became so popular."

"Has your grandfather got a grandfather clock?"

"Crikey, I don't know. He lives a long way away in another country called Italy."

"I've got a grandfather, but I don't know him," Annabelle said mournfully as she looked up at her father.

"But you soon will. Mummy and I will take you to London to meet lots of your family there next August, when the factory closes down for a week. We know that these little legs here will be strong enough for you to walk to the railway station, because you can already walk two and a half miles each way to school. You'll really like your grandparents. Grandpa can't speak English very well, but he loves his family. He'll want you to call him 'Bubble', just as grandchildren do in the region of Italy where he comes from."

"That's a funny name. I just have to say 'Bubble', not Mr Bubble?"

"Just Bubble, sweetheart. That will make him very happy."

To everyone's relief, eventually the headaches ceased, proving the doctor's diagnosis correct. After that, Annabelle was always excused from drinking school milk.

With full energy abounding, she was up and ready for school every day, hungry for more lessons. The interruption of half-term was a disappointment for her, but the misery of that intervention was immediately wiped away when her friend, Pam Angel, from London, came down to spend half-term with her nanny. For the entire week, those two girls were inseparable; like two peas in a pod. Poor Pat was left out completely by this sister-like friendship. Pam helped Annabelle when she had to do chores, or run errands for her mummy, and in between times they played games such as doctors and nurses, where their imaginations ran riot. Alice was often the patient.

For many of the nights, Pam slept in Annabelle's single bed with her and they stayed awake for hours, whispering to each other, despite being forbidden not to talk for too long. On other nights, Annabelle slept at Pam's Nanny's house, which was nice because there they had a bigger bed. In that house, Annabelle became fascinated by their piano. She had never seen one before and she couldn't leave it alone. It held an obsessive fascination for her. In fact, it wasn't far short of relegating Pam into second place.

TGA: (*It was pleasing to see Annabelle's life expanding beyond the home. With time, she had become confident that her mummy wouldn't die while she was at school and thrived on all the information she was learning. How long could that possibly last, I wondered?*)

On the day school broke up for the Christmas holiday, 1936, Annabelle was thrilled to take home a book she was given by the headmistress. Every child in the school was given one. They were bought from The Gale Trust, which was set up by Miss Gale, a Smannell school benefactor, and had a label inside recording that source.

It was the Alessandros' turn to spend Christmas night at the Geoghegans' home with their siblings and partners and children; a big family. To add to the numbers, Joe and Jane had six children, of their own: Nora, Tommy, Lucy, Mary, Patsy and baby Joe and they also had their silver-haired matriarch, Grandma Geoghegan, staying with them for Christmas.

Soon the beer was oiling the vocal chords and they were all enjoying the long awaited get together, singing their hearts out, with humorous songs, country and folk songs, show songs and modern love songs. It was customary for solos to be performed by anyone who had a party piece, whether they had a good singing voice or not.

TGA: (How anyone could sing a note in that cigarette smoke-filled room was beyond me, but the camaraderie of those two families, sharing their hard-earned break from work, was a pleasure to behold. They certainly knew how to let their hair down once a year.)

Annabelle was coughing her heart out in that smoky atmosphere and clung to her mummy until Lucy and Mary suggested taking her into the back garden for some fresh air. Out there it was dark and cold, but the bigger girls decided to play *Ring-a-Ring o' Roses, London Bridge is Falling Down* and other such rhymes to keep them all warm. Refreshed, three sparkly eyed girls reappeared into the sacred silence that had now filled the room. Alberto was about to start singing his tear-jerker song that was requested, without fail, at every one of these shared family Christmas parties. Never forgetting the chilling impact of the frequent incidences of still-births in the recent era, they absorbed and deeply felt the pathos of every word.

Now your mother won't be long, she's only gawn out for some tea,
And while she's gone ya' needn't fret, your safe enough with me.
And she's a good old mother too, ain't she Bill?
She loves ya fond and true, don't she Bill?
And ya seems to understand, when she 'olds yer tiny 'and,
She's the best mum in the land, ain't she Bill?

Now we all got in a pickle on the day we christened you;
We couldn't find a name to suit ya straight away it's true.
We thought of Gus Adolphus, and other such fine names,
Till all at once your mother thought of Bill, the same as mine.
And Bill's good enough for you, ain't it Bill?
It's short and nippy too, ain't it Bill?
And though some people think it ain't,

Well, there's nothing in an ain't,
Cos you're our kid just the same, ain't ya Bill?

Now when you grows up a big boy and starts
toddlin' about,
The way we're gunna dress ya lad, will be a
fair knock-out.
A pair of boots high up the leg, the best that's
made for boys,
And a great big hat with feathers in and a pair
of corduroys.
And you will look bloomin' smart, won't ya
Bill?
You'll give 'em all a start, won't ya Bill?
And when I takes you for a ride, or out walking
by my side,
I shall simply burst with pride, won't I Bill?

Now I had a dream the other night, as by my
side ya lay;
I dreamt the angels had come down and taken
you away.
My pillow was all wet with tears as I woke with
a groan,
But ya wouldn't go and leave ya Dad and
Mummy all alone.
So we're never gunna part, are we Bill?
T'would break your mother's heart, wouldn't it
Bill?
Cos if you went away you see, think how lonely
we would be,
So you'll stop with her and me, won't ya Bill?

The party and the singing continued long into the night. Annabelle fell asleep and had to be carried home by Alberto. Al C was different. Young as he was, he could never fall asleep while all the camaraderie and music continued, and took his turn at entertaining; tap dancing to many of the songs. His arm movements were quite natural and he was clever with his stick, albeit a small branch from a tree.

After Christmas, Annabelle was more than eager to get back to school. Second to her home, it was the place she loved best. Her thirst for knowledge was insatiable.

TGA: *(Long may it continue.)*

Chapter 4

Andre Rebels

Andre still tossed and turned every night. Her words, "One day, there'll be murder done in this house, Eugene Kliskey," were clinging and haunting. He felt feverish with the reality of it all. He was certain he was her victim. "She certainly wouldn't kill Ron or Daniel," he thought to himself. "No. It's got to be me."

The next day, after school, he walked away from home. He walked for a long time. When he reached a field bordered by trees he lay down for a rest, using his satchel as a pillow. Afterwards, he ate the two jam sandwiches that he hadn't eaten at lunchtime and assessed which tree would be his bed for the night. He chose the big oak with the hammock-shaped branch at the bottom. He dumped his satchel and shoes by the fence and managed to grasp the lowest point of the branch with his bare hands. Next, he swung his feet up, rather like a monkey, before sitting himself up straight. From there, he manoeuvred himself towards the trunk of the tree, finding footings that enabled him to make steady progress upwards. With rests in between, he reached quite near to the top of the tree. He liked being up there with the birds, but better than that, he liked feeling safe.

Early next morning, he was awakened by something licking his face. It was a dog with a wagging tail. The dog's bark made Andre jump. Very soon the dog's master was by his side.

A silver-haired elderly gentleman appeared and patted his dog. "Good boy, Paddy. Good boy," as he stroked the black Labrador's head. The dog continued to lick Andre's face until his master said, "Sit, boy. Sit."

"Well, well, you've found a little boy; and what's your name sonny?"

"Andre Kliskey, sir."

"And how long have you been laying here?"

"I don't know. I climbed to the top of the tree last night."

"Looks to me as though you fell asleep up there Andre and then fell to the ground. You're covered in cuts and scratches. Quite a mess, really."

Wondering what to do next, he asked, "Do you hurt anywhere?"

"No, sir."

"Well let's try to deal with this sensibly. Can you lift this arm?"

Andre lifted his left arm.

"What about this one?"

Systematically, the gentleman did the same with the legs before asking Andre if he could sit up.

"Well, Andre, it looks to me as though you've had a narrow squeak. You could have killed yourself falling from that height. You must have been in a relaxed state and that saved your bacon. Let's see if you can stand on your two feet."

The gentleman offered his hand and Andre stood up, somewhat shakily.

"Well done. Now tell me where you live and Paddy and I will take you home."

"I can't go home," Andre replied hastily. "I have to go to school. Miss Rees is expecting me."

"Well I think you need to go home and have something to eat first. Anyway, it's too early for school."

Andre didn't dare tell the man that he was afraid to go home. The last thing he wanted was for his stepmother to smell a rat that he knew about her murderous intentions. He put his shoes on his feet and satchel on his back and decided he must face the music and accept that his plan had misfired.

"Good God alive, boy. What have you been up to now?"

The gentleman explained where and how he had found Andre. "It was pretty obvious to me, Ma'am, that the boy had fallen out of the tree. He doesn't remember it, so perhaps he fell asleep up there. Probably best to get him checked out with a doctor. He was asleep on the ground when Paddy found him, so he could well be suffering from concussion."

"Well, I thank you for bringing him home. I'll decide what to do."

Andre thanked the gentleman for helping him and patted Paddy on the back.

Indoors, his stepmother let rip. "You're nothing but a worry to us, boy. Your father's been up all night looking for you and then had to go to work. If he doesn't get to work, there's no money coming in you know."

"I am sorry, Ma," said Andre, hoping to calm her. "I couldn't help it; I got stuck up the tree," telling the white lie for his own protection.

"I'll give you sorry, young man. You shouldn't have been climbing trees in the first place. Come here." She fetched a bottle of iodine from the scullery cupboard. "This'll sting and it'll serve you right."

Andre knew she enjoyed hurting him as she dabbed the iodine all over his hands, face and legs. He forced his tears back out of defiance; he would not give her the satisfaction of knowing it was hurting him.

Coming up to Christmas, Andre was excited because he was going to be a shepherd in the school nativity play. The teachers had asked all the 'shepherd' children to bring in a small tablecloth or a big tea towel to be draped over their heads as costumes for the performance. Round the dinner table that night, Andre was pleasantly surprised when his stepmother said she would find him something. In return, he decided – as he hadn't yet been murdered – that he would force down the yellow cabbage that was on his plate with the boiled potatoes and a sausage. To get it over quickly, he put too much in his mouth, kept chewing round and round, desperate to swallow it, but gagged on it instead and brought the whole lot up in his hands.

Tut-tutting while she cleaned him up, a frustrated stepmother said, "Will this child never learn? That's what comes of stuffing too much in your mouth at once, young man. There's nothing at all wrong with this cabbage. You can jolly well sit there until you've cleared your plate right up."

Andre sat there retching with every attempt and each time his stepmother wrapped him over the knuckles with a tablespoon.

After a long evening sat alone at the table in front of the cabbage, which was interrupted from time to time by taunts such as, "Ha, ha, can't come out to play again," and "Big sissy won't eat your cabbage," from Daniel, Andre was glad to head off to school the next morning, still rejoicing in the fact that he could actually run there in his new shoes.

Unfortunately, along the way, he tripped over an uneven paving stone and grazed his knee. More concerned about scratching his shoes than his sore knee, he was surprised when a lady who was shaking her front doormat against her street wall, spoke to him.

"Come indoors with me, sonny. I'll soon clean that knee up for you."

She was a kind lady and Andre instantly knew he had found a friend. She told him he was a brave boy not to have made a big fuss and gave him two sugar knobs.

Andre was quite excited when the nativity play day arrived. He'd been given an additional singing performance. During earlier rehearsals, the music teacher was astounded when she'd heard Andre sing.

"You've got a very good singing voice Andre. Is someone coaching you?

"No Miss, but my dad sings in the choir in St. Paul's Cathedral."

"Ah, I see. You are a natural. You've inherited it from your dad. You're a very lucky boy."

From that day on she wanted his voice to lead the singing of the Christmas carol, *We Three Kings* and gave him the following instructions.

"Andre, from now on I want you to stand to the extreme left of all the shepherds so you can easily exit the stage at the required time and go and stand behind the back stage scenery, close to the three kings, but hidden from the audience. The teachers had agreed that that would be the best method of utilising Andre's talent, without having to recast or disappoint other pupils.

That nativity Play boosted Andre's confidence to the extent that he felt proud to tell his father what the singing teacher had said about his voice.

Eugene Kliskey pricked up his ears and showed signs of taking an interest in his son. Kit Kliskey and Daniel were not amused.

Christmas 1936 had not been a particularly festive occasion in the Kliskey household. Kit was in a mood because Andre had impressed his father with his singing ability and, by doing so, had usurped her territory.

1937 did not start well either. In late January, Eugene Kliskey received a letter postmarked 'Wiltshire'. All eyes were upon him as he was reading it. His family had been trying to locate him ever since his move to Norwood, following the death of his wife, and now they had succeeded.

With the arrival of that letter, Andre was amazed to discover that he had a sister. At the time of his mother's death while bringing him into the world, his sister had been sent to live with her aunt in Warminster. That aunt was now making travel arrangements to send Elsa Kliskey back to her father.

"Where the hell is she going to sleep for God's sake? And thanks for telling me about her!"

Eugene looked about as henpecked as any male could be.

"I'm beginning to realise that there are only two decent things about you, Eugene Kliskey. Your singing voice and your, your…" Kit searched feverishly for the right word, "…your blasted tackle de boudoir," throwing both arms up in the air in disgust.

Eugene couldn't help grinning at the outburst, before retorting defensively, "Believe it or not, I thought everyone was happy with the situation. They took her on willingly at the time."

"But she's your daughter!" screeched Kit. "Have you never written to her?"

"She was only four at the time. She couldn't write."

Kit was appalled and went through the motions of spitting in his face.

While looking forward to his sister's arrival, Andre desperately hoped they would be staunch friends together under the Kliskey roof. Although his father was not in the class of 'a staunch friend', he was being kinder after discovering about his son's excellent voice.

Andre knew that Miss Rees was a good friend, as well as the elderly lady further up the street who had treated his knee. A bit of sunshine in mid-February had tempted her out to polish her front door knocker and handle. Andre said "Hello" as he passed and offered to do any jobs he could help

with. He wanted to help her and she looked
delighted with the offer. Over time she had sensed
that the boy was troubled and asked him if he
would like to call her Grandma instead of Mrs
James.

"Would that make you happier?"

Andre's face beamed.

"Yes please. I've never had one of those."

TGA: *(I cannot adequately express how
thankful I was to see Andre experiencing some
kindness in his young life.)*

The day Elsa arrived, Andre felt quite shy. He
couldn't stop looking at her, nor she him. They
could have been twins. Both had golden to gingery
hair, freckled faces and slate blue eyes, although
she was taller than he was and better nourished.
Eugene greeted her with an awkward handshake;
not exactly a warm welcome, and Elsa looked a bit
fearful. That fear magnified when she was
introduced to her stepmother. Wanting to protect
her from the frosty atmosphere, Andre said kindly,
"I'm your brother Elsa. My name's Andre," as he
stretched up on tip-toe to give her a kiss on the
cheek.

TGA: *(Considering Andre's upbringing, it was
astounding to see his innate sense of social
correctness when occasion demanded.)*

Sitting around the dinner table that night, it was
plain as the nose on her face that Kit was not a
happy lady. The main topic of conversation was

wondering how to squeeze Elsa into that already crowded household. The conclusion was that Elsa's bed would have to be in the living room. They could push the two armchairs together and Kit would make room in the cupboard for Elsa's few clothes.

Elsa said, "Thank you," followed by a nervous, "I don't know what to call you."

"We are Ma and Pa."

Elsa's head jerked as she looked directly at Kit. "But my Mum died. I haven't got a Mum," she blurted out, as tears rolled down her cheeks.

Andre was pleased to see that his father looked sympathetic, but Kit was adamant. "Eugene, **you** know more than anyone, that in this household we are Ma and Pa."

Andre's heart went out to Elsa. She had only been four years old when their mother had died. He had never known a mother's love, but his sister was obviously still bruised and hurt by the loss. Responsibility welled within him. He still hoped she would like him, so they could be a comfort for each other.

Elsa's first day at school gave Andre the opportunity to be alone with her; otherwise she was always busy indoors, helping their stepmother with the chores. On the way to school he asked, "Is living with us OK for you Elsa?"

Her freckled face coloured up. "I hate it."

"Was your aunt in Warminster kind to you?"

"Yes, she's really nice and she didn't want me to leave, but she said it wasn't right to keep me after she'd found my father's address."

"I hate it too and they all hate me, except for my stepbrother Ron. He's older and doesn't live with us now, but he was – and still is – my friend."

"SHE seems to hate everybody. I'm afraid of her. I'm thinking about running away. I don't mind having to help with chores. I always helped in my auntie's house, but she was nice and always said 'Good girl. Thank you'."

Although Andre was sad for her situation, he liked Elsa living with them and didn't want her to leave. She was his friend and he liked having someone else in the family to be called freckle-face, the same as he was. At nights, after dinner, it was Elsa's job to clear the table while Ma was washing the pots and pans. More often than not, Andre was left alone at the table with cold food that made him gag on the plate in front of him, waiting to be consumed cold. While Elsa was clearing the table, she would furtively stuff a forkful into her mouth, but fear prevented her from taking too much. She didn't gag on it like Andre, but she could never reduce the portion enough.

On the way to school the next day, Andre thanked his sister for trying again to help clear his plate, but told her he didn't want her to do it anymore.

"I couldn't bear to see you punished and you can't be in the room with me long enough to eat it all anyway."

"Do you have to sit there all night?"

"Only until they go to bed. Then I have to put the waste food in the pig swill bin, wash and dry my plate and go to bed. It's OK. It's not every night. Only when foods I gag on are on the plate.

Friday night is good though, when we have fish and chips. Anyway, I don't mind sitting alone. The quiet gives me a chance to think of all the things I can do after my escape from here."

While Elsa was still trying to cope with her new environment in the Kliskey household, the main drive of meaningful existence there for Kit and Eugene was trying to secure a move to a larger house. Kit always held onto the hope of getting Ron back in the fold, and she knew Elsa would soon outgrow the two armchairs. Hence, in the following days, Kit and Eugene were continually scouring the local papers for accommodation to rent. They even considered paying for an advert, stating what they were looking for in Norwood, the better side, or further afield if necessary.

You would expect all of the family to be excited about such a prospect, but not Andre. The thought of having to change schools and never see Miss Rees again was horrendous, which was made even worse with thoughts of losing his very own grandma.

With her in mind, after school one day, Andre knocked on her door.

"Grandma, can I come in and talk to you please?"

"Of course, dear. Come on in."

They had to go downstairs to the living room, exactly the same as in his home, but there was a difference; this place felt comfortable. Andre felt at home.

"Let's sit here, dear, but before you tell me what you want to say, would you like a drink of lemonade and a biscuit?"

"Coo! Yes please."

Sitting alone at the table with his back to the wall, Andre drank in the homeliness. On his right there were no thick net curtains to block out the poor light caused by the close proximity of the stone wall, but hanging each side of the window were some fawn coloured curtains with a design of climbing red roses and dark green leaves. The concrete wall outside was beautiful, even though it was closer to Grandma's window than theirs was at home. It was painted pale blue, looking as though the sky had dropped down to her house. To the left corner of the wall opposite to where Andre was sitting at the table there was Grandma's armchair and across to the opposite wall, to the left of the curtain, there was what looked like a made up armchair on the floor; a basket-woven, rounded back with a small, folded blanket on the floor for a seat.

"I like your room, Grandma. Whose chair is that?"

"Oh, that's Marmalade's chair. My pussycat."

"Where is she now?"

She could see that Andre was enthralled.

"Out playing somewhere, I should think. She'll come back when she's hungry," she smiled.

With lemonade and biscuits in front of Andre, she asked, "Now what was it you wanted to talk to me about, dear?"

Andre poured his heart out about his home situation; about Elsa's arrival and the prospect of having to move away into a bigger house.

Feeling for him, Grandma put her hand across the table and enclosed it over his.

"You poor, dear boy. That is such a sad story."

"It's OK. I'm used to it. I shall run away from home one day. The worst thing about it is that I shall lose you, and Miss Rees, my nice schoolteacher."

Grandma moved from the table.

"Poor Andre. Come over here and sit on my lap," she said, patting her knees as she spoke.

Sitting in the armchair, she cuddled him. Instant tears rolled down his cheeks. She kissed his forehead and wiped his tears.

"Andre, dear, that's a terrible story. How can anyone be so cruel to a little boy? You can come and see me whenever you want. You need someone to love you and I shall shower mine upon you; that's a promise." She kissed him again.

The little boy continued to sob.

"There, there, boy," Grandma consoled, as she cradled and rocked him in her arms. "Let it all out. It's alright now."

Later, when Andre's sobs were abating, he looked up with tear-drenched eyes and kissed Grandma's chin, the only part of her face he could reach while cocooned in her arms.

TGA: *(This was Andre's first real experience of love in his entire life. Such a tragedy that he didn't feel free to enjoy it.)*

With dread in his voice, he said, "I can't come too often. They might find out."

"Well, you know where I am. Come when you feel it is safe to do so, and bring your sister too, so she can meet her Norwood grandma."

"Thank you, Grandma. I will."

The revelation of a homely second home in the same street helped Andre and Elsa through their remaining days in Norwood. They grew to love and cherish Grandma, which enhanced their lives until the threat of a move away from the district became a formidable reality. They had been made aware that their bigger house was in Morland Road, East Croydon, around four to five miles away.

Inevitably, the day came when Andre had to say goodbye to Miss Rees. It was pure misery to watch, but in comparison, his goodbye to Grandma was heartbreaking.

Grandma greeted them with open arms. Her white hair, with its neat bun on the top of her head surrounded by little wisps, was arranged as usual and her pretty pink wrap-around apron, covering her motherly figure, was the same as usual. In fact, everything about her was normal, apart from her smile. That was different. It was a brave smile, shadowed by sadness and yearning. She cuddled them both for a few minutes, while they rocked together in a huddle. Then she pulled back and looked at them.

"Now, listen to me you two." She bent down to their level to look in their eyes, "I want you to remember that this is not goodbye, it's only *au revoir.*"

"What does that mean?"

"It means 'goodbye until we meet again'. Look, I've written my name and address here. Write to me when you can, both of you, and let me know how you're getting on."

At that point, she went across the room to the dresser and picked up two packets.

"Now here's a little parting gift for each of you. This one is yours, Elsa." She handed it to her with a little peck on the cheek.

"Thank you, Grandma." Elsa looked at her questioningly.

"Yes, go on dear, open it now."

Elsa carefully opened the brown paper bag to reveal a delightful pink enamelled umbrella brooch and became awestruck.

"That is beautiful Grandma," she smiled. "I love it already."

"Good, my darling. I'm glad. That little umbrella is to shelter you through your path of life."

Both choked with emotion, they gave each other a lengthy, comforting embrace.

"Now, give me another lovely smile. You've got a nice present to take away with you. Treasure it; and forget me not."

"Your turn now, young man."

Andre's hand was trembling as he opened a similar package and then froze when he saw what it contained. It was a wide, gold ring with one big, star-like diamond in the centre, but too big in size to fit him. With eyes popping out of his head, he asked, "Is that real gold?"

"Yes dear, it is."

"Then, no thank you, Grandma. I can't take it. You must give it to a real grandson, not me."

She cuddled him.

"Dear, lovely boy, you are the only grandson I've ever had. This was my husband's wedding

85

ring. I clearly remember the day we bought them." She put her left hand out to show her own wedding ring. It was an exact replica, but smaller. The memory choked her up, but when she regained her composure she continued, "When Lord Kitchener took him away to WW1, George took his ring off and gave it to me for safe-keeping until his return. But, Andre, he never came back. He died on the Somme, a big battle in France in The Great War."

Andre stretched his arms around her waist, laid his head sideways on to her tummy, and between the tears said, "I'm sorry, Grandma."

Bending down, this time to look into his eyes, she said, "I know dear. Grandma knows. Keep it safe and when you grow into a man, wear it with pride for Grandpa."

Andre was spent with emotion, but he comforted Grandma with, "I will Grandma. I'll wear it proudly, for both of you."

Pointing to the big head-and-shoulders picture of a soldier on the wall that he'd first noticed when he was being cuddled a few weeks ago, he asked, "Is that him, Grandma?"

"Yes, dear, that's him."

Andre lifted his hand as if to say goodbye to the soldier as Grandma led them up the stairs. On opening the door a pale ginger and white cat came running across the street.

"Oh, how lovely. Marmalade's come to say goodbye to you."

The children stroked her for a while and had fun rubbing her belly before she stretched, arched her back and, with tail up, swaggered off indoors.

Grandma smiled. "She's hungry."

Another quick peck and then they waved their goodbyes.

"Isn't it strange that we're marmalades, just like Grandma's cat, but she can't have freckles like us, because she's got fur."

Grandma overheard as they walked away and she followed the cat indoors.

Andre and Elsa dawdled back to their home, wondering what their future would bring.

TGA: *(I'm very glad to say I have a rival. A wonderful human Guardian Angel who can physically cuddle and comfort my charge.)*

Chapter 5

Annabelle Goes to London

After Christmas, when normality was returning, Annabelle longed for the day to come when school re-opened. She needed to be there. It was as though she was connected to it by an unseen piece of elastic. She was familiar with the route and no longer needed Mary to take her there. After waving goodbye to her mummy, she would run up to Anton Lane and join several other children wending their way to school. At the end of the school day, that same piece of elastic served to boomerang her back home to be there for her mummy, where they could both be contented and happy. It was a daily ritual that must have played on her subconscious mind, representing itself in the form of a recurring dream.

TGA: *(Not being human, it's easy for me to know what's going on in her mind, so I can tell you about that dream. It's always exactly the same.*

Annabelle is eagerly hurrying home across the cinder track when she notices, in the ploughed field on her left, that there are masses of shiny new coins laying in the furrows. Quickly, she opens her satchel and stuffs in as many half-crowns and florins, shillings and sixpenny pieces as possible, before scurrying home to surprise her mummy. Before she arrives home to that joyful reality, she wakes up. Crestfallen, Annabelle has to start a new day, eaten up with disappointment. Her visions of the money paying for help with housework for her mother, while she was out at school had been wiped away.

Many other things in Annabelle's life were routine, which all helped the clock to tick by to August, when she would be taken to London to meet her relatives.

Every Saturday, at about 10am, the postman delivered a parcel from the Andover Co-op, which contained Alberto's Woodbine cigarettes for the week. Also inside the parcel was a slip of coloured paper, the receipt, showing the price paid and giving Alice's dividend number, 1782. Alberto made good use of the wrapping paper too. "Waste not, want not," he often told his children. It was strong, brown paper with shiny lines running diagonally across it and with it he made superb flights for his darts. Weekly, Annabelle watched that process with fascination as her daddy painstakingly made clean, crisp folds in the paper with the aid of a weighty pewter tankard and Mummy's unheated smoothing iron.

The Tottenham and Edmonton Herald was delivered weekly and kept Alberto and Alice in touch with home. It was posted from Edmonton by Henry, Alberto's nephew (sister Jane's son), whose job it was to run errands for Alberto's parents. Another of Henry's jobs was to send parcels to Aunt Palmeira (Bubble's Italian sister). Her address – after emigrating from Italy at about the same time that Bubble stowed away on a ship, which took him to England – was 64 School Street, Yonkers, New York.

January 1936 brought doom and gloom, not only to the Alessandro household and the village, but to the entire nation and the world. King George V had died. Wireless broadcasts about his failing health had compelled Alice and Alberto to have their ears glued to the wireless as they heard such bulletins as, "The King's life is drawing peacefully to a close." Generally, he had been respected as a good king and now he was dead. Immediately, his eldest son, The Prince of Wales was pronounced King.

TGA: *(The ways of Royalty! One King, whose demised body was hardly cold, waiting for rigor mortis to set in, while the public's chanting outside could be heard loud and clear: "Long Live the King! Long Live the King!")*

The King's death interrupted all that was regular and normal in Annabelle's life. So did days when Alice was too ill to be left home alone. On those occasions, sadness filled Annabelle's soul because she could not go to school, but her love for her mother rose above all else. At such times, Auntie Dolly would teach her how to cook dinners, with whatever meat was in the safe. Auntie Dolly tried to keep the dinners as simple possible for little Annabelle to manage. One such dinner was to prepare vegetables and cook an all-in-one stew on the range, which was always lit by Alberto before going to work.

As usual, on dry weather days, Annabelle was waiting by the picket fence at the bottom edge of the lawn for her daddy to come home from work. On one such occasion, she couldn't stop herself from laughing as two village boys were mimicking disabled men as they approached each other on the pavement, the other side of the fence from where she was waiting. One of them swung his right leg in a wide semi-circle in the process of taking each step, while touching his imaginary cap and saying, "Watcha, Charles."

The oncoming boy, putting on a cockney accent, replied, "Alright, Guv, thanks. 'Ow's yourself?" with accentuated jerks and twitches of the head. He was imitating a shell shocked man.

"You two are very naughty boys," Annabelle scolded. "The poor men can't help being like they are. The war did it."

By contrast, another day Annabelle was frozen out of her senses, along with the rest of the village. Peter Basting, a boy who lived in Knights Enham and went to school in Smannell, along with the Enham Village Centre children, was riding his Colson Fairy Bicycle, of which he was very proud, down the golden gravel drive from Enham Place. Without pausing to look, he cycled straight out onto the main road from Newbury to Andover and collided with a passing motor car. For Peter, there was no second best scenario, like being wounded. His short life came to a tragic end early in 1936, when he was 8 years old.

The accident was witnessed by Steve Weeks, a wounded man who had trained to be a gardener in Enham Village Centre. He was mowing the lawn in front of the Landale Wilson Institute when he happened to glance up and saw what was about to happen. He shouted to Peter, but the motor mower engine was too loud. Peter couldn't hear him. The shocked driver said there was no way he could have avoided the boy, who had cycled straight out of the drive and into the side of his car. Mr Weeks, accompanied by the driver, carried the boy's body to the Village Stores, which was next door to the Landale Wilson Institute and opposite the scene. He laid the body on a bed in the home of the Village Stores' proprietor, Mr Willoughby, at the back of the shop and awaited the doctor's arrival.

Mr Basting, who worked as a basket maker in Enham Village Centre, identified his son's body. The Coroner recorded a verdict of accidental death and offered his profound sympathies to the family.

The whole village became subdued, but Annabelle was deeply affected. She was more than ever aware how final death is. Uppermost in her mind was always the life of her mother.

For a while after the accident, Annabelle became very protective of her mother and was constantly by her side. Totally out of character, she didn't even want to go to school. Together, Alice and Alberto nurtured her back to a more confident state, only to be faced with another setback.

Alberto and his troupe of tap dancers had been taking part in the pantomime, Dick Whittington, in the Landale Wilson Institute after Christmas. It was a resounding success and a second matinee performance was put on by popular demand because news of the good production had reached to the people of Andover. After that matinee,

Alberto had to share some more amazing news about the pantomime with his family.

The family were cosy and warm in the living room, when Alberto broke the news that the village authorities wanted the show committee to take their pantomime to Papworth Everard, in Cambridgeshire.

Annabelle asked, "Can we go with you, Daddy?"

"No sweetheart, you can't."

"But what about Mummy? What if she's ill?"

Lifting her onto his knee, Alberto gently whispered, "I was hoping to take you all with me, sweetheart, but kiddy-winkles are not allowed to go. Even the little fairies who danced in the pantomime are really upset because they aren't allowed to go either."

"Will you have to stay away all night?"

Cuddling her tightly to him, he replied, "Yes, I do have to, but only for one night. I'm sure Mummy with be fine, but I've chatted to Dr MacCallum about my being away for one night and how worrying it is to be leaving you." Alberto looked down at his daughter with great compassion. "The doctor told me to tell you that if you are at all worried, then you or Al C can run up to the surgery, day or night, and ring his doorbell and he will come quickly to check on Mummy. Does that make it any easier for you?"

Annabelle nodded hesitantly.

"Come on, sweetheart. Cheer up for old Dad. We know Mummy's not going to do anything as silly as bending over, don't we? She's been a very good girl since you've been at school. Shall we give her a big clap for that. Come on Al C, you as well. Let's see how much noise we can make."

Al C was up for that alright; banging spoons on his tattered old drum and stamping his feet.

"Thank you, thank you, family. That's enough!" shouted Alice, with hands over her ears. She knelt down in front of Annabelle who was still sitting on her father's lap and quietly coaxed, "Don't you think it would be nice to share your daddy with all the children in Papworth, just for one night, so they can enjoy watching the show too? Then they can have lots of fun shouting out 'Boo!' and 'He's behind you', and all those funny things, just like you did."

Rubbing her eyes sleepily, she said, "I do want them to see it, but..."

"I know, Annabelle. I know. But, just one night, eh?" Alberto put his hand out invitingly, "Shake on it?"

Annabelle put out her hand and they 'shook' for a long time. Alberto would not release his grip. Thankfully, that bit of fun, along with the explanations, took the stress out of the situation for Annabelle.

"Just one more little word of warning, sweetheart. I might not be home until late the second night, but I promise, as soon as I get home, I'll creep into your bedroom and kiss you goodnight."

A little brighter now, she chirped, "Put some of that stage lipstick on, so when I wake in the morning I can see where you kissed me," she giggled.

"You're nothing but a little imp, young lady."

The Cambridgeshire village where they were performing the pantomime had a link with Enham. Their village started in 1917 as a Tuberculosis Colony, providing a sheltered, fresh air environment with accommodation and vocational training, leading to permanent work if desired and medical services. Dr Pendrill Varrier-Jones was the catalyst for the foundation of this colony. It was his vision to create not just a hospital or rehabilitation centre for tuberculosis patients, but a whole community. As the settlement grew, it went on to build profitable workshops under the name of Papworth Industries.

Dr Pendrill Varrier-Jones was that link with Enham Village Centre. The Village Centres' Council, set up by the British Government in 1919, had plans to set up similar villages all over the British Isles for WW1 wounded soldiers and co-opted Dr Pendrill Varrier-Jones onto the governing body of their first such village, taking advantage of his knowledge in setting up a successful village settlement.

Now, with both villages prospering, Enham wounded soldiers were taking their pantomime to entertain the people living at Papworth. The following account of the show appeared in their local press:

PAPWORTH

EPOCH-MAKING EVENT – An event occurred at Papworth on Saturday, which did not shake the world, it is true, and yet, in its way, it was an epoch-making event, and one that is full of

*significance. The casual visitor to Papworth would
have noticed a poster declaring to all that the
'E.D.A.D.S.' were presenting a pantomime, 'Dick
Whittington', in the Village Hall. It was much more
than this, however. It was the first time that a
Village Settlement for the Disabled had entertained
another Village Settlement. An entertainment was
being provided at Papworth entirely by the Enham
Village Centre, the well-known Hampshire
Settlement for disabled ex-servicemen. Enham,
which is one of the settlements for the disabled,
controlled by Sir Pendrill Varrier-Jones, set out to
show Papworth what they could do, and Papworth
saw and was conquered. For Enham provided
three hours of music, colour and laughter – a
gargantuan meal, but eagerly devoured by
Papworth. What a wonderful show it was – most
ably performed by ex-servicemen and their wives
and daughters, led by the Rev. H J Webb, the
Chaplain of the Centre, who was not only the
producer, but took the title role also, in a most
gallant and dashing manner.*

*One would like to mention all the cast, but that
is impossible. Mrs Guest as 'Alice Fitzwarren'
deserves special mention, particularly for her duets
with 'Dick', and her performance as a 'vivandière'
in the wonderful number, 'The Guards are on
Parade' by the whole company, which brought the
house down. Mr Tempero as the 'respectable cook-
housekeeper', (dare we say, perhaps a little too
respectable for a pantomime cook) was responsible
for much merriment, particularly in his love
passages with Mrs Moody (otherwise Idle Jack,)*

who also was extremely funny in a part that did not allow much scope for humour.

Mr Alessandro, despite the handicap of an artificial arm, tap danced well and rhythmically, and Mr Lillywhite did some remarkable wizardry. The principals and chorus worked hard and sang well and much credit is due for the way the ensembles were arranged and the whole production dressed. If we have one criticism, it is that the show was a trifle long, and might be cut with advantage in the third act. The performance was well supported by a mixed orchestra of Enham and Papworth musicians. After the show, the players were entertained to supper by the Matron, Miss K.L. Borne, in the Scouts' Hut.

A very happy little girl found her lipstick kiss on her cheek the next morning and gave her daddy a 'smacker' before he went off to work, soon after which she went off to school. On the way there, she was told that someone else was going to give dancing lessons in the Institute; apparently, not tap dancing like her father. A lady named Dulcie Darke was going to teach ballet dancing. At the tea table that evening, she was eager to share that news and if Alberto had already heard it, he didn't let on to his daughter.

After tea, as usual on cosy winter evenings, Alberto and Alice would sit at the table playing easy card games such as Snap, or do jigsaw puzzles or homely things with the children. Sometimes Alberto had to go to the Institute to give tap dancing lessons, or rehearsals and other times he would go there to play billiards for the Club.

Other evenings, Annabelle enjoyed learning to knit. With Alice's guidance, she was knitting a simple style maroon-coloured dress for her dolly. It was a double-sided oblong, sewn together at the top for shoulders and down the sides, leaving slits at the top for armholes.

Al C's hobby was all-absorbing. He loved horse-racing, which he had learned about from Auntie Dolly and Mr Mesney next door. Mr Mesney was a bookies' runner. That meant he ran the facility for Enham villagers, but was linked to a bookmaker's office in Andover. Hence, they were one of the few families in the village who had a telephone; their number being Andover 2858. Auntie Dolly understood the business equally as well as Mr Mesney, so when he was busy with private basketry work in his shed, she could relay the bets to the office for him and work out the win payments.

As soon as Al C had learned to read, he used to grab the racing pages from the Express newspaper, which was delivered daily, and pick out his winners for the day. In the evening, he would nip out of the back door and run round to Auntie Dolly's to show them how much money he would have won, or lost, if he'd had money to bet on his chosen horses. He became quite skilled at working out the winnings too.

With Easter looming, Annabelle was hoping that her friend Pam Angel would come down from London to stay with her nanny. Because she was too shy to go and knock Mrs Piggin's door, her mummy took her. It was Pam's Auntie Ella who answered and invited them indoors for a cuppa.

Mrs Piggin greeted them and said, "I'm so sorry, dearie, you won't have your little friend at Easter, but she is coming down in August.

Annabelle blushed and looked up to her mummy.

"It's alright sweetheart. I expect Pam will be down for more than one week in the long summer holiday." She looked questioningly at Mrs Piggin.

"Oh yes. She's coming down for three weeks. Is that better, dear?"

Annabelle smiled as Alice replied, "That's lovely. We are taking the children to London to meet our families up there for the week of the factory closure, but that will leave two weeks for the girls to be together."

"I heard that your daddy had you and Pam tap dancing together when she was down last time. Is that right?" asked Auntie Ella.

Annabelle nodded.

"Well, I might be able to teach the pair of you some ballet steps in August. I'm having lessons with Dulcie Darke in the Institute."

"Yes, and our Ella is the star of the class too, so she'll be a really good teacher for you."

On a Friday night in August, a week before the London visit, Annabelle had the surprise of her life. Auntie Ella and Pam called to see them. Immediately, the two girls were in a world of their own. In minutes they were in the corner settling dollies in the pram ready for a walk in the garden and then, quite naturally, both pushing the pram, having one hand each on the handle. Before getting very far, both the girls rushed urgently back indoors.

"Mummy, can Pam sleep with me tonight?"

Auntie Ella raised her distinctive dark eyebrows in Alice's direction.

"That didn't take long, did it?"

Looking at Auntie Ella, Annabelle asked, "And…can I sleep with Pam tomorrow night, so I can play your piano again?"

TGA: *(Plans, plans, plans. This was more like a proper childhood for Annabelle. So different from the little girl who stood on the back door step gently dabbing her eyes with a cold flannel, but not rubbing them, as instructed by Auntie Dolly, after she had been peeling onions for an all-in-one-stew. "After that, you can continue peeling onions and your eyes won't sting any more. But, my darlin', you must remember that little tip each time you peel onions," said Auntie Dolly caringly.)*

On their first evening together, Alberto took the girls up the woods to find a couple of sticks to use for a new tap dancing routine. Back home, he unrolled the tap dancing mat onto the scullery floor and started to teach them. Alice was trying to do the washing up at the sink, but found the girls' attempts at coordinating the sticks with the dance steps quite hilarious. The sticks were dropped onto the dancing mat umpteen times until all four of them were weak with laughter. Between his own tears of laughter, Alby managed to say, "I think we'll put the sticks to bed for another year before you poke each other's eyes out."

Next night at Mrs Piggin's home, they were practising ballet positions by holding onto the 'bar'. The improvised bar was the edge of the draining board. In their happy state of just being together, facing one another in their ballet positions was not conducive to concentration, so Auntie Ella placed them in line, one behind the other. After half an hour of routinely hard work, Auntie Ella said, "Good girls. Now you can run along and laugh your heads off as much as you like and I'll teach you some more when Annabelle gets back from London."

Before getting into bed, Annabelle wanted to spend time sitting at the piano, which was pushed into the corner of the bedroom the girls were sharing. It was very dusty, but when she lifted the lid the piano keys were clean. She was trying to pick out the notes of the tonic-sol-fa scale, which she'd learned in singing lessons at school. She found that sometimes she could play it and sometimes she couldn't. Her perseverance was unrelenting as she desperately tried to find the correct note to start on. In parallel, pyjama-clad Pam was practising some ballet positions while standing on the bed, without a bar! Eventually, the ballet-without-a bar caper became too tempting to resist, so Annabelle closed the piano lid.

Tucked up in bed at the end of their last day together before the London interruption, Annabelle asked Pam, "What's it like in London?"

"It's ever so different to here. All the houses in our street are the same, both sides of the road. They are tall offices."

"So you live in an office?"

"No, we live in a flat."

"What's that?"

"It's our home. It's where we live, but it's in the basement of the office building."

"Whatever's the basement?"

"It's below the ground."

Full of pity, Annabelle went on, "How awful. You poor thing. Is it dark all day long?"

Pam laughed at Annabelle's quizzical face. "No, of course it's not. Demonstrating as huge a size as manageable with her small outspread arms, she said, "We have big windows that look up to the pavement and you can see the legs of people as they walk by."

Whispering, and blushing, "Can you see the lady's knickers?"

"Annabelle, you're incorrigible."

"What does that mean?"

"I don't know, but my mum says it to me sometimes."

Early next morning, Auntie Ella came to collect Pam and take her home, after separating the girls from their limpet-like goodbye hug. Soon after, Alby, Alice and the children started their long trek to Andover Junction Station, via the country lane to Charlton, a small village on the way. The day was bright and energising; Annabelle's strong little legs were up to the job and Alice's heart was coping, so long as she didn't have to carry any luggage.

At the station, Alberto bought their return tickets to Waterloo, after which the family waited on the platform. Arriving on time, the train came into view with a plume of billowing white smoke.

"Here comes the train, children," said Alice, who was excited at the prospect of soon being able to show off her children to both their families.

102

"It looks like a snake, Mummy."

"That snake will get bigger and bigger very quickly. You'll soon see."

The horrendous, deafening noise of the train's approach ruled out more conversation. Annabelle was petrified and clung onto her daddy's leg for dear life.

"It's alright, sweetheart. It won't be so noisy when we're inside it. Look at Al C. He's not frightened at all. He's excited."

When the train came to a halt at the platform, a station guard who had observed Alberto's artificial arm, was immediately at his side to help him get his family and luggage on board. Alberto, who was holding Annabelle in his arms, was first into the carriage, guiding Al C as he went. In a short time the family were settled inside. Alby and Al C sat opposite Alice and Annabelle, with each child sitting by a window. Before very long, they could see the guard outside on the platform again and heard the piercing shriek of his whistle as he bellowed, "Mind the doors; mind the doors!" He then walked the length of the train, slamming shut all the open doors.

That train journey gave rise to distinctly opposite reactions from the children. Al C was like a cat on hot bricks.

"Are we nearly there, Dad?" He was so eager to get to London, while his sister was scared stiff and longed to get to London, purely to get off the train.

Al C was taking it all in when the ticket inspector, who was distinctive by his big white, grandfatherly moustache, came into the carriage to punch a hole in their tickets.

"Why aren't you punching the hole in the middle of the ticket?"

"Because the other end will be punched when you go home on your return journey; so make sure your dad looks after those tickets, young man."

Alberto knew from experience that their journey was coming to an end as they passed through Clapham Junction. From that time, he was organising the drill for getting his family off the train at Waterloo Station. Beckoning them to huddle heads together, he said, "We don't want any accidents, so I want you both to understand that when the train stops and we have to get out onto the platform, you will see a bit of a gap between the two. I shall get out first and you will be second, Al C. I will hold your hand and you must jump down to the platform.

Next, I shall help Annabelle out, and when she's on the platform I want you to hold her hand, while I help Mummy. Now you look after her like a good boy, because she is very frightened and there'll be lots of people all rushing by with heavy luggage, anxious to get through the platform gates quickly. Are you listening to me, Al C?"

Al C appeared to be a bit bewildered at so much instruction being necessary, just to get off a train. He nodded his head as he said, "OK Dad. I'll hold her hand and look after her, but make sure she's listening to you too."

"Did you hear that, Annabelle? When I lift you off the train, you've got to stand still by Al C's side and hold his hand while I help Mummy."

A white faced Annabelle nodded, looking frightened and shaken at the very prospect of it all.

"Try to be brave, Annabelle," pleaded a worried Alice. "Your friend Pam does this journey all the time when she comes to stay with her nan and she's not frightened, is she?"

Continuing his instructions, Alberto said, "When you two are on the platform, I shall then help Mummy off the train and after that I'll get back into the train for the luggage."

A surprise voice cut in at that point saying, "Don't worry about your luggage, mate, I'll hand that out to you."

It was the middle-aged man who had been sitting by the window at the other end of the carriage.

"Thank you, sir. That'll be a great help."

Alberto succeeded in getting his family safely off the train and hastily found toilets on the station, to everyone's relief.

The next adventure was boarding the No. 76 double-decker bus outside Waterloo Station. Al C and Annabelle were wide-eyed. It was the first time they'd ever seen a bus with an upstairs.

"Do they have beds up there?" asked Annabelle.

"No, sweetheart. It's full of seats up there, the same as downstairs."

"Can we go up there, Dad?" asked Al C, raring to go.

"Sorry, son. Not this journey. I'll take you on one while we are up here, just you and me, and no luggage."

"Cor, thanks Dad. I like being in London. It's more exciting than the country."

The 76 bus took them all the way to their destination, where they alighted at the bottom of the turning to Workhouse Hill. Proud as peacocks, Alberto and Alice guided their children up the road to the alley, where they turned left. Four footsteps later, Alberto opened the front door into the warmth and familiarity of the parlour, impregnated, as of old, with the smell of something delicious cooking for dinner, and called out, "Is anyone at home?"

The small room was crowded. Lots of family members had gathered for this homecoming.

"Alberto, my son," greeted his mother with open arms.

It had been eight years since they'd seen each other and her tears of joy were running down his neck exactly the same as they had seventeen years ago when he returned home from the war.

"And what a gorgeous little girl you have here. I'll sit down in a minute and say hello to your children."

Before further greetings, Alberto responded to Annabelle's constant tugging on his trouser leg and lifted her into his arm. Papa was waiting impatiently in line. For him, it was the three-way cheek-to-cheek greeting. His eyes, too, welled up with joy.

"My-a d'son. My-a d'first-a born-a son."

Then, holding Annabelle's cheeks between his flat hands, he repeated the same motion. She smiled at him. It was obvious she could feel the genuine emotional outpouring from her grandfather.

"Annabelle, this is Bubble, your grandpa." I have a teeny-weeny feeling that you like him."

Her nod confirmed the assumption.

Even for Alberto, the large family gathering was overwhelming. Taking control of the situation, mainly for the sake of his children, he asked his eldest sister Jane if she would ring the cowbell that was still on the mantelpiece. That done, Alberto said, "Hello family. What a royal welcome and it makes me proud to be one of you. For my children though, who don't know any of you, it's a different kettle of fish."

"We're not blinkin' fish, Dad." Al C's remark cast a momentary hush over the room, followed by laughter and clapping and comments such as, "That's my boy," and "Blimey, you're a chip off your Uncle Jonty's block."

"Come here Al C. Come and show your face," laughed Alberto.

"Is it alright if I stand my children on the table here Ma, where everyone can see and meet our offspring?"

"Of course Alberto."

"Here we go then. It's 'Meet the Family' time."

Looking lovingly at Alice, who was standing by his side, he said, "Here is my lovely Alice and you all know what a risk it was for her to bear my children; but she went through it all successfully for me. The truth is, she's made my world and we are a very happy family together down there in the sticks.

"Now I want to show off our children. Here is *'my first-a born-a son'*, winking at Papa. We don't call him Alberto Junior as you were told when he was born. After starting school and learning his ABC, he decided he wanted to be called Al C; didn't you, scamp?" He pretended to strangle his son's throat. "That's because the blokes down there call me Alby."

"Yea, well," chipped in Al C. "He," pointing his thumb over his shoulder to his dad, "came first and me second. We haven't got to Al D yet!" he joked confidently, relishing in his spotlight on the table.

Antonio called out to his brother, "Blimey, your son's talented too. Reminds me of NOSMO KING; the one who got his name from the NO SMOKING signs. And, knowing you, I suppose he can tap dance?"

The showman in Al C responded immediately with a few steps.

"OK, OK, Al C. That's enough now. Let's give your sister a look-in."

Looking pretty as a picture dressed in her 'new for the occasion' lacy lilac dress, which Alice had crocheted, and rich plum, hand-knitted cardigan that accentuated her blonde ringlet bunches, tied with lilac ribbons each side of her head, many comments such as "Beautiful", and "She looks good enough to eat", spilled forth. But, there was not one iota of showman in Annabelle's little body. She was very shy and immediately turned round and buried her face in her daddy's neck to outbursts of, "Shame, she's shy. Leave her alone; she'll come round in her own time."

Bubble saved the day. He went to her at the table and said warmly, "Anna come-a Bubble."

Happy to escape the limelight, she clung to him and he took her to his low wooden stool, with the sash window behind. It was heart-warming to see how she had taken to him. He sat down, then lifted her onto his lap with her back to his chest. Placing his arms around her tummy, he pulled her closely to him as though she was more precious than anything else on earth. You could see she was feeling the warmth of this man's love as she looked up to his face and said, "Thank you Mr Bubble," which triggered laughter.

Sitting opposite in her wooden rocking chair, Grandma Aless smiled and said, "How sweet, but there's no need to say 'Mister', Annabelle. You just say Bubble. She then beckoned to Al C.

"Come, young man; come and get to know your grandma."

Al C put his hand out. Holding the proffered hand, she said, "A handshake won't do for Grandma now, will it? I want a nice long cuddle."

Al C cringed at that prospect from a lady he'd never met before. He stood straight and still before her while she said in her soft cockney voice, "Well I hope it's true that you do like London, Al C. It's where your dad grew up and he was happy here."

Grandma patted her knees. "Come, sit on my lap now, so I can give you a kiss and a cuddle and we can get to know one another."

Allowing himself to be lifted into position, Grandma asked, "And how old are you now, Al C?"

"I'm seven and Annabelle will be six at Christmas.

"Well, my boy, when you get a bit older, you might like to come up here in your school holidays and stay with Bubble and me? Your dad tells me you've taken an instant liking to London.

"Oooh, yes please, Grandma. I really want to do that." He excitedly volunteered another kiss.

The room became abuzz with chatter and laughter, while Jane and her thirteen-year-old daughter Hannah, Alberto's youngest sister, Lucia, and her fifteen-year-old daughter Francesca, busied themselves making cups of tea and biscuits.

Later, when Vincenzo arrived, after having finished his morning stint selling ice creams from the barrow on Edmonton Green, Mama said, "My goodness, it's time for dinner. Come on you lot. Off you go to your own homes. I expect Alberto will visit you all individually while he's here."

"We intend to do that Ma, don't we Alice? I've got door numbers imprinted on my brain. Jane and Richard and children still live in the family home here, of course, and Lucia and Nick and family are still in No. 24, next door to the ice cream parlour; where they were before I left home. I understand Vincenzo and Phoebe are in 26 and Antonio and Little Polly and their baby girls are further up the road in 76."

Alberto scratched his head as he looked around at them.

"So I'm still the only one of us to have moved away from Workhouse Hill! Yes, of course we'll spend as much time with you separately as we can, but you must remember that we've got Alice's family to visit too. There's Alice's mum and youngest sister Daisy in the shop at No. 40; her eldest sister, Emily and Tommy at 29 and Emily's eldest daughter Becky in 84, with her young husband, George. Unlike our family, who are all still here, Alice has two brothers, Tom and Justin, who have moved out of Workhouse Hill, but we're hoping they'll save our time by coming to see us."

Almost exhausted at the thought, Alberto continued, "Phew, that's enough to keep us busy for a month, but I'm afraid we only have one week. I'm due back at work on Monday."

After eating a delicious dinner of scrag-of-mutton stew with Papa and Mama, Jane, her husband Richard and their children Henry and Hannah, Alberto and Alice excused themselves to go up the road to see Mrs Howitz, Alice's mum.

No. 40 was just a distance of ten terraced houses up the road. Al C was in awe at what he was seeing in Granny Howitz' shop window.

"Jeeps, Mum. Look at all the sweets Granny's got. I can see sherbet dips and lollipops and aniseed balls. Oooh, and she's got blackjacks too. I really like those."

Annabelle was more interested in peering through the window into the shop.

"I can see Granny, Mum."

"Come on then. Let's go in and say hello." She entered the shop door, which was on the right of the window.

Excusing herself from two waiting customers, Granny Howitz lifted a section of the counter top and let herself into the shop to greet her family.

She had a quick kiss for each of them saying, "Go in and put the kettle on. I'll join you as soon as I can."

"Are all the rooms this small in London?" asked Al C.

"We're not in London yet," retorted Annabelle.

Alberto intervened, "I'm afraid you're wrong there, sweetheart. We definitely are in London."

"No we're not Daddy. In bed last night, Pam told me that all the houses in her street are high. They are all offices and people live in basements, which are under the ground and she lives in London, so she should know."

Alice laughed. "It's OK you two. You're both right. The difference is that Pam lives in the city. I know that for certain because Auntie Ella gave me her address, which is 3 Great James Street, High Holborn, London, WC1."

Alberto grinned at Alice. "I can understand Annabelle's confusion, coming from an Enham perspective; a very small village where everyone knows everyone."

Sitting with Annabelle on his knee, with her back to the range in Granny Howitz' flattened armchair by the side of the square table, which more or less filled the drab brown parlour, Alberto said, "Let me try to explain to you, Annabelle. I want you to think of the biggest circle you can imagine; a huge one, and that still won't be big enough. OK?"

She nodded.

"Then we shall call that circle London. Now your friend Pam lives in the centre of the circle, which is called Central London, and while we're staying up here with Granny, we are on the top of the circle, which is called North London.

Distracted, Annabelle noticed a piano to her right, which was squeezed into the room with the back of the table butting on to it.

"Mummy, Mummy, Granny's got a piano."

Immediately, she was gone from her daddy's lap and hurried round the table to get to the end of the piano, which was near the inner door to the shop. She slightly lifted the piano lid, which was covered in piles of clothes and played one single note, happy to discover that it worked.

Granny nearly squashed her as she entered the living room from the shop.

"Hello, my precious family. It's so good to see you again. Goodness me, you do all look well. Is that kettle on Alice?"

"Yes, Mother, it is, but I was so shocked when I went into the scullery. The big bowl of live eels has gone from the top of the copper."

Granny gave her familiar chuckle. "Well, what do you expect? You've all left home! There's only Daisy and myself here now. Quite often a neighbour will bring me a live eel, if he's been fishing up the Lea, so we still eat them. I just don't need my own livestock anymore. In between times, we have bread and Bovril, or fried eggs on toast."

The shop bell rang.

"Sorry, I'll have to go to the shop. Daisy will be back soon and then she'll deal with the shop while I get five minutes peace with you."

There are cream crackers in the tin and the cheese dish is in the cupboard. Help yourselves."

"No thanks, Granny, we've just had a big dinner, but can I have some blackjack chews from the shop please?"

"Of course you can, my boy. Come in the shop and I'll give you a handful. What about Annabelle; do you want some sweeties too?"

"No thank you," she replied politely, shyly shaking her head. I want you to sing me some more sea shanties, like you did at Christmas."

"Granny will be glad to, poppet. I remember you liked the stories the sea shanties tell, didn't you?"

"Well, I want Granny Howitz to do something for me, too," interrupted Alberto. "Listen, Ma, I have had this wooden carving made by Mr Shergold, who lives in the house called Vimy Ridge in the village. It's depicting the Roman God of Love, Cupid, aiming his golden arrow, and I'm asking if you will hang it on your shop door?"

"Aha, and I know why, Alberto Alessandro. You found all your romantic, shall we say, liaisons under my roof, didn't you? I remember them well, dear boy. Of course I'll hang it on my shop door. The customers talk about it to this day, so they'll have a laugh to see it commemorated."

It didn't take long for word to spread that Alice and family were indoors. Alice's eldest sister Emily was first to pop in from her shop over the road. Her pretty blue wrap-around apron was quite sooty and there was a smear of coal dust across her face. She'd just had a supply of coal bags delivered, which they sold in the shop.

"I've got ten minutes off; Tommy's holding the fort."

The two sisters were busy chatting ten-to-the-dozen about how the war had affected them and how Emily had married a Belgian wounded soldier while he was receiving medical treatment over here, before she returned to Belgium with him. Sadly Boris, her husband, had later been killed by friendly fire when he resumed Army duty again, leaving her alone in a foreign country with three children. On return to Workhouse Hill, she was fortunate enough to meet Tommy, a lonely man who had lost his family in a Zeppelin raid.

"Emily, I'm so glad there's been a happy ending for both of you," said Alice, giving her sister an emotional hug. "I'm longing to meet him. Send him over to meet us when you shut the shop."

"The war didn't affect me as dramatically as it did you, Emily. Marrying Alberto has been the making of me. I'm lucky to be living in a nice house in a country village. The village, as you know, is full of WW1 disabled men. It is both sad, and inspiring, to see how they cope with their daily lives. I wouldn't come back to Workhouse Hill if you offered me a fortune."

Their chat was interrupted by Daisy who suddenly dashed in the door from the shop.

"Daisy! My baby sister Daisy. Look at you!" You're so grown up. You look lovely."

"Well, I'm twenty-three now. Don't forget, I was only fifteen when you left home."

"That's right. And in those eight years I've got myself two children."

Calling them in from the yard with Alberto, Alice said, "You must say hello to Annabelle and Al C. They are growing up too fast for my liking."

"They're gorgeous children Alice. Lucky you."

"And what about you? Have you got your eye on anybody?"

"Don't make me blush, Alice."

At that point, Al C cut in with, "Mum, I'm bored. Can I go back down to Grandma Aless and see my cousins?"

Alice look at Alberto.

"I think we'll both go if that's OK with you Alice? I feel like a spare part myself with all this girlie talk going on."

"That's OK, Alberto, but make sure you both come back later to say goodnight to Annabelle and me, won't you?"

After they'd departed, Alice was eager to get back to her heart to heart.

"Come on then, Daisy. Tell me more. There is someone, isn't there? I can tell."

"I see you're still an old witch. You always did have a second sense about things. Yes, I am sweet on somebody and I think he's interested, but nothing's been said yet."

"Well you and I must have a quiet chat. I'm an experienced matchmaker you know. The only way I could put myself in Alberto's way was by going out with his brother first."

Daisy was wide-eyed with amazement, but could not pursue the conversation because Granny Howitz had summoned her back to the shop.

"So what's the plan for tonight?" asked Emily. "Are we girls going down the Eel Shop for a meal to celebrate your homecoming, Alice?"

"Sounds perfect to me. Will you come with us Mother?"

"No, thank you. It'll be nice for you girls to go off together. I'll stay and look after the shop."

"Granny, can I stay up to see the old people coming to the shop to leave their treasures?"

"Good gracious Annabelle! I'm surprised you remember such things."

"Mother, I can tell you, it's not the treasures that are attracting her. It's the poor old people. At home, she cries when the shell shocked men are twitching badly and she desperately wants to help the disabled men in winter when they are trying to walk to work on the icy roads. I'm sure she's got an overdose of compassion because of it."

"Come, Annabelle, come and sit on Granny's lap." She cuddled her closely and said, "If that's what you want to do my poppet, then you shall do it; but not tonight. You've had that long train journey and a very busy day, so I think it's beddy-byes for you soon."

"Where is my bed?"

"See that door the other side of the table?"

"I'll take her up and show her, Mother."

"Alright dear. You've got Daisy's room at the back. She's sharing with me at the front."

After the first step, the stairs had a sharp curve to the right and were very steep and narrow.

"It's dark, Mummy. Is there a light?"

"No, my love. These houses are very old and they're still using old-fashioned gas mantles, but only in the rooms. You'll see when Granny lights hers tonight. At home, we're lucky to be living in a new house with electric lights."

Later, when Annabelle was tucked up fast asleep, Alice, Emily, Daisy and Emily's daughter

Becky, all trundled off to the Eel Shop for a supper of stewed eels, mash and parsley liquor. Alice felt hungry, having eaten nothing since the mutton stew earlier in the day. To her, there was nothing to compare with the homespun uniqueness of the eel shops. They were eating houses for the man in the street; not a place for 'airs and graces', posh cutlery and napkins. They were places of down-to-earth, finger-lickin' luxury, where hard-working, hungry people were welcomed into the warmth of its confines to tuck into a good square meal and left feeling comfortably nourished and satisfied.

For those who didn't like eels, there was the alternative choice of pie and mash, with parsley liquor if required.

Despite her shyness, Annabelle liked doing jobs for her granny in the shop. On the floor opposite the counter where Granny and Daisy served the customers, there were sacks of commodities such as rice, sugar, flour, salt and soda crystals etc., each with its own individual scoop. When required, Granny would pass a brown paper bag to Annabelle who would put two full scoops into the bag and pass it back to Granny to be weighed before selling. There was also an area with crates containing Tizer fizzy drinks in different flavours, plus some empty bottles. Customers got a half-penny back if they returned their empties.

Alice and Annabelle didn't see much of Al C in Granny Howitz' home, although he did come at the end of every day with his dad to say goodnight to them. He was full of excitement about London and wanted to live there. On the other hand, Annabelle made it her business to see Bubble every evening for her cuddle.

"Daddy can't cuddle me the same as you, Bubble, because he doesn't have two nice soft arms."

TGA: *(Whether or not Bubble understood what she said, I'll never know, but he was touched to the core that he had made such a staunch friend of Alberto's daughter.)*

After her cuddle, Bubble always took her to the ice cream parlour to give her a cornet.

"Only a little pink one please. They're really too cold for me."

TGA: *(That statement was a white lie. Annabelle didn't like the ice cream, but being the compassionate child that she was, she wouldn't hurt her new-found friend.)*

During their week, Alberto and Alice fitted in visits to five family homes in the street, other than the family home in which they were staying, as well as pop-ins to old neighbours still living there, until their children thought it was OK to enter any house in the street.

Annabelle stayed up late one night and saw the old people coming into the shop to leave their little treasures, such as wedding rings or lockets containing pictures of loved ones, before getting to the workhouse by midnight for the chance of a bed to sleep on.

She also got up very early one morning to greet the old people who were chucked out at 6am. All of this swelled her heart with admiration for her Granny Howitz, who was such a kind lady to help them. On that early morning, she actually felt the gratitude of the old folk for her granny's help. It meant such a lot to them, because otherwise their treasures would have been confiscated at the workhouse to help pay for their night's bed. Every morning, these old folk would bless Granny Howitz' heart, call her an 'angel on earth', or say, "God Bless you, Mrs Howitz. You are a Saint."

Al C got his ride on a double-decker bus and wanted more, so Alberto took him on a sightseeing tour of London to see Big Ben, St. Paul's Cathedral, the Houses of Parliament and other places of interest.

All this activity made their week pass rapidly and, on the morning of their departure, there were so many people in the street to wave them off that it reminded Alberto of the day in 1919 when he was welcomed home from WW1 by a street full of neighbours.

On the train back to Andover, they were lucky enough to find an empty carriage. Holding her hand as though he'd never let it go again, Alberto asked, "Glad to be going home my lovely Alice?"

"I truly am, Alberto. I'm so glad you introduced me to life in the country." After a tranquil pause, she continued, "And I've missed you cuddling me, Alberto."

"I wonder how you and I managed to produce two children with such contrasting characters. On the one hand, we've got Al C sulking miserably because he can't stay in London to live and on the other, we have Annabelle happily snug in the corner seat here, glad to be going back to the peace and quiet of our home in Enham."

Two weeks before Annabelle's 6th birthday on Christmas Eve, King Edward VIII broadcast to the nation that he was abdicating his position as King of England, the Commonwealth and Emperor of India. *"I have found it impossible to carry the heavy burden of responsibility and discharge my duties as King as I would wish to do without the help and support of the woman I love,"* was the reason for his decision. He had been an uncrowned King for 325 days. Within hours, his brother Albert was proclaimed King, with the official title George VI.

That Christmas, Alice and Alberto opened their front door to a group of carol singers.

"Welcome all you carollers. So, you're about to sing for us again this year, yes? OK, so I'll leave the doors wide open, but Mrs Aless and I will sit in our living room to listen to you. Now don't forget, we want to hear every word."

The showman in him felt it to be good training for projecting their voices. The children knocked the door after singing all the verses of three different carols.

"Thank you all," said both Alice and Alberto. "That was most enjoyable, so we are giving you a good donation. Who's doing the collecting? Happy Christmas to all of you, and think about joining my tap dancing classes in the New Year. With good voices like yours, tap dancing would be such an asset."

Their festive season that year brought many a smile as one of the carols stuck in their minds. The carollers had replaced the words of the chorus of *Hark the Herald Angels Sing* as follows:

Hark the Herald Angels Sing,
Mrs Simpson stole our King.

Chapter 6

Andre Moves to a Bigger House in East Croydon

Andre couldn't believe his luck when he saw his new home. Morland Road, East Croydon, was a long road with lots of semi-detached houses. 152, in keeping with others, had a bay window upstairs and downstairs and an attic room with a gabled roof above. Their front door was painted dark brown and, when he entered the house for the very first time, he was taken aback by the daylight inside. It was so different from their previous basement accommodation.

His first thought was to run out and explore the area but, along with Elsa and Daniel, he had to help with moving belongings in from the big lorry. Andre wasn't strong enough to lift heavy stuff, but he was able to help carry such things as blankets, sheets and pillows. He enjoyed being able to help in that way; it made him feel important, until he bumped into his stepmother because the eiderdown he was carrying blocked his view. That episode reminded him that although the house had changed for the better, other things remained the same.

When heavy goods, like furniture, were being delivered into the bedrooms, Andre began to discover who would be sleeping where. Ma and Pa had the front bedroom with the big bay window, Daniel the biggest back bedroom and Elsa the back box room. When he discovered that his room was in the attic, he was overjoyed. He stood proudly looking out of the window, surveying not only the street, but the world beyond, with a plan for an escape route uppermost in his mind.

Andre couldn't rest until he had shown Elsa his bedroom.

"Andre, you're really lucky. Your bedroom is huge. There's room for lots of beds up here."

"I know. There's so much room that it sounds daft to say it, but I don't know where to hide the ring that Grandma gave to me. If Ma or Pa should find it, I know they'll think I've stolen it. I'm dead scared it'll fall out of my trouser pocket."

"It's OK, Andre. I found a safety pin on my window ledge. I'll give it to you so you can pin the ring inside your trouser pocket."

"Brill, Elsa. That's a bit of luck. Do you think you can come up here with me some time and help me to write to Grandma? We ought to let her know where we are living."

"OK, good idea. I'll come up to you tonight, after I've finished helping Ma to clear up in the scullery."

Quietly creeping in to his bedroom that night, ever fearful of drawing attention to themselves, Elsa brought the safety pin, a brown paper bag and her school pencil box with her.

"Andre, we'll have to write the letter on this brown paper bag, as I don't know where Ma keeps the writing paper and envelopes in this house. Then I'll have to keep my eye open until I can find an envelope; we won't be able to send the letter without one."

Two major things happened in Andre's life when Monday came around. Before going to her junior school, Elsa accompanied Andre to his new school, Woodside Infants. There, he had the shock of his life. His teacher introduced himself as Mr Grant. He was a very tall, thin man and towered above Andre. Andre felt scared. His new teacher was nothing like gentle Miss Rees.

"Hello, young man. What's your name?" he asked loudly.

"Andre Kliskey, sir."

"Speak up boy; I want to hear you."

Tittering sounds filled the classroom, which was full of boys.

Mr Grant was quick to face the classroom.

"QUIET!" he bellowed. "I will have discipline."

"Now, Andre, this time I want to hear you loudly and clearly, and I want the whole class to hear you too. Do you understand me?"

"**Yes, sir!**" Andre shouted abruptly, almost as though he were a soldier answering his commanding officer.

That sergeant major retort started the class tittering again. Andre felt somewhat smug as he watched Mr Grant glaring at the schoolboys again. Feeling confident that he could score here, and remembering Miss Rees' words that discipline was very important, he continued in a louder voice, "I'm Andre Kliskey, sir."

"That's better boy. I want you to remember this lesson. If we are to make progress with education, it is essential that we can all hear each other."

"Yes, sir."

"Have you been to school before, Andre?"

"Yes. I went to the infant school in Norwood, but my parents have just moved to East Croydon."

"Well, Andre, if you work hard for me, I'll work hard for you, but always remember, or perhaps I should say, never forget that word, 'discipline'." Mr Grant gave a long, positive nod, as though to register it on Andre's brain. "Now, this empty desk here, next to Martin Weston, is where you'll sit. Martin was the last new boy to join this class, so it will be good practice for him to show you around."

"Thank you, sir."

TGA: *(I was proud to watch Andre as he coped with his first day at the new school. I was relieved that the boy seemed to take strength from the strictness of his new school master. He certainly needed someone positive to look up to in his life.)*

The second major event in Andre's life that particular Monday, was managing to find an empty Reckitt's Blue Bag in the dustbin when he got home from school. On washday, Ma always used a Reckitt's Blue Bag. The little bag was made of white muslin with a drawstring at the top. The bag contained a one inch cube of what looked like blue chalk which, when dissolved in the washing water, helped to keep sheets and pillow cases nice and white. With the empty muslin bag safely in his pocket he would now be able to put Grandma's ring inside, draw the string tightly and then pin the bag inside his trouser pocket.

A fortnight later, when Andre and Elsa were having lessons in their new schools, Grandma in Norwood heard a rat-a-tat-tat on the front door. Marmalade raced her to the door where they were greeted by the postman.

"A letter for you, Madam, but I'm afraid there's no stamp on it, so I'll have to make a charge."

The quaint little lady, dressed in her pretty blue wrap-around overall, replied, "Of course, I'll just get my handbag."

Ten minutes later, sitting at the table opposite the picture of her long lost husband, she neatly cut open the envelope with a pair of scissors and was surprised to find a letter written on an opened and crumpled brown paper bag.

Dear Grandma,

We're sorry we didn't have a stamp.

Andre is sitting with me while I write to you. Because I am older I can write better than him, but he keeps telling me what to say.

152 Morland Road, East Croydon, our new house, is quite posh. We have a front door at street level and there isn't a basement. The house has a big bay window downstairs and upstairs, where Ma and Pa sleep, as well as an attic. Andre sleeps right up there at the top of the house. Daniel has the big back bedroom and I have a small back bedroom all to myself. We have a small front garden and a long narrow garden at the back.

The school is quite near to us. I am going to go to Woodside Juniors and Andre will go to Woodside Infants. He's dreading to meet his new teacher because he's sure she won't be as nice as Miss Rees.

I still love my pink umbrella brooch and will never forget you. Andre is trying to find somewhere to hide the ring you gave to him. He's scared of losing it.

We think it would be best if you don't write back to us. We might get into trouble because we've never told Ma about you. We will try to write to you regularly because we both love you, and when we are old enough, we will come to see you.

Big kisses to you, and strokes for Marmalade.
Elsa. xxxx

Hello Grandma. I miss you so much, and can still feel how nice it was when you cuddled me when I cried. One day I'll see you again.
Lots of love from Andre. xxxxx

Much to Andre's amazement, he was starting to like his new school. He was trying hard with his work, just as Miss Rees had advised, and he knew also that Mr Grant would then keep his word and help him to get on.

The walk to school in East Croydon was so different to that in Norwood. It was about the same distance, but here the walk was along an alley; Dalmally Alley. That alley was enclosed both sides by tall, upward grooved corrugated iron fencing. Every day on his journey to school, along with other schoolboys who were becoming his friends, he would pick up a stick and drag it along the corrugations. Collectively, the noise was magnified into deafening sounds, akin to a dozen racing motorbikes. Threats such as, "If you wake my baby up, I'll come down that alley and wring your bloomin' necks," came from the other side of the fence.

Threats such as that were a bit close to home, for Andre, which meant that he immediately dropped his stick and shot off to school as fast as his legs would carry him – only to be taunted for the rest of the day with names such as 'Scaredy Pants', 'Yellow Belly' and the like.

Andre continued to work hard at school, realising that his teacher was a strong friend to have and the more he could learn, the better things would be for him after his escape. Conversely, at the end of the school day, it was absolutely natural that the 'perfect pupil' became a tearaway kid, releasing all the pent up energies built up by the day's concentration.

After changing his school clothes and shoes, and doing the jobs set for him at home, Ma was glad to get him out from under her feet with the ultimatum, "Dinner is at 6pm. Don't be late."

Like an escaped animal, he then headed straight back to Dalmally Alley where, with other schoolmates, he had fine fun sharing one roller skate. Speed was of the essence. Two older boys, who were in charge of the races, were at the end of the alley preparing for the off. One of them was armed with a handkerchief for a flag, his dad's pocket watch, a scrap of cardboard and a pencil with which to record times taken to cross the chalk line at the other end. This activity brought out competitive streaks in all the boys, as they ever strived to prove themselves to be the best. An advanced improvisation of the race for more experienced boys was to skate the route as fast as you could with another boy balanced on your back. There was never a prize for the winner, but the accolade was worth more.

In his new environment, Andre was gaining confidence. It put space between him and his stepmother, apart from the still dreaded mealtimes. He had become aware that the house move had also served his stepmother well. He was certain she would not now be able to squeeze herself into her cramped space at the dinner table in their old home, as she was getting much fatter.

School was closed for the day on 12th May 1937. The children had been told that it was a day of historic importance and celebration for the Coronation of King George VI.

Andre didn't know the King, so he celebrated in his own style, playing in the street. The boys were rolling hoops along Morland Road when a loud, posh voice shouted, "Get those hoops off the road you boys! You'll upset the horse."

Andre became rooted to the ground. That voice was his father's. He was leading a brewer's dray horse, pulling a cart along the road. The cart was fully loaded with bottles of lemonade and the words on the side of the cart read: 'R. WHITE'. Andre stared in amazement at his father, and then at the apparition, as it continued its journey to the end of the road before turning left. The boys decided to make chase.

When they turned the corner, they were immediately distracted from their goal. They had entered a red, white and blue world. Pennant type flags of each of those three colours were hanging across the street as far as the eye could see, both ways. Billboards had been placed along the pavements with the words 'GOD SAVE THE KING'. Woolworth's front windows, as well as most of the other shop windows, were displaying a variety of coronation memorabilia, such as stacks of the same commemorative book with a royal blue hardback cover and a gold cameo side view impression of the King's head on the front. Other souvenirs, such as biscuit tins, chocolate boxes, tea caddies and coronation mugs etc. depicted both the King and Queen, dressed in the robes they were wearing for the ceremony. By the time the boys had feasted their eyes on the souvenirs in various shop windows which, all along the street, were swathed in red, white and blue drapes, they began to realise what important people the King and Queen were and had totally forgotten about the lemonade cart.

Andre had almost forgotten about time too. When playing in the alley he could guess the 6pm deadline for dinner by the two-way traffic of adult pedestrians using the alley to get home from work. Here, he had no way of knowing.

On arrival home, it seemed that no one indoors was aware of time either. Andre had walked into a strange, strained atmosphere. Ma had heard on the wireless that Croydon was in the grip of a Typhoid Fever outbreak, which meant all household water had to be boiled. She was in a frenzy trying to cook dinner. Oddly enough, Andre felt sorry for her, even though she was never nice to him. He especially appreciated the fact that she was working extra hard boiling lots of water to protect the family from illness, which was a great relief. She had managed to cook boiled bacon with onions, potatoes and carrots for them. Over dinner she told the family all she knew about the outbreak and that the authorities suspected the source was the reservoir on the Shirley Hills.

Andre was waiting for an appropriate lull in the typhoid conversations before talking about the surprise of seeing his dad leading the lemonade cart. He had no idea that was his father's job. His father never talked much indoors, mainly because he was nearly always upstairs in his bedroom repairing clocks. Now reminded of Grandma's nice lemonade, and with growing confidence, he plucked up courage to ask, "Can we have a bottle of lemonade one day as a treat, please Pa?"

His stepmother exploded.

"This boy thinks money grows on trees. How can you talk about treats, when we're having to burn gas all the time to boil water!" she yelled, glaring at him as she spoke.

"Sorry Ma. I forgot."

Daniel sniggered. Elsa passed a sympathetic glance to Andre and Andre went into his silent world.

In his silent world, Andre mulled over the extraordinary fact that he was not as frightened for his life at home as he used to be. He puzzled over why Ma disliked him so much, but could find no reason. Ron used to understand the problem; perhaps he could answer the question, but since the move, he no longer knew where they lived. After long deliberations, Andre decided that finding a better life for himself was a perfectly good reason to pursue his escape goal. Despite all that, he was sensitive to the misery Ma was suffering, having to cope with boiling so much water and promised himself that he would try to help her more. Who knows? Perhaps she would come to like him.

With that in mind and full of only good intentions, he walked the streets at the weekend looking for pretty flowers in front gardens. Most gardens were filled with shrubs; others had a small lawn surrounded by narrow flower beds. One garden attracted him; the border was filled with pink tulips and low ground-covering, rich blue flowers. Becoming intoxicated with the wonderful scent, he made his decision. He would walk up and down the road, watching the house for any signs of activity. The idea of giving Ma a bunch of pink tulips to make her like him a little bit was becoming obsessive.

Good fortune smiled. The postman knocked on that door with a parcel to be delivered. There was no answer, so the postman knocked next door. No answer. Third time lucky; he left the parcel next-door-but-one and returned to put a card in the letterbox of the house Andre was watching.

Biding time until the postman had disappeared into another street, Andre then plucked up courage, slipped in the garden gate and started to pick tulips.

"**You little devil**! I thought you were up to no good."

The man opposite had been watching Andre from his front window. He was limping across the road, waving his walking stick.

Andre was scared out of his life and didn't quite know whether to run, or what to do.

"Give those flowers back to me, or I'll report you to the police mighty quick."

Relieved for that God given opportunity, Andre returned the flowers to the man as he said, "Sorry, sir," and scampered as fast as his thin legs – which dangled from the wide leg opening of his short grey trousers – would carry him.

Back at home, Ma was still preoccupied with all the extra work of boiling water and Elsa was the unlucky one bearing the brunt.

Deciding not to take more stupid risks, the next day after school Andre paid another visit to his friend at the glassworks further down his road. He often chatted to him in the yard at the front of the factory, where sometimes he would be trying to remove scratches from mirrors.

"What's that red stuff you're using?"

"This," young man, "is a jeweller's rouge cloth. It's what they use to polish silver and gold."

"Crikey, does it work?"

"You bet, as long as the scratches ain't deep."

"Can I see?"

"Sure, have a look."

"Well, that's only a tiny scratch," he observed. "It's hard to see it anyway."

"But we can't sell flawed work, Sonny."

"Can I have a go?"

"Okey dokey. You've probably got more energy than me."

Andre worked hard with the polishing cloth and his face was beaming when he could see the result of his efforts.

"Ooh, that's good. Can I come again another day?"

"Come whenever you want, Sonny, as long as you don't ask for any of my wages."

Andre eventually got round to the area known as Woodside Green, where he would gang up with his mates to kick a ball about. That was good fun, although it often meant trouble. The ball was forever going over the high fence and into people's gardens. They had found various ways of dealing with this. One of the boys lived in the row of houses the other side of the fence. He used to bring a stepladder to the green. When the ball went over, other boys would look through knot holes in the wooden fence to see if anyone was about. The fastest runner amongst them would then be given the all clear to climb over, collect the ball, sneak out of the garden gate and bring the ball back.

There were many such escapades, but the day the ball smashed into someone's greenhouse, no one dared to collect the ball. That brought football to a halt until someone's birthday came around.

That saga was uppermost in Andre's mind the following day when 'Lanky', as the boys had nicknamed Mr Grant, asked him to go to the headmaster's office.

Frightened out of his wits for getting into mischief the previous day, Andre was petrified, but had no option other than to report to the headmaster's office. He was terrified of being expelled from school, which he didn't want to happen, since he was getting on so well with Mr Grant.

As it happened, sheer panic had magnified the circumstances out of all proportion. Within seconds of his knock on the door, Andre was being hugged by his stepbrother Ron.

Andre sobbed with shock. "I thought I'd never see you again when we moved from Norwood."

"Could I ask you two to tell me what this is all about?" interrupted Mr Channell, the headmaster.

"Yes, of course, sir," said Ron. Putting his hand out to shake, he introduced himself, "I'm Ron McKenzie and I'm Andre's stepbrother."

He went on to explain how he had left his overcrowded home in Norwood a few years previously after getting work as an apprentice accountant in the city.

"I found it hard to cope with all my studies in the crowded home in Norwood, as well as watching the appalling way my mother treated Andre, who had come into the family on the occasion of her second marriage. The worry of it was affecting my concentration and I had to put my future first. While living there, I used to help him with homework, stick up for him and show him kindness. When I left, I told Andre that I would always be his friend. Unfortunately, because of low apprenticeship pay and subsequent lack of suitable accommodation, I made the decision to join the Army, where I could continue my accountancy studies. The first thing I did when I got home leave was to go to the old home in Norwood to see Andre, only to discover that they had moved away. Then I was stumped."

"This is all very interesting, Mr McKenzie, but is there any way I can verify that you are whom you say you are?"

"Yes, sir, there is. I traced Andre to East Croydon via his previous school teacher, Miss Rees and an elderly lady who befriended him in the road where he used to live in Norwood. I met with Miss Rees and after our chat she kindly gave me the school telephone number, saying I might have need of it one day. Here it is written on this piece of paper."

"Good, then I would ask you to sit quietly in here while I make the call."

Mr Channell proceeded to give the operator the telephone number he wanted and waited for her to connect him. At the end of his conversation he looked at Ron and said, "You'll be glad to know everything's fine, Mr McKenzie. Miss Rees has identified you satisfactorily and told me more about Andre's unhappy background. We welcome getting such information on our files so we can keep an eye out for any personal abuse. Now I will take you to the staff room annexe, where you and Andre can spend a bit of time together."

"Andre, I will tell Mr Grant that you have been excused from lessons for the rest of the afternoon. You and your stepbrother may leave the premises when the school bell rings."

Andre, still in bewilderment, nodded, and Ron said "Thank you Mr Channell, but I do have one more thing to ask. It's not possible for me to send letters to Andre at his home address. I'm certain they'd be confiscated. Would it be possible for me to write to him at the school address? I don't want to lose touch with him again."

"Yes, of course, that would be possible. I'll make sure the necessary staff are informed."

Sitting together in the annexe, the brothers chatted away ten to the dozen.

"I'm glad you found me Ron," Andre kept repeating.

Ron heard news about Andre's other friend, Grandma, and about the ring, but a persistent Andre wanted to know why Ma didn't like him.

"You've got me stumped there, Andre. If I knew the answer to that one, I'd have dealt with it years ago. I can only assure you that you are a decent kid and you certainly do deserve a better deal in life. Grandma sounds like a perfect friend for you. I met her when I was trying to find you. Tell me more about how you met her."

Settling into the memories of that happier side of his life, Andre spoke with more energy and enthusiasm, concluding with, "She really loves me Ron. Honest. I could feel it. She cuddled me and was kind and I love her too. I've got to eat a lot of dinners though, before the ring'll fit me." He held out his widespread little fingers.

"You'll get there, kid. Concentrate your energies on your schoolwork. Remember, no one can take away from you what is in your head. I hear your studies are going well at school, so make sure you keep doing that. Promise? You know, I think you've got to stop worrying about Ma poisoning you. I don't think she'd go to those lengths."

Andre's eyes welled up with relief at his brother's words and, with both thumbs up, replied, "Promise."

After that, all the tensions of the day disappeared. Andre relished and appreciated his brother's support..

"Good. Now it's my turn to share news. I've found myself a new friend, too. She's a nice young lady whom I hope to marry one day. Then you could come and live with us. Her name is Dorothy and she lives in Gipsy Hill, not too far away from here. That's my really good news but, as I'm in the Army now, I could be sent overseas, which troubles me. If that happens, I want you to remember about Dorothy. I've told her all about you and she's your friend too. She wants to help you. I've written her address on this piece of paper and I'm giving you two florins as emergency money. That's a lot of money, Andre. Put it away safely with your ring. If you ever feel you can't stand being at home anymore, don't just run away. Remember that; DON'T JUST RUN AWAY, because that would mean losing each other again. Get yourself a taxi and go to Dorothy, who will look after you."

Taking his big brother's hand, Andre replied, "Thank you Ron. I know I'm lucky to have you and Dorothy. I shall guard the taxi money carefully and use it if I have to. Till that time, I wanna see if I can make Ma like me. I'll never like her yellow cabbage, but you're right, so far she hasn't hurt me."

"Andre Kliskey, I'm so proud of you and I think Mr and Mrs Eugene Kliskey are very stupid people."

Chapter 7

Little Miss Responsibility

Annabelle, now in her eighth year, was maturing in her private realms of responsibility and although basically shy, was beginning to blossom with domestic confidence and authority.

Looking after her father on this particular occasion, she asked him if he had known about the auction of reusable contents from the old Estate House before its demolishment.

"A load of oak panelling was delivered to Mr Guest's home today and then the lorry delivered some banister rails to Mr Close's house. The wood was all polished and posh. Pam and I saw it delivered when we were playing up the crescent. Didn't you know about that, Dad?"

"Yes, sweetheart, I knew, but what time have I got to be doing woodwork to improve the house, I ask you? I've got enough to do helping you and Mummy indoors, doing the gardening, teaching tap dancing and putting on shows, as well as enjoying my game of billiards. No, I didn't want anything Annabelle, thank you."

Alice still suffered a mix of good days and bad days, so Annabelle accepted that on the worst of those days she had to forego school. Missing school troubled her deeply, but looking after her mother still took priority. Auntie Dolly continued to help Annabelle daily by answering a host of domestic questions and their special relationship was going from strength to strength.

Towards the end of the summer holidays, after best friend Pam Angel had returned to London, Annabelle, with her second best friend Pat, both looking pretty in their crisp cotton summer dresses, one in green and one in yellow, hurried along the golden gravel drive to the workshops so as not to miss the excitement.. They were overtaken by some rowdy village boys, including Al C and his friends Ken, Maurice, Malcolm, Jack and Dougie, all dressed in their cotton shirts, some undone looking like jackets to let air in, and their short trousers, which showed off their black scabbed knees. The drive was crowded with village wives pushing their babies in prams with their toddlers running alongside, all anxious to have a nose at what was about to happen on that lovely sunny afternoon. They were gathering to see the big Estate House demolished so that a new factory, to replace the dilapidated wooden workshops, could be built on the land.

A fenced-off section had been provided at a distance as a safety area for sightseers who were guided into the enclosure as they arrived. The old building was gradually being detonated and, with each explosion, spectators screeched and covered their ears, or stuck fingers in them for better sound-proofing. It was an exciting occasion, not seen by the disabled men themselves, who were busy earning their wages in the existing workshops.

Later in the afternoon, when about half the building had been demolished, *Little Miss Responsibility* decided it was time she went home to check on her mother and make her a cup of tea.

As they were passing the Landale Wilson Institute, Alberto passed them in a frantic hurry.

"Daddy, Daddy! It's me, Annabelle," she screeched.

Alberto ignored her. Annabelle was shocked and frozen to the spot. Pat quickly took hold of her friend's hand and said, "It's OK Annabelle. He's ever so white. I think he might be hurrying home to be sick."

The girls, quick to follow, were frightened to death when they became within earshot of his rage.

"Those bleedin' Germans have raided us here in Enham now, my Alice. They're not only after me – they want my family as well. The bastards. What can I do? How can I keep us safe? Are we never to get peace?" Growling now, and shaking, which rattled his voice, he continued, "I can't think straight any more. I don't know what to do...I don't know what to do."

That loud, unrecognisable voice bore no resemblance to Alberto's normal speech.

On peeping into the living room, the girls became more perturbed. Alberto, broken-hearted, was on his knees in front of Alice, with his head in her lap, crying like a baby.

"No, no, Alberto. That's not true. You've got it all wrong. Look at me," Alice said gently and urgently, as she lifted his face up in her two hands to look into his eyes.

Another explosion sounded. A distraught Alberto yelled, "Quick everybody. Under the table! Quick!"

Alice slapped his face.

"Stop it, Mummy! Stop it!"

"Alberto; listen to me," pleaded Alice, as she shook him by the shoulders. "We're safe, Alberto. We're quite safe," she reassured, wiping his eyes with her handkerchief, before wiping her own. "You're **not** on the battlefield. You're at home with us. CAN YOU HEAR ME, ALBERTO?"

There was a slight reaction. Driven by the trauma of the occasion, Alice continued slowly, waiting for a reaction from Alberto after each sentence, "Look at me Alberto…can you see me?"

Alberto nodded.

"We are safe. Can you hear me?"

Alberto nodded.

"We are all safe, my darling. The authorities have been detonating the old Estate House."

A hint of a smile on Alberto's face encouraged Alice, who continued, "They are going to build a nice new factory for you disabled men."

Alberto, with tears running down his cheeks, allowed himself to be cuddled and comforted by his wife.

"Get Daddy a drink of water, please Annabelle. He'll feel better in a minute. Look, the colour's coming back into his cheeks."

Annabelle and Pat quickly ran to the scullery.

Handing over the glass of water, Annabelle asked, "What's the matter with Daddy, Mummy? He didn't see me up the road."

Back to reality, Alberto replied, "Nothing's the matter now, sweetheart. Daddy just had a bad dream."

Alberto looked helpless and Alice took charge.

"Annabelle, Daddy wasn't well today. The explosions up the Estate House reminded him of

144

something horrible that happened to him before you were born. He became frightened. That's why he didn't see you. The bangs frightened me too. I could hear them from here. Were you two frightened?"

"Yes. They were too loud, but the men told us we would be quite safe in the fenced-off area, so we tried to be brave."

"Well, let's have some nice hugs together, because none of us need be frightened anymore."

"Not even Daddy?"

"Not even Daddy," Alberto replied. "Mummy's made everything better, like she always does."

Not quite convinced, Annabelle asked, "Were you at that place where they hurt your other arm?"

Alberto and Alice looked at each other. Annabelle was starting to put two and two together.

Early on the morning of the first day of the autumn term, Annabelle kept looking out of the front window across the road to the two semi-detached black and white Tudor cottages. The plan was that five-year-old Rita, who lived in the furthest of the two cottages, would wave to Annabelle from her garden when she was ready for school. Eventually, the two waved to each other and Annabelle ran off happily knowing her mummy was having a good day. Across the road and up the small lane to their garden path, she called for her charge, five-year-old Rita Rose, who had a thick, fairish plait hanging down the centre of her back. She was starting school that day and Annabelle was going to look after Rita exactly the same as Mary had looked after her when she was an infant four years previously.

Annabelle took Rita to Miss Wells who was taking care of the new intake of infants. The bell rang in the playground and all children filed into school to assembly as usual, but things weren't 'as usual'. The children were being told about changes. Annabelle's name was called out, along with her old classmates, to let them know they were being moved up from the infants to the juniors. That meant a new classroom and a new teacher whose name was Miss Roberton. They were also told that Miss Wells, the infants' teacher had got married in the summer holiday and from now on they should call her Mrs Leach.

Round the tea table at the end of the school day, Annabelle told her parents about her move up to the juniors and Al C quipped, "That's no big deal. I've gone up to the seniors, Miss Kyles' class, AND SHE'S THE HEADMISTRESS, so there." He elevated himself to a more imposing height as he spoke.

"You're not being nice to your sister, Al C. You are the older of the two and should be a bit wiser, but you've just shown us how silly and childish you can be. Before you leave this table you will tell Annabelle you are sorry for being so stupid."

Alberto went on to tell them how quickly the new factory was being built.

"Before I came home tonight, I measured with my rule. They are exactly 2 feet above the ground level. The builder told me that it will shoot up more quickly from now on because they have stacks of light grey steel panels to be fitted in between the brickwork for windows to be fitted. And there's more to tell. Anyone want to know more?"

"Of course. We want to know anything there is to tell, Alberto."

"What about you, Al C?"

"Yeah, I'm all ears, Dad."

"Then before I tell anything, I want you to tell your sister you're sorry for being unkind to her."

"Sorry."

"That's not good enough Al C. I'll give you a choice. Either you can put your arm round Annabelle's shoulders, give her a kiss on the cheek and say 'sorry' nicely, or never hear the news I have to tell you. What's it to be?"

Al C conceded graciously, although it has to be said that Annabelle flinched at his gesture.

"OK, family, you'd never guess in a hundred years," said Alberto looking round the table at his waiting family who were tucking into bread and jam and cake at the same time, "so I'll tell you."

"You'll remember the story about the man on the governing body of Enham Village Centre and Papworth Industries, who congratulated me after I'd French Polished a table for him?"

"That's the one who remarked that you have to have lots of patience to make a good French Polisher and he thought you should make a career of it, isn't it? Yes, I remember, Alberto. He was the one who saw you in pantomime in Papworth a few years ago. He'd heard about your extreme and kindly patience when teaching children to tap dance."

"That's exactly right, Alice, and on the strength of that," looking at the children, "when the new factory is finished, your dad has got a very special job to do. Management have asked me to French Polish a..." Alberto widened his eyes and took a deep breath. "...**huge** dining table for an important man in Germany's Cabinet."

"Jeeps, that's good, Dad. Will they pay you more money for that?"

"Nail on the head, Al C. There'll be a big bonus for me when the job's completed satisfactorily, but don't forget, I still have to achieve that.

Full of compassion and getting hot under the collar, "Why do they keep him in a cabinet, Daddy? That's cruel."

Alberto and Alice laughed as Alberto caressed Annabelle's distraught face.

"It's alright, sweetheart. I didn't mean a piece of furniture 'cabinet' like I've made at work. Cabinet is another name for governments in many countries. They have what they call a Cabinet Office where ministers meet to discuss and make important decisions for their own country. Is that better now you understand?"

Getting less red, Annabelle shook her head as she whispered, "I didn't know."

Al C interrupted, "I didn't know either Annabelle, but it was a good joke."

"Right, so getting back to where we were, the man concerned is Herr Von Ribbentrop, Germany's Foreign Minister and Ambassador to Great Britain.

Annabelle clarified, "So the man in Germany is not as important as the King in our country?"

"Not quite, sweetheart, but he is a very important man." Alberto raised his eyebrows as he nodded confirmation.

Alice quietly gave her husband an admiring glance.

Annabelle was enjoying being 'little mum' to Rita. Every morning the two girls waved goodbye to Mrs Rose as they started their journey, hand in hand, to school. After about three weeks, Rita told her mummy that she wanted to walk home with children from her own class, but the teacher wouldn't let her. On the Friday afternoon at the end of that week, Mrs Rose invited Annabelle indoors with Rita.

It was cosy and warm indoors and Mrs Rose, a big, comfortably round lady, greeted the girls as though they were the most important people on earth, which of course, in a mother's eyes, Rita was.

"Annabelle, you've looked after my Rita so well, we have bought you a little present. "You get it for me, Rita. It's on the stairs."

Annabelle loved Mrs Rose. She had been her mother's friend since before Annabelle was born. In her young days, she had lived in London and used to catch a bus regularly to buy a delicious ice cream from Gino's shop. Years later, when living in Enham village, she heard the name of Alessandro mentioned. Excitedly, she knocked Alice's door to see if they were related to Gino, who, she said, sold the best ice cream in London.

"People travelled from miles around to buy it."

Together, that day, they had discovered that Mrs Rose knew Alberto's family in Edmonton and a close, lasting friendship was formed.

Annabelle blushed.

"That's a huge present. I don't know what to say."

"Try opening it," suggested Mrs Rose, as she cuddled Rita on her lap.

Annabelle carefully undid the pretty rose designed wrapping paper, which she had been told was left over wallpaper from Rita's bedroom, to reveal a small leather suitcase with its own keys.

Annabelle blushed again.

"Thank you, Mrs Rose, but you shouldn't have done that. I didn't do anything."

"Well, you looked after my precious Rita and she's worth more than all the tea in China to me, AND MORE, so you take your present home to show your mummy and tell her it comes from Mr and Mrs Rose and Rita, with all our love.

Smiling happily, Annabelle ran off excitedly with her suitcase, waving to Mrs Rose and Rita as she left. Indoors, she found her mummy lying on the bed, not feeling very well.

"What's the matter, Mummy? Why are you in bed?"

"I'm just not feeling very well today, Annabelle. Don't worry; I'll lie here today and hope to feel a bit better tomorrow."

"OK, Mummy. I'll make you a cup of tea in a minute and bring you a biscuit. That might make you feel better. First, look at my present, Mummy. Mr and Mrs Rose gave it to me for looking after Rita when she started school."

"That's lovely, sweetheart. It's real leather."

"Yes, and it's got keys, so I can keep my work private."

"Good Lord, how grown up you are becoming, child?"

Attending school after that day became a no-no for Annabelle. Her mother was suffering a terrible fatigue; she didn't want food and kept trembling. A couple of days passed, but when Alberto could see that she was not getting any better, he went to the evening surgery and asked the doctor to call.

The whole family were shocked at the doctor's diagnosis. He told them Alice was suffering from a nervous breakdown condition and that he was getting her admitted to Winchester Hospital. She would probably be an inpatient there for at least a month.

Alberto had to take time off work to make some arrangements. Those arrangements led to Aunt Daisy from Workhouse Hill, Edmonton, London, turning up one morning to take Al C and Annabelle to live and go to school up there until their mother was discharged from hospital.

"My goodness gracious, Annabelle, whatever are you doing?" asked Aunt Daisy, who had entered by the front door and appeared in the scullery to find the child chopping kindling sticks on the round log, just inside the open back door.

"I'm only chopping sticks to lay the range fire Aunt Daisy, so we can light it and keep Mummy warm when she comes home."

"You shouldn't be doing things like that," Daisy almost scolded. "You're far too young. You could chop your fingers off."

"But it's one of my jobs. I always do it. Daddy can't with one hand and Mummy mustn't bend over."

"What about Al C?"

"Boys don't have to do domestic work," replied Al C. "They have to learn skills to go out and earn the money."

"Well, I think that all seems a bit unfair. Anyway, let's get your bags packed, both of you. When your dad comes home at lunchtime, we can say goodbye to him, before I take you up to your families in London."

Aunt Daisy made some corned beef sandwiches for lunch while a tearful Annabelle ran round to say goodbye to Auntie Dolly.

"Be brave, my little precious. Your mum will get better you know. It wasn't her heart. She just needs a rest. You go and do what you have to do. I'll be waiting here for you. You know Auntie Dolly loves you a lot and will miss you a lot too."

Annabelle cried as she said goodbye to her dad. Alberto was at a loss as to how to comfort her and being the compassionate, sensitive child that she was, she attempted to put him at ease with, "I'll try to do some tap dancing practice every day for you, Daddy," she said, between sobs.

On the other hand, Al C was like a cat on hot bricks. He couldn't wait to get to London. He knew that Grandma Aless wanted him to go up and stay with them in the holidays, but to go to school up there was a dream come true.

Since she had to live up there for the time being, Annabelle decided to make the best of a bad job and began to get excited about the opportunity to attend school every day. Disappointment overwhelmed her when she became aware that she could not take advantage of the situation because they did not teach the same sort of things in London as they did in Smannell. For Annabelle, school in London was a nightmare.

Granny Howitz and Aunt Daisy tried to console her with hopes of her mum's recovery very soon. They also hit on something to cheer her up. Aunt Daisy lifted the piles of clothing off the piano onto the table and opened the lid. Annabelle momentarily forgot her troubles and played the tonic sol-fa notes as she gradually picked them out. After that, Aunt Daisy played a few songs and brought a big smile to Annabelle's face.

"Will you teach me how to do that please, Aunt Daisy?"

Annabelle had two cousins, Irenie and Joannie, at the same school. For playtime breaks she could meet up with Joannie, who was of similar age, but Irenie was a bit older and was in a separate playground. After school, out to play on the pavement in Gilpin Grove, which was a turning off Workhouse Hill by the side of Aunt Emily and Uncle Tommy's greengrocery shop, the girls tried to teach Annabelle how to play dibs.

Dibstones was a new game to Annabelle. It consisted of a set of five different coloured shop-bought stones, slightly bigger than the size of a dice, but elongated a little. Those who couldn't afford to buy dibstones could use five small pebbles equally as well. The object of the game was to score the most points. All three girls sat on the pavement and Irenie started by throwing all five dibs a short way up into the air and catching as many as possible onto the back of her hand. She caught all five, which gave her the advantage of using all five in her game. Next, she gently threw all five dibs onto the pavement. She picked up the most distant dib, threw it into the air, picked up one dib and then caught the falling dib before it touched the ground. She did the same with the other three. Next, she gently threw them on the pavement again, this time the objective being to pick the dibs up in twos, as opposed to singly.

If the dibs were too far apart to gather together in one attempt, she was allowed to throw one dib in the air and try to move the sprawled dibs closer together to enable her to pick up first one pair and then the second pair.

Having completed the pairs satisfactorily, she then had to pick up three and, finally, the entire four. Points were taken off the total for throwing up and moving.

Annabelle didn't do very well when it was her turn; she only caught three on the back of her little hand, which was a gross disadvantage. Immediately, the two stones left on the pavement were put out of play.

Sometimes they played hoops, keeping them rolling down Gilpin Grove and all the way back to the shop.

Although the games were fun and enabled her to get to know her cousins, it was foreign for Annabelle to have so much playtime. She was more used to domestic work and was much happier when she was helping Granny Howitz and Aunt Daisy indoors. One job she really liked to do was cutting up and portioning the big blocks of butter or lard for sale in the shop. Granny Howitz unwrapped the packaging from the top and sides of the block and showed Annabelle how to cut down through it at one side, then cut that side into about a dozen smaller blocks, which she then had to wrap individually in the squares of greaseproof paper they had prepared earlier. That process was repeated again and again until the whole block was dealt with. One big block portioned into half a gross; 72 packs. Those small portions were then stacked on a half-inch thick slab of cold marble on a shelf behind the counter in the shop, ready to be weighed as they were sold.

Life in London was very busy because of the shop, so there was never time for Aunt Daisy to give Annabelle a piano lesson. The closed lid of the piano was basically used as a linen depositary where items of dirty washing were placed on one end and, on the other end, nice clean folded washing from the line in the yard. That was disappointing for Annabelle. She would have loved to learn to play a little tune for Pam when back in Enham.

It had become a ritual in her London life that after tea she would go down the road to see Grandma Aless and Bubble; not for ice cream, but for her lovely cuddle. When half term came around, they expected her to spend some whole days in their home so they could get to know each other better. There she spent time playing with Rosie and Mary Ann, who were of similar age to herself. They were the daughters of her Uncle Antonio and Auntie Polly. Her older cousins,

Francesca and Hannah, made a big fuss of her, which she didn't quite understand because she was used to being a 'grown up'.

TGA: *(It was on one such day, when she was playing ball in the alley with Rosie and Mary Ann, that she saw a vision. That vision was her father. She stood stunned.)*

"Daddy, Daddy!" Looking back to Rosie and Mary, she said, "That's my Dad," unable to believe her own two eyes, before running to jump into his waiting arm.

"Hello, my little sweetheart. Are you missing Mummy and me?"

"I am, Daddy. I hate London. Have you come to take me home?"

"I haven't, my little one, BUT…" he said, as he kissed her salty tears. "Yuk!" He pulled a dreadful face as he said, "Wipe my mouth with your skirt, quick. Those tears are horribly salty."

Giggling at the face he pulled and preoccupied with the task in hand, Annabelle stopped crying.

"What I was trying to tell you my little one, is that I've taken the day off work today to come all this way to tell you and Al C that Mummy is getting better and will be coming out of hospital in about two weeks. I've only got time to have dinner here today with you and then I have to get the train home, but very soon we'll all be home together."

Annabelle was radiant.

"Thank you, thank you Daddy!" She kissed his cheek between each word. "I can't wait to get back home and go to my proper school again. Will you come and collect us?"

"I hope I don't have to. Before I go home today, I'll talk to Aunt Daisy and see if she'll bring you both home."

Following their dad's visit, the London families noticed a distinct change of personality in both of Alberto and Alice's children. Annabelle was all smiles, even at school. Al C was like a bear with a sore head. On one of his daily visits to Granny Howitz to say goodnight, he showed his bad temper.

"I'm not going back there with you, Aunt Daisy. I want to stay up here to live forever."

"Al C, your home is in Enham with your parents. That's where you belong and that is where I shall take you, even if I have to drag you in a harness."

"I hate you, Aunt Daisy!"

"Don't you dare speak to me like that when I'm trying to help your parents." She grabbed hold of his hand and said, "Come on, let's go and see what Grandma Aless has to say about this bad behaviour."

Grandma Aless let him know in no uncertain terms.

"You just listen to me, Al C. If you make trouble for your aunt and your mum and dad, then my offer to come and live here with us during school holidays is no longer open to you. Bubble and I only invite good children to stay with us. Do you understand?"

"Yes, Grandma," he muttered, with a sulky face.

"Then wipe that look off your face before you are stuck with it."

On the train going back to Enham, Al C told Aunt Daisy and Annabelle that it wouldn't be very long before he'd be coming back to London for the Christmas holiday.

"I think you'd better check that out with your mum and dad first Al C. I'm pretty sure they'll want you at home for that holiday."

Those words instantly brought back the sulky face, which remained for the rest of the journey.

Annabelle, of course, dashed indoors very excitedly to see her mummy again.

"Are you all better now, Mummy?"

"I'm fit as a fiddle, thank you, sweetheart," she laughed, crossing her eyes playfully. "I've had a lovely rest and am eating my food all up."

Clinging to her mother, Annabelle said, "That's good, Mummy. Auntie Dolly was right; she said you wouldn't die. Ooooh, Auntie Dolly; I'd better run round and say hello to her."

As she was going out of the back door, Annabelle heard Al C asking, "Dad, can I go up to Grandma Aless' for the Christmas holiday?"

A few days after the family had settled down into their daily routines, with Annabelle and Al C back at Smannell School, Alice answered a knock at the door. It was Sister Peters from the surgery. All the people in the village highly respected her. She had been a nursing sister in Flanders and was delighted when she got the job of working with the wounded men in the village.

"Mrs Aless, I've come to talk to you about Al C."

"Really? I hope he hasn't been up to mischief."

"No, no, my dear. I've come to suggest that you bring him to the surgery to see the doctor. I notice he is limping very badly."

"Oh that. It's alright, Sister. He's only copying the wounded men. All the boys do it."

"Well, I have to disagree with you, Mrs Aless. Of course I know they all pretend, but I can see that Al C's limp is real."

"Really? Then I'll do as you say and take him to the doctor, and thank you for coming to see me about it."

The doctor was in agreement with Sister Peters and requested an appointment for Al C to see a specialist.

The family were now busy preparing for Christmas in various ways; making presents, Christmas puddings and cake as well as decorations, etc. Annabelle had written her Christmas list and sent it up the chimney to Santa. In that regard, Al C had been sworn to secrecy about the myth.

"It's OK, Mum, I didn't even see what she was doing; I'm too busy rolling Dad's cigarettes."

TGA: *(Yes, I can confirm that he was doing that. It was his job every evening to roll 30 cigarettes using tinned A1 tobacco and Red Rizla papers. Al C boasted that he was being his dad's Left Arm.)*

It was on one such busy evening that Alberto revealed that while the family were all away from home, he had attended a meeting in the Institute where the disabled men had been invited to join an Association to do good for others.

"It's called the Ancient Order of the Buffaloes."

"But they're animals, Dad," said Al C with a puzzled, screwed-up face.

Alice, who'd previously been told of the setting up of the Lodge in Enham, laughed at the natural reaction of her son.

"I'm glad to know you do pay attention to some of the things you are taught in school, Al C."

"Well, Miss Kyles was teaching us some things about South Africa in our Geography lesson the other day and that's how I know about them."

Annabelle then piped up with, "But when they were selling off furniture and stuff from the big house, you said you didn't have time to be making things for the house with all the other things you had to do. Now you've got time to go out for another night of the week."

Alberto sat on his armchair and lifted her onto his knee.

"Now just you listen to me, young lady; you do a lot of work indoors to help Mummy and me under this roof. What I am going to do, if you don't mind, *Little Miss Responsibility*, is try to help other people who are worse off than us by being thrifty and building up funds to help make their lives better. Is Daddy allowed to do that, young miss?"

"You've joined, Daddy, so I suppose you're already allowed. How will you do it? Will you have to go away more often and take them baskets of shopping?"

"I suppose that could happen, because some families are starving for the want of a few shillings, but our first objective is to open a couple of orphanages. They are big houses where little children who don't have any parents can live and be looked after by kind people. I was happy to join and have the chance to be part of that. What do you think?"

Annabelle gave much thought to her answer before looking him straight in the eye. "I suppose I could have been an orphan if Mummy had bent over and died and you didn't escape from that awful place where you lost your arm, so yes Daddy, I like you doing that."

Amused by the fact that at that point in time Alice and he had not met, he continued, "Phew! Thank you for your permission young lady and I suspect you'll be glad to know that I won't be going to the lodge every week. We shall only meet once a month."

"So how come you get the name of Buffaloes, Dad?" asked Al C.

"Well, I don't know all the answers yet, son, because I've only just joined, but we were told that a true Buffalo believes in his brotherhood, so perhaps the animals have more strength when they are all together in the wild. Their own brotherhood, so-to-speak, which does seem perfectly plausible."

Al C still looked a bit puzzled as he finished rolling his dad's home-made cigarettes.

"There you are Dad; 30 of the best for tomorrow."

"Thanks, Al C. I'll really be glad of those in the break tomorrow. Herr Ribbentrop's table has

161

arrived in the new factory and I shall make a start straight away."

Just before Christmas, Alice was devastated when she received a letter from the bone specialist about Al C's knee. She waited for Alberto to come home from work so they could tell him the bad news together.

Alberto took charge as he said, "Come and sit down, son. There's no easy way to tell you this, but there'll be no London Christmas for you. The specialist says you've got a condition called osteomyelitis of the knee bone and you've got to rest your leg for a long time. Could take up to a year."

Al C cried. "I won't do it!" he said stubbornly. "He's made a mistake. He's got me mixed up with someone else, I'll bet. What about my dancing?"

Alice cuddled him and said, "Don't take it so hard, Al C. We'll get the doctor down to talk to us about it.

Dr MacCallum visited the next day and confirmed that if Al C didn't rest and let the bone heal, he could end up like some of the disabled men and never walk properly again, let alone tap dance.

"You must have knocked your knee badly at some time. Did you fall on it?"

"I know," said Alice. "That's playing football up the field with the boys. You used to come home pleased with yourself for being Sagar of Everton; copying the man who often went down on his knees and slid along the ground to save a ball. I'll bet that's what did it."

162

"Could well be that," said the doctor. "Anyway, you're going to have to get a bed in this room for him to lie on and a handy chamber pot."

At that, Al C started to snivel again and the doctor said, "Never mind, old chap, we'll all do our best to get you on your feet again as quickly as possible. You've got the easy job, remember. All you've got to do is lie there and be spoiled. Your mum and dad are going to find it mighty tough. You must try to be a good boy for them."

Al C's single bed had taken the place of the tool box in the front window, so he could wave to passers-by, or they could come up to the window to talk to him. That is where they had their present giving on Christmas morning, 1938. Al C was delighted with his present from Auntie Dolly. She'd given him a book all about horse racing, which he was anxious to start reading, as well as lots of pictures of race horses that she'd collected from the daily newspapers.

It was different for Annabelle. On her Christmas list she had asked for a piano and she could see that she hadn't got one. She was disappointed, but being a naturally gracious child she fought back the tears. She did have a big parcel to open and concentrated on doing that. The present was an imitation, wooden, one octave, baby grand toy piano with three screw-in legs. This time she could hold the tears back no longer.

This moment was interrupted by a knock at the front door. It was the doctor.

"Happy Christmas, everyone!" He handed Alice a bunch of holly with bright red berries from his walled garden at The White House.

Alice invited him to have a cup of tea, but he declined.

"I've just popped in to bring the children a little gift each. For you, young lady, now you've got two patients to look after and for Al C, a little bird told me you might need one of these."

Alice and Alberto were both proud of the way their children thanked the doctor and everyone looked on eagerly as the children opened their gifts. Al C had got a big scrap book to stick the race horse pictures in that Auntie Dolly had given him, and Annabelle had a larger nurse's outfit because she had outgrown her old one.

"Well, well, what a kind doctor we have to think of you children on Christmas Day. You can both amuse yourselves with your presents now while I cook the dinner."

Alberto sat with the children while Alice did just that. After dinner, as they settled down around Al C's bed to play some games, feeling disappointed that they could not go to the Geoghegans' house for the Christmas party, they saw Tommy coming in the garden gate.

Tommy came in to ask Al C a question. "Want to come to a Christmas party tonight, kid?"

"I'd like to, but I can't blinkin' come this year. I'm bed-bound."

"Oh yes, you can," said Tommy joyously. "We've fixed up a place in the living room where you can lay and mum says I can collect you in baby Joe's pram."

TGA: *(I watched those two families enjoy a wonderful Christmas together. They were the best of friends, all giving and supporting, especially in times of trouble. Tommy, who had two left feet, even tried to cheer Al C by doing a tap dance for him.)*

Chapter 8

Andre Escapes

Andre had just woken up and was looking out of his attic window. All was quiet apart from the Fyffe's delivery lorry travelling along Morland Road. Watching it disappear down that long road, Andre saw a huge bunch of green bananas fall out of the back, from over the top of the drop down wooden flap. Pyjama clad, he raced down the stairs, ran as fast as he could along the road and picked up the bunch. By that time, the lorry had reached the Fyffe's warehouse, beyond the glass works, where the bananas were stored to ripen before being distributed. Andre took the bananas into the scullery and told Ma how he had come by them.

"Andre Kliskey, that's the best thing you've ever done since you were born. I've been fancying a banana for ages," Ma said, as she started to peel one.

"But Ma, they're green."

"I don't care about that. I need to eat some. Thank you Andre."

After school that day, Andre was queuing in Dalmally Alley, awaiting his turn on the one roller skate when one of his school mates said, "My mum said your mum's expectin'."

"Expecting what?"

"Blimey, don't you know what 'expectin'' means?"

"Course I do. It means she is expecting something to happen, like waiting for a letter from a relative, or someone to be bringing shopping in."

"Nah, you dafty. When someone says your mum's expectin', they mean she's havin' a baby."

Andre gaped. "Your mum must be wrong. Ma hasn't said anything to us at home about a baby. My sister Elsa helps her a lot indoors and if she's got wind of anything, she'd tell me. I know she would."

After that conversation, Andre was ever on the alert at home, hoping to get the baby news denied, or maybe confirmed. Having pleased his stepmother with the bananas, he was also on the alert every morning looking for the Fyffe's delivery lorry again. He was determined to please her more, so she would learn to like him.

That opportunity arrived a couple of months later. This time he was already dressed and ran up the road as fast as his legs would carry him. It was his misfortune that no bananas fell off the lorry this time, but in his desperation to please, he loitered at the back of the lorry, hidden from the driver's view, until he disappeared into the store depot. At that point, quick as a flash, he clambered onto the back of the lorry and helped himself to the smallest bunch he could lay his hands on. Pleased with his success, he then sped home, hoping that no one had seen him.

"Ma, Ma," he said, excitedly, "I've got you some more bananas."

She was in the garden and by the time she'd returned to the scullery there was a loud banging on the front door. Bustling past Andre, she hastily opened the door.

"I've just chased a nipper up to this house. He stole bananas off my lorry. Does he live here Missus?"

"Andre; come to the door this minute!"

"That's him. I think he deserves a good clump round the earhole. And I'll 'ave me bananas back if y'please."

As soon as the door closed, Andre got the clump around the earhole. He cried.

TGA: (It was pitiful to watch the boy crying. Usually he fought back tears in defiance, but the disappointment at failing to win her approval was too hard to bear.)

"Stop your snivelling child. If you do wrong, you must expect trouble."

"But Ma, you were so pleased with the first bunch that fell off the lorry that I wanted to please you again."

"And after this lot, you expect me to believe the first bunch fell off the lorry?"

"But that's true, Ma. They did fall off the lorry."

"A likely tale. You fooled me once child, but I'm not going to be taken for a sucker a second time. Get out of my sight."

Elsa found Andre crying on his bed. With an old head on young shoulders, she mothered him.

"Don't get so upset, Andre. You always knew she didn't like you. I don't think she'll ever change."

168

"But when I gave her the bananas that fell off the lorry, she was pleased with me and I liked it. The first ones did fall off the lorry, honestly. I did steal the second lot though," he snivelled.

"Come on Andre, let's write another letter to Grandma. We know she loves us."

With nicer thoughts of Grandma distracting unhappy thoughts of his stepmother, Andre returned to school as a junior. His new master was Mr Channell. He was a shorter man than 'Lanky' Grant, with amazingly blue eyes, and he seemed to be a very kind man, encouraging all the boys to work hard. That was no problem for Andre; he always persevered with his schoolwork, never forgetting that no one could take away the knowledge you retained in your head.

As the year went on, Andre was enjoying his school life and was coping at home, with Elsa's encouragement. In October of 1937, both children had the shock of their lives. Ma produced a baby boy. As the nurse was leaving through the front door, she said, "Mrs Kliskey says you can go to her bedroom and meet your baby brother now."

Andre could not believe what he was seeing. It was a real baby with tiny fingers that moved and it didn't look a bit muddy, as though it had come from under the gooseberry bush.

Staring at their stepmother with wide eyes and in a state of shock, they heard her distant sounding voice saying, "You can say hello to him you know. His name is Brian."

They replied, "Hello Brian," but afterwards remained silent.

Pa's voice suddenly made them jump. "He's too little to answer you yet, but he'll gradually learn. Off you go now and you can see him again later with Daniel. He should be home soon."

TGA: (As the children lingered at the top of the stairs, they heard their father say, "Today Kit Kliskey, you have made me a happy man. You've got your kids, I've got mine, and now we've got one of our own."

At school the next day, Andre Kliskey received a big slice of education, and not from Mr Channell. It seemed his schoolmates knew a lot more about the 'gooseberry bush' than he did.

Having a new baby in the house made the days and months fly past and by the time Brian was a year old, people were talking more and more about the prospect of another war. Wireless broadcasts and newspapers had informed the public that Adolph Hitler from Germany and Benito Mussolini from Italy were planning to conquer Europe and establish a Master Race. Later, the news leaked that they were planning for *Fall Weiss*, the codename of an attack to be made on Poland in 1939.

Brian was brightening all this gloom, with his attempts to walk and talk and Andre, Elsa and Daniel enjoyed amusing him. One evening, he was having difficulty in settling down to sleep, so in an effort to appease Ma, Pa said he'd take the other three out for a walk and leave the house quiet. That night they saw a vision memorable enough to last a lifetime. In the sky above, they saw a Graf

Zeppelin silent missile. It looked like a huge cigar floating high above them. To them, with all the war talk going on, it seemed quite threatening. A couple of days later, the wireless told them that it had been on a spying mission over England.

Another memorable war-tainted day was when two big lorries dumped a huge pile of sand into the playground at Andre's school. The man in charge was a stranger and he soon paired all the boys up, one to hold a sack open, the other to shovel sand into it; swapping jobs from time to time as necessary. The objective was to provide sandbags to be used for protection purposes if war did come to pass. When their first sack was full, they were shown how to seal it with invisible tape.

"Excuse me, sir, there's been some mistake. That tape's not invisible. I can see it." Andre stated.

"Ah ha. I see we have a clever clogs in our midst and you are absolutely right, sonny. You can see it, but on a moonlit night pilots in enemy planes won't be able to. It's special non-reflecting tape provided by the Air Raid Precaution Department of the Government."

Touching Andre's head, he said, "A feather in your cap, son. Well spotted."

The next day Andre was summoned to the headmaster's office. He was horrified that perhaps he'd been too cheeky the day before about the invisible tape. Instead, he had a very pleasant surprise.

"Here you are, Andre, I've received a letter from your stepbrother, Ron. Would you like to sit in here and read it?"

Accepting the invitation, he sat on a chair by the door, opposite Mr Jones' desk and started to slowly decipher the handwriting.

"Do you need help, Andre?"

At Andre's nod, Mr Jones read the letter out loud:

Dear Andre,

I hope you are surviving at home with my mother. Dorothy hasn't heard from you, so we assume all is reasonably well.

I have news for you that isn't good. I expect you have heard that our country is expecting to go to war. Well, as part of that, I have been deployed to The British Expeditionary Force set up this year. It is highly likely that I will be sent overseas to Europe, but I cannot tell you where. I will try to keep in touch with you via your school.

When I joined the regular army, I never expected anything like this to happen so soon. I'm sorry I can't be there for you, but we will find a way to share life, one way or another. Don't forget to use the florins and get a taxi to Dorothy's if you're desperate. She will care for you.

Be a good kid and stick up for yourself, Andre. Life must get better for you. My thoughts are with you daily.

Love from Ron,

xxxxx

Another letter about the war was received by Mr Kliskey when he got home from work that same day. Looking at the postmark, he remarked that it was from his sister, even before he'd opened it. His sister was asking if Elsa could go back to Wiltshire and live with them if Great Britain did go to war.

Elsa looked at Andre. She would have loved the escape from Ma, but the wrench of separation from him would hit her very hard.

"I'm not happy with that idea, Eugene. Elsa has become very useful to me here, especially with Brian running around my feet all day."

"I absolutely agree with you Kit. I'll write and tell her our decision."

Elsa, who was now thirteen years old, was never asked what she wanted to do, but that didn't matter. She was happy to stay holding the fort with Andre.

At the end of March 1939, the government more or less committed Great Britain to war when, along with France, they offered Poland a Guarantee of Independence if *Fall Weiss* should come to pass. British people were beginning to feel more and more threatened by the thought of war. The exception generally was young lads who viewed all the war talk with an air of excitement, not realising what war could entail. Girls and their parents found the whole prospect very disturbing.

On the other end of the excitement scale, Andre was feeling miserable because he was very envious of his fourteen-year-old stepbrother, Daniel. He had now gone into long trousers. Andre, who was growing taller by the day, wanted to do that too, but wouldn't dare ask his stepmother. He still remembered the arguments when the school nurse wrote home advising his parents to buy him shoes to fit his feet before he became crippled. No, it was easier for him to keep quiet and let peace reign in the house.

Plans for the event of a war continued with a vengeance. The British Government were taking no risks. There was a fear that the Germans might start using gas warfare on our country, so every precaution was being taken. Schools were fitting children with respirators, which came to be commonly known as gas masks. The children in the Kliskey household couldn't wait to get theirs. Rumour had it that they made you look like Mickey Mouse.

The news on the wireless and in the newspapers was full of government plans to build warships, as well as armaments. Railings and wrought iron gates were being melted down to be used for ammunitions. Civilians had their part to play too. They were being advised to plant vegetables and fruit; in fact, anything edible that they possibly could to supplement possible food rationing. They were also being recruited into different divisions of the Home Front such as the Home Guard and Air Raid Wardens, to keep watch over our land, skies and coastlines.

No one escaped. Housewives were advised to play their part, using some recipes from Mrs Beeton's Victorian cookery books. In the event of war, there was a high probability that we would not be able to import sugar. Therefore, home grown carrots could be used as a substitute to make carrot cake and carrot jam.

Andre was very proud to be the first to take a gas mask home. Elsa and Daniel wanted to try it on, but Andre had been instructed not to let that happen, because he had been measured for a good fit, and that was very important in the event of a gas attack. Amusingly, Andre did not have to wait for war to use his appliance. The whole family were reduced to side-stitching laughter when Daniel let out a deafening fart and saw Andre scrambling to get his gas mask on to save his life!

Before long, the whole family had been fitted with gas masks and began to feel that their government was looking after them.

Mrs Kliskey put her thinking cap on and suggested that Eugene and the two boys should make use of themselves by digging up half the back lawn and starting to grow vegetables and fruit. The boys found that to be fun and called it their war work, while Eugene found it an intrusion in his life because he preferred tinkering with his clocks and making a bit of extra money that way.

"Eugene, sometimes you amaze me! Everybody needs to eat, and if we can't buy enough food to feed us, what do you propose to do for energy, may I ask?"

"Kit, it seems to me that our government is causing people to panic. There might not even be a war. Have you thought of that?"

"Well, I certainly hope you're right, that's for sure, but I'd rather be safe than sorry."

Although Andre had now resigned himself to the fact that his stepmother would never like him, he began to love doing the war work in the garden. In that way, for once in his life, he began to feel part of a family.

More preparation for war brought great joy as well as desolation to Andre. His ears pricked up when he heard on the wireless news that children living in the vicinity of London were going to be evacuated to live with families in less dangerous areas of the countryside. The desolation came when Ma started ranting, "I'm not letting Elsa go. I've had a baby late in my life and I need her here. I'm not well enough to let her go."

Andre was in deep despair; the wireless had said that the authorities were trying to keep children from the same home together in their placements. In his despair, he knocked the door to his father's clock workshop and pleaded, "Please Pa, could you talk to Ma about Elsa being evacuated with me. You are our father, after all."

"Yes, Andre, I am your father, but usually mothers know best about these things. Being separated won't hurt you. It will help make a man of you."

Not consoled, Andre asked Elsa to come to his bedroom when she could discreetly do so.

"Elsa, I've asked Pa to try to keep us together for evacuation, but he's weak-kneed. He never stands up to Ma and she usually gets her own way, so I want to give this to you, to help you make your escape."

He handed her the two florins with Dorothy's address and said, "You get yourself a taxi to her. I know she'll help you and then, through her, you can let Ron know I've been evacuated. I have copied her address, which I shall keep with Grandma's ring, so I can let you know my new address."

Andre left 152 Morland Road alone, carrying his small bag. Ma and Elsa watched him leave, Elsa with tears and Ma obviously overjoyed. His heart beat faster and faster as he boarded the charabanc in the school grounds.

With mixed emotions, he felt all alone as he sat in his window seat, totally overwhelmed by the sight of so much love, affection and tears on display from his window. Parents and children were distraught as they were forced to say goodbye to each other. He could see parting was almost too hard for them to bear. Tears rolled down his cheeks.

When all goodbyes had been said and the charabanc was motoring along the country roads, the evacuees began chatting, wondering what the immediate future would hold for them.

Andre sat in silence with his thoughts, which recurred constantly to the repetitive hum of the engine. '*Thank you, wonderful war; thank you, wonderful war*' for the entire journey.

Eventually, the charabanc came to a halt and the evacuation officer announced that they had arrived at their destination.

Andre, not wanting to draw attention to himself, remained seated and thought gratefully, within his own head, "HOORAY, I'VE ESCAPED." He repeated it several times, "HOORAY, I'VE ESCAPED. HOORAY, I'VE ESCAPED. HOORAY, I'VE ESCAPED", unable to believe and enjoy the fact that it was actually true.

Chapter 9

War Clouds Hovering

Annabelle was becoming frightened. Ironically, she wasn't sure what 'war' meant, because she'd never been told about WW1, but whenever anyone talked about it they were worried, so she declined to ask. Her mature, compassionate view was that their family had enough to worry about with her mother's health and Al C's knee.

That threat of war found the Governing Body of Enham making urgent appeals nationwide for funds and the response was outstanding. The amount raised was substantial and not only money; there were gifts as well, which ranged from fifty beds and mattresses, twelve chairs, etc. etc. to one Belgian hare. This news cheered the villagers who dreaded the demise of their life-changing, life-giving charitable refuge.

Life continued normally for the Aless family, apart from the dark cloud. 'Normality' in their household saw an ambulance arrive to take Alice and Al C to the Andover War Memorial Hospital for his knee check-up.

The ambulance was provided by the ingenuity of 'Nelson' Coxhill, who lost an eye in WW1, hence the nickname. He took responsibility to set up a Hospital Benefit Fund whereby villagers paid half-a-crown (two shillings and sixpence) every week for their membership. In this way, all the villagers helped each other in times of need.

The specialist's report on Al C indicated that the knee was improving, but he still advocated complete rest and arranged to see Al C again in three months. By this time, older village boys such as Tony Crabbe, John Moody and Jimmy Mulligan took turns to take Al C out for walks in the fresh air in an old pram, which gave the Aless family some welcome respite. Of those boys, Jimmy Mulligan became a close friend as he would spend all his spare time at Al C's bedside playing board games and generally help him pass time. More importantly, he would carry him to the lavvy when needed. That help was a Godsend.

As the summer approached, villagers were hiding their anxieties behind preparations for the forthcoming annual horticultural show to be held in July. Annabelle, who loved arranging primroses and bluebells, which she often picked from the woods in springtime for her mother and Auntie Dolly, decided this year that she would like to enter the wild flower arrangement competition in the class for eight to eleven-year-olds.

Chatting with her mum and Auntie Dolly, she felt quite adult to be taking part too. Alice was going to enter for the first time with her homemade strawberry jam and Auntie Dolly was going to enter one of her coffee and walnut cakes in the sponge cake competition. Al C, who was lying on his bed listening, surprised everyone when he boastfully said, "Don't forget me then! I'm going to do something too!"

All three of them looked at him with surprise, before bursting into laughter. "And how, young man, do you intend to join in, may I ask?" questioned Alice.

"Ha, ha. It's all arranged and wouldn't you like to know."

"Yes we would," laughed Auntie Dolly. "Come on, spill the beans, there's a good lad."

"I don't care what you're going to do," shrugged Annabelle. "If you don't want to tell us, then I don't want to know."

"Now, now, Annabelle. That's unkind. Of course we all want to know. Come on, Al C. We're waiting."

"OK, I'll tell you," grinned Al C, unable to conceal his secret any longer. "Jimmy's taking me up the field in the pram and I'm going to be in charge of the raffle stall. I'm going to sell thousands of tickets."

"A bit ambitious…and how do you propose to sell thousands?"

"By shouting out to people to come and see the prizes so they feel they can't pass me by, just like the greengrocers do in Petticoat Lane. I saw them working magic when Dad took me there on our London holiday. People were buying stuff they didn't really want; honestly, Mum. You can talk people into it. And I shall joke with people so I collect a crowd, then others will come to see what's going on; and that's how I'm going to sell thousands. You'll see," he gushed, enthusiastically.

"Ah well, that remains to be seen. Good luck to you, son. Let's hope you do raise lots of funds."

In bed later that evening, Annabelle was too excited to sleep, thinking about the flower arranging competition, so she went downstairs and was surprised to find Mr Spencer in the scullery with her mum and dad.

"I couldn't go to sleep, Mummy. Where's Daddy going?"

"He's just going out to help Mr Spencer do a job."

"Can't they do it tomorrow? It's dark now."

"No sweetheart, they'll do it tonight. You come and sit on my lap and Daddy will be back soon.

TGA: *(Mr Spencer, was a village settler who was not too badly disabled, having still got both arms and able to walk steadily, but slowly, with a limp because his knee was damaged by shrapnel. He had come to help Alberto empty his portable Elson lavatory into the cesspit in the garden on the small lawn the other side of the garden path, under the white lilac tree. That job was done once a week, when both children were normally asleep.)*

"Have you heard they've started digging up the road and laying sewer pipes from Andover, so we can have flush lavatories here in Enham, Alby?"

"Glory Hallelujah! Is that really true? I had heard a rumour."

"Yeah. It's a rumour no longer mate, which means, thankfully, that our nights of doing this job are numbered."

"Blimey, what a relief. A bigger one for you than me of course, Charlie. How many settlers do you help?"

"Practically everyone, unless they've got fit family members who can help. The only two who

181

can't be helped are living in the Tudor cottages. They both have commodes with a pail underneath. I know Mrs Rose deals with it because of Jack's one leg disability. She digs a deep trench in the garden and empties her pail daily. I expect Charlie Parsons does the same."

"Let's hope the workmen will be able to help them when they actually lay the sewers."

Next morning, while Annabelle was still on summer holiday from school, Al C called out, "Mum, a big van's stopped outside and the driver's coming up the path."

Mother and daughter were quickly at the bedside looking out of the window, just as the front door was knocked.

"Morning Ma'am, got a delivery for ya."

"I'm sorry, I think you must have the wrong address. We haven't bought anything."

"It's got No. 9 on your door, Ma'am. Are you Annabelle Alessandro?"

Hugging Annabelle close, Alice said, "My daughter is."

"Good gracious me; whatever has she got?"

"You don't know? Then before I offload, we'd better decide where you want us to put it Ma'am. It's a piano."

Alice put her hand over her mouth and gasped. Annabelle blushed crimson with eyes popping out of her head. From his bed, Al C could be heard shouting, "Brilliant! A piano, a piano!"

They were all agog to say the least.

"There ya go then! Looks like you've got a big surprise, young Missy."

Where to put the piano was not a problem. The front room was basically used as a junk room. There wasn't any furniture in there, so a quick decision was made to put it by the wall opposite the front window. Amidst all the flurry, Annabelle was like a yo-yo without a string, bouncing up and down with delight.

After the delivery, she was constantly sitting at the piano. She helped herself to a chair from the living room and concentrated on picking out the notes of 'Do-Re-Mi', although they didn't sound as good as on Aunt Daisy's piano. Totally absorbed, she spent time trying to pick out very familiar tunes, such as the *God Save our Gracious King* and *Rule Britannia* before dragging herself away to do a tea-time stint in the scullery. As soon as she heard the 5pm factory hooter, she asked, "Can I run up the road to meet Daddy now, Mum?"

"Of course you can, Annabelle, and don't forget to tell him about your piano!"

Annabelle stretched up, put her arms around Alice's neck, kissed her cheek and said, "Mum, you're incorrigible."

"And what does that mean, may I ask?"

Flying out the front door, she replied, "I don't know, but Pam's mum used to call her that."

Arriving home together, all smiles, Alberto asked, "Whoever's sent Annabelle a piano, I wonder?"

"My guess is my mother. She was so sad when she got my letter telling her the story of Annabelle's tears when she got a toy piano last Christmas."

As he set eyes on it, Alberto exclaimed, "Blimey, what an acquisition!" He opened the top and pulled out a drop-down music stand. Attached was an envelope.

"Yes," smiled Alice, reading the letter, "Mother has sent it in the hope that Annabelle will learn to play a few songs before she comes to stay next."

"Oh thank you, thank you, Granny Howitz," Annabelle cried, immediately followed by "What's that for Dad?"

"That's a music stand to put your music on."

"But I haven't got any music."

"Don't fret yourself about that Annabelle; Mummy will take you to Teague and Kings in Andover to see if they sell any 'Teach Yourself' music books."

The man in the music shop found the perfect book. It was a Wedgewood blue colour with black print showing a pianist sitting at a grand piano with lid raised. It was entitled *The Wright Pianoforte Tutor* by Albert H Oswald. He also made Alice aware that a piano needed to be tuned regularly. On asking the price, Alice arranged for the tuner to visit, but told Annabelle that she couldn't afford for it to be tuned regularly.

Having sneaked in to see the piano, Al was hoping to have a go on it, but Jimmy carried him back to bed saying, "Your priority is to tap dance again, so you've got to lie in bed for a bit longer; there's a good lad. You know that complete rest is working, so try to be content. It's not easy for me to be hard on you, but I want to help you to help yourself."

TGA: (*It was so pleasing for me to see Annabelle with a hobby of her own. I watched her studying from her music book and becoming excited about what she was learning from it.*)

As the horticultural show drew nearer, Annabelle was tortured by dividing her time between playing piano and picking wild flowers to practise arranging.

The night before the show, Alberto's younger brother Antonio turned up, which was a regular occurrence. No. 9 Newbury Road, Enham, was his halfway house, breaking his long journey from London to Devizes in his lorry to make a delivery. He was given lodging money by the company he worked for – James Stewart of Bruce Grove, London – and always insisted that Alice take the money, despite her protestations.

"And how's my little Annabelle here? Still the boss?"

"Very much becoming so, Antonio, I'm afraid. That's how it is."

"Uncle, do you know I've got my own piano?"

"You're kidding me."

"It's true. I have. Granny Howitz sent it to me. Mummy bought me a music book and I'm learning to play. Come in the front room and I'll show you. With proud Mum and Dad watching, she played a little piece called *Melody*, followed by a *March*, both by the same person, Lea Thorne. It told her that in the book.

Uncle Tonio was very impressed, gave her a big hug and a pat on the back.

185

"Goodness me, you are a clever girl. Wait till I tell Rosie and Mary Ann. They were so sad they couldn't come with me this time. I couldn't bring them because they've got the measles. If I get a Devizes job in half-term, I'll bring them down to stay for a couple of nights. Now let's go and see Al C.

"Hello cocker. What've you been up to then?"

"Hurt my knee, probably playing football, so I've got to keep resting in this blinkin' bed, but it is getting better, so they think I'll be able to walk and tap dance again. Then Annabelle will be able to play music on her piano for me to dance to."

"Sounds good to me, Al, and I've bought something to cheer you up. From his overnight rucksack he produced a big, full paper bag.

"How's this for the best medicine ever?"

"Brilliant, Uncle, thanks. Blackjack chews from Granny Howitz' sweetshop up the road. Want one?"

No thanks, Al; they're for you."

"Blimey, you as well. It must be catching. Everyone who comes to see me at the window calls me Al these days."

"Proper thing an' all. Not so longwinded, is it?

"Now, something for Annabelle. Sherbert liquorice dips. Do you still like those?"

"Ooh, yes please. Thank you, Uncle."

"And you've got something else young lady." The family were all ears with anticipation. "I saw this on the bank as I was driving along today. It's very old, but it might be useful to you."

It was a very old cookery book with the cover and front and back pages missing, so it was not possible to see who wrote it.

"I've never seen a cookery book before. Mummy and Auntie Dolly tell me how to cook."

"Well this book should tell you how to cook different recipes and then you can surprise both of them, eh."

"Don't you want to take it home to your girls?"

"What! It's no use to them. They never cook, so they don't know the difference between a wooden spoon or a whisk."

Alberto, as usual, took his brother to the Institute for a pint. Antonio had made many friends there over his years of driving. Bill Chant who lived in an original estate cottage at the start of Anton Lane, just across the road from the Institute, always seized the opportunity to talk to Antonio about North London. He asked, "Where you gunna kip tonight then, mate? Young Al's got his bed downstairs while he's laid up."

"That's all fixed, thanks, Bill. I'm going to get some shut-eye on the two armchairs in the living room with Al."

"The hell you're not! We've got two empty bedrooms now the kids have flown. You come and stay with us mate; you'd be most welcome."

"What say you, Alby?"

"I say, good ol' Bill. You need a decent sleep to drive all the way to Devizes in the morning."

"That's a lot of old tripe and you know it, Alby. I can do that trip with my eyes shut. I've been doing it for years and thoroughly enjoy it too, since I climbed the ladder and became a driver."

"Yeah. That's true. I remember the first time you went there. You were about fifteen, cleaning cars for the firm and someone went sick and you were asked to travel with the driver to help him offload. A long time ago; that was probably when I was getting weekends home from the Manchester hospital after my arm was amputated."

While they were out, Alice and Annabelle sat by the side of Al's bed and had a look through the cookery book for some dinner recipes. Much to their surprise, they had a hilarious time looking at weird recipes such as cow-heel boiled.

"Yuk! If you make that, Annabelle, I won't eat it."

"Don't fret yourself, Al C. I don't fancy making it either. And what about gravy soup? That's daft. You either have gravy or you have soup."

They were looking at random pages and next chose page 45; a selection of sandwiches.

"Wow! What a funny, festive treat. Christmas pudding sandwiches!

"That's not a cookery book. It's a joke book."

"No it's not!" retorted Annabelle. "It's serious. The title says *Success Cookery Book.* Let's try another page."

They were looking through a selection of sauces and preserves and on page 151 they found how to make walnut ketchup and pickled vegetable marrow.

"Perhaps I should try to make the walnut ketchup one day. I like walnuts."

"Somehow, I don't think you'll be doing that, Annabelle. There's a lot of hard work involved and you don't have that sort of time now you're learning to play piano. Listen, to start with, you've got to collect 2 gallons of walnut peelings and along the way you have to add three quarts of vinegar. Sounds disgusting to me. Here, you read it properly this time."

"You're right, Mum. I've changed my mind. Let's look further on."

On page 235, they came to *Household Tips*, where they could learn to clean bottles, clean silver, use up coal dust, deal with coats with shiny elbows, stop colours running when washing, etc. etc.

"Well, I think you should ask Uncle to throw it back on the bank where he found it. It's no bloomin' good."

"No, I'm not doing that, Al C. He was kind to think of me. I shall keep it forever, even when I'm a very old woman. Besides, I saw a recipe in there telling me how to cook tripe and onions, and Dr MacCallum told me once I should learn to cook that for Mummy, because it's very good for you."

"Well, I don't want tripe, whatever it is."

On the day of the show, Uncle Tonio came back early from Mr Chant's, just as Annabelle was about to go up the plantation.

"You going up there all by yourself, Annabelle?"

Responding to Annabelle's nod, Uncle Tonio accompanied her while she picked her wild flowers and a selection of grasses. At the same time, they were both constantly nibbling wild strawberries that were growing in abundance at their feet. Tonio wished her good luck and said, "When I come back on my return journey, I'll get your mum to give me a jam jar and I'll collect some of those wild strawberries to take home to the girls.

"That's good. I'll come with you, Uncle. They're really sweet and tasty."

Pandemonium reigned when they returned home. They all waved Antonio goodbye. Al had a bowl of water by his bed to try and wash himself, but craftily hoped that Jimmy would soon arrive to help him. After picking a few of the straightest runner beans he could find to exhibit, Alberto was helping Alice to pack a bag containing cardigans, lots of loose change, her nicely labelled pot of jam, the white vase for Annabelle and a Tizer bottle filled with sugar water to use in the vase for the flowers. Before long, Jimmy arrived to take charge of Al for the day.

Momentum was gaining pace. As soon as Annabelle was ready with her flowers and grasses laid in her basket, she went to call for Auntie Dolly.

"Oh, Annabelle, how lovely you look. What a perfect dress for the occasion. It's embroidered with buttercups and daisies."

"I know. Mrs Holley gave it to Mummy for me. She made the dress and embroidered the flowers on it and passed it on to me when Betty had grown too big for it. I love it."

"And you're using your trug that Phill made for you to collect bluebells. Go and ask him if he can see the colours of your wild flowers. He's up the shed still doing his basket work."

TGA: *(Mr Phill Mesney wasn't going to the show. He suffered near blindness due to mustard gas poisoning in the war and was advised by Enham Village Centre to take up basket making, where the sense of touch could enhance what minimal sight he had remaining.)*

The air of excitement and anticipation was palpable as the family and Auntie Dolly arrived at the field opposite the two pairs of cottages to the right at the top of King's Road. Already, there was a big throng mingling and many of them were making for the marquee to submit their entries. Other people were setting up outside events around the perimeter of the field; amongst them Jimmy, with Al in pram, setting up the raffle stall.

Annabelle was excited. "Can we go and see them, Daddy?"

"First things first, Annabelle. You've got to arrange your flowers before anything else. Let's go into the marquee and submit our exhibits."

When the business of entries was done, they made their way to see Al. Jimmy had brought a Union Jack flag to lay over their trestle table, with a big red tub in the centre into which the raffle ticket counterfoils were thrown. He also brought a long wooden spoon with which to stir up the contents, and a toy drum for Al to tap out rhythms and attract the crowds. The rest of the table was packed with various prizes, all donated to the village from Andover business people and from surrounding villages. Annabelle wanted to buy some tickets, but was not allowed because the show had not yet been officially opened.

While waiting for the opening ceremony, people were milling around in the glorious sunshine. Fantastic that the weather was so good, as there was a fancy dress parade – thanks to Mr Betts' inspiration – and a full sports' programme, as well as many other events. No one would ever have guessed by the enthusiasm of the villagers that afternoon that another war was on the horizon.

Alberto and Alice had a chat with Mr Cox and his wife Edith. They were enjoying every minute, proudly pushing Barry, their latest, in his pushchair, while the older ones ran around freely. Mr Fred Cox was unable to keep the confident smile off his face while waiting for the results of his garden produce. He was usually a prolific winner.

Next, they chatted with Mr and Mrs Tempero, who remarked what a miracle it was to see the Coxes with a lovely family of five around them.

"Do you remember the days when they had their first baby?"

Alice and Alberto shook their heads, saying, "We settled in the village much later than Fred and his wife."

"Oh my dears, it was so sad. They had to send their first baby, Marjorie, to live with her grandparents in Preston, Lancashire. Fred couldn't bear to hear her crying. It brought back terrible memories of the war to him and was making him a nervous wreck, finding it too hard to cope with his work."

TGA: *(What a horrendous war that must have been for Mr Cox and millions of others like him,*

192

not being able to cope with the cries of a newborn baby.)

"Poor Mrs Cox," replied Alice. "It must have been heartbreaking to make a decision like that."

"You're so right, Alice, but what a feather in Enham's cap," continued Alberto, "when you think how much the medical care here must have helped to enable him to go on and have five more children. I know how much they've helped me."

"Did Mrs Cox get Marjory back later?" asked Alice.

"No, they didn't, purely for the child's sake. She loved her grandparents dearly and was progressing with schooling, so they contented themselves with visits."

Loudspeakers abruptly silenced all conversations with the announcement that Mr Bob Bell, the Mayor of Andover, was about to open the show. Accompanied by a couple of councillors, he presented an impressive figure, dressed in his mayoral robes of red, trimmed with brown fur and his double chain of office with medallion resting on his 'comfortable' chest. It was all topped by a remarkable crown of thick, greying hair.

"Ladies and Gentlemen, it is an honour and a pleasure to come to this WW1 village today and see what you wounded men and families have produced in your gardens, despite the physical disabilities with which you have to cope daily. I often enquire about your welfare and I am reliably informed that the authorities are taking admirable care of you. I know from earlier days that it is all thanks to the generosity of the British public and of those who donated cottages."

The Mayor was interrupted by tumultuous applause. When the applause died down, he returned applause to the crowd.

"I am in awe of the results of your endeavours and achievements, which I've seen in the marquee and for which I give you my humbled congratulations. I think – well I know – you could give me a few lessons in horticulture!"

Following more applause, the Mayor raised his hand to calm the appreciation.

"Thank you. Thank you very much. Now I have to tell you that it is a source of great regret to me that my civic duties do not allow me to stay and mingle amongst you."

Blatant booing ensued to which the Mayor cupped his ears, wanting more. He was a bit of a showman himself in the local entertainment world and loved the camaraderie of it all.

He held up his right hand again. "But…I'll be back later to award the prizes and shake some of you by the hand. Now, all that remains is for me to do two things; firstly, to tell you that all funds raised at this event will be donated to the Enham Scouts, Guides and Cubs Packs and, secondly, that it gives me great pleasure to declare this Enham Horticultural Show well and truly open."

The atmosphere was electric and led to a scattering of people in ten thousand directions. Alberto and family went immediately to the raffle ticket stall and bought five tickets between them from Al and Jimmy. Their prize was a bottle of HP Sauce.

"Ohhhh...I like Daddies Sauce better than that," said Annabelle, totally ignoring the much more expensive prizes.

People were a bit dismayed to see a notice on the huge marquee informing them that the judging was not quite complete, due to the late arrival of two of the judges. Not to be outdone, they kept the momentum going by visiting some of the side shows, including coconut shies, bowling for a pig and a bit of a contortionist effort for some of the wounded men. There was a darts' competition, best score of three throws for a penny – run by Mr Skippings – and Annabelle's favourite, rolling the penny. A side show made by Mr Guest attracted lots of people and turned out to be a real money-spinner.

Annabelle was hooked on rolling pennies down the movable wooden ramp placed on the square patterned table top, trying to land the coin in the centre of a square to win herself a prize.

A loudspeaker announcement brought an end to Annabelle's fun. The marquee was now open, so she dashed off to see the results of the wild flower arrangement competition, catching up with Alice and Alberto along the way.

The family's reaction was a joy to behold when they discovered that Annabelle had won the silver cup for her flower arrangement. The excited little girl's emotions were subconsciously floating up a long stairway from disbelief at the bottom, through amazement up to delight; on and on up to a state of ecstasy, the likes of which she had never before experienced. The joy was infectious enough to obliterate all war clouds, and you could see other happy villagers zooming into the same euphoric state in support of Annabelle; in their eyes the little Cinderella of the village.

Back to earth, Alice wasn't displeased with a 'highly commended' for her jam, Alberto was happy with a 3rd for his runner beans and Auntie Dolly, of course, was delighted with a first for her cake.

After the judging, the excited atmosphere in the crowd could surely not exist with such intensity anywhere else in the world. The wounded men were buoyed with awesome appreciation of Enham Village Centre and all those people who had contributed to make the village a sheltered environment in which to live, to be able to compete and to enjoy the fruits of their labours.

Camaraderie was evident in the chatter that followed. Mr Cox shook the hand of Mr Ewers who had beaten him with his prize onions, and said, "But you still can't beat my tomatoes, parsnips or marrows yet, can you, mate?"

Mrs Rose, a very plump lady whose party trick was to be able to bend over keeping both legs straight and putting her hands flat on the floor, was thrilled to bits with second prize for her entry of 6 potatoes, which had to be of equal size and shape. She shared the gardening with her disabled husband, Jack, who had lost his leg from the thigh, so had to sit on a wooden box and dig from the handle just above the fork. It was awe-inspiring watching him deftly manoeuvring himself along the row as he dug.

So much was going on that it was a good job people from the surrounding villages supported the event with its numerous sideshows, because some of the villagers who had children in both events were torn between the sports and the fancy dress parade. The excitement, rivalry and sociability of the event made time fly; so much so, that most people were very surprised when Mr Bob Bell and his entourage arrived back at the loudspeaker area.

"Hello, you lovely people; here I am back for your prize giving, just as I promised."

At the same time, the showman in him was waiting for his applause as he opened his arms and beckoned towards himself. The crowd loved it and wanted more. This playful banter continued until the Mayor announced that it was time to get on with the business of the day, starting with fancy dress, the tiny tots' section.

"Mums and dads, please bring your little ones up so we can all have a good look at them in their costumes. First prize has been awarded to Susie Ewers as 'Little Granny', second to Lawrence Crabbe as a 'Mandarin', and third to Jacqueline Crabbe as a 'Tambourine Girl'. A sight worth seeing folks, don't you agree?"

"Now to the pushcarts and cars' section. First prize to John Cox, Motorboat, second to Molly Lowman, Basket Girl and third to Angela Tomlin as Miss Enham."

"Next, we have the special section. The clear winner is Mr Joe Geoghegan as Lady Godiva, no less! He's never been on a horse in his life, but being a naturally short man, if I may say so, he looks quite safe up there straddled across the back of Bob, the village carthorse. If we were in a house, he'd have brought the roof down upon us. There is only one other entry in this section, which is Mr Ewers, the village dairy farmer, displaying 'Drink More Milk'. Very astute chap, I'd say. What d'ya think?"

TGA: (*Mr Ewers, who delivers milk daily from churns into jugs at doorsteps to all the villagers, received his well-deserved ovation.*)

"Next we have the junior flower arrangement competition. The silver cup for this event goes to a very artistic 8-year-old young lady, Annabelle Aless."

As instructed by her dad, if her name should be called, Annabelle curtsied to the Mayor before accepting the cup. The Mayor bent forward and kissed Annabelle's forehead saying, "What a lovely little blonde bombshell she is," as the crowd applauded.

"Senior wild flower arrangements. Miss Mona Guest is the artistic one in this event. Are you out there Mona?"

There was a disturbance in the crowd as an attractive and confident 13-year-old ran eagerly forward.

"Mona, I am delighted to award you this first prize, an admirable crystal vase, which will last you all your life, as long as you don't drop it!"

Mona carefully carried it away to the laughter of the spectators.

"Now, we come to decorated bicycles. Well, well, well! First prize goes to Mona Guest, Enham Basketry. My goodness, you are a busy bee, Mona.

Second goes to Joan Dowling, Lavender Girl, and third to Mary Shergold, Enham Upholstery.

Next, we come to all the garden produce section."

Mr Fred Cox was back and forth like a yo-yo, picking up many firsts and umpteen second and third prizes and his proud young family were swarming about him like bees round a honey pot. Not to be outdone, though, Mr Ewers picked up a first onion prize as well as carrots.

When Auntie Dolly won first for her coffee and walnut cake, the Mayor said, "I know you. You're one of the cooks from the Estate House before they pulled it down."

"That's right, Mr Mayor."

"Well, I think your husband's a very lucky man."

"And you can jolly well tell him that whenever you wish."

Grinning broadly, the Mayor said, "There's always a cheeky one, isn't there folks? Now, it gives me great pleasure to award first prize to Mr Joe Woods for his stunning sweet peas – if you get my meaning?" He cupped his hand to his ear and rolled his eyes.

Joe happily collected his prize, still wearing his padded flat cap for protection.

TGA: (*Joe's skull had been wounded in the war and he'd had a metal plate inserted to protect his brain.*)

"Thank you, Mr Mayor," he said graciously, before adding, "We could tell better ones than that in the trenches, I can tell you."

"That doesn't surprise me at all," responded the Mayor. "I have to say that this list of prize winners has been huge, confirming the enthusiasm of the villagers, but the end is in sight now." He was interrupted by a few playful 'boos'. "Well, I don't know about you lot, but I for one want to go to bed tonight, so I will continue. Before I get to the crème-de-la-crème', I am delighted to give the dart prize to my one-armed showbiz pal, Mr Alberto Aless for the highest score of 180 with three darts. Well done, Alby, and here's your prize of a new dartboard and a set of darts."

The Mayor then came to the best kept gardens in the village.

"It is my great pleasure to award the runner-up prize to Mrs Rose for her beautifully neat garden, with plants on parade, just like regiments of soldiers."

Mrs Rose collected her prize – a new hoe – and thanked the Mayor.

"I'm afraid Jack hasn't come today, but this prize, sawn off lower down to accommodate his disability, is surely his. The other half can be a dibber for me; that way we both have a prize. He digs the garden and does the weeding and I do the planting. I'm always telling him that if he pulls out my plants for weeds, I'll knock his block off."

"Poor chap!" exclaimed the Mayor. "He's only got one leg, so he can't even run away."

"Now, now, Ladies and Gentlemen, calm down in order that I can present the most prestigious prize of the day. It is this magnificent silver cup and it goes to Mr Hall who lives on the Crescent. He is one of the most severely wounded men in the village and his garden is exquisite. I give him my whole-hearted congratulations."

The crowd waited and clapped while Mr Hall struggled to reach the table. His legs took turns in swinging a complete circle on the right and again, a complete circle on the left.

"Well done, Mr Hall. How you manage to do gardening with legs like that I'll never know."

"A damn sight easier than with no legs at all, I can assure you, but we mustn't forget my wife and daughter Eva. They give me a lot of help."

The enduring applause was deafening.

"Thank you, Enham village residents. You have given us an afternoon of great entertainment and pleasure, but before I hand you over to Mr Jack Crabbe and Mr Norman Cox, who will conduct the auction of your produce, there are people to be mentioned. We have to thank the following for their voluntary help in making this show possible. Mr E C Green, Hon Sec. Mr N E Cox, Treasurer, Mr G Bright, wireless for music and loudspeakers, and all the people, too numerous to be mentioned individually, always on hand to help as well as exhibit, including Miss People, Mrs Crimble and Miss Crimble, who deserve special mention because they have given extraordinary help this year. Also, our grateful thanks go to the village baker, Mr Cleverley, for providing sandwiches, tea and cakes here today. Perhaps we should also thank the good Lord for providing us such a beautiful day.

"Now, I shall hand you over to Mr Cox and Mr Crabbe for the auction of your produce, but never fear, unceasingly I shall go on admiring you courageous men and your lovely women. Thank you Ladies and Gentlemen."

Mr Cox's tomatoes were going like hot cakes. Mrs Basting bought lots of runner beans for her Sunday dinner and Mr Ewers' onions were bought by his sister-in-law, Mrs Dora Buck. Mr Ewers was heard to say, "You didn't have to buy those. I'd have given you some."

"Don't be silly, Ted, it's all in a very good cause."

Alberto bought a beautiful bunch of roses, one of Mr Hall's exhibits, and asked Annabelle to place them in her trug for later.

"Can we go home soon, Dad? I'm getting tired."

"Not yet sweetheart; I've got to buy a few more things."

So much produce was being auctioned that to Annabelle it seemed as though she was waiting forever. Eventually, her father bought a pot of strawberry jam and Auntie Dolly's coffee and walnut cake.

"Can we go now, Dad?"

"No, we can't Annabelle. Not yet."

As soon as the auction was finished, the crowds started to disperse. Officials were taking down the stalls as another Enham Village horticultural show was coming to an end. Alice, Alberto, Auntie Dolly and Annabelle went to collect Al from his raffle table. Alberto thanked Jimmy for looking after Al all day long and he gave Jimmy the pot of strawberry jam that Alice had made and the bunch of roses for him to take home to his mum.

"That's really nice of you, Mr Aless, but I like looking after Al. It's no trouble, honestly."

"Well it's been a very special, long, long day, so let's agree to make it an extra special one, shall we? You take these home with our love and thanks."

At home, Alice soon prepared a tasty tea for her starving family. She had bought 2lbs of tomatoes from Mr Cox's stall outside his home on the Crescent the previous Thursday, which Annabelle was slicing, while Alice was frying the rashers and the bread. The tomatoes were ready to go in the frying pan last of all.

For a pudding, they all enjoyed a lovely hunk of Auntie Dolly's coffee and walnut cake much to Annabelle's delight.

"Yummy. I'm glad we stayed on to buy this dad."

Over tea, there was much discussion on the day's events, with Al giving them a running commentary about his raffle ticket sales.

"You'll never guess what Mr Cox the treasurer said to me."

"You're right, we never will. So what did Mr Cox say?"

"When he's done the cashing up, he's going to tell me if I did well with the raffle. He said he heard me working hard to get people to my stall."

Alberto was delighted with his handicapped son's enterprise.

When the children were fast asleep after their busy day, Alberto whispered to Alice, "We won't switch the wireless on tonight, "We don't want any bad news to spoil this lovely day, do we?"

At the end of August, following another visit to the specialist, young Al was allowed to put weight on his leg again. His new routine was to stand on his legs for two hours every morning and two hours every afternoon, and to extend the times by half an hour every week. Should his knee start to hurt, he had to go back to bed rest. His next appointment was early December.

Before that date, every resident in the entire village became 'chilled to the bone' with dread. On 3rd September, 1939, at 11.15am, when Annabelle was still only eight years old, the following broadcast by Prime Minister Neville Chamberlain was heard on the wireless:

"This morning, the British Ambassador in Berlin handed the German Government a final note stating that, unless we heard from them by 11 o'clock, that they were prepared at once to withdraw their troops from Poland, a state of war would exist between us."

His speech went on for a long time, but Alberto and Alice, cuddling both their children, were too stunned to listen to more. It was terrifying. Their perfect existence in this village, had been crumpled at a stroke.

It was a sunny day and they went out onto the lawn hoping to see neighbours and share the horror of the news. All four of the ladies from the two pairs of British Legion houses, 3, 5, 7 and 9, Auntie Milly, Auntie Hilda, Auntie Dolly and Alice, congregated by Alice's garden fence, gaining some strange comfort from talking to each other. The distraught men gathered in front of the basketry shop window, too dejected even to go into the Institute for a pint.

One of the ARP (Air Raid Precaution) Wardens, Mr Jack Stuart, another one-legged man, wasted no time in visiting the houses in the southern end of the village to fit and issue gas masks for each person in the house. He also issued thick black material to be fitted at their windows, which would soon be inspected to establish that not one pin-prick of light could escape.

On Friday 20th October 1939, more doom and descended upon the villagers. Peter Ewers, son of the village farmer Mr Ewers and his wife, was killed instantaneously in a road accident not far from his home at 5pm. A tragic coincidence was that he was killed about 20 yards from the spot where his friend Peter Basting had met his death in a road accident a few years previously.

Peter Ewers was riding his bicycle down the lane from the farm and was killed at the junction of the lane with the main Andover to Newbury Road by a heavy GPO lorry. When Mr Ewers got to the scene, he was out of his mind with anguish and was trying to kill the driver. Ironically, Mrs Basting was passing at the time, pulled Mr Ewers away from the driver and stayed with him until more help arrived.

The entire village was stunned. Peter was a very popular boy with his many keen interests. He was a member of the 1st Enham Cub Pack, sang in Smannell Church Choir and took an avid interest in the Andover Young Farmers' Club, to which he belonged. On the Tuesday before his death, he won first prize in the class for young farmers' heifers at Weyhill Fair.

Who could have foretold that the following week his family and just about everybody in the village, including Alberto and Alice, would be attending his funeral at St. Michael and All Angels Church at Knights Enham, conducted by The Rev. H.J. Webb with Mrs Buck at the organ.

Still in a deep and unconquerable state of shock, not one of the villagers wanted – or indeed knew how – to celebrate the festive season. They were trying to put on a brave face and that was about the best they could manage.

It was the Geoghegans' turn to visit Alberto and Alice that year, and they decided that a booze-up to beat all booze-ups would at least drown their sorrows and help them to forget, albeit temporarily, that the nation was at war.

One little sparkle of brightness; young Al was able to tap dance again to their drunken singing accompaniment.

Chapter 10

Evacuation for Andre

Children from Woodside School and Davidson Road School were all evacuated to Brighton, each taking their gas masks with them. Two evacuation officials accompanied the children on their charabanc and handed them over to their billeting officials on arrival in Brighton.

Mrs Hopwood escorted Andre to the home of a Mr and Mrs Williams, designated as his guardians. She told them that she would let Andre's family know their address, so they should receive letters for him. Although in their late 60s, they were considered to be good, clean-living, contented people, well capable of looking after a nine-year-old.

Mrs Williams, a very old lady in Andre's eyes, with her curly white hair, said, "I expect you're hungry after your long journey, Andre. We've already had dinner. We had egg and chips." She smiled and rolled her eyes as if to say, 'yummy, yummy'. "But I didn't want to give you cold chips, so I'll cook you eggs on toast for today, if you'd like that?"

In response to Andre's nod, she put on her pale green patterned wraparound overall and went into the scullery.

Anxious to make conversation with Andre while they were alone, but at a loss as to what he should talk about, Mr Williams asked if he'd ever heard of the Langridge Brothers who played county cricket for Sussex.

Although feeling nervous in such a new environment, Andre remembered to speak up loud and clear, as a schoolmaster had once taught him.

"No, sir. I've never heard of Brighton, or Sussex until today. Well...I may have heard it mentioned on the wireless at some time."

"Well, I can tell you, lad, that Sussex have a superb cricket team. It's a good game Andre. Have you ever played it at school?"

"No, sir. We did try to play it in the alley where I live, but kept losing the tennis ball in people's gardens."

"A tennis ball's no good, lad," he chuckled kindly. "A real cricket ball is rock hard and that would've smashed many a window. It's played in a big field where there's lots of space; certainly not in an alley. My favourite player is John Langridge; he's a brilliant batsman. He plays for our county. If you like living here with us, I'll take you to see a county game one day when they're playing at home, if you'd like to do that."

"Yes please, I'd like that, sir."

"Glad to hear it, lad. Who knows, it could end up being your game when you grow to be a man."

"So where have you come from today?"

"From East Croydon."

"Well, let's hope you'll settle in with us. It must have been hard saying goodbye to your mum?"

"I haven't got a proper mum. I've only got a horrible stepmother, so I was glad to get away."

"Do you see your real mum?"

"I can't, sir. She's dead. Stepma told me she died when I was born."

"I'm sorry, lad. We'll talk about family things another day if you'd like to. In the meantime, you don't have to call me 'sir' all the time, you know. You can call me Mr Williams."

"There, did you enjoy your nice fresh eggs, Andre?"

"Yes, thank you; they were really nice. I've never had **two** eggs in one meal before."

"Ah well, we're lucky you see. We get plenty of eggs because we keep our own chickens. You can help me look after them when you're not at school or out to play. You can collect the eggs for me if you'd like to. Would you like to see your bedroom now?"

Andre entered a room that appeared small compared to the huge attic room at home. All the furniture was dark brown, apart from a pink stool with long wooden pink painted handles from front to back each side of the seat. He was surprised to see a dark red patterned eiderdown on the bed, having only been used to blanket covers at home, and was wide-eyed at the sight of the bed; it was as big as Ma and Pa's.

"I shall wash and iron your clothes for you Andre, but keeping them tidy is your responsibility. You can use these five drawers that are low down in the tallboy here for your belongings.

"That's a funny name. I've never heard of one of those before."

"Well, I can tell you it's a very useful piece of furniture to have, with lots and lots of drawers." Pointing to the pink Lloyd-loom stool, she continued, "And over there, the lid opens and that's where you can put your dirty clothes."

"At home I only change my clothes once a week."

"Well, that's OK, but it's not necessary for you to wear dirty clothes while you're with us. What I would like is for you to keep your room tidy. I can't bear untidiness."

"That's OK, Mrs Williams. Ma would've knocked our blocks off if we'd been untidy at home."

TGA: *(Andre found it extremely odd that Mr and Mrs Williams were speaking to him as though he were a grown up person. He'd never had such an experience with his own father and stepmother.)*

Andre naturally found the first night in his new home quite strange, but felt confident that he'd found a friend in Mr Williams. He was a tall man with grey hair, a slim, neat moustache, a big stomach and he wore horn-rimmed glasses. Andre drifted off to sleep wondering what a men's cricket match would be like.

In the morning, Mrs Robins called for Andre to take him to his new school. Outside, the sight of so many familiar faces boosted his morale considerably. He joined the queue, partnering Martin Weston, the boy who'd showed him around Woodside School when they first moved to East Croydon.

"Come and join us, Andre. Good boy; I see you've remembered your gas mask."

It was hanging across his body in its carrying case.

Along the way, Mrs Robins grouped them into the corner of a park to tell them that their new school was a home for dwarfs. The day was windy and Mrs Robins had to keep moving her brightly coloured headscarf away from her mouth as she talked to them.

"Dwarfs are very little people who unluckily don't grow as tall as most people do. What I want you to understand is that they are human beings with feelings, exactly the same as us. When you first see one, I know it will be a shock. That is understandable, unless you have seen one before, of course. Hands up, anyone who has."

As she half expected, not one hand went up. Shaking her head, she said, "Not a single one of you, I see. Well, you listen to me carefully boys and girls, the best way to cope is to say 'hello', which will save any embarrassment and hopefully stop you staring, which would be a very rude thing to do. You will see them around Brighton a lot, as they use the shops and facilities the same as everybody else and gradually you will get used to them. Their home that they are sharing with you is called Panza Mansions. Because other evacuees will use the premises in the afternoons, I'm sure you'll be pleased to hear that you will only go to school in the mornings. We have a lot of evacuees to accommodate for schooling here in Brighton."

Continuing their way to school, all the children were wondering what the strange smell was and eventually asked Mrs Robins.

"Funny smell? I can't smell anything. I can't see any doggy-poo on the pavement. Can you?"

"It can't be doggy-poo, Miss. We've been smelling it ever since we arrived in Brighton."

"Oh my goodness, of course. I know. You're not used to the sea air, are you?"

"Is this the seaside then, Miss?"

"Yes. Didn't anyone tell you?"

"No. Is the beach very far away?"

"Not very far. You could easily walk to it, but it's a pebble beach. There's no sand, so you can't build sand castles. And the smell you are talking about is ozone. It comes off the sea, so we call it the sea air. You'll gradually get used to that too."

As they entered the big house, a dwarf was leaving the building. They were all shocked at the sight of someone so little. Not one of them said hello, but some of them managed a smile.

TGA: *(I think that was a very good result. After all, these children were still feeling emotional and overwhelmed, having so recently been separated from their parents and a familiar home environment.)*

Entering the classroom on the first floor, Andre could see the sea through the window. That excited him. He'd never seen so much water before and decided that one day very soon he must go with some of his mates and see what a pebble beach was like.

A friendly looking lady with black bobbed hair and wearing a pink blouse with a deep purple coloured skirt welcomed the children and directed them to their desks, placing the tallest children at the back of the room and the shortest at the front.

When all were seated, she smiled and said, "I know you must all be feeling lost and alone in the world at the moment and missing your families dreadfully. You've now got to get used to a new school and a new teacher as well. I am that teacher and my name is Mrs Siers. It is my fervent hope that you will settle nicely at school here in Brighton and be safer if war does come to pass."

Clearing her throat, she continued, "Before we start lessons, we have many other things to do. First of all, I suggest you always keep your gas mask hanging over your bodies at all times. We don't want them getting mixed up, do we? Now I will take you along the corridor to show you where the boys' and girls' lavatories are. While there, you can seize the opportunity to go if you have a need; otherwise, in class, you must put your hand up and ask to be excused, but remember, you only speak when you are spoken to."

By the time Mrs Siers had given the class their induction spiel, showed them the geography of the building and taken their names and new addresses for the register, there was hardly any time left for lessons. We'll start lessons properly tomorrow morning. Until Mrs Robins comes to collect you, you can tell me what you have been learning at your own schools.

Before much more time had passed, Mrs Robins came to take the children back to their homes.

On the way, the children who were nearest to each other in the queue decided they would meet after lunch at the park where Mrs Robins had talked to them. They wanted to discover where

213

each of them was living so they could call for each other to go out to play.

When Mrs Williams opened the door for him, Andre could smell a nice dinner.

"Come on in, Andre. How was school then?"

"It was OK, but we didn't have lessons. We'll start those tomorrow; there were too many other things to do today, like 'induction', which I think meant showing us the ropes."

"Hello, lad. Are you hungry after your busy morning?"

"Not really, sir," Andre replied, quickly followed by, "I mean, Mr Williams. It smells nice though."

"Come and sit at the table with me then. Mrs Williams will be dishing it up any minute."

"Think you'll get to like the school, Andre?"

Andre shrugged. "It's a lot different to my school at home. Doesn't even seem like a school. It's a home for dwarfs and we only have to go there in the mornings."

Mrs Williams put a plate of sausages, fried onions, mashed potatoes and runner beans, all covered in thick gravy in front of him.

"Ah yes, I did read about that in the local paper a few weeks back. Have you seen a dwarf yet?"

"Yes. I saw one today. I didn't stare though, because Mrs Robins told us it would be very rude, but I wanted to."

"Only natural, lad, but you must try to put yourself in their position. If you were one of them, you wouldn't want anyone staring at you, would you?

"No, I wouldn't. I feel sad for them and am glad that I'm growing up properly. It's better to be as thin as me than little like them."

"Can't you eat any more than that, Andre? You've only eaten enough to fill up a little mouse."

Andre had a little smile and wanted to say, "I think I've eaten a bit more than that", but thought better of it and merely said, "No, thank you, Mrs Williams. I'm not used to big dinners, but I'll eat a bit more of it for tea. Your runner beans were nice. Ma usually cooks yellow cabbage."

"Well, I hope you'll learn to eat a bit more. You're so thin, a puff of wind would blow you over."

"I will try, Mrs Williams. Am I allowed to go out to play now, please?"

"Where do you want to go?"

"Some of us want to meet at the park we passed on the way to school, so we can show each other where we live. Then we'll be able to call for each other."

"Come and sit down at the table with me again, Andre. We have to have a little chat. What you're asking is essential really and something you have to do. What I need you to understand is that Mrs Williams and I are responsible for you and it's hard for us to let you go out unaccompanied for the first time. We've all got to learn to trust one another." Pausing and looking Andre in the eye, he continued, "Can you understand that, Andre?"

"Yes, Mr Williams. But I like being with you, so I won't be running away."

"Well said, lad. I suggest that you don't stay out too long for the first time. We will be worried sick and we don't want to get more wrinkles, do we?" He chuckled as he stood up and patted Andre on the back.

"I won't, Mr Williams. I promise I'll be back soon."

"Good lad; off you go then."

About an hour later, Mrs Williams answered a knock on the door.

"Why Andre," she exclaimed, with surprise written all over her round, jolly face, "you've come back with friends."

"I hope you're pleased with me, Mrs Williams."

"Goodness gracious, yes. Do you want to come in?"

"No, thank you. I just wanted to let you know you can trust me. These are friends from my school at East Croydon where I live. We all know where we all live now and we'd like to find the beach. Is that OK?"

"Yes, of course it is, Andre, now we know where you're going. Just wait there a minute." Returning, she held out her hand and said, "Here's a sweetie for each of you."

That reward was like gold dust to the children and before they scampered off, Mrs Williams pointed them in the direction of the beach.

"Don't stay there too long, will you Andre? We like to eat tea together."

"Did you enjoy your trip to the beach, lad?"

"Yes. We all did. It was brilliant. We kept throwing pebbles into the sea and trying to make them skim over the waves."

"Do you know, I used to do that when I was a little boy, but always managed to get my shoes wet. I see you managed to keep yours dry."

"I was very careful, Mr Williams. I didn't want to risk becoming crippled again."

"Crippled?"

"Yes. When I started school my feet hurt because I had to grip my toes to keep my stepbrother's old shoes on. They were miles too big for me. The school nurse wrote to my parents about it. It embarrassed my father and ever since then he has bought me shoes that fit. I don't know who will buy shoes for me now I'm not at home."

"Don't you worry about that, Andre. The authorities will make sure you are looked after for clothing."

At that moment, a chicken started clucking.

"Sounds like another egg, Marjory."

"I think you're right. Want to come into the garden with me, Andre, and I'll show you where to collect the eggs?"

TGA: *(Like a shot, Andre was gone. For the first time in his life he was really enjoying being part of a family.)*

Mrs Williams showed Andre where she kept the egg basket in the scullery and they tripped off down the garden path together. Lifting the lid of the nesting box, Andre was goggle-eyed to see three eggs laying in the straw.

"You look amazed, Andre. Are you alright?"

"Yes. It's just that everything's so different here. In Croydon we get eggs from the shop."

"And where do you think the shop gets them from?"

"Well, after seeing this, I suppose the shops get the eggs from the chickens."

"That's right, Andre. They get them from the chicken farmers." Mr Williams did not wish to confuse the issue with words like 'poultry farmers' at that moment.

The next day, Andre was pleasantly surprised at school when Mrs Siers gave them an arithmetic lesson. They had to work on fractions, which is exactly what they were doing at Woodside School.

In an English Grammar lesson, she asked them what they had learned so far. Lots of hands went up. One said "nouns", which led Mrs Siers to ask, "And what are nouns?"

"Nouns are the names of things, like chair, table, car. There are lots of them, Miss."

"Good. Next?"

"Proper nouns?"

"Are you asking me or telling me?"

I think they are proper names Miss. Names that need capital letters like London, England, Scotland and surnames like, Roberts, Singers sewing machines, Jones, even Siers."

Mrs Siers smiled, "Good girl. You're right. You must try to be more confident."

"Andre?"

"Verbs, Miss. They are doing words, so you should always be able to put a 'to' in front of it. Like 'to eat', 'to play' and to 'wash'."

After listening to a few more, she said, "Very good children. You've done well. Now tell me, have you ever learned about adjectives?"

218

There was a chorus of, "No Miss."

"OK, so now I know where you are in your London curriculum and that's where we will start today. Adjectives are describing words. 'Janet is wearing a pretty dress'. Hands up who can tell me which word is the describing word."

Mrs Williams' face was beaming when she opened the door to let Andre in at dinner time.

"A surprise for you, Andre. Look, you've got a letter."

Full of optimism she said, "Perhaps your ma and pa are missing you after all."

Andre started to rip the envelope open.

"Ah, ah, ah," she uttered, with her right index finger pointing upwards, hastily stopping him in his tracks.

"Tidiness; remember Andre?" said Mrs Williams, as she handed him a butter knife to open the envelope neatly.

Dear Andre,

I couldn't bear it at home after you left. Ma was like a different person, so happy I thought it was disgusting. When I asked her why, she said, "None of your business, Elsa Kliskey." That's when I decided to leave. I used the florins and I'm staying with Dorothy. She's really nice and I'm much happier.

Dorothy has written to tell Ron and you've got Dorothy's address so we can all keep in touch. Dorothy is giving me stamps etc., so I've written to Grandma too. I hope you like where you're living and that they are kind to you.

Please write back soon. I miss you and love you lots.

Elsa

xxxxxxx

Mr and Mrs Williams sat reading Andre's letter together.

"Good gracious me. That's terrible. So Elsa is your thirteen-year-old sister whom you told us about?"

"That's right, and I'm glad she's gone to Dorothy. She'll be happier now."

After discussing Andre's family life for a while, Mr Williams said, "Well cheer up, lad. As you told us on your first day with us, *you were glad to escape*. There's a home cricket match being played in Hove on 26th August and I'm determined to take you there.

"Thank you, Mr Williams. I'm really looking forward to that."

It was with great dismay that Mr Williams and Andre heard the announcement on wireless that the West Indies team were returning home immediately, all to do with the threat of war, following the Molotov/Ribbentrop Pact signed on 23rd August. Sounding as miserable and shocked as he felt, Mr Williams bemoaned, "That's our cricket match gone kaput, lad. Sorry. A big let-down I know, but it's not quite the end of the season. We have to hope we get another county game down here soon."

Andre, trying to ease Mr Williams' obvious disappointment, replied, "Well if they don't, there's always next season, I s'pose."

"Come on you two, it's not the end of the world. Here's a nice cup of tea and a biscuit to cheer you up. And here's some writing paper for you to send a letter to your sister, Andre. I can tell she'll be delighted to hear that you are with us and are happy here."

"Thank you, Mrs Williams."

Andre was eager to send good news to his sister.

Dear Elsa,

I'm glad you are with Dorothy. Now we can all be in touch.

Mr and Mrs Williams who I'm living with are very nice. They like me. Mrs Williams cooks nice dinners and wants me to eat more, but I can't. You know I never eat a lot.

Mr Williams wanted to take me to a cricket match, but it's been cancelled.

We only have to go to school in the mornings here.

I'm not as good at writing as you, but I want you to know I'm happy. Tell Grandma about me when you write again please.

Lots of love from Andre

xxx

Another wireless broadcast soon turned dismay into elation. On Wednesday 30th August, Yorkshire were going to play Sussex at Hove. Mr Williams and Andre were jumping around like two kids instead of one.

"We'll get there after all, lad. I must give you a few lessons about the game before we go, so you have a bit of understanding what to expect. Whacko, Andre. I swear you'll enjoy it."

"Charlie Williams, you're just like a child. Cricket's only a game, after all."

"But it's the best game in the world Marjory and I'm going to introduce it to Andre, if it's the last thing I do. Our own boys loved it, till WW1 took 'em. You surely don't forget that?"

"You know I don't Charlie. How could I ever forget that?"

"I'm sorry, love. If it upsets you, I'll give it a miss."

"Don't you dare do that," she said, putting her arms around him with a loving hug. "Andre needs someone nice to influence him and you're the one. Honest truth is, I prefer tennis and cricket bores the ass off me."

By the time match day dawned, Mr Williams had been in touch with Andre's school and squared it with them that the experience of a live county cricket match would be worth more to an evacuee for a morale boost at this time, as well as in his future life, than a couple of mornings' schooling. Andre had learned about the cricket ground itself; the 22-yard long pitch with wickets at each end, the umpire opposite the batsman, the wicket keeper behind, the bowling crease and the stumps – the leg stump, the off stump and the middle stump.

Mr Williams had arranged for them to arrive early and they were sitting directly behind the few front row seats reserved by the cricket club for the dwarves. Sitting there gave Andre a prime view of the ground. The day was overcast and breezy, but nothing bothered Andre. He was totally in awe of the spectacle before him.

"It's a huge ground, Mr Williams, and ever so clean looking with all these white chairs around it. Mrs Williams would love it being so neat and tidy. Whoever keeps the grass so short?"

"The groundsmen do, lad. They have mowing machines that they sit on and drive around."

"You wait till the players come out, Andre. Then it gets really exciting."

"Where are the players then?"

"They're in the pavilion over there." Mr Williams pointed to the wooden pitched roof building. "That's where they get dressed in their whites and caps."

"So the cricketers will be dressed in white then? Gosh, I'm really glad you brought me here. This is loads better than the beach."

Andre became quite overwhelmed when the cricket squad started filing out of the pavilion door. The ovation, along with the whistling and roaring, was deafening to everybody and excited Andre beyond belief.

Mr Williams explained that the players had gone into a huddle near the pitch to toss a coin to see how the game would start. Sussex won the toss and chose to bat first.

"So that tells you, Andre, that the batsmen in this over are all playing for Sussex and the fielders are playing for the Yorkshire squad."

"Look, there he is, lad; my favourite player, John Langridge. He's the opening batsman. He's brilliant."

Andre could see Mr Williams was very excited and he wondered if his own father had ever watched a game of cricket.

As the game went on, Andre became absorbed with Surrey's number of runs increasing.

Mr Williams explained that an 'over' was one bowler delivering six balls in succession to the batsman at the other end.

"After he's bowled the sixth ball the umpire calls out 'Over'. The fielding team then switch ends and a different bowler is selected to bowl from the opposite end of the pitch, but the batsmen do not change ends. That's the usual way the matches are played. For your introductory match, they are playing an eight 'over' game.

During the day, they surrendered to their hunger from time to time by eating the packed food Mrs Williams had prepared for them, with drinks of tea from the flask.

The scores were increasing and when the final innings of the day was declared, Yorkshire had reached a score of 330/3, chasing a Sussex score of 387.

"I told you John Langridge was brilliant, didn't I, lad? I wonder what tomorrow will bring?"

"Are we coming again tomorrow then?"

"You bet. We've got to see the end of the match, which will probably be tomorrow."

The match continued all day on Thursday 31st August, with no conclusion, so Mr Williams and Andre were back for more on Friday 1st September. Yorkshire continued and totalled 392 all out. Sussex deteriorated in their second innings and were all out for 33, after which Yorkshire made 30/1 to win by nine wickets.

"There, that's it, lad. Shame we lost, but it was a pretty close game. Did you enjoy it?"

"You bet. I'd like to come again with you next season, if that's OK."

"OK. You're backing on a winner there, lad."

It was a great shock to the Williams' household, and indeed the world, when Prime Minister Neville Chamberlain announced on the wireless on Sunday 3rd September 1939 that Great Britain was at war with Germany.

"It can't be true," said Mrs Williams, whose jolly face had become quite solemn. "It can't be true; we lost our Sammy and Johnny in the war to end all wars."

"I know, love. I know. The likes of us suffer for the greed of evil men."

Tears were running down her cheeks and Andre thought what a kind man Mr Williams was.

"Come on; buck up, Marge. We've got Andre to look after this time."

Monday 4th September changed the outlook. Mrs Hopwood called to say that on Wednesday the evacuees would be taken to a safer place, somewhere inland. The government had decided that Brighton was too near to the coast to be a safe place for them.

"I won't go," cried Andre. "I won't go! Mr and Mrs Williams are nice to me and I want to stay with them."

"Andre. Listen to me. I'm afraid you don't have a choice. I have to do my job and I mustn't defy the wishes of the government," said Mrs Hopwood as kindly as possible.

Everyone was in a state of shock. Mr and Mrs Williams cried and, together with Andre, they all huddled together on the sofa as Mrs Hopwood softly left the room saying, "The charabanc will be back in this street on Wednesday 6th September at 9 am."

At length, Mrs Williams interrupted the sobbing to say, "Such is life. Let's all have a cup of tea."

As their last couple of days were passing, Mr and Mrs Williams were trying to console Andre.

"Look, Andre, we know that your stepmother did you no favours. If you become a naughty boy and cause trouble because of this, you'll be doing yourself no favours either. The government are doing their best to keep you safe."

"And you're not the only one suffering, Andre. We lost our two boys in WW1 and now we're losing you in this war," choked Mrs Williams, whose jolly face had totally disappeared. "Having you to look after has been a short, but very sweet interlude for us and we don't want to lose you either."

The charabanc arrived promptly on the Wednesday morning, where all the children were gathering. Andre had promised Mr and Mrs Williams that he would smile as they said their goodbyes. He was bravely trying to honour that promise as he hugged Mrs Williams and said, "I like you and I'm sorry I couldn't eat bigger dinners."

To Mr Williams he said, "Thank you for taking me to the cricket match. I will never forget you."

Tears were shared and smudged during their last minute hugs.

There being no more to be said, Andre waved to the couple who were holding hands as the charabanc pulled away.

TGA: *(Devastating time for Andre. In the Williams' home he had experienced living with true love for the first time in his life. He really does need me now.)*

Chapter 11

Enham, First Year of WW2

The year 1940 started amazingly well for Annabelle, her family and everyone in the village. Sewer pipes had been laid and all Enham residents now had flush lavatories.

"Annabelle, you mustn't keep going in there and pulling the chain. It's not necessary."

Annabelle had grown out of her 'cute little girl' stage at nine years old and was starting to appear a bit more mature, dressed as she was in her red tartan kilt with complimentary red jumper.

"But I like pulling it, Mum. It's like magic. When I've 'been' I pull the chain and..." She opened her arms widely and raised her fair eyebrows as high as humanly possible, "*ABRACADABRA*, it's gone!"

Alice laughed.

"And best of all is that I don't have to go on top of other people's poop anymore."

"Annabelle, you're so outspoken, I just can't help laughing at you. And there's something even you haven't thought of young lady; I won't have to keep sending you to the shop to buy so much Jeyes Fluid. How about that?"

Alice, equally as thrilled, crossed her eyes as she happily sang, "WHOOPIE!"

Annabelle grinned and rolled her head round and round in circles, obviously overwhelmed by such a big improvement in their home and life.

"Come here, you; let's have a good long hug together. It truly is a miracle."

After the hug, Alice said, "But we must spare a thought for poor Mrs Rose. Because she lives in the old Tudor cottage, she's never had a lavatory facility. She told me they've adapted an old cupboard with a bucket under the wooden-holed seat. Every day she empties the bucket herself."

"What, full of pooh?" exclaimed Annabelle.

"Well, yes. She's dug out a deep trench at the bottom of the garden. She puts old newspapers down there to make layers between the pee and poo."

"Poor lady. How awful," said Annabelle, screwing up her nose.

"Well, Mr Rose can't do it. He's only got his one leg. It must be the same for Mr and Mrs Parsons, who live in the other half of the cottage."

"Unfortunately, the modern authorities couldn't put the old Tudor cottage on the sewer system because of its age and the condition it's in. The stairs are very rickety and it has uneven floors."

"Oooh, Mum. Let's tell them they can come and use ours."

Those words earned her another warm, speechless hug.

Mrs Rose's home caused another flurry of excitement to sweep through the village when the fire engine drove to her garden gate. For some time, she had been smelling smoke in her semi-detached Tudor cottage opposite St. George's Chapel. Becoming more and more worried and fearful for her 6-year-old daughter Rita, she decided to ask the fire brigade if they would call and see if they could detect smoke. Two firemen made an inspection and her suspicion was confirmed. It was then necessary for them to find the source as quickly as possible. It was a potential hazard, further impacted by the thatched roof. Before they could start investigating, it was essential for them to bring the fire engine to the garden gate.

The fire bell on that vehicle should have been called *The Pied Piper of Enham*. Villagers were popping out of their doors quicker than weathermen to see what was going on, and then trailing the fire engine to find the excitement. They waited patiently while the men were tearing down the fireplace frontage, which accommodated the grate. As they did so, combusting soot cascaded into the room and spectating villagers were asked to find as many wheelbarrows as quickly as they could. One of the workmen asked Mrs Rose for a glass of water. Although choking, he couldn't resist laughing, which made him choke more, when she asked, "What, to put the fire out?"

This work took a number of days to complete and the Roses and Parsons, (Mrs Rose's friendly name for her neighbours) had to be evacuated elsewhere in the village for their safety.

That event was a major historical one for Enham. Tons of soot had collected over literally hundreds of years in huge ovens – enclosed and inaccessible between the two homes – in the authentic Tudor building. The discovery of the ovens revealed that many years ago that building was the Enham Estate Bakery.

Still in January, everyone in the village had their first realisation of one of the knock-on effects of war. A lot of the food was imported from other countries in ships, which were now required for more sinister war uses. That necessitated the rationing of food so that people of all classes had an equal share of the supplies that did get through to British shores. The first items to be rationed were sugar, butter, ham and bacon. The shopkeeper would cut out the required coupons from customers' ration books, and that was their share of that product for a week. It was essential that everyone remembered to take their ration books, which had been distributed a few months earlier as a precaution.

An important government strategy in anticipation of food shortages as a result of war, was that everyone should be looking after their children. Hence, cod liver oil and malt was issued free to all children under five. Alice applauded the strategy and bought it at a price of ten shillings per large jar for her children. Fortunately, both Annabelle and Al liked it and looked forward to their teaspoonful every day after tea.

Following that government lead, Alice surprised her children by walking them to school one cold, early March day. She'd heard that Mrs Macknell, the landlady at the British Oak pub next door to the school, had started cooking hot soups for school children and went to ask if she would take on that service for her two children.

"Of course I will dear," replied Mrs Macknell willingly. "I will charge you sixpence for each bowl of soup and a pudding daily."

231

"Thank you so much, Mrs Macknell. It's a relief to know they'll get some hot food inside them, walking all this way on these bitter cold windy days. I'll give Al your money in an envelope on Fridays, if that's acceptable to you?"

"Of course, and I'll return the envelope to you on the same day with a signed receipt in it. We are pretty well off for vegetables because my husband grows a lot in the garden and I preserve a lot of things, so I hope I'll be feeding them to your satisfaction."

"That's wonderful. I hope they'll be well-behaved. You can let me know in a note if you have problems. It is important to their father and me that they know how to behave themselves when they're not under our wing."

That evening, Alberto and Freddie Cox, the compère, were holding a meeting about a future show. Their overriding attitude in this wartime environment was that *the show must go on.* The general consensus was that a revue should be put on in the LWI round about July, before the one-week factory holiday closure in August.

As usual, the regular helpers turned up and a date for auditions was decided upon. Mr George Guest was one such regular helper, doing jobs like scene shifting and controlling props, but he never took part in the shows. His confidence was minimal for performance, following his WW1 disability. He served on HMS Blenheim, which was summoned to the Battle of the Dardanelles, (North West Turkey) in 1915. Winston Churchill was First Lord of the Admiralty at that time and he was instrumental in implementing a naval bombardment of the Dardanelle Straits in February of that year.

In action, HMS Blenheim, normally a cruiser, was reclassified as a destroyer, carrying torpedoes in WW1, and suffered a direct hit in the engine room by light shell fire from the heavily fortified cliffs while trying to navigate through 'The Narrows', as well as the wild currents at the Dardanelles. The shell hit the ship in the engine room just below the spot where George was standing. Utter carnage ensued, with minimal survivors. Amazingly, George lived to tell the tale, except for the fact that he couldn't speak. He had been struck dumb, was badly shell shocked and a nervous wreck.

Along with other settlers, George was served well by the medical department of Enham. Gradually, with speech therapy, his voice returned, albeit with a stammer, which stayed with him until his demise. He enjoyed a long, contented, full and satisfying life in the village, together with his lovely petite wife, who was always a leading figure in the Enham shows.

In early April, Lord Woolton entered office as The Minister of Food and came up with what the general public thought of as outrageous food suggestions, such as whale meat, which had to be soaked in vinegar overnight to counteract the strong and odd flavour.

Following the governmental lead of looking after British children, he ensured that every child under the age of three received milk daily. He also came up with his Woolton Pie recipe, which had been devised by the Maître de Cuisine, François

Latry, at the Savoy Hotel, London. It was made by cooking diced potatoes, parsnips, cauliflower, swede, carrots and turnips, or any vegetables that were in season. Rolled oats were used to thicken the vegetable water, after which chopped spring onions were added to enhance the flavour. The crusty topping was made using mashed potato mixed with wheatmeal. An additional option would be to grate a bit of cheese on top from your family's weekly ration.

The month of May saw Winston Churchill succeed Neville Chamberlain, who resigned his Office as Prime Minister for Great Britain. In his inaugural speech to the House of Commons on 13th May 1940, with WW2 hanging heavily on his shoulders, he used the words spoken by Giuseppe Garibaldi many years before, "I have nothing to offer but blood, toil, tears and sweat."

By July, there was more threatening evidence that we were a nation at war. The German Luftwaffe had started bombing raids over Great Britain. Annabelle would lay awake all night long, trembling with fear listening to the long deep drone of the Messerschmitt aeroplanes flying overhead, about to drop their bombs on an unknown target, which would be revealed on the wireless news next day.

A bit lighter news in July was that the Enham Horticultural Show was without doubt a great success, even though a much smaller occasion than the previous year without sideshows or any sporting events, because it was held in the Landale Wilson Institute. The villagers, out of necessity, were growing more vegetables than flowers that year and the auction of produce at the end of the day boosted the funds. It was a longer day than the year before because after the hall had been cleared, a dance was held, which increased the funds yet again.

Way before the dance ended at 11pm, Annabelle was tucked up in bed with a broad smile on her face. The silver cup, which she had won for a second successive year for her wild flower arrangement, was proudly displayed on her chest of drawers and her first prize ticket, along with the previous year's one, was locked safely in the suitcase that the Roses had given her.

Late July saw a suffering Alberto back on the battlefield. Five minutes earlier, he had left home in high spirits raring to go with the Revue that he and Freddie Cox were putting on in the Landale Wilson Institute. In the entrance lobby, he received the equivalent of a slap in the face, which stunned him. The disabled comrade taking the entrance fees wouldn't let him through until he paid his sixpence. Immediately, he was back in a shellshock rage, turned on his heel and left bawling, "I'm not paying sixpence to PUT ON A SHOW! Where's ya brain mate? You can bloody well put it on ya'self."

Alice was astounded to see Alberto return home so quickly, but one look at his ashen face told her a familiar story.

"Sit down with me, Alberto, and tell me all about it.

"I can't do it, Alice. I won't do it. That stupid oaf from over the road wants me to pay sixpence to go in to put the show on!"

As always, battlefield tears were flowing down his cheeks.

"Stupid idiot!"

"Alberto, there's been a mistake. Annabelle, fetch Daddy a glass of water please."

Quickly returning with a glass of water, Annabelle pleaded, "Don't cry, Daddy. Mummy will make it better. She always does."

As the colour was returning to Alberto's cheeks, there was a knock at the door, followed by the voice of Freddie Cox, who had let himself in.

"What a stupid blighter they put on the door, eh mate?"

"You can say that again, Freddie. Bloody good music hall bloomer, if you're not on the end of it."

"That's the spirit. Sense of humour helps a lot. So how ya' feeling now mate?"

"Comin' round a bit. Alice has worked her magic on me, as usual." He gave her a long, lingering look of love, as well as gratitude.

"Good lass, Alice. Our wives have all been good girls. They must never be forgotten. They've played such a big part in helping us to survive, along with Enham Village Centre. Bless all their hearts."

"Up to coming back now, Alby? Need to rush. We've got a hall crammed full of people and we're stymied without you."

"Of course I'm coming back, but it was a lot to swallow; a big blow beneath the belt, I can tell ya. I give my time and expertise freely, but I'm damned if I'm paying to do it."

"Well, that won't happen. The committee are appalled and have already made the decision that

236

the same man won't be put on the door again, so come on. Let's get going. An announcement has been made that you've been delayed and George's wife is leading a sing-along in the hope that you'll be back soon. Remember the old adage mate, 'The show must go on'."

Together they went back to the Institute and as they entered the hall, an ear-splitting, appreciative ovation plunged Alberto straight back into the entertainment world where he belonged.

Freddie did a superb introduction, thanking Mrs Guest for filling the breach during the delay and welcoming the performers who were going to cheer them up, as well as the audience for coming. He went on to say that the Germans weren't going to stop them having fun.

"They might delay us, but they'll never stop us. The Enham shows will continue with a vengeance, whatever's going on in the outside world."

Winding up his introduction, he continued, "This is our first revue as a country at war, so we thought it might be appropriate to start with a very popular song, which I'm sure you'll all know."

Holding his right hand out to welcome them from the other side of the stage, he continued, "Mimicking Flanagan and Allen, I give you Mr Alberto Aless and Mr Joe Geoghegan."

As they entered, they received a standing ovation. Alberto was dressed smartly in a black suite, white shirt and grey tie, tall and smart, looking very much like Chesney Allen and a much shorter Joe made the perfect Bud Flanagan, dressed in his long, almost ankle-length, ginger-coloured fur coat, complete with black-banded Panama hat and upturned brim.

When silence eventually reigned, Freddie said "How easy can this business get? They haven't sung a note yet! Seriously though, don't they look good?"

The audience eagerly clapped again.

"They will open the show with the conventional version of *Run Rabbit Run* and then sing it a second time using the lyrics that were changed by Flanagan and Allen to poke fun at the Germans, i.e. *Run Adolph Run* etc. Ladies and Gentlemen, I give you Mr Alberto Aless and Mr Joe Geoghegan."

A better start for the show would have been impossible. Already there were shouts of "More! More!"

TGA: *(The villagers' very own 'Flanagan and Allen' were delighted with their success and sang the correct version two more times, inviting the audience to join them. It was pleasing to see these stalwart people enjoying themselves.)*

The applause was never ending, which meant they both kept taking bows to accept the adulation. When they finally were able to leave the stage, Freddie said, "WOW! What a start. We'll be seeing more of them later."

"We welcome our next act as a newcomer to the village. She has come to Enham from London to stay with her grandmother in Anton Lane. Her parents felt she would be safer here and, I must say, having heard her voice at rehearsals, we are very glad to have her. Ladies and Gentlemen, I give you Miss Doreen Morgan."

"Thank you, Ladies and Gentleman. I'm very happy to be here entertaining you tonight and I hope you'll like the song I've chosen. It's entitled, *With a Song in My Heart,* and, because I miss my mum, I'm going to sing it for her too."

Her delicate soprano voice was both lilting and uplifting. She meant every word she sang and made you feel she was singing for you alone. What's more, she was lovely to look at, dressed in a long royal blue dress, which matched perfectly with the royal blue velvet stage curtains. Although only looking about sixteen years old, it was obvious she was accustomed to stage work and very talented.

Thanking the audience for their wonderful ovation, she said, "Thank you, Ladies and Gentlemen; and now I'd like to sing for you a beautifully poetic song, *I Know Why and So Do You,* which has only recently been released."

The audience were entranced by her voice and the rapturous applause meant they wanted more. Freddie entered side stage and clapped with them.

"Doreen, your songs were beautiful. Thank you." Turning to the audience he said, "Doreen is one of the good things to come out of war for us, eh folks?"

In front of the closed curtains, Freddie kept the show rolling. To the audience, "How's about you and me becoming magicians? Let's say 'Open Sesame' three times and, shouting louder each time, see if we have magic powers."

On the third, deafening "Open Sesame", Alberto Aless appeared through the centre opening in the curtains with an impressive dancing pose, leaning forward, standing on one leg as still as the old oak tree at the end of the drive, and waving his top hat high in the air like foliage in the breeze.

"Alberto, what joy it gives me to introduce you today, performing a double act with your young son. You must be so thrilled, as indeed we all are."

A long duration of boisterous applause, foot stamping and whistling ensued, before Freddie could continue.

"Thank you, Ladies and Gentlemen. As I was saying Alberto, you must be so thrilled that Al pulled through from his knee injury to enable the two of you to dance again. Ladies and Gentlemen, I give you the chip off the old block, Al Aless, the younger."

This time it was Al's turn to leap through the curtains, using the same pose as his dad.

"OK, Al. We're gunna sock it to 'em, but first you must give the audience a wave and a 'thank you' because they're really glad to see you back on your feet again. When you've done that you can introduce our turn."

"Thank you very much everyone, and I'm really glad to be back here with my dad. We are now going to perform for you, *Little Mister Baggy Breeches.*"

Laura, who was still playing the piano for the concert party, then played the introduction and the tap dancing began. A very colourful turn with Alberto dressed in a bright orange satin shirt and white trousers and Al in a bright blue satin shirt and baggy breeches – all satin patched in a variety of brilliant colours. After receiving their ovation,

Alberto asked the audience, "Do you like our costumes?"

A mixture of clapping, stamping and whistling gave him his answer.

"That's good. Thank you very much indeed. So perhaps we can now give a big hand to my lovely wife, Alice, who spent hours trying to sew this goddamned satin…" He gave a little tug at Al's breeches as he spoke, "…which kept slipping all over the place."

To Al, "Did you enjoy that son?"

Al gave his dad a huge grin with both thumbs up.

"Excellent. Want to do another one?"

The clapping from the audience answered for him again.

"Thank you, Ladies and Gentlemen. So, dressed in our same costumes because we are running late and there isn't time to change them, we give you *Small Fry*."

"Thank you, Alberto and Al. Wasn't that brilliant to see them back together again?"

"Ladies and Gentlemen, we now have some more village youngsters to entertain us. They've been rehearsing an item for the Girl Guides, but one of the cheeky so-and-sos had the nerve to ask if they could perform for…guess who?" He opened his hands for a reply.

"Oh, you're so quick! You've got it in one. Well, the blatant truth is, if you don't ask, you don't get, do you?" This time he held his hand up to halt the applause. "Besides which, we like our youngsters to be enterprising, don't we?"

After the ovation, Freddie continued, "So, with the backing of Mrs Chambers the Guide Captain, it is now my pleasure to introduce Mona Guest, Kathy Piggin, Jocelyn Blackburn, Lucy Geoghegan, Eileen Cronin and Marion Crabbe with their act, *Mona and the Squad.*

Mona led the girls into a fascinating marching routine to *Something About a Soldier,* singing the words as they marched. Starting with a salute to the audience, they adeptly used swagger canes made by Mr Guest, and wore sleeveless tunics of bright red satin over short black skirts. The tunics were nipped in at the waist by black belts and were topped and tailed by black-trimmed, red pill-box hats on their heads, with white socks and black shoes on their feet.

You could see the girls were thrilled when the audience kept calling for more and were delighted to perform the routine again, each time ending with a well-practised salute.

"Well done, girls. We're all very proud of you. Next, Ladies and Gentlemen, we have two 'old girls', if you'll pardon the expression. Well, they are old girls compared to the last act. I give you Mrs Moody and Mrs Johnstone who are going to perform for you a skit entitled *The Washing Lines.*"

The curtains opened to the scene of two back gardens with a shoulder high dividing fence. Both women, one fat and one thin, were wearing wrap-around overalls as they pegged out the washing.

Mrs Moody, who was wearing a snood, called out, "I'm moving with the times these days, Mrs Johnstone. I'm being topical and calling my washing line the 'Siegfried Line'.

"Well, fancy that then," said Mrs Johnstone, "I'm topical too! I'm calling mine the 'Imagino Line'."

"It's the Maginot Line!" yelled the audience.

"Well, I never! And what goes on at the Imagino Line may I ask?"

"The best gossip ever." Beckoning Mrs Moody towards her with a curled finger, they both moved close to the fence where Mrs Johnstone started to whisper "Have you heard about Mr..."

Mrs Moody gasped, rolled her eyes and put her hand to her mouth in amazement before making a soft, slow upward curve of sound, "Oooooooh!"

The audience roared.

Mrs Johnstone to the audience. "Shuddup you lot. No interruptions please." Continuing, "They say it's huge."

Mrs Moody had huge bosoms and you could literally see them swell as she drew in a big breath; "Uuhhhhhhhhhh!"

"What's more, they say he's going to put it on display at the next flower show."

Mrs Moody uttered an exclamation of disbelief with a tapering down reply, "Nooooooooooo!"

Mrs M's one syllable replies, along with her very explicit facial expressions, were making the audience roar with laughter, but at the same time the one-sided conversation was driving them to distraction. They were beside themselves yelling out different comments such as, "Speak up!", "What the devil are you talking about?" and "You're supposed to be entertaining us, not yourselves."

Still ignoring them, waving her arm downwards and backwards as if brushing them aside, Mrs Johnstone continued, "What a rude lot we've got in here tonight, dear. They're not giving me two minutes' peace to answer you. Oh, OK you lot. Just to keep you quiet, I'll tell you that he's going to display it at the next flower show and tie a big orange bow on it too. There ya go. I bet that's whetted some appetites. I reckon you've got your money's worth now."

Amidst the laughter at the idiocy of it all, the audience shouted, "Tell us what he's going to show!"

Wagging her finger, Mrs Johnstone continued, "Aaaaaaaaaaaaaaaaah! I knew that'd get you going. You'll have to go to the flower show next year to find out."

Mrs Moody, nodding her head continuously as if to say, 'That's a good one, that is', and laughing fit to burst, reminiscent of *The Laughing Policeman,* infected the audience who were laughing their heads off too.

"Cor blimey, dear, what else does that Imagino Line of yours tell you for God's sake?" asked Mrs Moody, finding her voice for the first time since the start of the gossip. "It sounds like a better line than mine."

Their act continued for a while in a similar vein; the audience roaring with laughter at the nonsense to which they were being subjected.

The ladies brought their act to a close as the rain started pouring down (from watering cans being poured from a trap door in the stage ceiling). Brushing herself down, Mrs Moody said, "I'm

244

blinkin' fed up with this rotten English weather, dear. I'm thinking we should move with our Seigfried and Imagino Lines to Germany where we might at least be able to dry the washing. Then we'll escape the war!"

At that, the audience intervened with a huge ovation for this final absurdity.

"And we'll give them a third line to add to their collection: *The Washing Line.*"

"What a couple of nutters we had there, Ladies and Gentlemen. I'm glad they don't live next door to me! Let's give them another burst, shall we? And after all that fun, it saddens me to disappoint you. Because we're running late, we won't be able to include the shorter, second half of the show today. The clouds outside are threatening and it's starting to get quite dark. It's very important that we all get home safely in these 'blackout' days when we're not allowed to use torches. So, Ladies and Gentlemen, we are going to bring the show to a close now, with Enham's very own 'Flanagan and Allen'."

"Thank you, Ladies and Gentlemen. We thought it would be nice to round off the previous act by singing for you, *We're Gonna Hang Out the Washing on the Siegfried Line,* and we'll follow it with *Strolling*, which, of course, we'll all be doing very soon."

They couldn't put a foot wrong and Freddie had to bring the applause to a halt so people could start making their way home.

"Tonight, I will just say a big thank you to everyone concerned; get yourselves home safely and watch for notices on the oak tree telling you when you can see the second half of the show. No admittance tickets required. Goodnight, one and all." He waved his hand.

Before the second half could take place, the factory closed for the week's summer holiday. That enabled Alberto and family to go to London to see their families. Their first port-of-call was Alberto's home, where he found his father distraught. Shaking his head negatively, "Non-a gelato, mio sarn-a. Non-a d'egg. Non-a d'ice-crème'a."

"That's awful Pa; ice cream was your major money spinner."

Nodding his head, "Mio life-a work-a."

Mama explained that because of rationing they could no longer buy enough of the ingredients with which to make the ice cream. This reduced the income of both Papa and Vincenzo. They still did a bit of business with jacket potatoes, although they could no longer provide butter from the barrow. He still sold hot sarsaparilla drinks and hoped to be able to do the hot roast chestnuts in the winter, but nothing was certain any more. A double blow for him was that his adoptive country was now at war with Italy, his native country. Alberto felt overwhelmed by his emotions as his father appeared to be a broken man.

Rationing was affecting Mrs Howitz too, in her provisions' shop up the road. Alice found her mother trying to cope with ration books and having to measure out goods more accurately. Normally, when she portioned big blocks of butter into half pound packs, she would add or minus the charge to accommodate the discrepancy. Now accuracy was of the utmost importance.

"Have you had any bombing near here yet?" Alberto asked Mrs Howitz.

"They're not far away, Alberto. We can hear the explosions. It's very frightening. I'm surprised you've come up here this year."

"I expect you are, but Alice and I like to see our families when I get a holiday from the factory. It's our only chance to make the fare worthwhile."

As usual, Alice and Annabelle stayed in her mother's home and Alberto and Al went back to his parents' home. The only Aless family members left at home were Jane and Richard with Henry and Hannah who had grown into teenagers. Ma and Pa were absolutely lost with a quieter life, as well as no ice cream business to run. Nevertheless, Ma still managed to put a good breakfast on the table.

Alice and Alberto had decided to spend their first couple of days sharing time with both families. Alberto and Al spent a lot of time with Bubble, trying to lift his spirits with ideas such as drying out the ice house so that it could be used as an air raid shelter. Bubble appeared to be perked up by the thought that his ice house could still be useful, so they decided to leave the trapdoor open to let some warm air in and start melting the remaining ice. There'd not been a delivery since food rationing first began.

Catching up with the family was a delight for them all. Al still wanted to become a Londoner and live with his Granny and Bubble.

Granny Aless laughed. "I thought you were a smarter lad than that, Al. You're much safer to be in the country, far away from London."

In the strange quietness of the Aless household and no ice cream business going on, Annabelle got more cuddles from Bubble. She secretly loved those because he had two proper arms, but Alice had schooled her never to let her dad know the reason.

On Tuesday 20th August 1940, they stayed in their respective homes to listen to Winston Churchill broadcasting a speech about the Battle of Britain. It was in recognition of the enormity of the contribution made by the Boys in Blue, the Royal Air Force Crews, in defeating the Luftwaffe in the skies at the Battle of Britain with their Spitfire and Hurricane aeroplanes. You could have heard a pin drop as many families listened intently to his words, including, "Never in the field of human conflict was so much owed by so many to so few."

During their week, Alberto took his family to Edmonton Green to show them the tailor's shop where an employee used to do the bookwork, including taxes, for most of the stallholders on the Green. Inside the shop, Alberto greeted the man concerned and said, "Pa wants me to tell you he's sorry for your lack of income from his ledger work and thanks you wholeheartedly for your past loyal services."

"Thanks for coming in, mate. Tell him I understand that the war has knocked his business on the head. And you can tell him as well that we all miss the ice cream from his barrow on the Green here."

The loss of Bubble's authentic Italian recipe ice cream from the local vicinity was highlighted to

Alberto and his family when they saw a large notice in the window of the local Tunnes pub: *We apologise to our customers for no longer stocking Gino's ice cream here. Blame the war and food rationing. He can't get enough eggs.*

Another sales loss was via Ben Riley, a near neighbour, who used to buy large quantities of Bubble's ice cream to sell from his own cart, as long as he displayed the name Gino (Bubble's business name) by the product, in accordance with their agreement.

Visiting all their London relatives in turn made the family's week in London fly by. (In reality only six days because of travelling time.) Al was glad he could still get sweets from Granny Howitz' shop and was horrified when she forecast that they would eventually be on rations too, because of vulnerable sugar imports. Annabelle still took delight in helping her Granny in the shop and also enjoyed her first experience of joining her mum and aunties to have a dinner of stewed eels with mash and parsley liquor at the Eel Shop in the High Road.

Before they could blink an eye, their last day in London arrived, for which they were relieved as hearing bombs exploding in the near vicinity was very frightening and upset a shell shocked Alberto. To make their last night memorable, Alberto bought tickets to take his family to see a show at the Alcazar Theatre in Fore Street, Edmonton. He chose that theatre because it was local as well as an interesting landmark for his children to see. It was an Asian style, colonial building, with distinctive verandas, based on the design of a Moorish palace.

The next day, amidst teary goodbyes, after offers to come and stay with them in Enham (sleeping in tents if necessary) had been refused, they wended their way homeward.

Back in Andover, they walked from the Junction Station to the bus station in the town and boarded the double-decker bus downstairs, standing room only, for the last lap of their journey. On that bus it didn't take two seconds for them to hear devastating news. The previous evening, while they were enjoying the show in the Alcazar, the Germans had dropped a large number of incendiary bombs around Enham. After the bus had turned Lillywhite's corner at the bottom of the hill, they saw, on the left side of the road, a large number of craters scattered around the ploughed field on the approach to the village. It was a relief to hear that although there was damage, no one had been hurt by the raid. On entering the village, they could see many broken windows and were utterly relieved to see that their own home had not been damaged by the impact.

"What a shock and there we were, offering safety to our families back home. Wait till we tell them," remarked Alice.

A bigger shock came when they put on the wireless and heard that the Alcazar Theatre had been bombed to the ground.

"Blimey, we were sitting in there last night," said Alberto in shock. "That must have been the huge explosion we heard before we left home this morning. We all knew it was pretty close. Scared the hell out of me. What stalwarts our families are to stick with it."

"Well, I can remind you Alberto, you had your fair share in the First World War. Don't you ever forget that."

Having seen what family relatives were coping with in London and with bombs dropping so close to home, Alberto decided to join the Home Guard and go back into uniform. Feeling motivated by his own positivity in a second war, with a wife and children to protect, he volunteered his name at the Andover Police Station. Disappointment weighed heavily when he was rejected by the fact that he would not be able to handle a rifle with only one arm.

Desperate to help with Civil Defence in some way, Alberto signed up to do a couple of nights fire watching.

TGA: *(Might sound simple enough, but these WW1 veterans were conscientious in their efforts and walked the village all night long, including going to the top of King's Hill, where they could get good views of the surrounding areas.)*

Annabelle and Al were in their element on their dad's fire watching night. They took turns to sleep in their dad's bed space in the big double bed on the very soft and comfy feather mattress.

"I'll swap your bed for mine any time," Al told his dad after his first night in the bed.

"Not a chance, Al. You and your sister can take turns in keeping it warm for me, and that's your lot."

A knock at the door interrupted the conversation. It was Annabelle's friend, Pam Angel. Immediately she was invited to sit at the tea table with them and told them her exciting news.

"I'm going to live with my nan while the bombing is going on. I'm really glad about it because I'm frightened of the bombs."

"Is your mum coming down too?" asked Alice.

"No, she's staying up there with Dad, who has to go to work. I wish she was coming down, but she said they'll come and see me often."

Annabelle was absolutely thrilled to have her best friend living in the village and said, "You'll be able to come and sleep with me lots of nights."

"Hold your horses, young miss. That won't be able to happen. I've got other plans."

Before September was upon them, Alberto had got help from his Civil Defence pals to move all three beds into the corner front room downstairs, having first had the piano moved into the living room to allow much needed space.

"If it's our misfortune to get bombed, we'll all go together. I expect your nan will feel exactly the same, Pam."

Going to bed in one room was a strange occurrence for all the family. Alice and Alberto's bedhead was alongside the staircase wall with the small open grate fireplace in the corner at the left of their feet. Al's bed was by the front window and Annabelle's was by the side window, overlooking the bakery, with her feet pointing to the open grate. Annabelle had to squeeze between her dad's side of the double bed and Al's bed to get through to her own, but she could not sleep. She lay there awake, continuously shaking with terror, which began when the droning Messerschmitt planes first started to fly overhead.

An awesome threat came to Enham when three of its young lads played a prank, which started as innocent fun. Al, Doug Saunders and Kenny Woods often used to play 'diving', as they'd jump from an overhanging branch of a tree, into the huge pile of sawdust up the dump, which was offloaded there daily from the carpentry department in the factory. They were becoming quite expert, as they'd learned by experience to close their eyes, pinch their noses and keep their mouths shut. The dump was situated at the perimeter of a big field opposite the factory and an Enham lorry deposited sawdust there daily, via Dunhill Lane.

The threat came the day that council workers were re-surfacing the lane. To do the job, they spread tar on the road and then evenly raked grey gravel on the top. The next time the boys went to play on the dump, they found 40 gallon empty drums with tar residue at the bottom. Boys being boys, they went home and nicked a box of matches. Back at the dump, they rolled a couple of drums to the sawdust pile and removed the bungs. They then set light to the tar and were absolutely shocked, and scared, at the size of the fire. They did a bunk as fast as their feet would carry them and counted their blessings that there were no houses nearby.

The blaze caused panic amongst the villagers because of the blackout. Its visibility from the sky was an ominous threat. It took three visits over a period of two weeks for the Andover Fire Brigade to finally extinguish the source of the combusting sawdust, for which everyone was truly relieved and thankful.

31st October brought the end of the Battle of Britain and the whole nation were very proud of the good job done by our boys in blue. But the joy was short-lived. The Germans didn't give up and started a bombing campaign over Great Britain, which became known as The Blitz. On the wireless, everyone heard that British towns and cities, including Birmingham, Bristol, Coventry, Liverpool, London, Portsmouth, Southampton and many more, were all suffering the loss of many lives, as well as gross destruction. The closest of the bombed towns to Enham was Southampton and the exploding bombs could be heard in Enham when the wind was in the right direction.

Trying to live a contented life during all the threats of war, was nigh on impossible, but things worsened in November when Alberto received a letter from home telling him that his mother was very ill, and his family feared the worst. She actually passed away on 22nd November 1940 and Alberto travelled alone to London to attend her funeral. Because of the Blitz, he had no intention of taking Alice with him. He was paired with his father to head the family, following the coffin up the aisle of the church. During the service, his mind dwelt on the hard life of his beloved mother, who never had the chance to take life easy, but always found time for her family. She was a mother to be proud of.

It was very hard for Alberto to leave his father, who had now lost his lifetime's work and his loving wife. In a few short months he had become a broken man, his only consolation being that his ice house was now useful as an air raid shelter for his family and that was where Alberto slept on his one night's stay.

Before leaving, Alberto begged his father to return to Enham with him.

"Alice and I can help you, Pa, and the children are at a wonderful age to lighten your spirit, and you know as well as I do that Annabelle would absolutely love it. Please, please, Pa. I've got a lovely home that you haven't seen yet, and now Mama never will." He became choked up at the realisation.

Putting his hand out to Alberto, he replied, "Papa know-a mio sarn-a. But you-a appy. Mama say-a, 'Alberto appy'. Papa no leave-a Mama on-a own-a with da bomb-a. You good-a man-a. You know-a."

Alberto, along with the rest of his family, had tried hard to convince Papa to have a break in the country, but he was rigid in his conviction that he should stay close to Mama. Saying goodbyes and departing alone was tough for him, but he reminded himself that he had to return home without showing the heavy weight on his shoulders.

In that frame of mind, he went into a store in Edmonton and bought a game of Bombardo to entertain and occupy his family over long and frightening winter nights. He remembered the game becoming popular a few years after his discharge from the Army. It was well advertised as it was produced at the Lord Roberts Memorial Workshop for disabled soldiers and sailors.

Basically, it was a gambling game and he thought the time was right for Annabelle to learn about such things under her own roof. Al, of course, had a head start because he still hogged the Daily Express when it was delivered, in order to tick off the runners in the horse races. When the results were announced on the wireless, he'd then run round to tell Auntie Dolly and Mr Mesney (the bookies' runner in the village) how much he would have won or lost, if he were backing with money.

Bombardo was a totally different type of gambling. It consisted of a dozen ping pong balls, all different colours, which were sitting in individual thin wired stands, so you could see the bottom of the ping pong ball as well as the top. The stands stood about two and a half inches high from the green baized base of the game. There was a small fortified circle in the centre of the base, big enough to contain a spinning top. Hanging from a metal arch arrangement, straddling the entire board, was a fine cord with a marble-sized wooden ball at the bottom end. When the diabalo top was set spinning in its contained circle, it sent the hanging ball flying in different directions and it knocked many of the ping pong balls off their stands in one spin. The ping pong balls were attached by a silk thread to their wire stands, which meant they could not fall to the floor. The winner of the game would be the player who backed the last ball left in its stand. The family placed their bets with matchsticks, twenty-five of which were bought for a half-penny.

There was another winner at the end of the evening's play, when the matchsticks were sold back. Some players would more than likely have handed back a lot more than the twenty-five they'd started with.

Another game to help pass the winter nights was darts. Alberto was a good player and had a board hanging on the left side of the range, where play didn't get in the way of access to the scullery. Al was a pretty nifty player too, for such a short child. Besides these games, there was always singing and tap dancing going on and these activities helped pass the time until Christmas.

Christmas 1940 was spent in the Geoghegans' home, where everyone toasted the fact that they'd survived a whole year of warfare. In fact, more beers were brought out to make toasts to the New Year's survival as well as 'oil' the vocal chords for all the singing that ensued. When the sandwiches were brought out, the adults were asking the children what presents they had received that year.

Annabelle was bursting to tell everyone that she'd received a desk, which fitted into her bedroom nicely, even when there was a bed in it, so she could write in peace and quiet.

"Well, I think that's the perfect gift for you Annabelle. Your mummy tells me that you love writing everything down and that your Auntie Dolly has given you a diary."

Everyone could see by Annabelle's face that she was thrilled with her gifts.

"And what about young Al, here. What did you get?" asked Tommy Geoghegan.

A proud young Al said, "I've got the best present ever. I had a bike."

"And can you ride it?"
"Yeah, Clive Broughton tried to teach me, but his bike was a bit big for me then."

Alberto smiled to himself. Clive's bike had been put up for sale because he had outgrown it and Alberto bought it. Al had no idea that he'd got Clive's bike, which had been painted a different colour.

TGA: *(Well, there is a true saying, 'What the eye can't see, the heart won't grieve over'. Those parents managed to give their children very useful and much needed presents in very difficult times. Another adage comes to mind, 'Where there's a will, there's a way'. You'd have thought Annabelle had received a desk fit for a king. In actual fact, it was not much wider than fifteen inches, with a bureau top that pulled down to give a writing surface and revealed pigeon hole slots behind for filing small books etc. When the bureau top was in place, there was a drawer with two slim doors below, which reached down to the ground. When opened, she was delighted to see more storage space.*

I felt privileged to see how these relatively poor and disabled people could rise above all things and circumstances, to enjoy a Happy Christmas.)

Chapter 12

Andre's Evacuation to Ripley, Surrey

The billeting officer at Ripley was a blonde-haired lady named Mrs Wilmot. Before she started taking the children to their guardians, she told them that there was no room for them at the Ripley Church School so she would be organising to take them to school at Send, another village about two-and-a-half miles away. She said she would be notifying their guardians as soon as a start date could be arranged.

The children all had to follow her as, one by one, she delivered them to their billets. On the way she told Andre that he would be living with a Mrs Cook.

"You must try to be a good boy for her, Andre. She's quite sad at the moment because her husband's had to go to war. I hope the two of you will become good friends."

"I don't want to stay in Ripley, Mrs Wilmot. I want to go back to Mr and Mrs Williams in Brighton."

"Well you can get that out of your head straight away, my boy. The coastal areas are dangerous for fear of invasion by the enemy. You'll be much safer here. Chin up. There's a good boy."

One thing Andre liked about living with Mrs Cook was that she didn't like cooking. "It's not the same without a husband to cook for", she kept saying. That didn't matter to Andre; he never felt hungry. Other than that, he felt very insecure and unhappy. She never made him feel at home like Mr and Mrs Williams did. In fact, she was always miserable, so Andre had no idea if she liked him or not. She had her wireless on all day long, so conversation was non-existent. She told him that his bedroom was third off the landing, but she didn't say which furniture he could use, so he just left his clothes lying on the floor. It troubled him that he couldn't feel friendly towards her as Mrs Wilmot had hoped, but excused himself with the thought that she wasn't easy to be friends with.

He was very much surprised one day when she said, "Sit down, Andre. I have to speak to you."

Andre sat opposite her at the table, covered in its dark green chenille cloth with tassels dangling. She was a thin lady with plaited hair that she coiled into a bun at the nape of her neck with hair pins stuck through it and a hair net over to keep it in place. Her face was long and drawn and Andre wondered if she was eating enough now her husband was gone, because she looked quite ill.

"I've had a letter from Mrs Wilmot to say she will be calling for you at 8am on Wednesday and will be walking you evacuees to Send School.

"How far away is Send School?"

"About two and a half miles."

"Will you wake me up so I'm ready, please Mrs Cook?"

"I can't promise that, young man. I've got nothing to get up for these days, but I'll give you an alarm clock and you can see to yourself."

Andre felt numb.

"Do you mind having me to live with you?"

"I had no option child. It's a governmental ruling. They take your husband away then give you more mouths to feed."

"I'm sorry, Mrs Cook. I'll talk to Mrs Wilmot and see if she can help."

"Don't you say nothing of the sort. I don't want no trouble."

Andre was glad to get to school. There he met friends from home and began to think that perhaps he'd have been better off staying with Ma and not being evacuated at all. That thought was only fleeting. Nicer thoughts of living with Mr and Mrs Williams chased it away.

Because the school was being shared with local children, they only had to attend in the mornings one week and afternoons the next. Andre was happy with that, but he didn't go home for the half day off, ever. He'd always loved the pond at Norwood, but in Ripley they had a river. The River Wey. Andre spent all his spare time there trampling through the ferns where, on hot days when he took his shirt and vest off, imaginations of *Robinson Crusoe* ran riot in his mind.

In the area where he played there was a weir on the river, which actually divided it in two by a system of boards making an upright barrier. That barrier effected a waterfall that dropped and continued as the river. The divided half became a manmade canal. Andre became fascinated by the weir and often watched the lock keeper operating it; always from a distance because he didn't want anyone to find his hideout.

That became his habit until the day he heard on Mrs Cook's wireless that the beach at Brighton had been closed to the public and that mines, barbed wire and other defences has been put in place.

The next day, following afternoon school, and remembering to carry his gas mask, despite his excitement, he quietly took the ten shilling note he'd seen Mrs Cook slip in the dresser drawer the previous night and started eagerly to make his way to Woking Station, the first lap of his journey to Brighton and Mr and Mrs Williams.

TGA: *(Oh dear, Andre. This is not the way. I'm here watching you, but I can't physically stop you. I'm desperately hoping you'll remember in time to 'keep your nose clean and you won't go far wrong', which Grandma once told you.)*

When he didn't go home for tea that evening, Mrs Cook reported it to the local policeman, the Copper as he was familiarly known.

"Is there anything missing in your home, Mrs Cook?"

"Not that I've noticed."

"Then I'll accompany you home and you can make a proper search."

After she'd searched for a while, the policeman asked, "Found anything missing yet?"

"Doesn't look like it. I haven't got any other jewellery, only the few bits I'm wearing."

"What about money?"

She went to the dresser drawer to get her purse and there she discovered that the ten shilling note was gone.

"Ten bob, eh? What about inside your purse?"

She counted the money and said, "That looks about right. The little devil. He was in last night when I slipped that note in the drawer."

"Well, it looks as though he's hot-footed it somewhere Mrs Cook. We'll look into it and see if we can catch him and get your money back to you."

"Blinkin' London evacuees. Let them all go back to London and get bombed, I say."

"That's not a nice attitude, Mrs Cook. They've all been taken away from their mothers, let me remind you. Is he happy here with you?"

"How do I know?" He rarely speaks and us people didn't get a choice, you know."

The policeman walked away with a smirk on his face after hearing the last snippet.

Andre was making his way on foot to Woking Station. He'd made it his business to find out that it was about four and a half miles away. He wanted to hold onto the ten shilling note for the train journey to get himself back to Brighton. Feeling tired after four miles, he had a rest on the verge.

He was awakened by a lady walking her dog.

"Are you alright, sonny?"

"Ooh," he said, rubbing his eyes. "Yes, thank you. I must have fallen asleep. I'm walking to Woking Station."

"Are you an evacuee?"

Andre nodded.

"And missing your mum?"

"Yes," was Andre's answer because it seemed the simplest.

She pointed him in the right direction for the station, but continued her walk with the dog in the direction of the police station. She felt it to be her duty to let them know.

It didn't take long for the police to find him. Woking had already received a phone call from Ripley saying an evacuee named Andre Kliskey had gone missing and they soon found him and drove him back to Ripley Station where he was met by the policeman who had seen Mrs Cook.

"Come in here, lad, and tell me your side of the story. Mrs Cook told me you'd done a bunk."

"I wanted to get back to my guardians in Brighton. I heard on Mrs Cook's wireless that they've put mines and barbed wire and stuff on the beach, so the Germans won't be able to invade there now. Mr and Mrs Williams wanted to keep me and I know they'd be glad to have me back."

"And did you have enough money to get yourself there?"

"I don't know. I didn't know how much it would cost, but I saw Mrs Cook put a ten shilling note in her drawer yesterday, so I nicked it. I was walking to Woking to save all the money for the train, but I didn't use it, because you caught me."

With that, he put his hand in his pocket and gave the note to the policeman.

The policeman scratched his head and said, "There's so much good in you, lad. You're very honest, but call it nicking or stealing, whatever you will, it's still a crime you know."

"I do know that, sir. All I could think about at the time was getting back to Mr and Mrs Williams. I don't know if I'm sorry about that or not. They really cared about me and living with them was much better than being at my real home."

With tears welling in his eyes, he said, "What I do know is that Grandma wouldn't be pleased with me."

"Well, what are we going to do with you? I think right now I should take you back to Mrs Cook, so you can return her money. Then we'll have to find you another placement. Till then, you'll have to sleep in the station. It's for sure Mrs Cook won't want you back."

Mrs Cook was glad to get her money back, but spared not one glance in Andre's direction. On the way back to the station, Andre started to cry. "Do I have to stay the night in the police station, sir? I feel ashamed."

"Well, honestly speaking, so you should. Tell me what you liked so much about Mr and Mrs Williams?"

"They liked me and were kind to me. They talked to me and Mr Williams took me to a cricket match. Then I got moved. All three of us cried. We'd had plans for Mr Williams to take me to lots more cricket matches. The teachers at the school even thought it was a good idea and decided to let me have three days off in a row, if the match took that long. And Mrs Williams packed picnic lunches for us and flasks of hot tea. I'd never known anything so good. My own dad never took me anywhere like that."

"And what age roughly were they?

"Older than Ma and Pa. Mrs Williams had white hair."

"And what about Grandma, whom you said wouldn't be pleased with you?"

265

"She was a friend I made when I fell over outside her home and cut my knee on my way to school, when we lived in Norwood. I used to like helping her when I could."

"Sounds to me as though you get on well with older people. So what about Ma and Pa? How do they fit into the picture?"

"Pa is my real father. My mum died when I was born and for some reason my stepmother didn't treat me the same as her own boys, even though I tried to please her. Miss Rees, my teacher at my first school knows. She could tell you the truth."

"And what school was that?"

"Norwood Infants."

"Look, sonny, I don't want to lock you up in the station because I'd like to check out what you're telling me. As the police officer in charge, I can't put you up in my own home, but I could ask my sister, Mrs Goodman, if she'd put you up for a night. She's not a fit person; she's got heart problems, so she can't have evacuees with her, but I'm sure she won't mind for one night. Give you a little chance to prove yourself. What do you say to that?"

"Yes please, and thank you, sir. I promise I won't give her any trouble. I'll help her if I can."

The next day the policeman called at his sister's home and told Andre that Miss Rees had confirmed his indications that his stepmother was unkind and told him, "I've spoken to Mrs Wilmot about you and she is leaving it to me to find you a suitable placement."

"Thank you, sir."

Andre finally got settled with an elderly lady named Mrs Winter, who was kindly and looked after him a lot better than Mrs Cook had done. She was warm and motherly towards him and he was settling in nicely.

Wandering home from school happily one day, he saw an elderly man pushing a barrow up a steep hill and offered help. The barrow was very heavy and because his sock had 'gone to sleep', he rubbed a blister on his heel.

The next day Mrs Winter went to the surgery and asked the doctor to call because her evacuee had a big abscess that had come up in his groin. The doctor was shocked to find an inch-wide red poison line running up the back of the boy's leg from the open blister, gradually travelling up the back of the leg, across the stomach and into the groin where the abscess had formed. Mrs Winter did lots of fetching and carrying, providing boiling water and bowls etc. for the doctor, who sedated Andre before lancing the abscess.

That procedure had to be repeated twice more. Andre was very weak and even the weight of the sheet was too much for his leg.

A few days later, the policeman visited Mrs Winter to check on the reason for Andre's absence from school. He then went upstairs to say hello to Andre.

"How's it going then, son? Been through the mill a bit, I understand."

"Yes, sir. It hurt a lot, but feeling so hot was the worst. I'm lucky to have Mrs Winter. She's been really kind to me."

"Oh God, Andre. I'd rather be anywhere else in the world at this minute than sitting here knowing I've got something awful to tell you."

"Don't bother to tell me, Mr Policeman. I can guess."

"Go on then."

"You've got to find another home for me."

"How the hell d'ya know that?"

"Because every time I like where I'm living, someone has to move me on."

Scratching his head, the policeman said, "What rotten luck. You've suffered all this because you were trying to help someone. So off we go again. Not going to be easy because the doctor says you must be fed and nourished properly. BUT, never fear, I'll do my very best for you."

"Are you alright, Andre dear?"

"Yes, thank you, Mrs Winter. I know I can't stay with you. The policeman told me."

"I'm so sorry. I liked having you, but the nursing was a bit too much for me."

"I know, Mrs Winter. I saw you limping after a few days up and down the stairs. Perhaps if I'm not moved too far away I can come and visit you."

Andre's next move was to the Holt family with two girls, Vera and Connie, and one boy, Jeremy, whom the family called Jerry. They were a healthy family and certainly not undernourished. The hope was that being with other children might encourage Andre to eat more to help him get stronger.

For a while, the policeman kept a close eye on Andre, fearing that he might try to escape again.

Living with Jerry enabled Andre to get to know the village boys as well as the evacuees. He and his friends were always up to pranks, as they were the day they took Andre to the local farmer's field.

The farmer and his wife had twenty-four sons, ranging from toddlers to young men. His wife desperately wanted a daughter and never gave up hope. All the boys who were old enough worked on the land with their father. The local children were aware of their routines, so knew when it was safe to play in his field.

That particular day was the day they knew they could have undisturbed fun. There were lorry and aeroplane tyres strewn all over the place. The boys would stack the tyres one upon the other as high as possible and the challenge was that each child had to show his courage by climbing on the backs of others to the top and then climb down the centre. Once inside, the boys would put a lid of corrugated iron, old wattle fencing or whatever was available, on the top and then bombard the stack with stones or old bricks; anything they could find laying around. Andre didn't like being inside, but proved his courage along with the others. He didn't think the policeman would mind because they were only playing with rubbish. He liked being popular with the boys and began to gain confidence.

At home he was learning to eat up his food, which he knew was making him stronger, but best of all he liked going scrumping. Pulling a carrot out of the farmer's field, wiping it on his trousers and then eating it raw was the best thing he'd ever eaten. He couldn't help wondering why people ever bothered to cook them. With the boys he also scrumped apples and pears from the orchard. Altogether he was starting to enjoy life in Ripley.

Another caper was going to the barn with Jerry and his friends when the farmer and his sons were not about. In the barn, the hay was built up high and their game was to climb up to the rafters and jump to see who could sink deepest into the hay. One day things went wrong when a boy landed on another boy's head and he became unconscious. The farmer got to know and they all got a beating.

It wasn't long before the policeman was at the Holts' door. He reprimanded both boys, telling them that they were trespassing on the farmer's land. He then asked Mrs Holt if he could speak to Andre privately.

Together they walked up the stairs to the boys' bedroom. "So, you're in trouble again, son?"

"Yes, sir. I was having a good time with the boys. It seemed like just good fun at the time."

"I know. That's something you haven't had much of in your life, isn't it?"

"I haven't had any fun at all compared to living here, apart from Mr Williams and the cricket. At home when we played games, the ball kept going into other people's gardens and we always got into trouble. In Ripley, there's a lot more space and freedom and I like living with the Holts. They include me as part of their family and Jerry and I chatter in our beds at night, and he's a good playmate." At that point he started to cry.

"What is it, Andre?"

"Well, I'm eating a lot better now and feeling stronger and I'm frightened you're going to move me again."

The policeman put his arm around Andre's shoulders.

"Look, son, get this into your worried little head. I'm not here to move you on. I'm very glad that you are happy with the Holts. I am here because I know more about your hard life than others do and it is my judgement that I am right to befriend you, but this mischief can't go on forever. I have a serious job to do, and that is keeping law and order. Do you understand what I am saying?"

"Yes, sir."

"Then don't you forget it. Your stepmother didn't do you any favours, but now you're not doing yourself any. You toe the line and you can rest assured I'll be your Guardian Angel. Deal?" He put his hand out to shake and Andre reciprocated.

"Yes, sir. Thank you very much, sir. And thank you for not moving me again."

TGA: *(Goodness, gracious me. I've got help. A human Guardian Angel. Thank you Lord. It might well take two of us. My charge is in a very precarious position. I hope the authorities will realise that Andre is only a young lad, and that 'boys will be boys'.)*

Chapter 13

Enham Feeling the Effects of WW2

The war continued to weave its inimitable web and Enham Village Centre did not escape; the women were required to do five half days' war work, providing they didn't have children under five years old. In addition, because the Blitz was taking its toll over British cities, people living in the British Isles were required to house families who had been bombed out of their homes. Hence the village got a new intake of residents.

Village members of the Civil Defence did the organising, which meant that Alberto and Alice had their home inspected to see how many people they could accommodate. The fact that they were now all sleeping in one room meant that they had three spare bedrooms upstairs – room for a small family – to be allocated as two bedrooms and a lounge. The scullery, range, lavatory and bathroom would have to be shared. The inspector informed Alberto and Alice that the authorities would be providing beds and bedding in due course when a family had been allocated.

Alice's health was slowly deteriorating and she was worrying herself silly about all the pressures WW2 was putting on her. One such worry was alleviated when Mr Crabbe from the Enham Industries' office paid her a visit.

"Look, Dr MacCallum told us you are not fit to work in the factory, but we think we have a solution that you might consider worth a try, bearing in mind we are being pressured by the government for more and more output. We are aware of your sewing expertise and we need machinists. How's it sounding so far?"

"Well, if I can work from home, I'd be foolish to turn it down. Sewing is a sitting job that I can manage, although my heart races a bit when I treadle too much."

"Oh, I see," he said with surprise. "You've got a treadle machine under the back window there. D'ya mind if I have a look?"

As he was studying the machine, which had an ornate wrought iron framework and was floor standing, Alice asked, "Do you know what sort of sewing I would have to do?"

"I'm afraid some of it would be quite heavy work, but...I would say this is an industrial machine and I think Enham Industries Engineering could fix a motor to it; then you wouldn't have to manually use the treadle, only to control the starting and ending of a piece of stitching. So what do you think?"

"Very relieved. It's been a big worry, but I can manage sewing."

"Well, I'll look into getting the machine powered and then you'll be able to get started. Don't forget the best bit; you'll get a pay packet at the end of the week. Those parting words brought a welcome smile to Alice's face.

Around the tea table, Alice shared her news with the family who thought it was brilliant that she could work from home. They were used to her doing sewing jobs, so they knew she would be able to cope.

As usual that night, Annabelle laid awake in her bed shaking like a leaf as she heard the low drones of the German Messerschmitt planes flying overhead, fearful they might drop bombs on Enham. Her fear caused thumping palpitations and even when the droning ceased, the thumping continued. Peculiar sounds were coming from her mum and dad's bed. There was a lot of heavy breathing going on and she was frightened her mum's heart was the cause. Despite her fears, an innate second sense told her not to make a sound. She lay wide-eyed staring into the darkness of the room, hardly daring to move, or indeed breathe. Then she heard her mother giggle, which brought relief and the little girl started to relax.

(TGA: *It's amazing how the war affected people in so many different ways.*)

Alberto was the next with war news. The factory had received a government contract to manufacture gliders to be used for troop carrying. That gave the WW1 wounded men a feeling of great satisfaction in making a contribution to WW2.

In fact, repercussions of war were hitting everybody left, right and centre. Next came part-time school for the children. Annabelle was so disappointed because she desperately sought education. She could not go regularly anyway because of her mum's health, which was indeed getting worse and limiting her schooling more and more. Now, she would only get a half day, when she was able to attend. It was the same for Al who had moved up from Smannell School to the Andover Secondary Modern School for Boys, but he was delighted about the half day.

Because of Annabelle's disappointment, Alice and Alberto encouraged her to join the Girl Guides to get her out mixing and still have the opportunity to learn. She was a bit shy about it, but when her friend Pat Shears said she would join too, they went along together. They had to go to the dressing room on the right of the stage where the village Buffalo Lodge held their meetings.

Mrs Chambers, the Guide Captain, welcomed and introduced them as they were lined up side by side in the front row of the group.

"There's no need to be nervous, girls; you will soon learn the routine. If you are serious about becoming enrolled as Girl Guides you will need to learn the Girl Guide Laws and the Girl Guide Promise. We meet here every Wednesday night for two hours in school term time."

At that meeting, Annabelle and Pat were separated into different patrols. Annabelle into the Poppy Patrol of the 'Flowers' group; Pat in the Panda Patrol of the 'Animals'.

Annabelle enjoyed being in the Guides more and more each time they met. She loved it when they went out tracking. In advance of the meeting, The Guide Captain and her leader had laid a trail of 'twig arrows' along country footpaths and roads, and the guide patrols had to find their way to the end. Another thing she liked was when they were divided into their patrols and had to walk round the village gardens seeing how many shrubs and flowers, wild or otherwise, they could name. Later, back in the meeting room, the various patrols would share their knowledge with each other. At the end of the meeting, Mrs Chambers suggested they should continue learning about flowers and shrubs by borrowing books from the library.

"That will come in useful for a winter meeting when we have to be indoors."

Soon Mrs Chambers issued the girls with their navy blue uniforms and before they knew it, they were attending their enrolment ceremony.

"I will do this in alphabetical order girls, so that means you'll be first, Annabelle," she said, with a serious, confident nod. "Think about what you are promising, then go ahead in your own time."

"I promise that I will do my best, to do my duty to God and the King, to help other people and to keep the Girl Guide Law."

At the end of her promise, Annabelle gave a three fingered salute to the Guide Captain, which represented the three-part promise. Mrs Chambers then pinned a gold coloured trefoil badge on her tie and Annabelle saluted again.

At the end of the meeting, both girls dashed home to show off their trefoils.

Before Annabelle had been to very many Girl Guide meetings, Alberto and Alice had a visit from Mr Holley, the Head Civil Defence Warden to warn them that beds and bedding would be delivered the next day and that a Mr and Mrs Budgen and their 12-year-old son, Wally, would be coming to live with them.

And so it was that on Saturday afternoon they arrived. Mr Budgen was a brusque and stocky man dressed in a black suit with check shirt, brown bow tie and brown boots and his wife, Mrs Budgen, was a plumpish lady with brown, frizzy hair who was wearing a navy blue belted dress and fawn cardigan. Their son, who was also plump like his parents, was clad in a navy blazer and long grey trousers.

Mr Jack Stuart, the Civil Defence Warden who had delivered gas masks in 1938, had accompanied the family with an abundance of luggage to No. 9, Alberto and Alice's home, and took them upstairs, on his one leg with crutches, to see their rooms.

"These drawers are full up with other people's bloody clothes. Where shall we put ours?"

"You'll have to live out of suitcases for the time being I'm afraid and I'll see what can be done. Mr and Mrs Aless keep their clothes in the upstairs furniture."

Mrs Budgen went puce and exploded, "So they'll be coming into our rooms to get their clothes. Is that what's gunna happen?"

"Look Ma'am. This has to be done by trial and error. None of us have had such an experience before. The good thing is you're safer out of London. There is a war on you know."

"Don't you be bleedin' sarcastic to 'er, mate."

Later, Alice and Alberto, who had heard the rumpus from upstairs, started the welcoming process by lighting the primus stove to boil a kettle and make a cup of tea.

"Do you have to do that every time you want to boil a kettle? asked Mrs Budgen.

"No. We've got the range in the living room, but we don't waste the coal on mild days like today."

"Oh gawd. I'm gunna miss my old gas cooker, that's for sure. What d'ya think about this Bill?"

"No more than I expected. They've sent us to the soddin' sticks after all."

"I'd rather you didn't swear in front of my children, Mr Budgen. They're not used to it."

"High and mighty eh?" And who made you a bleedin' nob?"

"I don't want to have to get bitter about this, so I ask you respectfully not to swear under my roof."

"Well a bleedin' pint might help. Any good pubs down 'ere?"

Enjoying his own reply to this obnoxious man, Alberto quipped, "Yeah. In fact we've got three. All within two to three miles' walking distance."

"Bugger me. Sod that!"

"There is a bar in the Landale Wilson Institute, our village social centre, just up the road a bit."

At that Mr Budgen looked a bit relieved.

Over a cup of tea, the children were introduced to each other. Wally seemed shy of Annabelle and Mrs Budgen was shocked to learn that she would often be sharing cooking facilities with a ten-year-old child. Al said he would take Wally out to meet some of his friends. Chatting went on for a while, but the atmosphere was strained.

TGA: *(This disastrous situation was obviously the total opposite of a fairytale for both families.)*

Living with such chaos under his roof became appalling for Alberto. Alice and/or Annabelle took responsibility for providing meals for seven for the first three days and during that time Alice

278

discussed with Mrs Budgen whether they should take turns in cooking.

"No bloody fear. I've never cooked for that many in my whole bloody life."

"Then I'll make spaces in the larder for you to keep your shopping separately from mine, and I'm afraid I must choose to cook in the morning because Alberto comes home for dinner between 12 and 1."

Mrs Budgen continued to use vegetables from Alice's basket, despite having been told that she could buy supplies from the Enham vegetable gardens or from the door-to-door delivery service twice a week. She dominated the primus stove when Annabelle was working in the scullery, which made Annabelle cry because she couldn't get dinner ready in time for her dad's dinner hour. Alice was suffering hours of palpitations, whether she was in bed worrying about Annabelle, or trying to deal with food herself in the scullery.

After two weeks of living hell, everyone under the roof was becoming demented, apart from the two boys who went out to play a lot.

The last straw came when Mrs Budgen said, "Bugger this. It's like living in the year dot. I'll go out and get fish and chips every day. Then I won't have to use your bloody scullery. I can do cereals and sandwiches in our room upstairs. Where can I get fish and chips?"

"You'll have to get the bus to Andover, but I warn you, you won't be able to get them on Sundays and Mondays."

At that she was speechless and you could see her anger rising.

"A bloody bus to Andover every day," she screeched. "Bill, I can't live in these bleedin' sticks anymore. Let's get back to London quick and if we get bombed again, then anything'll be better than this."

Mr Budgen went out to look for Wally while Mrs Budgen packed up their belongings. Mr Budgen returned with the boys, saying, "I've booked a taxi from Withell's Garage up the road. He'll pick us up in half an hour."

With that, all the Budgens disappeared up to their rooms.

Al was all ears. "What's going on, Mum?"

"Be patient for half an hour and then we'll tell you."

Amazingly, because Mr Withell never did seem to understand clocks and times, he turned up on the dot and without a word of goodbye, they were gone.

Relief abounded. The family got into a circle with arms around each other's backs and started singing any songs that came into their heads, rejoicing for their freedom.

Over tea, Alberto said, "I shall take you all out on Friday night to celebrate."

"Where, Dad?"

"Not very far away I'm afraid. I'll take you to the Institute to buy you a packet of crisps and a lemonade."

"Oooh, yummy!"

"The authorities have decided that because women are now working as part of the war effort, they can have the use of the meeting room on Friday nights. They're still not allowed in the bar, but husbands can take drinks into the meeting room and I know your mum will enjoy a glass of stout."

Still overjoyed at having their home to themselves again, Alice was pleased to greet the engineer who had come to attach a power motor to her sewing machine. She was amazed at how easy sewing was without having to use the treadle so much. Very quickly afterwards, she was supplied with a roll of silver material with matching lines on pairs of pieces that she had to cut out first and then stitch together. She found it really easy and began to enjoy the work, which was making sections for barrage balloons. The fact that she, Alice Alessandro the puny one, was contributing to the war effort made her feel very satisfied and proud of herself.

Auntie Dolly popped round one afternoon while Alice was busy doing her war work in front of the back window.

"Just had to come to tell you dear, we've got an elderly lady from Southampton coming to live with us at the weekend. She's been bombed out. They're getting hit so bad in Southampton, you know."

"Well, I can only wish you better luck than we had, Dolly. I'll look forward to meeting her."

Our Richard, who will soon be five, can't wait to have a granny in the house. He's driving me mad persistently asking, 'Will she play with me? Mum, will she play with me?' Anyway, I mustn't hinder your work now."

On her way out the door, she said, "I suppose when Richard goes to school in September, I'll have to go to work too. What a life. See you later dear."

Al, who was now thirteen, was thrilled to tell the family that he'd got a weekend job. He and Dougie Saunders were paid two shillings and sixpence each for two nights' fire watching, but the joy was short lived. After a couple of weekends, they got bored with walking around looking for fires and found something more exciting to do.

Two huge brick containers had been built to store water each side of the factory because cellulose was being used inside. That was a requirement of the wartime government regulations. One of the containers was in the spinney, hidden by trees, and that was where the boys found their fun. They took the lid – with a quarter inch lip – off an empty five-gallon cellulose drum, then emptied the dregs from the drum into the lid. Next, they carefully placed the lid on top of the water, wondering what would happen if they set light to it. Doug had a box of matches in his pocket and struck one. It ignited immediately. When a certain temperature was reached, the lid automatically skidded along the surface of the water for about two feet, had a short rest, then skidded off again. They'd discovered such a thrilling game that they totally forgot altogether about fire watching and at one time had as many as eight lids skidding over the water.

Unbeknownst to them, Mr Moody, a fire-watcher who lived on the Crescent just across the road from the spinney, had been put in charge of monitoring the boys. That night he caught them red-handed, fired them on the spot and escorted them to their homes.

And so it was that in the middle of the night Alberto was disturbed by the loud banging of the door knocker. After listening to the fire watching saga, he was immediately in a rage and the whole family were disturbed.

With a deathly white face, which in itself was frightening, Alberto yelled, "Where's your sense of responsibility boy? Giving flame signals from the middle of this village to German pilots. Whose side are you on for Christ's sake? Because I'll tell you this, if you're on the side of the Germans, then you and I are enemies."

Al began to cry. With tears streaming down his cheeks he said, "I'm really sorry, Dad."

Ignoring Al completely, Alberto continued, "And then accepting money for a job you weren't doing. How low can you sink?"

"Al was becoming broken-hearted and between sobs, pleaded, "Dad, please, Dad; I am your friend. I must be your friend. I'm sorry, sorry, sorry, sorry, sorry!" Pausing for breath between sobs, he continued, "You and I are tap dancing partners and …"

At that point, Al broke down completely and Alice stepped in as usual.

"Al, what you did was very naughty and you must apologise to Mr Moody tomorrow. As for your Dad; I hope you can understand that he's unable to control his rages. As soon as something upsets him, he's back on the battlefield. He lost his arm while fighting the Germans in the First World War, where shells were exploding around him all day, which caused the shell shock. It seems to me that the blood drains from his face when the shell shock kicks in. Can you begin to understand that?"

"Sort of. Lots of the men here have shell shock, but I don't know if they have rages too. I know Mr Cotton twitches," he said, still sobbing from the ordeal. "His face and his arms and even his walking is unsteady, like he is drunk. And I know Mr Baker, who usually jokes and laughs with us, goes into his shell shock and doesn't even know us."

"Well there you are, and so your Dad gets rages. I think it's all to do with nerves and has affected different men in different ways. Look, he's starting to get some colour in his cheeks now."

She soothed Al's face with a cool flannel before he sat on his dad's lap.

"I'm sorry, son. I was horrified at what you did, but I should have put you straight in a sensible, fatherly fashion instead of frightening the life out of you like a raging bull. You and I, Al, will be tap dancing partners forever. Come on, let's put the mat on the scullery floor and do a few routines now."

(TGA: *It was pitiful to watch Alberto, who was immediately sorry after such an outburst, but didn't know how to stop them or turn the clock back.*)

Al, who was gradually getting over that episode and happy as a lark to still be friends with his dad, was overjoyed when he awoke on Empire Day, 24th May, because it was celebrated as a school holiday for children. But that joy was short lived. A dinner time radio news bulletin told them that HMS Hood was struck by several German shells when serving in the Battle of the Denmark Strait and it exploded and sank immediately. It was stated that 1,415 men had lost their lives, with only three survivors. Jimmy Mulligan was one of the 1,415; he gave his life to that battle. It was Al's special friend Jimmy who had looked after him for a year when his leg was bad. Al, along with every other person in the village, was in mourning.

While all these things were happening, Auntie Dolly's lodger arrived. She was a very grateful old lady who loved living with the Mesney family. Richard got his adored grandma and, yes, she did play games with him; but only seated games at the table where she sat for most of the day.

"I prefer a dining chair, thank you Dolly, and you're so kind. You're making me so welcome that I won't want to go home – when they find me one."

"You're welcome, Grandma. This works two ways you know. I don't have to keep playing Snap every half hour!"

Grandma hadn't lodged with Auntie Dolly for many weeks when Adolph Hitler recognised the fact that the Blitz (code named Operation Sea Lion) wasn't achieving its objective, which was to facilitate the Nazi's plan to invade Great Britain's coastline. Instead, he turned his warfare onto the Soviet Union. A bit too late for Grandma though. She'd been bombed out of her home and she was very happy to stay with Auntie Dolly.

It was wonderful not to be bearing the brunt of the Blitz, but the war was still hitting hard. More food had been put on ration over the months and now, on 1st June 1941, everyone was allocated a maximum of just 66 clothing coupons per year. Alice and Annabelle came off badly in this situation, because Alberto's false arm straps frequently wore holes in his vests and rubbed his shoulder sore. Despite frequent patching with soft lint, his vests needed to be renewed often. The situation worsened with Al's growth spurt. He'd always been quite a 'little shrimp', but all of a sudden he'd started to grow bigger, which meant he often needed bigger shoes and longer trousers. No sooner had he got a new pair of shoes than he needed a larger pair. Keeping up with these essential requirements used up the whole family's clothing coupon allowance for the year.

Alice coped with her existing clothes, but Annabelle was still growing and gradually needed bigger clothes. Village ladies chipped in and helped by handing down their older daughters' clothes and, in between machining for her war work, Alice was altering the clothes received to fit her own daughter. She was also unravelling old knitted garments to knit up into bigger ones with two different colours, usually as horizontal stripes, which her children liked.

One Saturday afternoon when Al was showing off his new long trousers and 'big' black shoes, he asked his father if he could go to London the following Saturday to watch his cousin Tony playing schoolboy football at Spurs.

"Kenny Woods has got a job with Anna Valley Motors and he said he'd pay for me to go because he's desperate to see Tony play. Mr Woods is very happy for him to go because he comes from Tottenham and has always been a fan of Spurs."

"So, Ken's learning to be a motor mechanic?"

"I suppose so. He said they are contracted by the government to maintain Army vehicles."

Alberto was happy to agree because he was glad for anything that might help Al to get over Jimmy's death.

"You'll be sure to say hello to Granny Howitz and Bubble while you're there, won't you? We haven't visited as a family since the Blitz. I'm the only one they've seen in all that time, when I went to Granny Aless' funeral."

"Yeah, I will go and take Kenny. I've already warned him that Bubble can't make ice cream anymore, because of the rationing."

On the night before they were due to go, Kenny and Al caught two buses to get to Anna Valley. There, Kenny took a jeep from his firm's forecourt and drove it back to Enham. He parked it on the White House lawn in the laurel bush area at the bottom. Early on Saturday morning, Kenny and Al drove the jeep back to the forecourt, then walked to Andover Junction Station and caught the train to Waterloo.

On return to Enham, both boys were anxious to get home; Ken to No. 5, the other side of Auntie Dolly and Al to No. 9, to report on their day. Spurs' boys won their match, which made their day extra special and afterwards they were invited by Aunt Phoebe and Uncle Vincenzo to have tea with Tony. Ken had taken a newspaper cutting with him, which had reported on how Tony was very clever with the ball and forecast a great career ahead for him. Over tea, Tony signed the cutting and Ken couldn't get back home fast enough to show his family, the village football team and anyone and everyone else in the village who was interested that he'd got the signature of a Spurs' schoolboy football celebrity.

When all had been said about football, Al told the family about his visits to the London grandparents.

"Bubble's not the same any more, Dad. I tried to comfort him, but all he wants is to be with Granny Aless." He continued, imitating his grandfather, 'Non'a d'work'a, non'a d'marney, non'a d'Marianna'.

"Dad, he opened his arms to cuddle me and he cried. Yeah, he actually cried with tears. 'My'a life'a gone'. I didn't know what to say or do, so I asked if we could show Ken the air raid shelter. It's all so different down there now. There were chairs, a small table and lots of cushions and boxes of biscuits, dried fruit, bottles of Tizer; loads of stuff. I just couldn't resist telling Ken the story of how Bubble dug the ice house out when he was a young man because I was proud of him, but after I'd said it, I knew I was wrong. All Bubble said with a shrug was 'Gonn'a, Amen'. He was so dismal.

"I asked him if he came down there when the siren went. And he doesn't, Dad. He told me, as best he could because he was so upset, that he sleeps in 'our' bed, as though Granny Aless was still in it. I hated it. I wish it could be like it used to be. Granny Aless always said I could live with them, because I like being up there in London, but that idea's dead now. It was horrible having to leave him, but as he hugged me goodbye he did say one cheerful thing, 'Give'a Anna'bella d'one'a'' as he gave me a second hug for her.

"Then we went up the road to see Granny Howitz. She hates the rationing because she thinks people are being starved, but good old Granny tells them her solution. 'For goodness sake, go down the Lea and catch yourself some eels. They're not on ration, and they're the best nutrition in the world.' She told us most of her customers reply, 'Yuk, I'd rather starve'. Anyway, she sends her love to everyone and when we said goodbye she gave Ken and me a bag of sweets each and a bag for you too, Annabelle."

Alberto was devastated by the news of his father. He said to Alice, "I think I'll have a quick trip up to see him at the weekend and bring him back down to stay with us, if that's OK with you?"

"Of course it is, Alberto. You know that."

"Just getting the OK from the boss," he joked, with a peck on her cheek.

Turning to his son, he said, "As for you, young man, I'm sure we've got enough relatives in London who will give you a home, but that can only happen when your schooling has finished and when you're either 21, or earning enough money to support yourself, whichever comes first."

"21 years old? That's a blinkin' long time!"

Because of Alberto's anxiety, Saturday seemed a lifetime away. Once there, he spent the rest of the day trying to convince his father that he should come and live in Enham with him and his family.

"Please come, Pa. Annabelle can't wait to get you down there. Come to that, neither can I.

You've never seen where your 'first'a born'a son'a' lives'."

"Alberto, mio figlio, Papa know'a you appy. Papa need'a go'a Mama. Io be'a there when'a d'bomb'a drop."

Alberto stayed in Papa's home, 18 Workhouse Hill, where Jane and Richard and their grown up children looked after Bubble. He opened his heart to his sister Jane, saying how hard it was to bear seeing his father a broken man.

"You can't do any more than you're trying to do Alberto. Yes, the war has stolen his livelihood and the responsibilities of that. Now he has nothing to get up for each day and he'll never get over losing Mama. Going to the cemetery to sit with her does get him up every day now. He's very happy there. We, or other members of the family, pop down to keep an eye on him and bring him home when it's time to eat, so he's being looked after. I think the only thing you can do now is go home to your family and thank the Lord he thinks he's happy there. He wants to be with her if she gets bombed.

Alberto could do no other than accept his sister's advice.

The beginning of July saw him go into another rage so quickly after the last one. This time it was at the Enham Horticultural Flower Show. Annabelle won the silver cup for her wild flower arrangement for a third year in succession. When the presentations were made, the cup was presented to her and Alberto heard over the loudspeakers that she had to return the cup at the end of a year. He went berserk.

"You can't take that cup away from her. She's won it three years in succession. It's called a hat-trick. Common bloody knowledge and you don't bleedin' know it." He was in a fighting rage.

While Alberto was being held off, the presenter and official said, "Rules are rules, Mr Aless. I'll let you have a set of the conditions under which you enter competitions in our horticultural shows and you can see them for yourself."

Still angry, as though he couldn't hear what he was being told, he shouted, "If anyone comes to collect that from her next year, I'll wring his bloody neck!"

There were 'oohs' and 'ahhs' from the crowd, most agreeing with Alberto and calling out that there should be a change in the rules.

Al was the first to rush to his dad's side, saying, "It's alright Dad. Let's go home now and talk about it there. You'll soon start to feel better."

As the reader may have guessed, Alice was soon behind him.

On the 19th July 1941, Winston Churchill broadcast to the nation once again. He had been in negotiations with the US military, trying to enlist their support in the Middle East campaign. The outcome of those negotiations was the signing of The Atlantic Charter. Boosted by the confidence that solidarity brought to him, he started his 'V for Victory Campaign' by signalling a letter V with the index and middle fingers of his right hand, with palms outwards, to avoid confusion with rude gestures. As with all his speeches, he proved himself to be a strong leader.

He said, "The V sign is the symbol of the unconquerable will of the occupied territories, and a portent of the fate awaiting Nazi tyranny. So long as the peoples continue to refuse all collaboration with the invader, it is sure that his cause will perish and that Europe will be liberated."

Thereafter, he was always seen displaying the V sign on newsreels or pictures in the daily newspapers.

That speech certainly uplifted people in Enham where residents were using the signal as a morale boost for each other.

Social activities continued in the village to help keep up the spirits of the elderly. The Enham Branch of the Women's Institute gave a tea for the old folks, which was held in the Institute on a Wednesday afternoon. Competitions were held, which were enjoyed by all and tea was served by the Women's Institute Members.

A fundraising dance was organised by Mr Freddie Cox. It was held in the Institute on a Saturday evening when the splendid sum of £12. 10 shillings was raised for the Andover Spitfire Fund. The White Wings Dance Orchestra played to a company of about 200 dancers. The Mayor of Andover, Mr Bob Bell, was in attendance and wished the dance every success. A competition for a large box of chocolates, given by Mrs Piggin, was won by Mr Rodrigues. Refreshments were served by Mrs Piggin and a band of willing helpers.

Throughout the evening, Mr A F J Knight sold badges on behalf of the Spitfire Fund. Overall, it was a fantastic evening enjoyed by everybody.

At the end of July, Alberto was busy with the summer show. He was interested to see how the new experiment would go down with the villagers. Mr Tempero was masterminding a new project.

On performance night, the secret was let out of the bag when Mr Freddie Cox announced that Mr Tempero would be producing a two act Comic Opera by Gilbert and Sullivan entitled *The Mikado*.

The first half of the show was a revue with individual singing and comic turns, which were received with great enthusiasm in accordance with usual standards. The second half opened with the Comic Opera, which gave Mrs Guest (Ada to her colleagues on stage) a chance to really show off her wonderful soprano voice. You could practically 'hear' the amazement of the villagers in the audience when they heard her voice being used to its full potential, and they wanted more. Feet were stomping and there were deafening calls for a repeat of the episode.

Basically, *The Mikado* was a resounding success and in response to the demanding ovation, Mr Tempero announced that the cast would respond with an encore of a couple of the most popular arias. The finale followed the encore in a euphoric atmosphere, which prevailed on stage as well as in the auditorium.

When conker time came around in September, the Aless family had no trouble in hearing what was going on in Auntie Dolly's house. After the usual rumbling sound, they could hear Grandma laughing her head off. With his mum, young Richard used to collect conkers in the little basket his dad had made for him from under the horse chestnut tree in the North Park. In the evening, Mr Mesney would sit against the adjoining wall with the Aless family and let Richard empty the conkers all over his head.

An appalled Alberto exclaimed, "I don't know how he can sit and let the boy do that to him,"

"Well, I can tell you," replied Alice. "Last year Dolly told me Mr Mesney explained that because of his near blindness with mustard gas poisoning, there's not a lot of fun he can have with his son. For him, sitting on the floor knowing what's going to happen, is nothing like as bad as the battlefield and well worth it that he can make his son laugh. After she'd told me the reason though, she chuckled as she said, 'Mind you, I've told Phil that he's not allowed to make Richard a bigger basket'."

Over the autumn months, Pam spent a lot of time with Annabelle, mostly in the evenings. The fact that she went to a different school in Andover meant they saw less of each other than they would have liked, plus she had to help her nan, Mrs Piggin, because her feet were giving her trouble since she became insulin dependent with diabetes.

What she loved to do, when spending time with Annabelle, was to play the game of Bombardo. That year she was determined to put the game on her Christmas list. Both girls were disappointed when evenings drew to a close. They didn't have space for another camp bed in the front room.

"After the war, you can sleep together again; you'll have lots to giggle about then, won't you?" Alberto comforted.

Clutching at straws in the hope of reducing Pam's responsibilities, Annabelle said, "But your nan was alright to do the teas at the dance the other night."

"No she wasn't. She should give it up, but she keeps arguing that she must do her best for Enham because they helped her husband after his wounding in the First World War."

Even at Christmas, Pam had to spend a lot of time in her nan's house because her mum and all her mum's sisters came to spend the holiday with Mrs Piggin, and it gave Pam a chance to get to know her many cousins.

On Christmas day 1941, Alberto and Alice hosted the Geoghegan family for a Christmas party in their home. They spent the evening eating, drinking and singing their hearts out because they had lived through another year of war and the bombing had stopped. The V for Victory sign became a form of salute, although sometimes drunkenly performed the other way round, and at midnight, after the usual big circle to sing Auld Lang Syne, Mr Geoghegan led the singing with, *There'll Always be an England.*

TGA: *(I'm not doing very well in looking after my charge. Poor Annabelle. What she wants more than anything in the world is an education, but what with the war and her sick mother, all the odds are against her. I watched her work and study and practise all the way through her music book and now she can fluently play every piece. If any child deserved an education it is this one.)*

Chapter 14

More Trouble for Andre

Not knowing what to do with themselves, Andre, Jerry and a group of village boys, all about ten years old, were wandering around Ripley Square one evening and loitered outside the fire station.

"I want to be a fireman when I grow up," said one of the boys.

"We could all be firemen now if we could get inside. They keep their uniforms in the back room."

"Getting in is easy," said another. "A window is always open at the back to stop the uniforms from getting musty, so we could 'piggy-back' one of us in and he could unlock the back door."

No sooner said than done. They dressed themselves up and exited the building as dusk fell. The next day, with smiles all over their faces and very proud of themselves, they trundled into school wearing helmets, belts and badges, with their own trouser pockets full of brass buttons that they'd cut off the uniform jackets, which were too big for them. True to form, they were carrying the axes, which were normally used by firemen to assist in rescues.

Very soon the village bobby was on the scene. Each boy was known to him by name. Every one of them was caned in front of the class and had to stay after school to sew the buttons back on the uniforms. They also had to do good deeds around the village for people who were having difficulty in managing their home because their menfolk were away at war.

That village bobby was soon on the doorstep of the Holt family.

"I'd like to talk to Andre please."

Directing the two of them up to Andre's room, the policeman said to Mrs Holt, "Not this time, thank you. What I have to say to Andre affects you all."

Addressing Andre, the policeman said, "Well, tut, tut, tut," shaking his head. "The last time we met, you and I did a deal. Do you remember?"

Nodding his head, Andre said bleakly, "Yes, sir."

"And we shook hands on it?"

"We did, but I forgot. I'm sorry, sir. I was having fun with the boys and it made me forget, but I know what you're going to say to me. You're going to move me somewhere else." He started to cry.

Looking at Mrs Holt, the bobby said, "The boy's pre-empted me. I shall be moving him. It's got nothing to do with you or your family, but before he gets much older this boy's got to learn right from wrong and to honour his promises. I know he's got a good side and I don't want him to turn out being a no-gooder."

Jerry was soon by Andre's side trying to give him comfort as Mrs Holt said, "But he's paying his punishment exactly the same as the other boys."

"Ah yes, but the other boys haven't got Andre's history."

"Seems a bit harsh to me. He's lived with us a number of weeks now and he's a very well behaved little boy with good manners."

Breaking into a laugh she couldn't control, she spluttered to the policeman, "Well you have to admit that what they did was so funny, wasn't it?" Still giggling, she continued, "Obviously stealing wasn't their intention. Seems to me the police are making a mountain out of a molehill. Such a shame because the whole village has had a good laugh; a welcome good laugh in the light of all the bombing and war bulletins."

"Nevertheless Ma'am, the law is the law."

TGA: *(How can he hold a ten-year-old boy to a deal? If only he knew Andre's background as well as I do, he'd surely re-think.)*

Andre's good deed was to do digging and other work in the garden for a nice lady, Mrs Pilkington, who lived in Send, the same village where he lived. Her husband was away at war and she had a little toddler daughter named Esther. That lady was kind to Andre, so he continued to help her in the garden long after his punishment was served.

Before Andre was moved to a new placement, he asked Mrs Holt if he could write a letter to Dorothy at Gipsy Hill.

"She's my stepbrother's girlfriend and my sister Elsa lives with her."

When the letter was written, Mrs Holt suggested that Andre write her address on the back of the envelope, just in case Dorothy had been bombed out of her home.

Andre's next placement was with a Mrs Carter; her previous evacuee fretted so much for his home that he was eventually returned to his parents. She already knew about the mischievous boy, Andre Kliskey, and didn't want to take him, but accommodating evacuees was a government order.

Andre settled in and was behaving himself. Mrs Carter looked after his physical needs, such as food and clean laundry etc., but spent minimal time talking to him, so he never felt welcome. The move away from the Holts' home where he was very happy began to affect him deeply and a rebellious spirit made him decide to become a loner, so he could no longer be influenced into more mischief.

When not in school, he went to his old hidey-hole high up in the tree that overlooked the weir on the River Wey, which held a fascination for him. There were punts on the canal, but no one was there to charge so he enjoyed many a short trip in one. In fact, this was a minor crime, but Andre didn't know that and luckily never got caught.

TGA: *(For a young lad with an enquiring mind, there were so many pitfalls awaiting him around every corner.)*

Much more serious was the day he could not stop himself from operating the weir, which he'd watched the lock keeper do on many occasions. Immediately, he was down the tree and attempted to operate the weir, but the pressure of the water was too great for him and it shot the lock boards out of their containment. What hadn't occurred to him was that the lock keeper was physically much stronger than he was. Try as he might, he couldn't get the lock boards down again and the water quickly started flowing into and flooding the fields. Andre fled for his life and luckily escaped without getting his socks or clothes wet.

The village bobby was soon making enquiries in Send and in Ripley. Eventually, he called on Mrs Carter where he discovered Andre's clothing was dry, so the bobby could find no evidence against him. On enquiring what he was doing at the appropriate time, Andre said he was climbing trees, which was true. On inspection of his clothing, smudges of lichen were found, in keeping with tree climbing!

Excitement came into Andre's life with The Battle of Britain dogfights between British and German aeroplanes; the perfect scenario for young boys who had little sense of fear. Because of blacked-out windows, the viewing had to be done from outside. This he liked to do with Mrs Pilkington when Esther was tucked up safely in bed. Andre preferred the sound of the British Hurricanes and Spitfires, not only because they were English, but the droning sound of the German Messerschmitt's was very threatening.

While working in Mrs Pilkington's front garden one afternoon, Andre was surprised to see his friend, Jerry Holt, who looked hot from running.

"Can you come and see Mum, Andre? She wants to see you."

"What for?"

"She wouldn't tell me, but she said it is very important and she wants to tell you herself."

After squaring with Mrs Pilkington, the boys ran back together. Suddenly remembering, Andre said with great excitement. "Ooh, I expect she's had a reply from Dorothy and my sister."

Getting back to Mrs Holt's familiar cosy room with the piano in the corner brought tears to Andre's eyes. She gave Andre a loving hug as he asked if she'd got a reply to his letter.

"Sit down, Andre," she invited, pulling out a chair for him as she knelt by his side at the table. "The answer is going to shock you, I'm afraid."

She showed him the unopened letter. It had a note written on the back. 'Your letter could not be delivered. The addressee has been evacuated to Ireland'.

"So, where's my sister?" he sobbed. "And what about my stepbrother? He loves me. He'll **never** find me now." The boy's heart was breaking. "Nothing ever, ever, ever goes right for me. Why did my mum have to die when I was born?"

"I wish I knew the answer, Andre," comforted Mrs Holt as she cuddled him.

She then asked Jerry to run a flannel under the tap and wring it out so she could put it across Andre's forehead.

"Just cry it all out, dear. You've been badly shocked by this news and I think you should stay with us for the night."

They moved to the settee so he could sit on her lap and she rocked him in her arms.

"Jerry, I want you to do two things for me. First, go to Mrs Pilkington and tell her Andre won't be able to do any more gardening today and then go to Mrs Carter and ask if she minds if Andre sleeps at our home tonight."

"Ooh, that's good, Mum. I hope she'll let him stay."

"Andre, you're shaking now. I think it's the state of shock and distress you're going through, so I'm going to make you a little drink. I'm only going to leave you alone on the settee while I make it. I'll sing softly while I'm in the scullery so you can still hear me. I won't be a minute."

While softly singing *Always,* she dissolved a teaspoon of brandy and two teaspoons of sugar in a cup with boiling water and then added some cold water.

"OK, Andre, I wasn't too long was I?"

Mrs Holt manoeuvred herself until Andre was comfortably laying on her lap again with his head resting on a cushion on the arm of the sofa. She put the cup to his lips, which was no easy task because he was trembling so much.

"Try to sip this, Andre; it will do you good."

After a few sips, although still choked with tears, he whispered, "Grandma cuddled me once."

Before long, he was fast asleep in her arms.

They were still in that position when Jerry returned.

"Mrs Pilkington was sad about Andre and sent him this curly stick of barley sugar. She said the sweetness would do him good and Mrs Carter didn't mind at all. She asked if we'd let her know tomorrow how long he would be staying in case the bobby called to check on him."

When Connie and Vera came in from play, Mrs Holt asked them to make some cucumber sandwiches for tea. The family all tucked into a mountain of them, with a nice ripe tomato each, while Andre was asleep on their mother's lap.

TGA: *(My charge must have been exhausted as well as broken-hearted. He slept soundly through all the noisy, excited fun of healthy children playing Snap with the playing cards.)*

Maybe it was the noisiness of the children that eventually disturbed Andre, but his mood did not match theirs. Although in a daze, he was aware that his surroundings were wrong. Starting to move off Mrs Holt's lap, he said, "I've got to go back to Mrs Carter's house quickly. She'll be cross with me and so will the policeman."

"You're doing nothing of the sort, Andre." Lifting him back onto her lap, Mrs Holt reassured him. "Mrs Carter knows you're staying with us tonight and if the bobby finds out, she'll send him here and I'll tell him how unwell you've been."

The boy had no fight left in him as he responded, "I want to go to the lavvy."

In the morning, despite the food rationing when eggs were usually shared by scrambling, Mrs Holt took a boiled egg and toast soldiers up to Andre and fed him as he lay in his bed. She then gave him a full glass of milk, which he sipped as she told him she had asked the doctor to call.

"I think I'm alright now, thank you, Mrs Holt. I really want to stay with you, but the bobby banned me, so I'd better get back to Mrs Carter."

"Andre, that's the very reason why I want the doctor to come. I shall show him your letter returned from your family and tell him how shocked you've been and that I think you need to be living where you're happy. Perhaps then we'll be able to convince the bobby."

Those words brought a brief smile to Andre before he replied dismally, "but the bobby won't break the law."

"Well, I'm hoping the doctor will put up a big fight for your health, if nothing else."

Mrs Holt was overjoyed that the village doctor agreed with her as he said, "We must do our utmost to keep these evacuees happy while away from their homes. You are quite right to keep him here. Keep him indoors for a few days; make sure he's eating and drinking, and then let him run free with your children. The fresh air will do him good."

"Thank you so much, Doctor, and will you let our bobby know?"

"Of course, and don't hesitate to call me again if the boy is still troubled."

Soon after tea that day, the bobby called. You could see Andre recoil into himself as he was approached.

"It's alright, Andre, there's no need to be afraid of me." He ruffled the boy's hair in a friendly manner. "The doctor's been to see me and said that you've now lost connection with the members of your family who care about you."

Andre nodded, but did not say one word.

"That's tough luck, kid. You've certainly had your bloomin' share of that, haven't you? Anyway, I'm happy to tell you that with the doctor's report and my senior's approval, I've been to see Mrs

Carter and told her that you won't be going back to her to live."

Andre was wide-eyed, but still speechless.

"And I am happy to tell you that you can stay here and live with the Holt family."

Immediately, the atmosphere in the room changed from one of gloom to one of great joy. The Holt family were hugging Andre, the policeman and each other.

When Andre eventually found his voice again he asked the Bobby, "But what about the law?

"This time, son, the law's on your side."

"Thank you, sir, thank you."

After a few days, when Mrs Holt thought Andre was ready to go out to play, the first thing he did was to go and thank Mrs Pilkington for the stick of barley sugar.

"Oh, Andre, that's the least I could do dear." She gave him a hug and a peck on the cheek. "Esther and I have missed you, so you must ask Mrs Holt if you can come and spend the day with us sometimes."

"I'd like to do that, Mrs Pilkington. Thank you."

He stayed a while playing 'catch' with Esther using her soft homemade woollen ball and then stacking her building bricks before saying, "I'd better go back now as this is my first outing."

"I think that's quite right, Andre. You're a very sensible boy. Here you are; you suck this as you go home. It'll help give you energy."

"Oooh, another stick of barley sugar, thank you."

For the first time since being taken away from Mr and Mrs Williams in Brighton, Andre felt a sense of contentment and security.

TGA: *(Can this be a turning point in Andre's life? I'm thrilled, and I am sure you are too, that he is now living with a family where he is happy.)*

Although Andre was thrilled to the core to be back living with the Holt family, who had a jolly sing-along around the piano nearly every night, his private thoughts were always sadly coloured by the fact that he'd lost touch with Ron and Dorothy and his sister, Elsa. What the war dealt them next puzzled him as to why children were ever evacuated.

Not only did they get dogfights in their area, they were also being bombed. The Germans were targeting various aircraft production sites in Great Britain. One such site was the Vickers Armstrong factory in Weybridge, not far from Send and Ripley, where the Vickers Wellington, the Vickers Warwick as well as Hawker Hurricanes were manufactured.

The British were very protective of their aircraft production sites because fighting in the skies was one aspect of war in which they were starting to excel. With this in mind, they attempted to camouflage those areas with such decoys as dummy haystacks, canvas lorries and quick growing trees near the factory. Also the east-west runway was grassed and unlit.

Typical of most children living through the bombing in WW2, girls would sit indoors hushed and scared, longing for the bombing to stop, while boys would be outside trying to see something of the 'spectacle'. That description was very apt when search lights were criss-crossing the skies trying to spotlight German planes. When successful, that made the targets more visible for our anti-aircraft fire operators in their endeavour to attack the bombers before they dropped their bombs. Andre always stuck his fingers in his ears to protect them from the extremely loud noise of the anti-aircraft fire.

Despite the government's camouflage tactics, the Vickers Armstrong factory at Weybridge was eventually bombed by the Luftwaffe on 4th September 1940 and was extensively damaged. Several people lost their lives and hundreds were injured. The bombing was so close to Send that even Andre and Jerry felt scared to death, but once the all clear siren was heard, they were immediately on their bikes and racing along lanes to get to the bomb site to see the destruction.

On one raid, Andre watched German aircraft flying across the sky to drop their bombs and then return by the same route. As they turned to fly home, three Spitfires flew in from out of nowhere and shot German planes down. Andre and Jerry became so excited that once again they were on their bikes to get to the scene to collect shrapnel and aeroplane glass and find pilots. The village bobby rushed to the scene also, armed with a baseball bat to apprehend any pilots who were alive.

A short while later, the crash spectators witnessed a single German plane, guarded by a

Spitfire on each side, come flying back over the scene. The Spitfires were very close to the German plane, their objective being to force it down intact and hopefully take a live German prisoner-of-war. The plane did not come down in that particular field, but villagers read later in the local press that the mission had been successful.

Andre found Mrs Pilkington very distressed next time he visited her. Her parents, who lived near to Weybridge, had been injured in the Vickers Armstrong bombing raids and had been moved to temporary accommodation because of their damaged home.

"Can't they come and stay with you?"

"I'm afraid they're stick-in-the-muds and want to stay in their own area amongst their friends. I can understand that and it's for the best really. I've only got my bedroom and a box room upstairs and Esther's just got settled into that. If they decided to come to me they'd have to sleep in the living room and they certainly wouldn't want that. I can cycle to see them every other day and I can take Esther in her chair on the back of my bike, but it's not safe for her there with all the rubble around, so I just sit here being worried sick."

"I want to help you, Mrs Pilkington. I could cycle with you and play with Esther if that would help and if Mrs Holt would allow me."

"Andre, you're such a kind boy. Esther is very happy with you, and I've got a pushchair at my parents' house, as long as it isn't damaged. You could take her out for walks; she loves being pushed and sometimes falls asleep."

"Shall I run back to Mrs Holt and ask what she thinks?"

"OK. See if we can work something out. Mums and dads are very precious people you know."

Smiling sceptically, Andre nodded his agreement with the maturity of a much older person.

Mrs Holt thought it was wonderful that Andre wanted to help Mrs Pilkington and approved of his wish.

"We've got plenty of children in the village who are helping the farmers with the potato picking, so you go ahead and arrange things with Mrs Pilkington."

"What about the bobby? Will he tell me off?"

"Andre, you've got to stop worrying about him. He told you last time, the law is on your side now, and he'll be pleased you're trying to help Mrs Pilkington. He knows how you've continued to help with her gardening. Run and tell her it's OK with me and you can go with her whenever she wants. You'll probably learn more there than missing your half days' schooling sometimes."

The following day, the three of them set off for Weybridge. They found Mrs Pilkington's parents, Mr and Mrs Fowler, sitting in armchairs with a cup of tea in front of them in the old school. Due to these exceptional circumstances, summer holidays had been extended.

Andre felt warm inside from the affectionate greetings they had for one another. Mrs Pilkington cried, as she said, "Well, whatever you've got to put up with, thank goodness you' re still alive."

They were very pleased to see Esther again and took turns at having her on their laps. Mr Fowler said to her, "Well young lady, I'm a bit surprised you've got a boyfriend at your tender age," as he winked at Andre.

As Esther was becoming fidgety, the school teachers, who were helping out in the old school, found a pushchair in the store room and Andre took her out for a walk.

On returning home at the end of the day, Andre was tired and downcast.

"Didn't you have a very good day, Andre?"

Yes, it was good. I like helping people, but…."

"But what?"

"Am I allowed to swear?"

"If you've got something on your chest, it's better to let it out," said Mrs Holt kindly."

"Well, I'm miserable, miserable, miserable!" There was a long pause, as though he'd forgotten what he wanted to say. "I hate this bloody-bloody war. People are suffering and being killed and all that comes out of it is soddin' misery!"

Chapter 15

Enham Continues Coping with WW2

Early in 1942, George Guest introduced a little light relief from war news for the Enham disabled men. He arranged snooker tournaments between them and an Army team at the garrison location of Tidworth. He organised transport to take them and their expertise was at least on a par with that of the boys in khaki.

Alberto sat next to Arthur Brooks on the journey to Tidworth, where he learned about Arthur's citation from his commanding officer. Arthur invited Alberto to visit him and see the actual citation, which was framed and hanging on the wall of his home, Princess Mary Cottage, The Crescent. I can tell you right now exactly what it says, word for word. I was out there, I earned it, was very proud of myself and even more proud of my commanding officer for recognising me.

Alberto could sense the man's pride in his achievement and said, "Go on; tell me more Arthur. I'm very interested."

(QUOTE)

32 Division
British Expeditionary Force,
No 22258 Private A.J. Brooks,
Dorset Regiment.

Your commanding officer and brigade commander have informed me that you distinguished yourself in the field on the 11th August 1918.

I congratulate you upon your performance and thank you for the credit you have brought to the Division.

O.S. Lambert

Major-General Commanding, 32nd Division.

During the attack on Damery on 11th August 1918, PTE Brooks took charge of his platoon when all the NCOs in it had become casualties, and led them forward under heavy fire.

(UNQUOTE)

Before Alberto could pay a visit to Mr Brooks' home, he received a telephone call from his family in London. In 1942, not many families had a phone at home, but Auntie Dolly's husband was a bookies' runner for a bookmaking company in Andover and for that reason they provided him with a telephone. It was a candlestick telephone with the number 'Andover (telephone exchange) 2858', so he could phone through to them the bets that the Enham villagers made. All the phone numbers were made up of four digits.

The candlestick phone was about twelve inches high with the speaker section at the top. On the left, just below that speaker, was a jutting 'arm', from which an ear piece dangled, and on the base of the phone was a round dial. The dial was a metal ring with holes in it through which you could see the numbers 9, 8, 7, 6, 5, 4, 3, 2, 1, 0. At the zero point, the finger could turn no more. As an example, if you wanted to dial the telephone number 'Andover 7427', you would put the ear piece to your ear and put your finger into the 7 hole, turn it to 0 and release and so on with the remaining numbers. You then heard the ringing tone and waited to hear either the voice of the person being called, or an engaged tone.

As with everything else, Auntie Dolly was very kind to everyone in the Aless family about the telephone. She said that as Alberto's family all lived away in London, he could pass on her phone number for use in emergencies. If she got a call for them, she would knock on the chimney wall between their semi-detached houses and one of them would go round to take it.

The call in question came on 17 February 1942, when Alberto's brother Vincenzo, one of the twins, gave him the terrible news that Gino, their father, had died. After explaining the circumstances to his work manager, Alberto hot-footed it to his family home at 18 Workhouse Hill.

Jane and Richard welcomed him and explained that Jane had found him dead in his bed the previous morning. In an effort to ease Alberto's shock and obvious distress, Jane said, "You know, it truly is a happy release, Alberto," as they hugged. "All he's done since you were last here is sit by Mama's grave, so now we rejoice that he's where he wants to be."

"How I wish I had the belief that you have, Jane. At times like this, it must make life easier to bear. All I can do now is get back to the home that neither my mother or father saw. I'll come back for his funeral when we know the date."

Arriving late back home, Alberto was greeted by Alice with one of the friends she'd made in Enham, Mrs Basting. She came round nearly every evening after Annabelle and Al were tucked up in bed. She liked to have the company of her friends for the compulsive necessity of listening to the late night propaganda programmes of William Joyce, under his broadcasting name of Lord Haw-Haw.

Mrs Basting had already lost three of her children. Her eldest son, Mons, in WW1, her second child, Mary, who had been crippled at birth, bedridden and nursed by her mother all her life, and her fourth son, Peter, who had been killed on the road in Enham a few years back. Now she was left with two sons only; Leslie who was in the Royal Air Force and had been reported missing and her youngest son, John, who was too young to go to war.

Thus it was that on most nights Mrs Basting, Alice and Alberto would sit as quiet as mice, listening intently to the upper class English speaking voice of Lord Haw-Haw, saying "Germany calling, Germany calling, Germany calling," while drinking hot Camp coffee to warm their chilled souls. Unbeknown to her parents, there was always a fourth listener sitting on the bottom stair the other side of the living room door. Annabelle never slept very well through all the years of the war.

The listening time was considered well spent, even though they'd had to sit through Haw-Haw's threatening comments such as, "Herr Hitler has not forgotten sleepy old Andover."

The prize of enduring so many such hours came when they heard the name, "Leslie Basting" loud and clear filling the room. That night, Leslie was one of the six British POWs mentioned. Leslie Basting was still alive! The aura in that room changed from the deathly hush that had prevailed to one of indescribable joy.

The wireless was switched off immediately, way before it was time for the inevitable "Heil Hitler." Together, the three of them cried with relief at the fact that Leslie was not dead. In way of celebration at the good news, Alberto put a tot of whisky into three fresh cups of Camp coffee, before seeing Mrs Basting home.

Hearing all the happy celebrations, Annabelle very quickly got herself back into bed before her dad and Mrs Basting left by the front door. The front door was opposite the stairs where she had been sitting.

Following the joy of that evening, it was a bit of a shock for Alberto to see Alice's serious face when he came in for dinner next day.

"Why the gloom, my lovely?"

"I had a visitor this morning."

"Who the hell was he, dare I ask?"

"It was a she, actually. That nice Mrs Crabbe with the big family who lives in Anton Lane. She came to remind me that it's the 11 plus exams at Smannell School this week, and that she could arrange, through the Enham Women's Institute, for an adult to accompany me all day if I'm unwell, so that Annabelle can go to school and sit the exam."

"Well, that was really nice of her. What did you say?"

"I thanked her, of course, but said I'd discuss it with you. Annabelle is a lovely, natural girl and those grammar school children all end up swanking. I'd hate her to be like that. Anyway, as things are, she could knock spots off every other girl in this village putting hot dinners on plates. She's doing brilliantly with her piano playing, can grow vegetables and practically run a home on her own. What more could she learn at any grammar school?"

"I can see your point, my lovely. Grammar school is an unknown for the likes of us. Shall we just play it by ear?" he suggested, more as a statement rather than a question.

Still looking troubled, Alice replied, "I suppose so," which led to a tear as she whispered, "I do wish I was healthy, like the other mums. She's always been desperate to learn."

Consoling his wife, Alberto pulled her into his arms and whispered, "You forgot, she can tap dance too!"

Next day, in contrast, Alberto found Alice having a little laugh to herself when he came home for dinner. She'd just heard on the wireless that more severe clothes' rationing was to be introduced.

"Let's hear the joke, then?"

"The joke is that you're going to have to wear three-quarter length trousers in future."

"What?????"

"We've got a new lot of clothing ration limits to face. The longest inside leg measurement anyone's allowed to have from now on is 19 inches and…guess what? No turn-ups allowed! You'll have to be content with trousers that have rowed with your socks. How's that for you Mr Daddy Long Legs?"

"You little minx, Alice Aless. You're laughing at me, aren't you? That wicked sense of humour of yours made me fall in love with you a long time ago, along with those lovely high cheek-bones. I ought to pull those bloomers down and smack your bottom young lady," he laughed. So, what other restrictions are they putting upon us? I suppose we've got to use shirt tails for hankies."

"That's a good idea, or you can give up a half a clothing coupon for one. What else was there? As far as I can remember, a man's suit can have no more than three pockets and only three buttons. A new dress would take 11 coupons and pyjamas, 8."

"Ah well, we can easily do without those," Alberto quipped, with a wink.

"Not for me, Alberto! For the children! Anyway, you can read about it all for yourself in tomorrow's newspaper."

"Sorry, Alice. I just can't resist being saucy around you. I'll buy you a nice glass of stout at your Glamour Girls' Club in the Insty, (Institute) tomorrow night. It's for sure you'll be the most glamorous girl there."

"Alberto, you're still the most romantic man in the world to me." Alice pecked him on the cheek.

"And with you I always will be."

Ever since women had started doing war work and had been allowed into the meeting room in the Insty to have a drink, village women had met there every Friday night. They'd formed themselves into a club and sat knitting items such as socks, balaclavas, scarves, gloves and mittens etc. or sewing kettle or iron holders to sell locally in support of forces serving overseas. For them it was not a chore. The Glamour Girl Club was a very friendly, productive group who always enjoyed a sing-along as they worked.

About that time, village talk was revolving around the hardships of rationing. Customers in the Village Stores were all highly amused when Rita Rose was at the counter questioning Mr Willoughby, the elderly proprietor, about what sweets she could buy and how many coupons she would have to give up. He put on his horn-rimmed glasses to enable him to assist, but being new to the system himself, he was becoming fraught and by the time the child had made her purchase, he totally forgot to take her sweet coupons! Needless to say, she made a hasty exit as the remaining customers tittered.

By that time of the year, Alberto was up to his eyes in rehearsals for the summer show. Lots of revue items were rehearsed in his living room, with Alice and Annabelle being tea ladies. Someone was always available to play Annabelle's out-of-tune piano, which offended many ears, but accepted that they were living in a 'make do and mend' era after all.

Saturday dinnertime brought with it great excitement. George Bright, the village handyman, regularly did his rounds in his big blue van on Saturdays. He always managed to call at the Aless's just as they were finishing their weekly ritual dinner of chipolata sausages, mash and baked beans.

"My God, it always smells good in this house," George greeted, rubbing his hands together in a business-like fashion.

His normal business was to deliver paraffin oil and methylated spirits for use with Primus and Valour Stoves; swap re-charged accumulators for wirelesses, (for which he charged 6 pence delivered,) sell bicycle puncture sets and tyre pumps, or return bicycles that had been left in his shop for repair etc. On his van he carried a multitude of hardware goods such as nails, screws and tools, and had built up a sizable and essential village business. You were always welcome to browse his shop when open, which had the familiar smell of a hardware store.

After dealing with all the usual business, George said to Alice, "I've got your new acquisition in the van. Is it convenient to deliver it now?"

"Already? My goodness; yes please."

He carried the big cardboard box in through the scullery door. It contained a radio.

"You'll have no need for accumulators anymore!"

When George had finished setting it up on the small wooden polished table where the wireless has stood, he plugged the radio into the power socket. Turning a knob, he showed Alice and Alberto how to find two short wave programmes as well as the medium wave and the long wave along a straight dial, while the children watched.

"How can it work without accumulators?" asked Al.

"Because it's plugged into the electricity, which does a better and more permanent job than the accumulators. This one's called a radio, because of course it is no longer wire-less. Look, you can see the wire cable attached to the electric plug here," winked George. "You are now the proud owners of a modern radio and will be billed on your monthly Central Electricity Grid invoice for power used, which will be minimal."

The new radio often had to be switched off because of rehearsals indoors for the summer show. Everyone was excited because that year five village boys were going to act out a short sketch, which was performed on national stages by Will Hay, a popular comedian of the 1920s.

The first half of the show was a revue with individual singing and comic turns, which was received with great enthusiasm in accordance with usual standards.

The second half included *THE FOURTH FORM AT ST. MICHAEL'S - THE NEW BOY.* Script as follows:

Village Boys

HEADMASTER: Al Alessandro

DEAF OLD MAN, Dressed as schoolboy: Doug Saunders

NEW BOY, Watt: Kenny Wood

Shared parts at different venues: Maurice Waite

Shared parts at different venues: Jackie Greener

Stand-in who knew all the parts: Clive Broughton

(QUOTE)

Street scene. Boy enters from left, crosses stage as though going down a street, meets a man coming the other way. As they pass, the headmaster, in mufti, calls him back.

HEADMASTER: Hey boy…where are you going?

BOY: I'm going to school.

HEADMASTER: Bit late aren't you? You should have been there half an hour ago.

BOY: I haven't found it yet.

HEADMASTER: Found what?

BOY: The school.

HEADMASTER: What, has someone moved it?

BOY: I've never been there before.

HEADMASTER: A boy of your age never been to school before…

BOY: Not this one.

HEADMASTER: Which one?

BOY: The one I'm going to.

HEADMASTER: Which one are you going to?

BOY: St. Michael's.

HEADMASTER: Oh, that's a good school. You'll have a good time there.

BOY: I don't think I shall.

HEADMASTER: Oh? Why not?

BOY: The headmaster's a mingy old beast.

HEADMASTER: (SNIFFS): Who said so?

BOY: One of the boys told me.

HEADMASTER: One of which boys?

BOY: St. Michael's boys. Wait till I get there. He'd better not come any funny stuff with me.

HEADMASTER: What do you mean by funny stuff?

BOY: Rough stuff. He'd better not bully me.

HEADMASTER: Why not?

BOY: I'll spread him all over school. If he knew what's in store for him, he'd skedaddle.

HEADMASTER: What?

BOY: Vamoose.

HEADMASTER: If you're talking slang, I don't understand you.

BOY: Clear off.

HEADMASTER: Oh bunk.

BOY: I'll show him how many beans make five.

HEADMASTER: Why, doesn't he know?

BOY: Whether he knows or not, I'll show him.

HEADMASTER: (SNIFFS): I'm going that way. I'll walk along with you.

LIGHTS DIM AND GO UP ON SCHOOLROOM, DESK, CHAIRS, BLACKBOARD AND EASEL. HEADMASTER ENTERS, TAKES OFF HIS COAT, PUTS ON GOWN AND MORTARBOARD.

HEADMASTER: Welcome to St. Michaels. I'm the mingy old beast. (WALLOPS THE NEW BOY WITH HIS HAND. HE FALLS OFF CHAIR.) So, you're going to spread him all over the school. (WALLOPS HIM AGAIN) Now you're here, we'll have your name.

BOY: Tom.

HEADMASTER: I suppose your full name is Thomas.

BOY: My name is Tom; T-O-M.

HEADMASTER: Oh, What's your second name?

BOY: Yes.

HEADMASTER: Yes, What?

BOY: That's right.

HEADMASTER: What's right?

BOY: That's right.

HEADMASTER: Now don't start that all over again. What's your second name?

BOY: Yes, Watt; that's my name.

AN OLD MAN ENTERS LEFT, DODDERING. SITS ON A STOOL.

OLD MAN: I'm 'ere.

HEADMASTER GLANCES VAGUELY TOWARDS HIM, TURNS TO BOY, DOES A DOUBLE-TAKE.

HEADMASTER TO BOY: Does this belong to you?

BOY: Nothing to do with me.

OLD MAN: I've come to school.

HEADMASTER: (DISDAINFULLY): You want the infants. Where have you been all year?

OLD MAN: Been working on the railway.

HEADMASTER: Were you a sleeper?

OLD MAN: I was tapping wheels.

HEADMASTER: Slapping what?

OLD MAN: No, tapping wheels with an 'ammer.

HEADMASTER: Emma? Who's she?

OLD MAN: Hammer.

HEADMASTER: Oh, you've been working on the railway tapping wheels.

OLD MAN: Yes, for seventy-five years.

HEADMASTER: Been on tap all that time, have you? (TURNS TO BOY) I've seen them do that. (TO OLD MAN) Why do you tap wheels?

OLD MAN: Er? Oh dear, I don't know.

HEADMASTER: (TO BOY) Would you believe it? He doesn't know why.

BOY: Well, do you know why?

HEADMASTER: Of course I do – to see if they're cracked.

BOY: Oh no, they don't. It's to see if they're sound.

HEADMASTER (SNIFFS): Oh, do they?

(WALLOPS BOY) What's your name?

OLD MAN: Jimmy Harbottle.

HEADMASTER: Bluebottle? Where do you live?

OLD MAN: That's right.

HEADMASTER: Where?

OLD MAN: Yes.

HEADMASTER: What do you mean, 'yes'? Where do you live?

OLD MAN: Ware, That's in Hertfordshire.

HEADMASTER: Where in Hertfordshire?

OLD MAN: On the left.

HEADMASTER: Going in or coming out? I think we'll take Scripture. What are the chief mountain ranges of the world?

BOY: What have mountains got to do with it?

HEADMASTER: You've heard of Mount Ararat, haven't you?

OLD MAN: I have.

HEADMASTER: You would. You ought to know who made it.

OLD MAN: I like it.

HEADMASTER: Like what?

OLD MAN: Arrowroot.

HEADMASTER: Arrowroot isn't a mountain.

BOY: Then what is it?

HEADMASTER: It's a sort of...well, it's like celery.

BOY: What is?

OLD MAN: Rhubarb.

HEADMASTER: Who's talking about rhubarb? I never mentioned rhubarb.

BOY: That reminds me. At my last school the teacher was telling us about Noah.

HEADMASTER: Noah what?

BOY: Noahing (gnawing), nothing. But not what mice do.

HEADMASTER: Then why mention it?

BOY: I've got to.

OLD MAN: I've got three.

HEADMASTER: Three what?

OLD MAN: Three mice.

HEADMASTER: You keep out of this. Let's get this straight. You say your teacher was telling you about Noah, not what mice do, you've got two, he's got three. Where in heaven's sake are we?

HE THROWS DOWN HIS MORTAR BOARD IN DISGUST. THE OLD MAN BENDS TO PICK IT UP.

HEADMASTER: Not you. You'd never get back up. Where were we?

BOY: I'm talking about the fellow who built the ark.

HEADMASTER: You mean Noah.

BOY: Yes, well, who was his wife?

HEADMASTER: Who was Noah's wife?

BOY: Noah's wife.

OLD MAN: I know.

HEADMASTER: You ought to. You tell him.

OLD MAN: Joan of Arc.

HEADMASTER: Idiot…that's Lot's wife.

THE HEADMASTER GOES TO THE BLACKBOARD, STARTS WIPING IT CLEAN. BOY TAKES A PIN FROM HIS JACKET, BENDS IT AND PUTS IT ON THE HEADMASTER'S CHAIR. HEADMASTER GOES TO SIT DOWN; RISES.

HEADMASTER: Remember. Always do unto others as others do unto you.

HE SITS, JUMPS UP. WHACK, WHACK, WHACK.

CURTAIN COMES DOWN ON BOY AND OLD MAN BEING WALLOPED.

(UNQUOTE)

The sketch was a rip-roaring success and brought half-a-dozen curtain calls. That response was well deserved as the boys were slick and quick with their delivery. What's more, the sketch was put on twice more in the Insty on different occasions, once in Preston Village Hall, once in

329

Whitchurch, once in Hurstbourne Tarrant and all local villages, as well as once at the Senior Boys' School in Andover. It was also lined up to be performed before a talent scout in London, but conscription of some of the organisers concerned put a stop to that excitement.

Doug Saunders had the ominous task of following that superb sketch with an individual performance of *The Wandering Vagabond.*

1942 saw the end of the family's annual summer trips to London. After their near miss when the Alcazar Theatre was bombed the night after Alice and Alberto and children were in it, Mrs Howitz preferred that the family stayed more safely in their own home. Alberto agreed with this, knowing full well that Mrs Howitz would visit them, giving Alice the opportunity to see her mother. Things had changed for him now that he had lost his own parents.

Feeling settled about that decision, Alice and Alberto had a fearful shock when Annabelle who, after tea had all been cleared away, had been playing two-ball on the Insty veranda with her friends, ran straight into the communal bedroom in the front room, slamming the front door behind her and crying broken-heartedly.

Quickly by her bedside and hovering over her as she lay on top of her patchwork eiderdown, Alberto asked gently, "Tell old Dad what's the matter, sweetheart. Who's upset you?"

Alice was soon beside him.

"Annabelle, it's so out of character for you to slam doors. Whatever's the matter darling?"

TGA: (*It was pitiful to see these two caring parents tearing their hearts out over Annabelle's distress.*)

Annabelle wouldn't speak and Alberto called to Al to bring in a cold wet flannel to soothe her hot, flushed cheeks. The tension and suspense of the drama started to aggravate Alice's heart condition.

"Get on your bed my lovely; this is too much for you," Alberto urged.

Alberto was torn between the two of them, but felt compelled to stay by Annabelle's side. He instructed Al to lay with his mother to get her resting on the bed.

After Alice's heart episode, Annabelle sobbed more and more and started to panic.

"I don't want Mummy to die. I'm sorry, Daddy. I'm sorry, sorry, sorry." She turned on her bed to face the wall.

"Mummy's not going to die, Annabelle. She's resting now; she's got her tablets and the doctor is just up the back garden path. Al is with her, but she's worried sick about you. Now you tell Dad what's upset you and maybe then we'll be able to calm both of you down."

Alberto then whispered, "Come on, Moosh. You can tell your old dad, can't you?" He kissed the back of her head.

With her mother's life in danger, she volunteered, "Pat's just told me that the 11 plus exams were held when I wasn't at school, so I won't stand a chance of getting to the grammar school now. I really wanted to go. They teach French there and a lot of other things."

"Does that matter so much to you, sweetie?"

"It did. Or I thought it did. There's so much to learn and I want to know it all. But I don't want Mummy to die. I'd rather look after her and keep her safe."

TGA: *(Even more pitiful than seeing her fraught parents in this situation, it was heartbreaking to watch a child being deprived of her education because of the demands and bonds of loving a sick mother.)*

Being a resilient child, Annabelle pulled herself together and faced up to her home-driven responsibilities. For Alice, it was harder. She was haunted by Mrs Crabbe's visit and the knowledge that with the help of the WI, Annabelle could have gone to school on 11 Plus exam day.

Alberto did his best to console Alice with various suggestions, none of which really helped. Coming home for dinner one day, he went straight to the radio and switched it on.

"All my mates at work are talking about a lively programme of music called *Workers' Playtime*. I thought we'd give it a go," he said to Alice. "There; how's that? I've always said the best thing for the doldrums is music."

"It's really cheerful, Alberto, and I'm sure we'll enjoy it as a family, but you must understand, it's going to take me a little while to get over my selfishness, or short-sightedness, or misjudgement; whatever it was, about Annabelle. The last thing in the world I would want to do is upset her."

Alberto looked at her despondently.

"Don't bear it all on your own shoulders, my lovely. We shared the decision and reasoned that it was the right one – and it could still be." He gave her a long, loving hug as he said, "Time will tell."

Ironically, the next person to cross the threshold was Mr Crabbe. He was changing Alice's war work from making barrage balloon parts to making Bandolier Belts.

"What are Bandolier Belts?"

"Belts that soldiers wear around their waists, on top of their uniforms. It's complicated work with lots of stitching. This khaki material is very tough. Needs to be hard-wearing, but I'm sure your industrial machine will cope well. The idea is to make rows of slots, which will contain bullets for ready access for gunfire on the field."

"Good heavens. My machine might cope, but will I?"

"I'm sure you will. They are already cut out and are marked with tailor's chalk so you can see exactly where to stitch."

Alice felt overwhelmed. The table was piled high with khaki material and there was a bag containing accessories such as strong thread and buckles.

Mr Crabbe seemed in a hurry to leave, but before he could get away, Alice asked, "Hey, what about the barrage balloon job?"

"That contract's finished, so we won't need any more of those."

"What about all this spare material then?"

Keep it. It's no longer required by us. Use it up personally if you can, or dispose of it."

He was gone. Alice looked at her living-room-come-workshop in despair.

Things changed for Annabelle in September. Firstly, a girl named Ann Waite moved in with Auntie Milly, (Mrs John Smith). Auntie Milly's sister, Dimp, was married to a warrant officer in the RAF and he was being stationed away, so Auntie Dimp and Ann were going to live with Auntie Milly for the time being. That meant there were now six children living in the two pairs of British Legion houses: 3, 5, 7 and 9, Newbury Road. There was Ann in No. 3, (Auntie Milly didn't have any children,) Ken and Hazel Wood in 5, Richard in 7 and Al and Annabelle in 9.

Annabelle was keen to be friends with Ann because she was going, by service bus, to the grammar school in Andover. She had the black and yellow horizontal striped scarf to prove it.

In parallel, Annabelle started school at the Andover Secondary Modern School for Girls in London Road, Andover, opposite the Boys' School. She boarded the school bus outside George Bright's shop every morning when Alice was well enough. Unlike the grammar school, they only had half day's schooling in the mornings, leaving the school available in the afternoons for the education of Southampton girls who had been evacuated to the area.

"I hated it, Mum," she blurted out to Alice. "They started with Scripture and I couldn't understand a word of it."

"Well perhaps they'll explain it better tomorrow," Alice comforted, as Annabelle changed her clothes and dashed off for a stint of potato picking before having to get tea ready.

"Busy afternoon?"

"Yes, but the field's cleared now. All the potatoes have been picked up and sacked. Mr Ewers is pleased and wants us all to go up to his other field tomorrow to dig out dock roots. He'll give a halfpenny to anyone who can carefully dig out a dock and give it to him with the root intact. If you can show him the tiny tip of the root, he'll pay you the money.

When tea was over and done with, Annabelle dashed down to Auntie Milly's to call for Ann. Together they sat on the inner grass edge of the pavement, leaning on the white picket fence.

"Did you do French at school today, Ann?"

"Yes we did. Why?"

"I wanted to sit the 11 plus exam and get to grammar school, but missed it because my mum was ill. I so wanted to learn French. Will you teach me?"

"I'm not a teacher, you know."

"But if you tell me what you learn every lesson, then you can be my teacher. Please, Ann. Please."

TGA: *(Not to be outdone by circumstances, this determined child intends to progress with her education, by hook or by crook.)*

Christmas 1942 brought another war year to a close with the usual boozy party at the Geoghegans' home. Whether in the Aless's or the Geoghegans' home, the parties were practically a repetition of the previous year. Now, over three years into WW2, confidence was building that the war couldn't go on much longer.

There were inevitable changes in that both families' children were growing up. Nora, the eldest of the Geoghegans, had become engaged to be married to a very good looking young man named Trevor Phillips. They made a stunning couple and harmonised Irish songs together. They actually closed the Christmas celebrations of 1942 with a haunting rendition of the song *The Rose of Tralee*. The magic of the song could be heard by villagers, resting cosily in their homes, as party-goers staggered their way home in the early hours, drunkenly singing that beautiful song.

Rationing continued with a vengeance in 1943. 1 egg per person a week was a joke, but true nevertheless. Alberto said that he would look into making a chicken run in the garden with small meshed wire, which would contain a chicken house with nesting box.

"We'll show the Hun how we can provide for ourselves."

Alice had never seen him so uptight before.

"That's a lot of work for you, Alberto."

"I never let work beat me before. It can be a project for Al and myself. We'll show 'em."

There were other forms of rationing to cope with too. New furniture was designed to use as little wood as possible and only available to purchase by newly-weds or people who had been bombed out of their homes. Cosmetics such as soap were restricted too. Al's reaction was that anyone who wanted to use his soap ration could. He was happy not bothering to wash!

Another year of war was passing with so many restrictions, but all citizens were 'fighting the good fight'.

A good bit of news over the radio helped to cheer them along when it was announced that Field Marshal Montgomery's Eighth Army had made progress in Tunisia, and the British Government had publicised the week 1st to 8th May 1943 as Wings for Victory week. It was a campaign where every county in Great Britain should donate as much money as possible to help build Spitfire aeroplanes. Enham did their bit enthusiastically, as can be seen by the text of the following cutting from the local paper, The Andover Advertiser:

(QUOTE)

ENHAM – Help from the "Glamour Girls".

A small party of married women in the village who style themselves "The Enham Glamour Girls" have been very successful in their efforts to raise money for national and charitable causes during the past three years; their initiative is worthy of emulation in other places. They have given £15 for a rubber dinghy, £10 for the Merchant Navy, £5 for Wings for Victory, £10 for Hampshire prisoners of war, £10 for the Red Cross and St. John Joint Prisoners of War Fund and recently (by means of a dance) £20 for the Merchant Navy Comforts Fund; a total of £70.

(UNQUOTE)

Later in 1943, the government set up a department for the issuing of National Registration Identity Cards. To comply with this, Alice had to take all the family's birth certificates to Smannell School, Enham's designated National Registration Office, to register the family for their identity cards.

To everybody's great relief, the threat of bombing night after night had gone away, but life was becoming more and more restricted. Nevertheless, the radio was bringing great joy with *Workers' Playtime* at dinnertime holding many surprises. It was broadcast from various factories all over the British Isles, thanks to the Ministry of Labour. That brought hometowns to many WW1 survivors, wherever they had settled.

After dinner, when Alberto had gone back to work, Alice switched on to *Woman's Hour*, which she listened to while machining her bandolier belts. A big family favourite on Saturday evening at 7.30pm was *In Town Tonight*. It was a lighthearted news/celebrity programme where people who happened to be visiting London at the time were interviewed by a roving reporter with a microphone.

TGA: *(Yes, if ever there was a life-saver, or should I say life-giver, it was the radio for the entire United Kingdom, as well as Enham. Everyone was whistling or humming 'The Knightsbridge March', the signature tune for In Town Tonight, as they went about their daily business.)*

The chicken shed project was coming along well. Alberto remembered that his first job in Enham was making chicken sheds, so he checked with Freddie Cox, the woodwork foreman, to see if there might be any old stock tucked away. Luckily, they found one in an old shed and Freddie said, "It's yours, mate. I'll be glad to get rid of it."

"What a start," said Alberto at the tea table that night. "We've got a big job ahead of us, but you and I will make a great team." He and Al chinked teacups to seal the deal.

They did make a great team. The mesh wire cage went up to seal off the area, which had a full length mesh gate in it. The ground was levelled and a raised board flooring structure with a damp course was positioned. It was given a new coating of creosote and before long the family were the proud owners of a chicken house and chicken run.

Full of excitement, they went to see Mr Ewers, who had plenty of young hens for sale, so they bought eight. They had a double nesting box in the chicken house, so Mr Ewers gave them a sack full of hay with which to line the boxes.

Annabelle had the delight of finding their first fresh egg on 13th November 1943. She'd gone to lock the chickens in their house to make sure they were safe from prowling wolves and rats. While there, she checked the nesting boxes and found the egg.

Coming down the garden path, she saw a light in Auntie Dolly's bedroom window and was shocked to hear a baby crying.

Indoors she almost forgot the excitement of finding an egg.

"Mum, I heard a baby crying in Auntie Dolly's house. The bedroom light was on."

"Oh my goodness, she's had it, has she?"

"Had what?"

"The baby. If it's a little girl, she's going to call it Stella."

"Where did she get the baby from?"

"Under the gooseberry bush!" Alice winked at Alberto.

"Auntie Dolly hasn't got a gooseberry bush."

"That's true, sweetheart. There's a bit of magic about babies, which you'll find out as you grow up."

Chapter 16

Evacuation Ends for Andre

Although Andre's mind was continuously tortured by the knowledge that he was no longer in touch with the most important people in his life, he was a very settled evacuee living with Mrs Holt and her family. He looked forward to and enjoyed the sing-along evenings with her playing the piano. News of his forgiveness by the bobby and, ultimately, of his unhappy life, had travelled fast and furiously along the Send grapevine, and he was now more readily accepted by the residents.

Boys still got up to mischief, but Andre was no longer singled out from the others and accepted his just rewards. Such an occasion was when the boys went scrumping for apples and stuffed as many down their shirts as they possibly could.

"What's this?" asked the bobby, pointing with his truncheon to the shirt tops.

"Nuffink," was the communal reply.

Getting the cane at school was the punishment, which the boys considered to be a fair deal, since they were able to take the apples home, rather than be wasted.

Send and Ripley schools, being situated reasonably close to London, had gathered a cosmopolitan assortment of foreign students. As a result of this, there was a need to store plenty of international foodstuffs. During one of their escapades, Andre and his friends raided a food depot and got away with a horde of dried figs. The natural punishment befitted the crime; they ate more than their fair share, much to their later distress.

Andre, now thirteen years old, had lived this semi-contented life for nearly two years, during which time he moved up to a senior school in Ripley where he was a good pupil. He never forgot his stepbrother Ron's words that no one can take away what is in your head.

Also, hovering in his head at that time, were constant thoughts about Ron and Dorothy and his sister Elsa and it was as though Mrs Holt sensed this. It was she who broached the subject one day when they were indoors alone together.

"Do you ever think about your home, Andre?"

"Yes, I do; a lot. I keep wondering about Elsa and where she is."

"You know, quite a few evacuees are returning home now that a lot of the warfare is taking place in the East. I wouldn't be offended if you wanted to do that too."

Andre's reply was to put his arms around her neck and hug her for a long time.

"Andre, as far as my family and I are concerned, this can always be your home; and I speak for my husband too, if – God willing – he comes home safely from the war. You are a very good boy and we've all grown to love you. You can always come back to us. Do you understand?"

Choked up, Andre nodded as tears rolled down his cheeks.

"Good. Good boy. But…we always knew that one day you would have to go home."

Andre put his arms round her neck again.

"I love you too, Mrs Holt."

"Oh, it's you. So you've come back home 'ave you'." The old 'chill' was still there when Ma answered his knock on the door at home in East Croydon.

"Yes. The authorities arranged it. Lots of us are being allowed to go home."

"You'd better come in then."

"Where's Brian?"

"He's at school. He's seven now."

"Gosh. He was almost three when I was evacuated."

"Yeah, well you've got older too. Let's hope you're better behaved now."

"Is my bed still in the attic?"

"It is, and remember to keep it tidy."

Glad to escape, Andre unpacked his few belongings and checked that Grandpa's ring was still safely with him in its Reckitt's Blue Bag, having been pinned to the pockets of a various number of different sized trousers over the years. He stood for a while and looked out of his attic window where he used to plan his escape. His evacuee escape had enabled him to see other parts of his country and he was contented in the knowledge that, at some time in the future, it should be possible for him to find both happiness and love.

As he was looking out of that window he began to wonder what the rest of the day had in store for him, having been away for four years. The first one to come home was Brian, a very energetic little seven-year-old who looked very like his father. He was mystified by that fact that he had another brother. He couldn't remember Andre and was asking questions incessantly as to why he went away and where he went.

Andre's father was the next to appear. After asking many mundane questions about his placements, he then became more animated as he asked, "Done much singing while you've been away?"

"Yes, I have, Pa. Mrs Holt played her piano most nights and her children and I would sing along. I really enjoyed that."

Pa looked disappointed as he said, "I was hoping for quality singing really, like joining a school or church choir."

"Well, I was chosen to sing in school concerts as well." That statement seemed to please a bit more.

Encouraged by his father's minimal support, he asked, "Do you still drive the R White's lemonade lorries?

"I don't, actually. My vehicle got damaged in one of the raids and while it was being repaired I found myself a better job. I now work for the NAAFI."

"What's the NAAFI?"

"It means the Navy, Army and Air Force Institutes. It's a more satisfying job; much more worthwhile so-to-speak. Almost seems like part of the war effort."

Still in awe of his father's 'posh' speaking voice, Andre felt a sense of warmth sweep over him during this conversation. It was as though his father had more time for him now he was a teenager. Pity it was interrupted at such a high point, apart from the fact that the interruption itself was a delight.

"Elsa! Elsa! My sister Elsa. You're here. I thought you were in Ireland."

Both the shock, the joy and the suddenness of the moment rendered him speechless.

Elsa cuddled him.

"Andre, I didn't go to Ireland with Dorothy. I came back home so I didn't lose touch with you."

"...And all this time I didn't blinkin' know. Anyway, I've found you now, but you're so grown up."

"Yes, I'm seventeen and I've got a job. I'm a bell boy." Her gentle, freckled face broke into a broad smile.

"A bell boy?"

"Yes. I think the name originated in America, but girls can do the job too. I operate the lift in Grant's Department Store in Croydon. It's easy. I press the buttons by the sliding doors to operate the lift and say, 'Going up', or 'Going down', whichever it is. Then, as we stop at floors, I have to announce the floor number and name, like Haberdashery, Women's Clothing, Gent's Clothing, whatever it is."

"All day long? Isn't it boring?"

"No. It's exciting. I meet very, very rich people who sometimes give me a tip. I feel quite important really. I have what they call a 'blue' costume, although I call it bluey-grey, with red piping, brass buttons on the jacket and a pill-box hat to match."

"Blimey, you make it sound important; so where's your uniform now."

"Oh, I'm not allowed to bring it home. I have to change in the Staff Ladies' Dressing Room every morning and evening."

The smell of dinner cooking began to disturb Andre because of fearful old memories. He fancied he could detect the smell of the dreaded yellow cabbage of earlier days, but when dinner was put on the table he discovered it was the hateful boiled swede, camouflaged by being mashed with carrots and served with sausages and fried onions. Much to his amazement, he found it quite tasty.

"Where's Daniel?" he asked.

Ma explained that Daniel, who was her son by her first marriage, had got himself a job too.

"You might remember, he always loved his cycling and on leaving school he managed to get a job in a cycle shop in Sutton, Surrey. He no longer lives at home. Sometimes he does spend a weekend with us, but a lot of the time he goes away on cycling weekends with his friends."

"I expect he's a lot bigger than me."

"That's because he eats up all his food. You were never good at that, were you?"

When Elsa had finished her washing up chore, as of old, she joined Andre in his attic bedroom.

"It's so good to have you back home, Andre, but things don't seem the same, do they?"

"No, they're certainly not. I enjoyed my dinner for a start! Why did you come back home when you were so unhappy here?"

"Because I was afraid of losing touch with you. That was the only reason. I hated Ma even more for being such a nice person after you were evacuated. I expect you'll find it hard to believe that she really can be nice. How could she hate you so much? Will we ever find out, I wonder?"

Deep frown lines showed the extent of the enigma written all over both their faces.

"Anyway, did you have a nice time when you were away?"

"Some of it was really horrible. I stayed with so many different people. The best bits were that I loved Mr and Mrs Williams in Brighton and Mrs Holt and her family in Surrey and they loved me as well. I've been with Mrs Holt for the last two years and that's where I came from today. She really loved me, just like Grandma did."

The mention of Grandma made Elsa sit up with a start.

"Have you written to her?"

"I have, and I've got sad news Andre."

"I won't prolong the agony for you," she said gently. "Grandma's home got bombed in the Blitz. Apparently it was a direct hit, so I consoled myself with the thought that she was asleep in her bed, with Marmalade beside her. The raids were often at night."

Andre was stunned. "Are you sure? How did you find out? We never gave her our address because of Ma."

Putting her arm around his shoulder, she said, "Yes, I am certain Andre. It is definitely true. When I wrote to her I gave her a school friend's address for replies. It was a bitter blow to get an answer telling me that she had been alive and well prior to the raid, but that she would have had no chance of survival with a direct hit on her house and damaging two others."

Andre laid his head back on his pillow. "Is it in man's blood to kill?" he asked from the depths of his soul. "Grandma wouldn't hurt a fly."

"Neither would you, Andre." Trying to change the subject, she asked, "Have you still got Grandpa's ring?"

"I have, Elsa. It's been with me through all my travels, but it doesn't fit my finger yet."

"Then you must eat bigger dinners and put some weight on. You're still as thin as a rake. Anyway, try to cheer up a bit, otherwise Ma and Pa will be asking questions. And don't forget, you have found me! I hope that pleases you."

Andre lay there lifeless, almost as though he hadn't heard.

"Come on, Andre. Cheer up a little bit. I know, I'll tell you my secret. I wasn't going to tell you, but I can't bear to see you so unhappy."

With her head beside his on the pillow, she whispered excitedly into his ear.

Andre soon got settled into Woodside Senior School. In class, there was a mixture of familiar and unfamiliar faces. There were now more mistresses than masters and when he enquired after Mr Channell, Andre was told that he had gone off to war.

Schoolwork bore no relation to what he was learning at the senior school in Ripley, but he persevered in order to catch up with their syllabus.

Having returned from the safe haven of evacuation, it came as a tremendous shock to him that his return home did not signify a peaceful experience. On the contrary, there was a resurgence of war on the Home Front. Doodlebugs.

Doodlebugs were treacherous weapons. Doodlebugs, or buzz bombs, were the common names for them, but officially they were V1s (Vergeltungswaffe 1) meaning 'revenge weapon'. Whilst travelling in the sky they made a terrible droning sound, followed by silence. During the silence, they were still travelling to a destination, but no one had any idea in which direction. You just waited and prayed for your safety.

The first night of the Doodlebugs was imprinted on Andre's mind with threatening reality. He was awakened by the warning siren, which was situated virtually alongside his bedroom wall. There was a heavy throbbing engine sound. Immediately, he went to his attic window and peered between the blackout curtains. It was pitch black outside, but about every three minutes he could see some sort of craft passing by overhead and each one appeared to be on fire. Andre became excited by this, assuming it was German aircraft going down in flames and got back into his warm bed.

The next day, the family heard on the BBC News that they were in fact German V1 Doodlebug bombs.

Night after night Andre watched these missiles flying across the sky and was deafened by their long awaited explosions. His father, stepmother, Elsa and Brian would go into the air raid shelter in the garden, but Andre refused to do that. It often used to get half-filled with water and was always damp. Early one morning, Andre went down the stairs, turned into the passage at the bottom to go into the kitchen and the front door caved in on him. This was caused by the blast of the Doodlebug that hit The Old Windmill at Croydon. All schools were then closed because of the danger from daytime raids.

From that time onwards, Andre and a friend used to cycle to the Shirley Hills; a natural range of seven hills. They would climb a tree at the highest point there and watch Doodlebugs all day long. They got very excited watching the American Mustang aeroplanes attacking the Doodlebugs. They would hover over the unmanned missiles, tuck a wing under the Bug and tilt it over. This made the inbuilt gyroscopic navigator ineffective, resulting in it dropping to earth in the hills, thereby avoiding inhabited areas.

TGA: *(It was a great relief for the suffering public to know that a deterrent was available, but as yet, not enough to stop the raids.)*

On one occasion, Andre was reading the paper over his father's shoulder as he was sitting on the back doorstep. He looked up and saw a Doodlebug hovering over the big oak tree in the park opposite. A few minutes later, the blast from the explosive blew down half of their house and propelled Andre through the fence into next door's garden. Undaunted, Andre was quickly on his bike to go into the field and look for shrapnel. In the field, although it was summertime, the bare charred oak tree skeleton stood there without a leaf and the row of houses bordering the other side of the park were all demolished.

Later, they discovered that the oil lamp in the air raid shelter had burst into smithereens and suspected it was caused by the same blast. Thankfully, no one was in there at the time.

With half their house blown down and uninhabitable, the family were billeted with a family in Braintree, Essex, while their house was being repaired.

Elsa was the exception. She chose to find digs near to Grant's Department Store as it was cheaper than travelling to and from Braintree every day.

Chapter 17

Victory in Europe in Sight

On 6th June 1944, an invasion of France was initiated, known as the Normandy Landings, along an 80 kilometre stretch of the coastline. It was reputed to be the largest seaborne invasion in history. Over 150,000 national and allied troops were deployed and it was the beginning of the liberation of German-occupied North Western Europe.

This news greatly uplifted spirits in Great Britain; Enham included. Truckloads of American soldiers, who were now one of our allies in the war, were brought to the Insty from their nearby camps, which balanced the shortage of men while our boys were fighting the good fight overseas. This meant that girls who were old enough to be allowed on the dance floor were having the time of their lives.

The Yanks, as they were commonly called, had access to supplies of nylon stockings from the USA and when local girls got the know-how, they would tap the breast pockets of the soldiers' uniforms as they were dancing to listen for the crinkle of the cellophane wrapping. If they were lucky enough, they went home deliriously happy with a pair of nylons; an immense improvement on the British Lyle stockings, which were unattractively thick.

In August, news reached the world that the Normandy Landings had now re-occupied all of

Northern France and the icing on the cake was that Paris had been liberated.

Another national boost came in September when Field Marshal Bernard Montgomery commanded a daring operation by seizing a bridgehead north of the Rhine at Arnhem. On the 17th, the largest airborne and glider operation in history was carried out by three Airborne Divisions. 'Operation Garden' was the ground side in which the Thirtieth British Corps were to link up with the British First Airborne at Arnhem by thrusting north along a narrow corridor opened up by the US 82nd and 101st Airborne Divisions. These operations enabled The British Second Army to rapidly assault the Ruhr, thus hastening the collapse of the Third Reich.

TGA: *(No wonder British spirits were rising. The incoming news, whether by newspaper or radio bulletins, was becoming very uplifting.)*

While this was going on, Alberto had his own good news. His name had been put forward to enter a News of the World (national daily newspaper) Darts' competition to take place in the Insty. On 12th December 1944, he won the championship for the third time; each time getting a score of 180. On that occasion, he was presented with a set of silver darts from the News of the World.

Annabelle became 14 years old on 24th December 1944, and left school. Because of the dates, she actually left school while she was still 13 and very quickly got herself a job in the cash office of the Co-op in Andover.

That office opened her eyes as to how one big department store operated. Many times she had shopped in the Co-op for her mother. On those occasions she paid at the counter and the assistant put her money and a duplicate copy of a little pink receipt, with Alice's Dividend No. 1782 written on it, into a container about four inches long. She then put the container into a chute on the wall and it magically travelled by a suction process into the cash office. Not many minutes later, her change would come down the chute together with her copy of the pink receipt to take home to her mother.

For her combined 14th birthday and Christmas presents, Alice and Alberto gave her a tweed reversible A-line belted coat. One side was plain blue and the other side, although basically the same colour blue, had a check pattern all over it. The reversible effect became apparent when turning back the cuffs and collar.

Proudly wearing that nice warm coat to work after Christmas, Annabelle looked forward to learning more about her job.

In the office there were four cashiers whose stools were placed on an elevated ridge by the back wall and each had a chute in front of them. They sat there all day untwisting the containers that kept appearing down their chute. Having put in the correct change, if change was required, they'd return one dividend receipt in the container and the second was kept in the office for the next process by the sorters. A colour coding system was applied to the divi receipts, which enlightened Annabelle to the fact that pink was the colour for the 1700s, matching her mother's number.

One of the cashiers, named Beryl Baker, was very fat with an extremely jovial personality, laughing at every single thing. It amazed Annabelle how she could balance all day long on her stool, which was totally obliterated from view by her girth. Another was Joyce Slater; she always made the morning cocoas at break time because she said she was the only one who could make it properly. Their dinnertimes were staggered so that two of the four cashiers were always manning the tills.

Annabelle, along with four other girls, was a sorter. They sat in pairs on two sides of a huge square table. In front of each sorter was a large tray with one hundred pigeon holes. Their job was to sort dividend slips into their tray. The Chief Cashier, Miss Annetts, explained the job to Annabelle. She gave her a pile of yellow slips and showed her how to sort them into her tray. They covered the block of numbers 1201 to 1300. Annabelle had to place them into her tray starting top left with 1201, so the top row contained 1201 to 1210; the second row, 1211 to 1220, and so on.

When all the yellow slips in that group had been sorted, Miss Annetts took the tray to her own desk and keyed in to her comptometer the amount spent on individual numbers to enable her to calculate how much dividend each customer had earned.

It was an exceedingly busy office and Annabelle's conclusion was that Miss Annetts must have earned every penny she was paid. As for her own future, she made up her mind that sorting was a dead end job and she must look in the Andover Advertiser for something better.

Ironically, a chance conversation with Mrs Rose at the bus stop led her to more optimistic horizons.

Mrs Rose was seeing off her elder daughter, Betty, who was getting on the bus that Annabelle was alighting after work. Betty was starting her bus journey to Swindon.

"I hear you're a working girl now, Annabelle," said Mrs Rose. "How's the job going?"

"It's OK, but there's no future in it so I shall be looking for something else."

"You want to do what our Betty did. She learned shorthand and typing and she earns good money now in an office in Swindon."

Annabelle was fascinated by the idea of speedwriting and soon enrolled in a class of girls who were being taught Pitman shorthand by a white-haired lady named Miss Hart, who held her classes at her home, 66 Junction Road, Andover.

As luck would have it, when Annabelle was at Mrs Piggin's home one afternoon with Pam, she told them her news about learning shorthand and Pam's Auntie Ella offered to teach her how to touch type for free.

Annabelle arrived as arranged and Auntie Ella had her old Imperial typewriter on the table. She also had a learning book propped up by the side of the typewriter. She showed Annabelle the home keys and then explained that Annabelle's hands must always hover over these keys and she must never look at the keyboard. Auntie Ella wanted her to look at the book and read out loud exactly what she was typing, using first the left hand and then right. Without moving from the home keys, she then had to find the top bank and say the letters aloud as she typed. Annabelle blushed with embarrassment at having to read out loud, because the room was always crowded with the big Piggin family. But studying was by no means a chore. She was enjoying both the shorthand and typewriting, and learning more and more subjects was satisfying her ambition.

In April 1945, Alberto received a letter signed by Mr D.J. Crabbe, Hon. Treasurer, Youth Organisation Council, Enham, thanking him for all the hard work he and his friend Mr Joe Geoghegan had put in to help set up the Youth Club and give guidance to members in putting on events and organising their own fun. The letter was also signed by a number of the cast members as follows: Ray Budd, Maurice Waite, Geoffrey Crabbe, John Cox, Betty Johnson, Dorothy Pearce, Gladys Johnson, Doug Saunders, G Colebourne, P Cutting, Al Aless, Annabelle Aless, Jackie Greener and Clive Broughton, among other indecipherable names from the old letter.

Supreme joy abounded on the afternoon of 7th May 1945, Winston Churchill made a radio broadcast from No. 10 Downing Street to British citizens, which was relayed to the crowds that had gathered in Trafalgar Square and around Parliament. He informed his listeners that Germany had signed unconditional surrender papers, bringing to an end six years of war in Europe. This led to a later news bulletin when the Minister of Information confirmed that an official statement declaring the end of the war would be made simultaneously in London, Washington and Moscow the following day, 8th May 1945.

"The day has been declared a National Holiday to mark 'Victory in Europe', (VE Day). The 9th May will also be a National Holiday."

On VE Day, Winston Churchill made another in-depth speech to the nation, but villagers in Enham were certainly not listening. They were losing no time in enjoying the euphoria of the moment.

Nationwide, people were out in the streets dancing, hugging, crying and kissing through their tears. For those who had lost loved ones, the tears readily fell from a melting pot of emotions; heartbreaking sadness, relief, weakness, disbelief, joy and a whole gamut of appropriate descriptive words you could find in any Thesaurus.

TGA: *(How can I describe such a momentous occasion to you readers? Some members of your family may have lived through it. See if they can do better than I. In my 'elevated' status I had a prime view, but even so, I am struggling. Truly, all the emotions had to be lived through to be believed.)*

The WW1 disabled men in Enham preferred to celebrate on their own Home Front; quieter perhaps, but nonetheless exuberant. Many other able-bodied people from the village celebrated more rigorously. Therefore, on the afternoon of Tuesday, 8th May 1945, Annabelle and Pam, with parental approval, went off to Andover in company with many other Enham residents for the Mardi-Gras celebrations. It had been announced in local papers that such an event would be held on the day of victory.

They had to force their way through the crowds down the High Street to get to the hubbub of proceedings in front of the Guildhall. The scene itself was breathtaking as well as deafening. Union Jacks flying from all windows created the perfect backdrop. Red, white and blue streamers were flying from above, as well as from all other directions. People were dancing to the music, which could not be heard because of the cheering, celebratory shouting and singing. Songs such as, *Kiss Me Goodnight Sergeant Major, You are My Sunshine, Roll out the Barrel* and the like did their bit to release a wealth of victory joy. Many of the crowd were dressed in red, white or blue, which heralded the patriotism that was breathed in through the air and exhaled for all to share. Drunken young men were trying to climb up the Guildhall pillars and falling off without a care in the world. The war was over.

In this exhilarating atmosphere, Annabelle kept her eye on the large Guildhall clock with its Roman Numerals. In her head, she kept hearing her father's words, "Yes, of course you can go, but just make sure you catch the last bus home. It's at 8.30pm; don't forget that. Enjoy yourselves. No more war is something well worth celebrating."

Neither of the girls wanted to leave all this infectious camaraderie, but Annabelle said, "I think we should leave here at ten past eight."

Pam pulled a face.

"Don't forget," said *Little Miss Responsibility*, "I'm not fifteen till the end of the year and you're younger than I am. We were lucky to be allowed to come."

With that, they dragged themselves away to the bus stop in New Street. They could see by St. Mary's Church clock over the high wall that it was not yet 8.30pm. Breathing sighs of relief, they waited and waited and waited. When St. Mary's clock said 8.40pm, they started to panic. They agreed they should start walking home, hoping that as the war was over the bus driver might be kind enough to pick them up along the route. Still the bus did not come.

When they reached the top of Lillywhite's Hill, Annabelle gasped, "That's my Dad on that bike. It's Auntie Dolly's bike; I can tell by the basket on the front. He's in a terrible rage, Pam; I can see by his white face."

Alberto let the bike fall on the grassy bank as he made his way across the road to the girls, unstrapping his belt. Pam attacked him as he started strapping her friend across her bottom with his eight-plait leather belt. Small as she was, she used all her might to drag him away.

"It's not her fault! We waited for the bus but it didn't come!" she shouted. "You're cruel. Stop it, or I'll report you to the police!"

"Leave him alone Pam! He can't help it. It's the war. He's in a rage."

"The war's over."

"Not this war; the other war. It gave him shell shock."

By the time that was all said, Alberto had started to cry.

"I'm sorry, my lovely, lovely, special Annabelle." He smoothed her tears down the side of her face with his one hand. "Please forgive me," he pleaded. "The rage controls me so I don't know what I'm doing. It's like I go out of my mind." Still in a state of bewilderment, he asked tenderly, "Have I hurt you?"

The three of them sat on the bank calming down, while the girls explained about the Guildhall and St. Mary's Church clocks and the fact that the bus didn't come. As they all walked peaceably back into Enham village together, they were told that the buses had been re-routed because of the Mardi-Gras.

The next day the nation was overrun with street parties. It wasn't the brightest of days, but that did not mar celebrations. The sun was shining brightly in the hearts of all citizens.

Union Jack flags covered long trestle tables in thousands of bunting adorned streets, with happy people buzzing about everywhere. Eating, drinking and singing was the order of the day. What else could they do? The war was over.

Celebrating together in the streets was a way to let the joyous emotions escape gradually and make room for normality to slowly seep into their souls. It was a transitional period in time, which each and every person had to live through before blood could flow naturally through their veins again.

Those essential activities and releases were echoed for millions of war torn people in Great Britain. Simultaneously, they were rejoicing the end of the war, Enham Village Centre included. It was such a relief for the WW1 wounded men and their wives to have personally escaped harm. The icing on the cake for Annabelle was that she'd had two days off from the boring sorter job at the Co-op.

TGA: *(Before moving on with this story, I'd like to try once again to describe the overwhelming joy and elation felt by citizens. It was as though they were in a place where dark clouds and rain would never exist again. Suffice to say, 'on top of the rainbow').*

Royal balcony pictures of King George VI, with Queen Elizabeth and their daughters came out in abundance in the newspapers, with a story to enthral the nation. The princesses had begged their parents to be allowed to join ordinary people in the street celebrations. Against advice from the Palace, the King and Queen gave their permission. The sisters slipped out of a side entrance, chaperoned by a Horse Guards' official and mingled and danced with the general public. Princess Elizabeth was wearing her army uniform with her cap pulled down over her eyes. She was just another pretty girl in khaki out in the street with her sister, celebrating victory.

Before very long, young soldiers returning from the war soon became a common and recognisable sight, dressed as they were in their Montague Burton demob. (demobilisation) suits.

The Ministry of Food wasted no time advertising its contribution to the magnificent victory with the following poem:

362

The Pail

Because of the pail, the scraps were saved,
Because of the scraps, the pigs were saved,
Because of the pigs, the rations were saved,
Because of the rations, the ships were saved,
Because of the ships, the island was saved,
Because of the island, the empire was saved,
And all because of the housewife's pail.

Further benefits to the overriding joy of peace reigning for Alberto and family was the thrill of getting their beds moved back upstairs so that they could regain privacy, as well as being able to remove blackout curtains, which had robbed them of evening sunsets and moonlight and generally cast gloom and doom.

The elation of the end of the war became clouded for some when, at the General Election on 26th July 1945, just about eleven weeks after VE Day, Winston Churchill found himself without office. The Labour Party won a landslide victory over the Conservatives and Mr Clement Atlee became Prime Minister. The consensus was that the Conservative Party had been virtually leaderless in all directions other than war.

Many citizens of Great Britain were naturally delighted with that outcome. They had a Monarchy and a Parliament and they play by the rules.

TGA: *(But the joyous fact remained that the Labour Party could now rule the country with peace in Europe.)*

Chapter 18

Civvy and Military Employment for Andre

On the war front in Essex, Andre watched gliders being taken up into the sky for the D-Day invasion of France in June 1944. At the time it was popularly, and significantly, believed that D-Day stood for Deliverance Day, but the newspapers quickly confirmed that D-Day was a military term for the first day of a planned attack.

Prior to that, soon after the move to Braintree in 1943, he started work for the first time at the age of 13 years working for a firm called Bradbury's Ltd. He was paid 24 shillings a week, of which he gave his stepmother £1 (20 shillings) for his keep. His workmates were mostly women and teenagers, because menfolk were fighting for their country.

Bradbury's made items such as car jacks and box spanners. Andre was put on a machine that punched the holes in spanners. To do that he had to stand from 7.30am until 6pm, which made him feel faint. During his lunch hour, the foreman said, "Eat some grub, lad. You look like you need a good feed up. Make a man of ya. Then you'll be able to stand all day and all bloody night."

"I know I'm not a good eater, but this job bores me stupid. School was a lot more interesting than this."

"True, but they didn't pay you money every week, did they?" the foreman grinned.

Andre stuck the job for some time, but the final straw came when a lady operating a big commercial drill to the right of him got her glove caught under the drill and she lost two fingers. Even though he never saw her again, the sight of her face became imprinted on his mind. Thereafter he sought and obtained a variety of jobs, all within the engineering field.

During that period in his life, WW2 in Europe came to an end. Essex people went mad. They certainly knew how to let their hair down. Dancing in the streets became the norm and Andre wished like crazy that he was old enough to drink a glass of beer. He enjoyed the camaraderie and was singing his heart out with the rest of the nation, but it gave him an unnatural thirst.

"Give us a swig of your beer, mister, please," he begged. "I need to oil my vocal chords."

"There you are, son," said the reveller. "Now you can sing your heart out."

His ploy had worked and it had been easy, so he tried it again and again. He ended the day somewhat tipsy and VE Day became the catalyst for his partiality to a pint.

He and his mates found more celebratory fun by setting off firecrackers amidst the crowds and their memorable night out continued into the early hours.

Soon after VE Day, the family heard that their home in East Croydon had been repaired and they were able to return. Once settled, Andre got a more major job at Kennedy's. It was a garage/engineering workshop. In the workshop they made machines for the butchery industry such as sausage makers, pie pressers and mincers.

Andre hated the first job they put him on. He had to clean such machines when they were returned for refurbishment and they absolutely stank.

In the way of recreation for teenagers, the local councils were setting up youth clubs. Andre was interested, favouring individual sports where he could excel under his own efforts and signed up for boxing tuition. Because of another keen interest, the council looked into the possibility of setting up a chess club. It turned out to be a viable proposition and Andre became an avid member, always aiming high. He loved swimming too, which he used to do in the rivers and streams in Ripley, but that was a non-starter in East Croydon because he would have to pay to go to the swimming pool.

Progressing jobwise, he learned other facets of engineering such as welding, drilling with machines and using a lathe, etc. He was succeeding in his work and became an apprentice engineer, which encompassed learning draughtsmanship. Realising his potential, the company eventually sent him on day release to study the subject at college.

He stayed with the company when they moved their factory to Balham, which entailed a big change for him. He had to travel to and from work by train as opposed to cycling.

Although he enjoyed his technical drawing work, taking copies of it was a different matter. It involved using a cumbersome box, approximately 5' 2" long by 2' 6" wide by 6" deep, with a quarter inch plate glass lid on top of it. It was necessary to darken the room by closing the office curtains to keep all sunshine and light out before putting print paper under the plate glass and his drawing on the top of that. A frame would clamp the whole lot together before two people carefully carried the box into the sunshine to develop the print. The duration of development was a hit and miss process to say the least and the entire business took about half a day.

It was while working in Balham that the company, now re-named Kennedy Instruments, started to produce cameras. They made one called The Ilford Advocate, which was the first camera ever to be made out of die-cast metal and the first one off the production line was presented to Her Majesty the Queen.

As the years were passing, Andre was making a name for himself winning county boxing championships as a flyweight, and found the added bonus of self-defence gave him a confidence boost. He was also enjoying his chess nights, which was more a battle of the minds.

A momentous day of interruption to that ordered life came for Andre at work one day. He'd been quite settled and interested in his job for a number of years. On the occasion in question he'd left his office in the roof to go to the canteen on the shop floor for the sole purpose of getting a cup of tea for his boss. Regrettably, he came face to face with the owner of the company while carrying the cup of tea on a tray to his boss.

"So what's going on here, young man? Am I paying people in this company to time waste?"

The owner ranted on for some time.

Andre became angry at the insinuation and started to defend himself by swearing at the presumptuous boss. Instant dismissal ensued, before he could either blink or deliver the tea.

The shock of dismissal was great and hard to bear. Even harder to bear was the lack of support at home. Ma continued the process of reading the riot act.

"So now I'm expected to feed you again for nothin'. Blimeeeey! Will this ever stop?" she screeched.

At the end of his tether, Andre replied, "Don't fret yourself. I won't blinkin' eat anything," and cleared off to his room.

True to his word, Andre starved himself rather than be subservient to his stepmother. The price paid was a nasty boil appearing on the back of his neck and what felt like one on his back. He lived in hope that they would soon burst and ease the pain.

Fortunately, the home situation did not prevail for too long because it was time for Andre to be conscripted into the Services. He chose to enlist in the Army.

Feeling weak and unwell, he was happy on the appointed day to be escaping home for the second time in his life. Before leaving, he ensured that he'd got Grandpa's ring still contained in its Reckitt's Blue Bag pinned safely in his trouser pocket. He weathered the biting wind on that bitter cold day in late winter and arrived at Fleet in Hampshire where, along with other raw recruits, he was issued with his kit, which included his army uniform and heavy black boots.

"I don't think I can wear those heavy boots until I get rid of these boils," Andre said, as he touched the boil on the back of his neck. I was nearly poisoned once with ulcers on my feet."

"Cor blimey! There ain't no mummy to wet-nurse you here, sonny. This is the Army for God's sake."

That retort hit Andre between the eyes and he saw stars. He wanted to punch the sergeant on the nose, but common sense told him it was better to keep his own nose clean, despite the confidence he had gained from his boxing lessons.

Before many days passed, he was in an army hospital suffering with boils, ulcers and a carbuncle on his back. The diagnosis was under-nourishment and he was put on a high protein diet. Thanks to the massive doses they pumped into his body, he became clear of all the infections and was able, at long last, to start his army career.

After an initial six weeks of training, he was approved for army service and decided to join the Royal Army Medical Corps. He easily passed some simple tests and was given the choice of four options to pursue. He could either undertake normal hospital nursing, special nursing for venereal diseases, mental nursing or training to become a hygiene inspector.

Andre chose hygiene inspector, which was the highest category and involved a further three-month training course.

The course was held in Ash Vale, near Aldershot, and involved the ins and outs of hygiene and sanitation, field work, the building of primitive incinerators and the creation of hot water supplies.

Working in pairs, the instruction they underwent to provide hot water in the field was to cut off about a third of the depth of a 40 gallon drum and make a hole toward the top of it, large enough to insert a piece of angle iron in a V-shaped position. They then had to place a bricklike structure in the centre, covered with the combustible substance provided, before placing that lesser section of drum in position on a flat area, open side uppermost.

Next they placed the larger section on top, open side uppermost, and filled it with water. The heating process began by running a mixture of three parts water and one part oil down the angle iron so that it could drip onto the combustible material and explode.

A similar arrangement was used as an incinerator to burn human excrement, which dried out very quickly in hot countries and then became combustible.

TGA: *(Not being human, the importance of this snippet is lost on me, but for interest's sake I think it should be brought to your attention that each soldier serving there was allowed five pieces of toilet paper a day. Pity the poor man who got diarrhoea!)*

During the RAMC training lectures, Andre brought his draughtsmanship knowledge into play by making first class drawings to assist himself. This skill did not go unnoticed and a female officer seconded him to do drawings for her own lecture purposes. The final two facets of the course involved learning about tropical diseases, which interested Andre immensely, and the last, received with great relief was that – in accordance with the Geneva Convention – the Medical Corp were only allowed to use firearms to defend their hospital or patients.

Those personnel who completed the course satisfactorily were then posted to Egypt and they actually landed there on 29th April 1951, the day Andre was 21 years old.

The moment his troopship had moored at Suez, they were besieged by bumboats, containing local people trying to ply their wares. In this instance they were unlucky because the squaddies had gambled all their money away on the ship.

After two days in Port Said, the troops were taken to a place called Gebel Maryam on the banks of the Suez Canal, midway between Port Said and Fayed. That place was to be Andre's permanent location for the next eighteen months and he was eagerly looking forward to putting his newfound knowledge into practice.

Chapter 19

Peace and Joy Followed by Heartache for Annabelle

William Joyce's life came to an end on 3rd January 1946. Better known to the British public as Lord Haw-Haw, his execution for treason took place on a damp and cold morning at Wandsworth Prison. Undoubtedly deserved, it was still a chilling event whether you were a spectator, a listener or a newspaper reader. With the full understanding that he was executed for the crime of treason, Mrs Basting still couldn't help feeling a twinge of gratitude to him for reading out her son Leslie's name as a prisoner-of-war, thus saving her many days' and nights' worry.

During that cold winter, Auntie Dolly and Annabelle found a way of saving fuel money. They'd heard that the woods opposite the plantation, up beyond the farm at the back of them, were undergoing a husbandry operation. Hundreds of self-sown saplings, or maybe young trees at that stage, had grown quite tall and reached a diameter of three to four inches. They were being sawn down and left lying on the ground.

"How's about you and I starting our own logging business, me little darlin'?" asked Auntie Dolly with her usual twinkle in her eye.

For Annabelle, the seed was sewn. Thriftiness should have been her second name. It was too dark in the evenings after work, but the pair of them were anxious to get on with their task on Saturday.

A learning curve was to see how many saplings they could manage to carry under each arm. Usually they managed about six, one carrying from the front and one from behind. By the time they got home, they were mighty glad to drop six outside each back door.

Very soon they'd fixed themselves up with trestles and were both sawing away, filling sacks with logs that would help keep them warm in winter. They were company out there for one another because they could chat over the five-foot weather boarding fence or run round to each other for a breather.

Alberto helped Annabelle choose an appropriate saw from his WW1 tool chest and showed her how to grease the teeth with lard for ease of use. Annabelle passed on that tip to Auntie Dolly.

Looking for a more interesting day job was becoming a priority for Annabelle. She was doing well with her shorthand and typing and knew she was superior to other girls doing the same studies. An advert in the Andover Advertiser for a legal secretary at Jones and Trethowan Solicitors in Bridge Street, Andover, prompted her to apply for the position.

Mr Trethowan was a dark-haired man looking quite formidable in his smart business suit, but this didn't deter Annabelle. She was starting to mature, knew she looked good too, and had some qualifications behind her that boosted her confidence. Thanks to Auntie Ella, she was able to take her Royal Society of Arts Commercial Examination, Advanced Stage, Certificate in the

First Class in Typewriting with her. Miss Hart had told her that her studies in shorthand were exemplary, although as yet she had not been put in for any exams.

"Pleased to meet you," said Annabelle, as Mr Trethowan put out his hand across the desk.

"Do sit down," he invited, gesturing to the posh red leather seat the other side of the desk. "Have you ever done legal work before?"

"No, sir, I haven't, but everyone has to start somewhere."

"I really like to employ people with experience."

"The advert didn't state that. Look, sir, I'm in my first job in the Co-op at the moment and it's so boring I can't stand it. I've bettered myself already."

Annabelle unrolled her RSA certificate from its cardboard container.

"I'm also studying shorthand and am quite confident in applying for this position."

He gave the certificate a cursory glance as he acknowledged, "Well done."

Annabelle sensed that the interview wasn't going well, so boldly said, "If you'll forgive me, sir, I've calculated how much money I need to earn and if you can't match it, then I'll stop wasting your time."

Somewhat bowled over by this young lady, Mr Trethowan asked, "How much?"

"Five pounds."

"I'm sorry. No match, but thank you for applying; it's been quite interesting."

"You're welcome," she replied, with her nose in the air. She felt proud of herself for handling such a businessman.

When Annabelle stepped out of the street door, she was surprised to come face-to-face with Alan Baker (colleague Beryl's brother). She'd noticed that such an encounter was becoming a bit of a habit and on that particular occasion he asked if he could take her to the pictures.

"No, thank you. I don't really like the pictures and I'm far too busy with my studies anyway."

Looking crestfallen, Alan walked away and Annabelle thought no more of it.

It was two years before Annabelle was able to move on from the Co-op, the job she started before Christmas 1945, at thirteen years old.

During her last days there, winter spirits were lifted on 20th November 1947 when Princess Elizabeth married her blond-haired prince in Westminster Abbey. It was easy to see how she could fall in love with such a handsome naval officer and the nation was delighted with the match. The King bestowed on him the title Prince Philip, Duke of Edinburgh.

After the marriage ceremony and the wedding breakfast, with radiant smiles and waves from the balcony of Buckingham Palace, the couple departed for their honeymoon at Broadlands in Hampshire, the home of Prince Philip's uncle, Earl Mountbatten.

Very soon after the royal wedding on 8th December 1947, Annabelle's office training studies earned her the privilege of becoming a shorthand typist at RAF Maintenance Command in Amport

House, which entailed two bus journeys from her home. Her job was classified as a civilian working for the Royal Air Force. It sounded grand, but to her it was the opposite. After a few weeks she wrote a little poem for her family, summing up the gist of the job.

I go to work in a typing pool,
We sit at desks, just like at school;
So much so that to me it seems funny,
At the end of the week they give me money.

She soon earned herself a good reputation and was often requested by the typing pool supervisor to attend meetings to take notes for officers. That was real work for Annabelle. She utilised her skills to the utmost and they paid her good money for it.

On one such occasion, the leader gave her an appointment to attend such and such a building and report to Wing Commander Rees.

Introducing herself, she asked him, "Would you like me to take notes verbatim, or will you give me a signal to record the bits you're interested in?"

"I'll signal you. You keep an eye on me and I'll put a finger up, like this, when I want you to take notes."

At the start of the meeting, Winco Rees (the office jargon for a wing commander) introduced everybody. Annabelle gave herself a master page to lay on the board table in front of her, with attendees' names, then drew a table plan allotting them each a number to be used for speed when taking notes, to enable her to record which person said what.

The meeting had been in progress for maybe twenty minutes or so and her eyes and neck were becoming fixed on the wing commander. Out of panic, she then put her pencil into use.

She had no idea for how long she was taking notes, but at the close of the meeting Winco Rees said, "Oh my God. I forgot to signal you, didn't I?"

"Don't worry, sir; I soon got that message and I took down verbatim notes for the whole meeting."

"You're a little gem. Thank you," he said, with relief.

"I'm afraid the transcript will create extra work. I'll type a draft for you and you'll be required to edit it. Then I'll have to re-type it."

"Marvellous. Some very important stuff came up. Thank you for your initiative."

Annabelle soon got the draft to him and he personally brought it back to the typing pool and got the OK from the supervisor to go directly to Annabelle's desk.

"As my work has helped you, sir, I'd like to ask if you would kindly explain to the supervisor at the desk today why your job has taken me double time."

"It will be a pleasure young lady, and at the same time I'll recommend an incremental raise."

At such an unexpected outcome, all Annabelle could think to say was "Phew", with a beaming smile.

A big change had happened at home while Annabelle was enjoying her job. Al had been conscripted for his army service and was now training to join the Royal Corp of Signals at Catterick Camp in Yorkshire. Home was a strange place without him; he was of no help whatsoever domestically but he was a very live wire, always joking and fooling around. Alberto missed the games of darts they used to play together in the living room while Alice, now free of war work, would sit in her armchair doing sewing for local clients.

Alberto, who had received a bonus in his wages, decided to buy the family a nice Christmas present. They all loved music and Annabelle often played an out-of-tune melody on her piano from sheet music. With coal fires being lit daily and cold nights creating contrasting atmospheres, it was hopeless trying to keep the piano tuned.

The communal Christmas present turned out to be a radiogram. Alberto had ordered it through George Bright who allowed him a little discount for taking the old radio away.

George plugged the appliance into the electric socket and then showed the family how to tune into the radio. More exciting was the vinyl record player. George raised the lid of the 'Ultra' radiogram to reveal a turntable with an 'arm' sitting on its rest. The arm contained a stylus (needle) which, when powered and placed in the revolving record groove, started to play the music. You had a choice of playing either a small single record, or you could place as many as eight long-playing records (LPs) onto the central spindle and they would drop one at a time and play music for hours without attention. Pure magic. Annabelle was beside herself with delight.

A temporary snag was that they didn't own any vinyl records, but George kindly left a few of his own with them.

"You sure know what to write on your Christmas lists now, don't you?"

Christmas 1947 was better than typical for the Geoghegans and Aless family that year. They celebrated in the Aless's home and there was no need to use the radiogram. No more war was a lasting joy and, when the beers were flowing, the war songs flowed with it. Friendship added its own elation and heralded a trouble free 1948.

How could anyone have known the bitter truth? A harsh winter was in front of them; very difficult for the village men. Much caution was needed on the icy roads and sometimes they could not get to their work in the factory. Conscientious Annabelle was hit hard too with two bus journeys to face in order to get to work.

Conditions were worse than appalling. Temperatures were freezing and iced-up roads played havoc with bus timetables. You daren't walk under a tree because there were inch thick ice-coverings on leaves, which could slide onto the head of anyone who ventured beneath.

On those icy cold mornings, a warmly-dressed Annabelle waited stoically at the bus stop with Jocelyn Blackburn who worked at the post office in Andover.

"Poor you," Jocelyn, sympathised. "I'd dread getting to Amport after Andover." Her eyes nearly popped out of her head when she added, "And then you've got to get home again!"

One morning, much to her parents' horror, Annabelle got up at five in the morning and said she was going to cycle to Amport.

TGA: *(At 17 years old, Annabelle was her own determined person and her parents knew it was futile to intervene. Alberto comforted Alice by saying that she would learn more by her mistakes than they could teach in a million words.)*

"I'll be OK, honestly. I won't take any risks and I won't go under trees."

Annabelle didn't get very far. She encountered 10 foot snowdrifts which were impassable. To her own, and her parents' relief, she got back home safely and realised that any more attempts would be stupid.

In parallel, Al was suffering worse conditions up in Yorkshire. The appreciable difference was, he was stationed in camp so training wasn't interrupted.

It was while discussing the benefits their logging expeditions had provided during the harsh winter, when the coal lorries had the same problem as all other traffic, that Auntie Dolly suggested Annabelle should telephone the operator to see if she could get a telephone number for HQMC. That way she was able to contact the authorities, whose advice was to get back as soon as she could; her job was still waiting for her. Apparently, because Amport House was such a remote location, many other people were having similar difficulties.

The severe weather conditions began to ease in March 1948 and it was a relief for all people when things got back to normal. Annabelle was worried sick about leaving her mother every morning, which was hard to bear after such a long time off work, but Auntie Dolly remained a true and loyal neighbour. Because her young daughter Stella was now at school, Auntie Dolly had time to watch over Alice in the daytime.

Annabelle received a royal welcome at work and soon was thoroughly enjoying the mental exercise and stimulation.

Having gained her shorthand theory certificate, Annabelle was now able to continue studies with Miss Hart in a speed class. First lesson back after the bad weather she was presented with Pitman certificates dated 7th January 1948 and 25th March 1948, 80 words and 90 words a minute respectively. Full of confidence, Annabelle knew she was better than that. She loved the subject and it still held a strong fascination for her. At home she would take down political speeches from the radio for practice and read them back fluently. She also took down the words of all the latest songs and was able to transcribe them in longhand for her parents.

A huge surprise came to the family one Friday when Al turned up unannounced. He had passed out of training successfully at Catterick and told his family that he was being sent to Suez in Egypt for a tour of duty as a signaller.

He and Alberto played darts nearly all the time during that short weekend. To ease the shock of his departure, they agreed that they would continue to play darts by post if there was a dart board in Al's camp.

In November, two things happened. The young Queen Elizabeth gave birth to her first child, a little boy. The names chosen were Charles Philip Arthur George, a son and heir for the British Throne. Secondly, Alberto had to go to the surgery because a large swelling had appeared on his neck, just under the back of the right ear. Dr MacCallum had arranged very quickly for Alberto to be seen by a consultant professor at University College Hospital, Denmark Hill, London.

Alice held Alberto's hand for the entire journey in the ambulance that had been provided by the National Health Service, which had been founded that very year.

Back home, the wait for the consultant's report seemed endless. During that time, Al's letter arrived giving Alberto his first score. Alberto concentrated on that, practising darts before playing his turn and posting back his score.

Dr MacCallum signed Alberto off from work, which meant that although his job was still safe, there would be no wage coming in. Annabelle was the main bread winner, boosted by Alice's sewing income, Alberto's army pension and a bit from the Enham Sick Fund, which they'd paid in for all year at the same time as they paid into the Christmas Club.

Life was very hard for Annabelle, but devastation set in when Doctor MacCallum explained that the consultant could not help her father. He was suffering from cancer of the lung and his life expectancy was round about six months.

From that time on, Annabelle and her mother lived in a dazed bubble. They were exceedingly grateful to Dr MacCallum for not telling Alberto the score. He was told that there wasn't a clear diagnosis and that they would try different medications.

It was always Annabelle's suspicion, nagging away at the back of her mind, that her father knew the truth. His rapid loss of weight did not tell lies.

Relatives visited practically every weekend and tried their utmost to cheer Alberto, but truth always came out in the living room when Vincenzo and Antonio, as well as Alberto's sisters, and other in-laws, could not hold back the tears.

Mr Geoghegan was a constant visitor. Extra hard for him because he'd recently lost Jane, his wife, and now he was suffering the ordeal of watching his best friend die. Many other village men paid visits too, for which Alice and Annabelle were more than grateful. If nothing else, they helped pass a few minutes of the formidable life sentence.

Christmas 1948 was harrowing. It was the Geoghegans' turn that year, but with Jane gone and Alberto dying, realisation set in that Christmas 1947 had been the Grand Finale.

Annabelle coped with the situation as best she could, but with Alice now in bed beside Alberto, she was finding it difficult to be able to earn money too. She'd already had the bed moved back downstairs into the front room, where it was in the war, to make her days easier, but felt the need to discuss the worsening situation with Dr MacCallum. He suggested that he could apply for

National Assistance money for her and so, in January, she tendered her resignation to HQMC. Her final work day there was 14th January 1949 when she was just 18 years old.

Annabelle greeted the man from the National Assistance Board. They sat at the living room table where he asked ten thousand questions, sometimes requiring evidence such as her birth certificate or employment papers. Eventually the paperwork was complete and Annabelle signed accordingly. Later she received a book containing a number of orders, which she could cash weekly at the post office for the grand sum of £3-16-5d. Annabelle was deflated. It was a drop in the ocean compared to her HQMC wage.

News of Alberto's illness spread rapidly around the village and soon reflected people's kindness. Mrs Chambers, the Guide Captain, was the first at the door offering a quarter of a pound packet of tea to Annabelle.

"Thank you, Mrs Chambers. How did you guess that we've run out of tea?"

"Easy, my dear. We all head for the teapot in times of trouble. I bet you're really glad that you passed the Red Cross Home Nursing exam when you were in the Girl Guides aren't you? Must be coming in very useful with your mum and dad both sick in bed.

"Yes, it's been a help. Nursing my dad is a lot different to nursing my mum. He needs bedpans and stuff, but Dr MacCallum tells me what to do and Sister Peters comes in every day."

"Well, I'm pleased to hear it and if you need the help of myself or my girls, you know where to find us."

"Thank you, Mrs Chambers."

"Who was that?" asked Alice as Annabelle went into their bedroom.

"It was Mrs Chambers, the Guide Captain. She brought us some tea, so I'll go and make a cup."

Many more similar gifts were brought to the door and Alberto remarked to Alice, "I always knew that Enham was a very special place to live, my lovely. I'm so grateful you married me."

Annabelle knew they were holding hands under the covers as she quietly left the room with her undisclosed tears.

It is said that as one door closes another one opens, which was confirmed in Annabelle's case. An opportunity for Annabelle to earn a bit of money came from no other than Dr MacCallum. His secretary, Betty Moody, had broken her leg and the doctor asked Annabelle if she thought she could fit in a few hours' work for him.

"As long as you can cope with irregular working hours, yes please."

With his broad grin he replied, "The world's your oyster. We can help each other out."

The first thing that sprang into Annabelle's mind was "no bus journeys". Her route to work would be up the back garden path, through the loose planks in the six-foot fence, through the hole in the laurel hedge and into Dr MacCallum's office. It was exactly the same route that the doctor used regularly to care for her parents.

"Weekends?" enquired Annabelle.

"If it helps, yes, of course."

"That's good. We have relatives visiting at the weekends, so I'd feel free to concentrate on your work knowing there were people at home to look after Mum and Dad. Same thing in the evenings really, with villagers' visits."

"That's settled then."

"Not quite, Doctor. We haven't talked about wages yet."

"Good God; you're a wee canny lass, young madam. I thought I was the only Scot! Tell me what you were earning in your last job and we'll work out an hourly rate."

The job arrangement was perfect. Annabelle loved the work and Dr MacCallum was delighted with her capabilities, but all the time she was watching her father's life ebbing away and it was now becoming a 24 hour a day ordeal. She had the benefit of calling Dr MacCallum any time of the day or night to give Alberto morphine injections and although they took away pain, they gave her father hallucinations and he was screaming at all hours, thinking he was in a snake pit.

Annabelle's loyalties became one-sided, erring on her father's care, so she had to give the doctor notice that she was too tired to keep doing his job.

"Not to worry, Annabelle. I could foresee this situation, of course. Betty is now on crutches and she will come back to me part-time. What I must do immediately is get in touch with the Army and get Al home on compassionate leave."

"Yes please, Doctor. He'll be no help whatsoever domestically, but he should come home to see dad before…" Annabelle became too choked up to say the words.

Over the next few weeks, things deteriorated so badly that Annabelle found herself praying for the end. All Alice could do as she lay beside her screaming husband was to hold his hand and say "It's alright Alberto. You're having a nightmare. I'm still with you. I'm squeezing your hand. Can you feel me?"

Whether he could feel it or not, Annabelle never knew and never would know. She left them together while she went to the scullery to rinse out some washing that had been soaking and when she came back, all was quiet. She felt for her father's pulse and couldn't find it. Immediately she ran up the garden path.

"He's gone, dear. He'll suffer no more," said the doctor as he gave her a comforting hug. "Your mother's exhausted so I'll give her a sedative. What about you?"

When Mr Geoghegan came in the early evening, he cuddled Annabelle as he said, "I've lost a very good friend."

"So have I," wept Annabelle.

Annabelle found solace in going to her writing desk in her bedroom and writing from the heart.

26ᵗʰ May 1949

Dear Dad,

After all the suffering so quickly you fly, before I could even say goodbye; and all I can do is cry and cry.

387

Was it awful to be so alone, with mum asleep beside you and me momentarily gone?

But before you could have flown very far, I was holding your hand, just like before.

Oh Dad it was awful, I lingered awhile, but then got scared 'cos you did not smile.

Oh Dad, it was awful, I felt the chill, and all my feelings just stood still.

Then through streaming tears I woke my mum and we hugged each other with feelings numb.

But now, 'peace for you' dear dad is my plea, I'll take great care of mum, you know me.

From your ever-loving daughter, Annabelle.

Al had arrived home in time to say goodbye to his dad. When the end came he was shocked and choked up, but wasn't good at showing his feelings. Annabelle was grateful for his presence because he did the immediate jobs, such as registering their father's death and finding a funeral director.

Mr Geoghegan visited every day after Alberto had gone. After comforting Alice, he found Annabelle up in her back corner bedroom still crying her heart out.

"I want to get him back. Tell me how I can do that?"

"There's no way I'm afraid, darlin'. He's gone. It is very final."

"Mr Geoghegan, help me. I can't think straight. I'm nearly out of my mind. What have I got to do for the funeral? Do I have to arrange buttonholes?"

Touched by her trauma, he replied, "No darlin', you can do that for your wedding day. I'll tell you what you've got to do. You've got to pull yourself together for your dad's sake and get yourself to the shops. You have to buy yourself something black to wear. Find something nice so you can look lovely for him, and find something black for your mum too. I'll come at the end of every day to see what you've chosen."

"Yes, of course. I should have thought of that."

So many villagers attended the funeral, which comforted Annabelle, because her dad was amongst friends above the ground as well as those below it.

Settling into a different life was hard. Al had gone back to Suez and Annabelle was left nursing her sick and mourning mother. At that time, tortured by the loss and emptiness in her life, she again found solace in her writing:

Dear Dad,

Did I ever tell you I loved you so? Dear, dear Dad, perhaps till now I didn't know.

Mr Geoghegan still visited the two of them and Annabelle voiced that she would have to get out and find another job soon. Fortunately, Dr MacCallum saved the day for the second time in her life.

"There's a vacancy in the office in Enham Industries and I've recommended you as the ideal person. Mr Crabbe suggested you call into the office some time and he'll make the necessary arrangements."

That news cheered both Alice and Annabelle.

"Dr MacCallum, it's like you're my Guardian Angel."

"Well I certainly haven't got wings!"

TGA: *(No, but I've got mine, and today I feel as though I've got a second pair, seeing things starting to get easier for this broken-hearted young lady. All her life she's cared for a sick mother. Whoever would have thought that Annabelle would have to cope with her father being the first to be taken, leaving her mother a grieving, sick widow?)*

Annabelle had no problem in securing the job at Enham Industries. It was far less interesting than working for the doctor in the medical world and less demanding than HQMC, but they paid her fairly and it was only a short walk up the road. She could go home at dinnertime to look after her mum and then go back home at 5pm. Her life was blighted by loss, but getting easier.

No matter what, life goes on and Enham underwent the most amazing development in the late 40s.

The British Government had received a huge gift of £250,000 in the form of three separate cheques from the Egyptian Government in recognition of the gallantry of British Forces, including The Desert Rats, at the Battle of El Alamein in WW2 and their resultant freedom from Axis countries' domination.

The British Government decided to donate the money to Enham Village Centre, which brought about the renaming of the village to Enham Alamein. At the same time, Field Marshal Montgomery became a proud Vice President.

The money was put to good use by building new houses on an Alamein estate at the top of Kings Hill, where new roads such as Alamein Road and Tobruk Close came into being. This meant a new intake of disabled people, mostly suffering from tuberculosis, which was the scourge of the early 50s era.

At that time, on 15th August 1950, it was announced that Queen Elizabeth II had given birth to her second child, this time a little girl, Princess Anne Elizabeth Alice Louise. The nation rejoiced that the Queen had got her pigeon pair.

Annabelle became 21 years old while working at Enham Industries. That was Christmas time of course, and that year they had Uncle Ted and Aunt Nell, Alice's younger brother and his wife, down to stay for the holiday, much to Alice's delight. She was still mourning not only Alberto, but also her younger brother George, who had recently been reported missing, believed dead, during his active Service at Dunkirk as part of the D-Day landings.

Annabelle had festively decorated the room for their visit and was planning a few things to make the season merry.

On 24th December, her birthday, she was officially allowed to have the key of the door.

TGA: *(The reader will know that Annabelle had qualified for that many years ago. She had been practically running the home since she was about eight years old, which is exactly the reason why I am her Guardian Angel.)*

To celebrate her birthday, Uncle Ted had carved out a wooden key, shaped in accordance with a key of the era. It was the same as their front door key, but about fourteen inches long and covered in silver paper. Aunt Nell had decorated it with some pressed pink flowers and pink ribbon, some of which was long enough to enable Annabelle to hang the key round her neck. She wore it proudly for the entire Christmas, feeling as important as the Lord Mayor of London.

It turned out to be a good Christmas. Uncle Ted loved sing-alongs and brought his piano accordion with him. Annabelle introduced her own sense of fun, catching her uncle out several times by suddenly saying, "What's that?" and looking somewhere specific, like under the table. With all attention held, she would then sing, "I taut I taw a puddy tat…" It was a novelty song released fairly recently about a big black cat called Sylvester who wanted to catch a canary called Tweety Pie. It was an infectious tune and it must have been sung a hundred times in No. 9 that Christmas.

New Year started in an amazing and totally unexpected way for Annabelle. Dr MacCallum asked her if she would like to take on Betty Moody's job permanently, as she had handed in her notice. She was getting married to Tom Blackmore and emigrating to Australia. He explained that the job would be a bit more complicated than before because he was now the Chest Physician for all the tuberculosis patients that were coming to the village for rehabilitation, as well as being the village doctor. The Egyptian money also paid for a hostel to provide living accommodation for the new influx.

With even better qualifications, having achieved her 120 words a minute shorthand in March 1949 and 130 in September, Annabelle knew she could cope with whatever was thrown at her and eagerly accepted the position.

She became employed as secretary to Alan C Smith, Company Secretary for the Governing Body of the Village Centre's Council and as medical secretary to Dr MacCallum.

Annabelle was still ambitious with her shorthand. She wanted to equal Emily D Smith (250 wpm) who issued a monthly magazine incorporating exercise tips, counted dictation passages and short form phrases that shortened the shorthand even further. With this in mind, Annabelle went to see Miss Hart to ask if she would coach her at such high speed rates. There was no answer to her door knocking and a neighbour came out and beckoned her to the fence.

"I know this is going to shock you dear, but I have to tell you that Miss Hart committed suicide last week."

That information, which came as a terrible shock, knocked the ambitious stuffing out of Annabelle.

"Why would anyone want to do that?" she pondered, her father's death uppermost in her mind.

As the weeks passed, she settled down to her new job, in which she was more than happy and proved herself well qualified.

Chapter 20

Andre's Life Threatened in the Suez Canal

After a short period of service, Andre was promoted to a corporal and began his army career as a hygiene inspector. His duties were to travel the length and breadth of the Suez Canal to check on the sanitation of all camps within the area. Cockroaches and flies were the main enemies.

At the camp next to Ismailia, there was a NAAFI warehouse that had become infested with cockroaches. Andre and another hygiene inspector, John Crotty, were assigned to deal with this infestation.

Their first job was to seal all windows and doors, with the exception of the door from which they would make their exit. Secondly, they lay gammexane smoke candles (similar to nightlights) on the floor at strategic points, row upon row, until they had laid the last row near their exit door. Finally, they put on their special masks and started lighting the candles from the front row to the last one until each was lit. They then made a hasty exit as the building was rapidly filling with yellow oily gammexane smoke. From the outside they sealed their exit door and were glad to leave the building overnight.

It was an appalling sight to behold next morning when they opened the door. The floor was completely covered with dead and dying cockroaches, small and large. The sight was hard to be believed and Andre had to pinch himself to make sure it was real and not a nightmare.

The appalling evidence of their work was soon cleared up and incinerated by other Egyptian staff.

At Gebel Maryam, where Andre was stationed, a stone monument had been built to commemorate the first time the Suez Canal had been breached by a foreign force. That had happened in 1915 when some French troops had supported the British Allied effort to fight the Turkish forces who were attacking the canal.

Apart from reading and playing draughts, which was quite popular, there was nothing much you could under canvas. Andre preferred chess, which was not popular, so an opponent was hard to find. Feeling fed up one day, he decided to take a dip in the canal.

Being a sea level canal, the height of water levels can differ slightly, but the extreme tidal range can be as much as 65 cm in the north at Port Said to 1.9 meters in the south at the Gulf of Suez. These extremes are influenced by the pull of the Mediterranean Sea at the opposite end of the canal to the Red Sea.

Unknown to Andre, such conditions cause strong currents within the canal and he got swept away by them. He was helpless and was convinced his number was up. The currents were too strong for him, but thankfully some Egyptians on the canal path spotted him and managed to haul him out.

"Not good idea," said one, wagging his finger at Andre.

"You're tellin' me," gasped Andre. "I know that now, for my sins. Thank you; thank you for saving my life."

They got him back to Gebel Maryam in an old truck where they found his pile of clothes still on the canal bank. He shook his rescuers' hands before saying "Praise be to Allah," not quite sure if he was saying right or wrong thing.

As he was dressing himself, he realised that Grandpa's ring was missing. He'd been able to wear it ever since he'd put on a bit of weight when the Army hospital had pumped protein into him. After all those years of keeping it safe, it was now lost somewhere in the Suez Canal. He was mortified and silently told Grandma so. He knew there was not one iota of hope of ever finding it.

Andre had difficulty in getting the loss of Grandpa's ring out of his mind, but eventually something happened that began the process. An unknown Egyptian came to his tent one day when his day duties were finished.

"Corporal Kliskey, I understand you play chess."

"I do, but it's hard to find someone on the camp who will give me a game with such a mix of nationalities and languages. We have Greek and Cypriot soldiers as well as some from the Seychelles."

"Would you like to give me a game at some time?"

Andre was delighted. He was invited into the Egyptian's luxurious tent. Before Andre had played any more than four moves the Egyptian said, "Corporal Kliskey, you have lost."

Andre was baffled. The Egyptian explained that he played three or four moves ahead, which told him what would happen next. Andre could do no more than concede after the Egyptian had shown him his reasoning. The two of them met on eight more occasions and each time Andre was thrashed.

Sometime later, Andre saw the Egyptian playing chess with another person outside his tent and stopped to watch. They started by playing mental, or theoretical, chess. Both sitting with their eyes shut, they would call out the number of the square and the piece that would occupy it. They would play out the entire game in this way and Andre was in awe of their astounding expertise.

It was while relating this amazing story to others on the camp that Andre discovered that his Egyptian opponent was an Egyptian chess champion. He never invited Andre to play again.

Andre attained the rank of Sergeant before his conscription service came to an end and had enjoyed all the new things he'd mastered.

On return to East Croydon, he called on his father and stepmother to notify them that he was back in England and that he had found himself digs. He packed his few belongings and said goodbye.

Thereafter, he concentrated on the sports that he loved by going back to the youth club. Boxing was still a favourite and he trained hard, running three times a night round the Shirley Hills before going back to the gym and fighting six rounds. He was now a featherweight and was beginning to get back to his previous standard. He proved his progress by winning the Croydon Youth Club Championships.

Now he had to prove himself as a draughtsman all over again and started looking for civilian employment. During his local travels, he seized the opportunity to go into Grant's Department Store in Croydon and headed for the lift. His intention was to give Elsa a big surprise.

Instead, he received a huge shock.

"I'm sorry, sir. Elsa left us about a year ago and we haven't heard from her since."

"Do you know where she went to work after she left you?"

"Afraid not."

"The little monkey," thought Andre, remembering the last thing she whispered in his ear before he joined the Army. "I bet she's gone off to Gretna Green to marry that chap she fell in love with."

Concerned, he went back home to ask his parents, but that just drew a blank. She hadn't communicated with them in a long time.

On nights when he wasn't training in the gym, Andre's adult life started to open up. He was hitting the town with some of his old mates with whom he'd formed fond memories of the VE Day celebrations. By this time, they were all grown young men, most of whom had conscription service to their credit.

Now they were a divided group; Ken Pick, with whom he used to cycle around the Shirley Hills in younger days, was in the group chasing girls, while Andre was in the group chasing whiskies.

Invariably, such nights would end with Andre and his mates walking back to their digs on the top of suburbia's neatly cut privet hedges.

TGA: *(What an action-packed two to three years Andre experienced. I, for one, am grateful to the Egyptians who saved his life at Suez. Had his life ended there, I would have lost the opportunity to finish telling you this story.)*

Chapter 21

'Jack of All Trades' at White House in Enham

Conscription service came to an end in 1951 for Al and he returned home from Suez. It was good to have him back. His humorous spirit cheered the house. Alice and Annabelle were enthralled when he was telling of the entertainment skills he had developed out there. Naturally, his tap dancing was very popular, but there was more and he was itching to get back on stage in the Insty with horizons set further afield.

In the meantime, he had no problems in getting himself a job in the paint spraying department of Enham Industries.

On his second day home, he wrote a letter to the BBC saying he was interested in becoming a horse racing commentator whenever a broadcasting position became available. He explained to them how he'd successfully entertained the troops in Suez with mock horse races and commentating on them; qualifying the statement with the fact that the soldiers thought being a commentator was his real job. The subject was second nature to him because, with Auntie Dolly's influence, he'd studied the race horses, their stables, their owners, jockeys, weights and colours and forms since he was a little boy. Now back at home he had his nose stuck into the racing page of the Daily Express every spare second of the day, trying to bridge the knowledge gap that occurred while serving in the Army.

Every day Al patiently waited for a reply from the BBC, but it seemed they were preoccupied with General Election broadcasts, which came to a head on 26th October when, by a small majority, Winston Churchill was voted in as Prime Minister again.

It was when all that hubbub had settled down that Al received his letter offering him an interview.

TGA: *(I've heard humans speak of 'cats with two tails', but seeing Al so happy helped me understand what that phrase was all about.)*

He thought he got on OK at the interview. The gentleman told him he certainly knew his subject, so Al came home somewhat confident, but still apprehensive.

The letter was on the table waiting for him when he got home from work a week or so later. It said all the right and polite things you might expect, but those comments didn't hide the negativity. He was informed that his knowledge was impeccable, but regretted that he didn't have a good enough BBC voice for broadcasting!

"Cheer up Al," encouraged Alice. "You're a talented young man and you should keep trying in the entertainment world. Your father would want you to do that."

Al heeded his mother's words. There wasn't a pantomime organised in the Insty for early 1952, but Mr Freddie Cox with Mr Geoghegan and others decided that a revue would be better than nothing. That was an entertainment outlet for Al's newfound dream and on performance he proved to be a sensation.

He decided to put on 'Have a Go', based on the very successful radio show of the time being broadcast by Wilfred Pickles and his wife Mabel. It was a show where participants were encouraged to tell moving or saucy stories of their own family's lives and then answer very simple questions for money prizes. That could have been any denomination up to £2 at the most, which was considered to be their fee for taking part.

Al's image was of a confident professional, looking smart and raring to go as he stood centre stage with a microphone on a stand in front of him.

Laura played the upright piano, still on stage left, and a chorus of cast members sang out the opening song of the radio show:

"Have a go, Joe, come on and have a go.
You can't lose out; it costs you nowt
To make yourself some dough.
So hurry up and join us;
Don't be shy and don't be slow,
Come on Joe, have a go."

"Ladies and Gentlemen of Enham, 'ello, ow are ya?"

Eager applause ensued and Al responded with "OK, so what's keepin' ya? Without a contestant, there ain't no show."

There was a tentative pause before a sea of hands were waving at him.

403

"That's better. Come on up here, Mr Gamblin. You and me are gunna make these people laugh, I hope."

Mr Gamblin was a wounded WW1 man, who couldn't get up on the stage.

"Don't you worry, sir. We'll come down to you. That's a brilliant name if I may be so bold as to say so, Mr Gamblin. Do you back the winners every day?" He moved his eyes from side to side.

"Never gambled in me life and proud of it."

Al silently encouraging the audience to boo.

"So you haven't got rich quick then? Maybe you should give it a try. What do you reckon, audience?"

Swift participation was spontaneous.

"What's your Christian name, Mr Gamblin?"

"Joe."

"Blimey, so you're really ready to 'ave a go, Joe. Good 'ere, ain' it," said Al, smiling to the audience. "I'm beginning to feel like Wilfred Pickles himself."

"So, Joe, have you got any good family secrets to share with us?"

Welcoming responses, Al motioned both of his hands toward himself and the audience did not disappoint.

"Come on, Joe, tell us about the night you got married," someone shouted.

"Can't remember."

"Blimey, who's the comedian around here?"

"Ooh, yes I can; yes, I can. We caught the train to Frimley and we went to bed together."

"Well done, Joe. Thanks for telling us something we already know. Ladies and Gentlemen, a big hand for Mr Joe Gamblin, please."

As Joe returned to his seat, Al called out, "And there's no prize money here, Joe. You'll have to go on radio to get that."

"Let's see if we can get more out of the next contestant. Anyone else willing to come up? Ah, I can see pretty little Lucy there. Come on up Lucy."

As soon as she was on stage, Al asked, "Are ya' courtin'?"

The audience roared. It was a typical Wilfred Pickles question.

Lucy giggled, "Let's say I'm dabbling."

"Dabbling in what?"

"In the hayloft."

"Sounds ominous," Al winked. "We all know you like to help out at the farm. And Lucy, you've got the prettiest of speaking voices. Come closer and tell me, do you whisper sweet nothings in his ear in the hayloft?"

"No fear. We've got better things to do."

Al, to the audience who were agog, "Whoever would have expected this from our little Lucy?"

"More, more, more!" shouted the audience.

"Lucy, I've got the jitters. Tell me, what are the better things?"

"Balancing ourselves so we don't roll off the stack."

"Come on, Lucy. Give. We want more."

"Well, what would you do in that situation?"

"Hey, who's Wilfred Pickles in this outfit? I'm the one asking the questions. Does he take you anywhere else besides the haystack?"

"Yes, he takes me behind the cowshed."

"Blimey, I wonder if the farmer knows? And what does he do there, may I ask?"

"Tries to avoid the cowpats." Lucy giggled uncontrollably.

"Lucy, I give up. You've entertained us beautifully, and I guess we'll just have to use our imaginations."

"Make sure you do me credit then," Lucy laughed, as she kissed him on the cheek.

That brought Al's slot in the revue to an end, so Laura played the closing song to which the audience sang along:

Have a go Joe, you've been and had a go,
And you can tell your friends as well
You've been on radio,
So listen in again next week
And hear another show.
Have a go, Joe, Have a go!

As the applause died down, Al said, "Ladies and Gentlemen, before we part I'd like to share a good book title with you. You'd be wise to look out for it. It's called *The Long Drop* by P Overcliffe." With both thumbs up and grinning broadly, he concluded with, "Goodnight and God Bless."

On 6th February 1952, not many days after all the excitement of that revue, people around the world were shocked by the announcement that

King George VI had died peacefully in his bed from a lung condition at the age of 56 years.

Surely the most severely shocked of all was Princess Elizabeth. She and Prince Phillip were on a visit to Treetops, a game viewing lodge in Kenya. Prince Phillip received the message first and took his wife for a walk in the quiet garden where, at 2.45pm on 6th February 1952, he told Princess Elizabeth that her father had died and that she was now Queen of the Commonwealth.

Annabelle was doing one of her many and varied jobs in her office when Dr MacCallum came through and told her the news. It was one of those occasions when you remembered exactly what you were doing at the time. Everybody did. She went from the table where she was working and sat at her desk in the bay window.

"So, what job have they got you doing now?" asked the doctor. "I thought you were a secretary."

"Secretary, telephonist and Jack of all Trades would be more like it."

Returning to the table in the centre of the room, she said, "I'm working on this head and shoulders' bust of Field Marshal Montgomery; trying to patch his nose that got damaged. We want it as an exhibit for the prospective museum. I must get on with it before this alabaster dries." She studied the picture in the newspaper cutting in front of her.

Ever since the introduction of the Alamein aspect to the village, artefacts had been arriving in Annabelle's office from Egypt. Leaning against a wall in her office, there was a railway station sign, about 4' wide by 18" deep, with the words EL

407

ALAMEIN in white letters on a dark green background.

"You OK now?"

"Yes, thank you, Doctor. When I've finished this I'll make us all a cup of tea. I'll give you a phone signal and you can come back in if you want one."

Although Annabelle put on a brave face in the office, she was really glad when it was time to go home to have a cry. Alice cuddled her. "Why are you so upset, Annabelle? I can't bear to see you breaking your heart."

"Well, it hurts. The King had the same illness as Dad."

"He did, but I'm sure they kept him as comfortable as possible."

"Do you think he thought he was in a snake pit?" she whispered.

"I've no idea, sweetheart, and you mustn't dwell on that all over again. The King would have had the best care in the world, the same as your dad did. The King may have had a posh bedroom with beautiful eiderdowns and things, but the love is what matters, and I'm sure his family gave him plenty of that. Now come along and buck up. Al popped home in his break to tell me that other villages are wanting him to do 'Have a Go' for them. He's really excited. Wouldn't it be good if that could start him off on an entertainment career? Shall we drink a cup of tea to it?"

As a mark of respect, before Parliament adjourned, Winston Churchill offered their condolences and announced that he would broadcast to the nation the following day. It was common knowledge and generally accepted that Winston Churchill wrote his own speeches, devoting much of his sleeping time to the cause when required. I detail sections of the speech so you can judge for yourselves:

(QUOTE)

When the death of the King was announced to us yesterday morning there struck a deep and solemn note in our lives which, as it resounded far and wide, stilled the clatter and traffic of twentieth-century life in many lands, and made countless millions of human beings pause and look around them. A new sense of values took, for the time being, possession of human minds, and mortal existence presented itself to so many at the same moment in its serenity and in its sorrow, in its splendour and in its pain, in its fortitude and in its suffering.

The King was greatly loved by all his peoples. He was respected as a man and as a prince far beyond the many realms over which he reigned. The simple dignity of his life, his manly virtues, his sense of duty – alike as a ruler and a servant of the vast spheres and communities for which he bore responsibility – his gay charm and happy nature, his example as a husband and a father in his own family circle, his courage in peace or war - all these were aspects of his character which won the glint of admiration, now here, now there, from the innumerable eyes whose gaze falls upon the Throne.

Now I must leave the treasures of the past and turn to the future. Famous have been the reigns of our queens. Some of the greatest periods in our history have unfolded under their sceptre. Now that we have the second Queen Elizabeth, also ascending the Throne in her twenty-sixth year, our thoughts are carried back nearly four hundred years to the magnificent figure who presided over and, in many ways, embodied and inspired the grandeur and genius of the Elizabethan age.

Queen Elizabeth II, like her predecessor, did not pass her childhood in any certain expectation of the Crown. But already we know her well, and we understand why her gifts, and those of her husband, the Duke of Edinburgh, have stirred the only part of the Commonwealth she has yet been able to visit. She has already been acclaimed as Queen of Canada.

We make our claim too, and others will come forward also, and tomorrow the proclamation of her Sovereignty will command the loyalty of her native land and all other parts of the Commonwealth and Empire. I, whose youth was passed in the august, unchallenged and tranquil glories of the Victorian era, may well feel a thrill in invoking once more the prayer and the anthem, 'God save the Queen!'

(UNQUOTE)

Alice, Annabelle and Al listened intently to that speech, along with many other people all over the world. It truly was, as the Prime Minister had said, a solemn event that chilled the soul, but over the

410

next few days, thoughts started turning to their new, young and beautiful Queen and her momentous task.

Annabelle's job at the White House had changed immensely since the time she stood in for Betty Moody. At that time, Dr MacCallum looked after the WW1 disabled men and families, either in the surgery or by walking round to make home visits. The Alamein connection with the village, which coincided with the tuberculosis epidemic in the early fifties, brought about significant changes.

The Governing Body made the decision to take over Weyhill Hospital, which was about three miles west of Andover, where tuberculosis patients were initially admitted for assessment. Within those premises there were also isolation units for contagious patients and those suffering relapse.

When considered fit enough to do three hours work a day, they were transferred to Enham Alamein to live in the hostel, which had been built courtesy the Egyptian donations. It had been built with a flat roof to enable more storeys to be added in the future.

With the advent of Weyhill Hospital, Dr MacCallum was provided with a chauffeur driven car to enable him to visit the hospital daily. His chauffeur was Mr Franky Betts, a WW1 settler in the village.

Catering for the hospital and the hostel became another new aspect. Mr Bob Hipperson, who had married Doreen Pilkington, daughter of a WW1 settler, was employed as Catering Officer. He was a competent chef, who had responsibility for employing staff to cater for all meals at both institutions and was provided with a white hatchback car, which was essential for the job. He did all the purchasing himself and was yet another person to pass through Annabelle's office daily, taking all invoices to Mr Cox, who had become the accountant for the village since its inception.

To cope with all the extra secretarial needs, Annabelle had to reorganise her workspace. Previously she had one desk with a typewriter and enough space to handwrite when required. She faced the opposite wall with a door leading into the small boardroom, which doubled as Mr Alan C Smith's office, with her right shoulder into the bay window. Mr Smith was the company secretary.

Now she had two extra work spaces and one swivel chair, which served all. Turning to her right, she could operate the PBX Switchboard, which had two outside lines and several internal lines to facilitate contact with all factions of the village.

Over the top of the switchboard, she could see into Dr MacCallum's walled garden, which he kept in top-notch condition, gardening being his all-consuming hobby. Turning right again, she had another desk, which backed onto the adjoining wall of Dr MacCallum's living accommodation, his surgery being on the far side of the building. There she could deal with the constant daily flow of post. Large envelopes would arrive containing chest x-rays with applications from county councils or their chest physicians all over the British Isles, applying for their patients to come to the village for treatment.

Many more staff had to be employed to support the new influx. Dr MacCallum was, of course, the chest physician. Newly employed were Miss Buxton, the Matron, Mrs Jeffery, the Almoner and support staff of all vocations to run the newly built hostel where the patients would live after being transferred from Weyhill Hospital. Just like the WW1 intake, those TB patients would be assigned various numbers of working hours in a choice of work environments and upgraded to more hours as their health improved. When patients were certified fit, they had the option to return home to find employment, or settle in a house in the village and become self-sufficient.

David Henry, one such patient, found his new livelihood working as a medical orderly for Dr MacCallum, whose workload had increased beyond measure.

Lil Robson, who was married to Frank, eldest son of a WW1 settler, became housekeeper and cook to Matron Buxton who had been provided with the top floor flat in a thatched farm cottage at the north end of the village, next door to the Geoghegans' house. Lil passed through Annabelle's office every Friday afternoon to collect her wages from Mr Cox and nearly always admired Annabelle's beautiful long blonde thick hair as she passed.

"I wish that was mine," she would say.

Another new, essential employee was a young Mr Ted Wesley who had come from Skipton in Derbyshire to work as Assistant Accountant to Mr Norman Cox. He was going to take on all the catering finance work and new Alamein connection accounting as well as learning Mr Cox's job to hold the fort in times of sickness and holidays.

Ted usually brought sandwiches to eat at lunchtime because, although he lived up in one of the new Alamein houses, he felt that by the time he'd walked down the hill from The White House, up King's Hill and beyond to his home, it would be time to come back again. One such lunchtime he brought his Scrabble game with him. It was new on the market and Annabelle was impatient to learn how to play the game.

The next day she made a special lunchtime arrangement for her mother and stayed in the office to play the Scrabble game. Loving words as she did, Annabelle was absolutely fascinated and found it hard to wait for Saturday to come, when she could go to Andover and buy a game for herself.

Many of the above people had occasion to use – or pass through – Annabelle's office, which very often gave rise to the thought that she was working in Clapham Junction. That situation was compounded more so by the constant interruptions of operating the switchboard.

As she entered through the conservatory door and unlocked her office, Annabelle never knew what unexpected things would happen in her office from one day to the next. One day, fairly early in the morning, Matron Buxton and Mrs Jeffery arrived through the inner door of her office from Dr MacCallum's surgery. An outside phone call summoned Annabelle to the switchboard and she offered the telephone to Mrs Jeffery. "It's for you."

"Pardon, am I hearing you correctly?" she questioned as she sat on Annabelle's chair.

A long pause ensued while she listened intently.

"I thought that's what you said," Mrs Jeffery said, looking round to everybody in the office with surprised, wide eyes. "Why yes, darling. The answer's 'YES'. Of course I'll marry you."

Matron and Annabelle gazed at each other as the conversation continued.

Congratulations abounded when twice widowed Mrs Jeffery came off the phone. By that time, quite a congregation had gathered in the office. Matron Buxton broke the ice, if there was indeed ice to be broken, by declaring loudly, "Three proposals in a lifetime and I can't even get one!"

Another time, early in the morning, Alan C Smith barged in Annabelle's office from the conservatory with hardly a second to breathe. He had driven his Ford Popular car from his home in Andover and asked Annabelle to get Bartley's for him.

"You're through," said Annabelle efficiently.

Barging very soon from his own office into Annabelle's he said, "Thanks to you I've just discussed all my bank details with my garage. I asked for Barclays!"

Annabelle kept her tongue between her cheek and put Barclays Bank through to him.

At 10.30am, when Annabelle made tea for all the regular staff, she purposely put two heaped teaspoons of sugar in Mr Smith's tea. Very quickly he was back at the adjoining office door pulling the most unimaginably contorted face and said, "There's sugar in my tea."

Cool as a cucumber, she replied, "No more than you deserve today, I'm sure."

Mr Smith got his comeuppance for assuming that Annabelle could tell the difference between two such similar names as Bartley's and Barclay's, garbled at her as he was disappearing into his own office when, through no fault of his own, he had the task of placing an advert in every national newspaper in Great Britain.

One of the new tuberculosis patients had the idea of building up his bank balance substantially by making sit-in swing seats for toddlers out of plywood, rope and cotton reels. Therefore, he had advertised in a national newspaper asking for cotton reels to be sent to him at The White House, Enham Village Centre, without giving the registered charity number of the village. His reasoning was that he'd be more likely to get a response by giving an official address.

Before many days passed, thousands of sack loads of cotton reels arrived from all over the country. About a hundred sacks arrived from a glove factory in Cornwall alone. The White House was being swamped. The conservatory and a lot of the boardroom space had been filled as well as some of Dr MacCallum's personal accommodation.

The patient concerned was 'called over the coals' for not seeking advice and Jack of all Trades was being buried under cotton reels! Everyone concerned was greatly relieved when lorries started removing the sacks.

One thing was constant in Annabelle's office life. Mr Gee, the gardener, always found a little bunch of flowers, or maybe only leaves in wintertime, to provide an arrangement to go on the table in the centre of her office every Monday morning that he was working, throughout the entire year.

In the autumn of 1952, Annabelle felt as though her heart had been pierced by an arrow. A notice on the oak tree at the bottom of the Insty drive announced that a Mr John Constable would be auditioning for acting parts in *Jack and The Beanstalk*, a pantomime to be put on in the LWI in January 1953.

In her mind, Mr Constable was a usurper. That was her father's domain.

"Will you apply for an audition?" she asked of Al.

"Of course I will. You should too. Much better to be involved from the beginning, otherwise you'll find it hard to join in another time. Dad's gone, but he'd want you to apply."

Annabelle deliberated long on the suggestion.

Chapter 22

Lust or Love for Andre

Andre was on the streets of London searching for work as a draughtsman. He had a small portfolio of his own and would settle for employment or private work, whichever appeared on the horizon first. He was just one of many qualified men looking for work in London.

In the meantime, he was prepared to do anything to earn money to pay for his lodgings. He was quite successful in picking up odd jobs like a bit of gardening, which in one instance was made available by a man in full-time employment who was paying to keep his elderly mother independent in her own home. There were also window cleaning jobs to be found, although his faint heart forced him to turn down one good job. It was a huge swimming pool complex, but horrific memories of dicing with death in the Suez Canal prohibited any consideration. He was terrified to go near the place.

On a cold January day, he had a flurry of excitement during his travels by public transport when he spotted a young lady with a wonderful head of auburn hair walking down the street. Compelled, he tore down the stairs from the top floor of the double-decker bus, trying to keep his eye on her while grabbing onto the support pole waiting for the bus to slow down. Alighting as soon as he could, he raced back along the pavement like an untrapped hare at the Dogs in White City.

"Excuse me, miss," he blurted out, gasping for breath. "I saw you from the top of the bus and I just had to meet you."

He could see her two front teeth were crossed as she grinned and said, "This can't be true. They only do that sort of thing in pictures."

"Do you want me to pinch you then, so you know it's real?"

"No thank you very much," she laughed. "That won't be necessary."

"Can I see you some time? I'm so attracted to you. Pleeeeaaaase," he begged.

After a bit of haggling, she agreed. "Oh, alright then. I'll meet you outside the Odeon cinema in Croydon High Street on Saturday at 6pm."

"Thank you, I can't wait," he enthused, as he watched the rear view of her disappear down the street. She had very straight legs in black court shoes and her long auburn hair glowed brilliantly against the green velour coat she was wearing.

That evening Andre went to the pub to down a few whiskies with his mates. Shocked at himself, he told the boys, "I've got to tell you blokes that I've changed sides from the drinkers in this outfit to the Ken Pick lot. I've got a date!"

"Never! Not you, of all people."

"Don't do it mate. Keep your freedom. You're way too young yet."

"I know all that reasoning," confessed Andre, "but this was compulsion. I couldn't take my eyes off her." He shrugged his shoulders and shook his head from side to side. "So I've got a date."

Bridging the gap until Saturday, he decided he should go to London again to try to find work. He knew he was a good draughtsman and was anxious to become a technical illustrator, so he headed to the publishing companies in Fleet Street. He found that to be a formidable task.

His first enquiry was at Reuters. The receptionist asked him to take a seat in the foyer opposite her desk where he watched hundreds of people walking in and out of the glass swing doors.

"Excuse me, miss, I've been waiting here for over an hour. Will someone see me soon?"

"I'll remind them that you're here. Editors are very busy people you know."

Feeling hungry after three hours, Andre walked out. Venting his frustration at home, he went for a good long run round the Shirley Hills.

Two days later, feeling refreshed, Andre went through a similar experience at The Telegraph.

Disillusioned, he cheered himself with '*Rome wasn't built in a Day*' and this time vented his frustration on a punch bag at the Youth Club.

"Oh, thank goodness, you've come," Andre said, with a huge sigh of relief when she appeared. From the display board outside they discovered that the main film showing was a romance, *April in Paris* with Doris Day and Ray Bolger.

"Would you like to see it?" Sounds perfect to me," winked Andre.

"Yes, I would, but I'd rather wait for the last full programme to start. Look, that's at ten past seven, it says here."

"Still perfect. We've got an hour, so how about going to the Milk Bar further along the road?"

"Ooh! Yes please. Then I can have a strawberry milkshake."

Standing in the queue to be served, Andre almost choked out, "Hey, I've just realised, I don't know your name. I'm Andre and I'm very pleased meet you," as he held out a hand to shake hers and then covered hers with his left.

"Thank you. I'm Myra. You don't sound French."

"You're right. I'm not, but wish I was."

"Why?"

"I'd like to have an accent, that's all."

Arriving at the counter, Myra said, "Well, it sounds as though you've got a Cockney one to me."

"I'll have a glass of milk and a piece of chocolate Swiss Roll please...and for you, Myra?"

"That's easy. I want a strawberry milkshake and two chocolate biscuits."

At the cinema kiosk, Andre asked for two 'one and nines'. That was buying him two seats at the back of the auditorium and he was glad to see in the beam of the usherette's torch that there were seats available in the back row.

Seated there, he put his arm around Myra's shoulders and they chatted quietly. All conversation in the auditorium ceased abruptly as the lights dimmed.

Comfortably holding hands together, the two of them enjoyed the lighthearted film. Afterwards, while walking Myra to her bus stop, Andre asked for another date. She agreed, so Andre dared to give her a quick kiss on the lips and felt on top of the world as he ran all the way home to East Croydon.

Andre had been making enquiries and reading up in the newspapers about getting started with a publishing company, which led him to The Pergamon Press in Fitzroy Square, London, this time giving Fleet Street and the big boys a miss. He explained his business to the receptionist and before very long he was shaking hands with the publisher himself, a tall dark-haired man with very distinctive eyebrows.

"Pleased to meet you, Mr Maxwell."

An abrupt, fidgety voice said, "Come on then; I haven't got all day!"

"I'm looking for work as a technical illustrator. Here's my portfolio so you can see examples of my work. I'm hoping you can give me a few leads."

"Not that easy to get started in this business," Mr Maxwell replied gruffly.

"I fuckin' know that. That's why I'm here, grovelling to you."

Robert Maxwell raised his black eyebrows to heaven.

"I think I've impressed him," thought Andre.

"Like your spirit boy. Come back and see me in a couple of weeks."

"I will. Good day."

TGA: *(You'll notice that Andre did not attempt to shake hands with Robert Maxwell, nor did he say thank you. He decided to treat like with like.)*

"At last we meet again Myra," Andre greeted on their next date. "Would you like to go for a walk up on Farthing Downs?"

"I'm really too lazy to enjoy going for walks, but I don't know what else to suggest."

"I do," he joked, rolling his eyes.

"I'll choose the walk, thank you very much."

"OK, let's hop on a train to Coulsdon Station. We'll be able to find huge snails up on those downs. People collect them and cook them, just like the French with their escargots."

"Charming."

"Your hair looks more beautiful than ever against the green backdrop of the downs, and your coat looks lovely and warm.

"Thank you. You're not so bad yourself you know. Those fawn trousers and dark brown jacket blend in handsomely with your fair hair and freckled face. Are you warm enough?"

Ignoring the question, Andre asked, "Does that mean you approve of me a little bit?"

"I didn't say that, did I? I was just talking about what you're wearing."

"Yes, I am warm enough, thank you. I've got a thick jumper under this jacket and I'm hoping you'll see me again and get to like me better each time. Hey look, there's a snail. For some reason they call them Roman snails, although I'll never understand why."

"Does it matter?"

"Not really. What matters is where you're going with me? Up the aisle?"

"You don't waste any time, do you? I want a lovely white wedding."

"Well, I wouldn't complain. Can your parents afford one?"

"I haven't got any parents. My grandmother brought me up, but if I say 'yes', you can buy me one."

"What happened to your parents?"

My father died when I was small and my mother had to go out to work, so my gran looked after me. After about four years, my mum married another man and she emigrated with him. She and my gran decided that as I was so settled with her and the school, she would keep me.

"Does she write to you?"

"No, but it doesn't matter. My gran is a mum to me. She's the one I bonded with."

"I haven't got a real mum either. She died when I was born. I was brought up by a horrible stepmother."

"A likely tale."

"No, it's actually true. I'll tell you about it one day."

On the dot, Andre went to see Robert Maxwell. He thought he was the bees knees because he'd come up with a couple of illustrating jobs, which surprised Andre and he was very grateful. He got them done as quickly as possible to start pulling in money. He was also studying the newspapers looking for draughting work. He was prepared to do anything to boost his income, but naturally preferred to find his own line of work.

During this time, Andre was slowly finding clients for his technical drawing as well as progressing his romance with Myra. It was obvious that she reciprocated his feelings by the way she was becoming very amorous towards him, although no one had declared love.

On St. Valentine's Day 1953, he took her to the Orchid Ballroom in Purley where he would have the opportunity to hold her close. To make a real night of it, they decided to live it up by starting with fish and chips from the chippy and do a bit of window shopping while eating them. Soaked in vinegar and covered in salt, their feast was comforting and warming on the chilly night.

The Orchid Ballroom was a fantastic place to go on Saturday evenings. There was a revolving stage and often there were two bands playing there on the same night. One evening they were entertained by Frankie Laine singing *Jezebel* as well as many of his other famous songs.

As their relationship had been building over time, Andre asked Myra if she would like to go to the woods, where they could look for hazelnuts. As a result, he took her on a bus to Addington Bridle Way, which gave them access to Three Half-Penny Wood at Shirley Hills, Croydon.

"I'll have to have a poke around in the pond while we're there," he told her. "I've been fascinated by all the living things that inhabit them since my childhood."

Uppermost in his mind though, was to find a secluded area of the woods where they could have a kiss and a cuddle.

Carrying a paper bag full of hazelnuts, they found a reasonably private spot, but Myra was not happy.

"I don't feel comfortable being kissed in a public place, Andre."

"Do you know of anywhere else we can be private then?"

"No. My grandmother certainly wouldn't let us be private together."

"Well, let's walk until it gets dark. Then you won't feel so exposed. Fingers crossed, everyone else will have gone home."

"Don't like the idea of it, but it's tempting just the same," she said, squeezing his hand tightly. "Are there any snakes up here?" She shuddered.

"Don't even think about it, Myra. You've got me to protect you. Who gave you the name of Myra?"

"Apparently my Dad liked it. He said it was the name of a river in Nova Scotia, Canada, where he was born."

"How amazing. That's absolutely true. I know about it. Allister MacGillivray who wrote it was an absolute poetic genius, purely for his simplicity. He knew how to pull at the heart strings. It's called *Out on the Mira*. It's a folk song and I can sing it to you. I like singing and I love poetry too. I want to buy myself a guitar when I can afford one."

"So one way or another you're a very arty person. I'd like to hear you sing it."

Andre looked into Myra's eyes as he sang a rendition of *Out on the Mira*.

"Andre, that's beautiful. Will you sing it again for me?"

The entertainment made time pass rapidly and before they knew it the light had faded, leaving a clear starry sky and they were able to get their private kiss and a cuddle. Thereafter, Three Half-Penny Wood was quite a popular location for dates.

Perusing the Jobs Vacant section in the local paper one evening, Andre saw a job that was of interest. It was listed under Draughtsman and said the successful applicant would be required to design special camera equipment. He immediately put in an application to the company – Applied Optics.

He ran all the way to the post box with the letter before running on to his local pub for a whisky.

"Well, well, well. Look what the wind's brought in. Casanova himself."

"How's the romance goin' then, mate? Has she trapped ya' yet?"

"Have you managed to score, more likely?"

"Fine bunch of mates you are. As soon as I come in the door, I'm bombarded with innuendos. I might tell you that it was me who chased her, so lay off."

"Okay, okay! Keep yer 'air on. How's Fleet Street?"

"Slow, but I just posted off an application for a full-time draughting job at Applied Optics in Coulsdon, so you can all wish me luck with that. I really need the backup of regular money. That would give me leeway to continue slowly building my technical illustrating business and become an independent freelance operator."

"There's an ambition for ya. We'll drink to that, Andre."

Mr A G Bach, the Director of Applied Optics, didn't take long in replying. At the interview he explained that he preferred to think his technical thoughts out loud and would expect his

427

draughtsman to be able to produce technical drawings accordingly.

"Think you could cope with that?"

Andre knew this man was a boffin.

"Sounds interesting and a real challenge. I'd like to give it a go."

"Then the only way we'll be able to find out is by giving you a trial period of a month and see how you get on."

"So, I understand you design cameras to fit inside other products. I assume you'll always tell me at the outset what that product is?"

"Of course. I do tend to get caught up in my own head designing that way, but with my eyes shut I can clearly see the design I want and you are going to capture it on paper and turn it into a product for me."

TGA: *(Tony Bach reminded Andre of the master chess players in Egypt, thinking their game in their heads, saying their scores to the open air while playing without a chess board. Andre hoped sincerely, and desperately, that he would prove himself to be a better draughtsman than he had been a chess player.)*

"I've never worked that closely with someone before, but I'm looking forward to the experience."

That experience was going well. Andre found that by listening to Tony's thoughts he was able to visualise the concept. Session by session he was able to get technical information down on paper which, after having been seen in black and white, helped Tony to know the next move. Andre's sense of achievement was sky-high when he left the office every day.

It didn't take Tony Bach long to make his decision. He was delighted with Andre's outstanding ability and soon offered him a permanent job. At the same time he offered one to Ted Wells.

Ted Wells was a new colleague at Applied Optics and his job was to double check Andre's work.

"This is an important project and I don't want any errors creeping in," said Tony. "It has the potential to make me a millionaire."

The two speechless draughtsmen raised their eyebrows and suspected they'd got a job for life.

Andre was thrilled to share his permanent job news with Myra and her response was, "So you'll be able to take me to The Ritz then."

"You should be so lucky. More likely a cup of coffee at The Lyons Corner House."

Nearing the end of the year, Myra knocked Andre into a flat spin.

"My grandma wants to see you. She said I was to tell you that you've got to make an honest woman of me and marry me quickly, before it starts to show."

"Are you telling me I'm going to be a father?"

She smiled back broadly. "I'm telling you exactly that."

"Of course I'll see your gran. Thank goodness I've got a good job now, working for a very clever man. How do you feel about it?"

"I'll be happier if, and when, you marry me." She looked into his eyes with desperation.

"Of course I'll marry you!" He gave her a passionate kiss. "Bloody wars! How long before it's due?"

"I've only missed one period, so probably seven to eight months. Maybe next August, but I'll have to go to the doctor soon to get a proper idea."

Andre had no inclination whatsoever to desert her. If he was the father of her child, then he would want to bring the child up and certainly would do the responsible thing.

Grandma wasn't disapproving at all. She liked and accepted Andre, whom she considered to be quite a catch for Myra. To celebrate, she made a lovely homely smell by baking some rock cakes in her tiny kitchen in her typical suburban home.

"Myra's a good cook. You'll have to watch she doesn't make **you** fat when you're under the same roof. She's far better at it than I am."

"Could be my lucky day then?"

At lunchtime in the pub the next day, with cap-in-hand, so to speak, Andre told the other chaps from the office about the baby.

A big cheer went up.

"Another sucker bites the dust," and similar comments ensued.

TGA: *(Those raucous young men, with a beer inside them, enjoyed their momentous deviation from the mundane 'norm' and joked that they should all work at putting more 'buns in the oven'.)*

By end of April 1954, Myra was beginning to show and her grandmother had been busy knitting baby clothes; she was crocheting a patchwork baby shawl in different pastel colours, which they had admired on their previous visit. All this made the whole thing more of a reality to Andre and triggered the pair of them to look in estate agent windows. It was becoming popular for couples to buy their own homes, rather than renting, which depended on the male income. Females were not allowed to take on a mortgage.

Finally, they made an offer of £1,750 on a £1,999 semi-detached house in Woodmansterne, a village close to Andre's job in Coulsdon. He was desperate to get the house as he would be able to run to and from work over that short distance.

On the mortgage application form, Andre had to give names of mortgage guarantors and was successful in getting the agreement of Tony Bach, his employer and Myra's grandmother. Once the application was completed and signed, it was purely a waiting game.

Both Andre and Myra were scouring second hand shops for furniture and equipment that they would be needing and were concentrating on kitchen, dining room and bedroom items. They'd placed postcards in various shop windows in Coulsdon, East Croydon, Banstead and Sutton, as well as the post office in Woodmansterne.

Myra's grandmother had offered them the huge oak table that was filling her room.

"Now I'm alone, I only need a small table, so this lovely one will be of more use to you than me. You might have yourselves a small tribe to sit round it. Who knows?" she laughed.

"That's a beauty, Gran. I know quality when I see it. Thank you."

By the time the house became theirs for a haggled price of £1,800, they had a whole collection of possessions. From the specification, Andre noticed that the rooms had more modern names these days than when he was a child.

They collected the keys and were very excited to open their own front door. Andre carried his bride-to-be over the shallow-stepped threshold and found themselves in the small hallway. Immediately on their right they turned into an L-shaped lounge, which led into a dining room at the back through which the long narrow back garden could be seen. Turning to explore more, they saw a hatch on the side of the dining room wall through to the kitchen. Just beyond the hatch was a door on the right, which led into the back end of the hall and from there they turned right into the modern kitchen, which was a vast improvement on the old sculleries.

Upstairs, they had three bedrooms, the master one having a bay window, a smaller double room and a box room. The bathroom and toilet were combined. They also had a small lawn at the front with a low hedge to enclose it, over which there was a kerbed pavement bordering the modern suburban road.

Andre enlisted as many friends as he could to help collect their belongings from many sources, but even with their help his small savings were diminishing fast as he paid someone to collect bigger items on his truck. The oak table from Gran was the killer. He was terrified that the weight of it would crush the truck. That was a big sweat, but as it turned out, well worth it. It looked quite classy in the dining room, even though it stood on unpolished floor boards.

The truck had also collected Andre's drawing board, angled-light, his straight-edge and a whole collection of other office equipment, as well as his swivel chair. That was all put in the box room, which they decided would be used as his office.

Finding homes for their new acquisitions and emptying cardboard boxes became an overriding occupation. Although their home was sparse, it was a start. Myra, who was desperate to get a posh home, asked whether they had any jobs available at the local pub. She was lucky in that they'd just had to fire someone for drinking the profits.

When Andre returned from work, he discovered that Myra was a barmaid.

"That's a turn up for the books. My wife's a barmaid!"

"But I'm not your wife yet, remember?" she laughed.

"Golly, no. We must get on with that. Mind you, I'm not sure where a white wedding is coming from now. I'm stony broke, living from hand-to-mouth, with a mortgage on my back."

"Don't forget I'm earning too," Myra proudly offered. "We'll talk to Gran and see what she says."

Gran offered to give them a small buffet affair at her home. "It'll have to be a buffet because you've now got my big table!"

The two of them agreed that would be fine as, because of time delays in getting the mortgage through, Myra was obviously expecting and a white wedding would look ridiculous.

"I've also got some curtain rings in my sewing box, if you can't afford a ring. It's better than getting a gold one on tick."

Myra laughed. "OK, let's try one." She was quite a thrifty young lady. She knew exactly what she wanted and would stop at nothing in order to achieve that. "That'll do," she said.

Turning to Andre, she joked, "You can buy me a 22 carat gold one on our first wedding anniversary."

"One day I'll certainly buy you a gold ring. Whether I'll ever be able to afford the best for you remains to be seen."

All appeared to be going as well as could be expected. Andre was running to and from work, paying the mortgage in the estate agent's office in Coulsdon every month and doing some technical illustrating work in his own office at home. He was satisfied to be getting his daily run as well as saving fares by doing it. He could no longer fit in his boxing, but that was worth forfeiting to own his own home.

Myra was bringing in her small wage with which she was paying deposits on things like a cot and a pram. No one expected you to buy these items before a safe delivery.

With his new life under control, Andre arrived at his office one sunny morning in July and got fired. He and Ted Wells both got the bullet.

"I'm really sorry, chaps," apologised Tony Bach. "My client in Germany who is paying me instalments for work I've already done for him has got a cash flow problem. He can't pay me, so I can't pay you."

"Blimey, that's an almighty shock," said Andre, while Ted Wells looked on, speechless.

"Jesus wept," whispered Andre. "This means my mortgage is up the chute."

"No. I hope not." comforted Tony.

"It does in my book," retorted Andre. "No job, no mortgage."

"Listen to me," commanded Tony. "As soon as my money comes through, I'll reinstate the pair of you. Andre, you are like my second brain and Ted works well with you. You're not going to lose me that easily, I can assure the both of you. Meanwhile, you might be able to keep up your mortgage payments with your private work."

"Phew! Thank you. "In the meantime also, I'll be living my life on a knife-edge."

Chapter 23

The Spreading of Annabelle's Wings

Annabelle thought about it long and hard before putting her name down for an audition.

Lots of the villagers who were in Mr Freddie Cox's and her dad's shows were present and, as audition night progressed, Annabelle began to realise that she had done the right thing in attending.

"How did you get on?" asked Alice from her bed.

"I've been given a part. I'm going to be the Fairy Queen."

"Proper thing an' all for my beautiful daughter."

TGA: *(Annabelle was 22 years old when she attended the auditions and had grown into a beautiful young lady. Many of the village boys were after her as well as lots of the tuberculosis patients who were living in the hostels. The world was her oyster, but nothing deterred her from caring for her mother.)*

"Al's got a part as well, but I left him in the Insty. He seems to be smitten by one of the two leading ladies that Mr Constable brought with him."

"Ah well, he can't escape forever," said Alice with a wry smile. "He's so good looking, just like his dad was."

"What's her name?"

"Daphne. She's attractive and I think she's the best of the two. Her sister Doreen is quite hefty. I didn't really take to her."

"Ah well, early days."

"I've got my own news too. One of the TB patients at the auditions asked if I would go to the pictures with him."

"I hope you're going. You must never let me stand in your way."

"He's a Welsh boy called Matthew Griffiths. He's very handsome, so I might go."

"What? Didn't you say you'd go there and then?"

"No, I said I'd think about it."

"You jolly well go. It will do you good and then you can come and tell me all about it. Your Dad used to take me to see all the Fred Astaire films. Did us both good. So uplifting because you're taken into a different world."

In the end, Annabelle succumbed. Matthew took her to the Odeon cinema in Andover where the feature film was *Lili*. The male and female leads were the French ballet dancing star, Leslie Caron, and Mel Ferrer.

Annabelle enjoyed the film, but got the feeling that Matthew, although he said he enjoyed it, preferred holding her hand and looking at her, which made her feel uncomfortable.

At her gate, he asked if they could go out again.

"I'm sorry Matthew, it wouldn't be fair for me to say yes. I've enjoyed this evening, but there is somebody else."

TGA: *(Annabelle was telling porky pies! She thought he was very nice, but declined because she was very wary of illness. She'd seen too much of that in her own life.)*

Matthew retorted, "Well if you're not actually engaged to anyone, I really would like to take you out again."

"I'll think about it," she called out, as she ran up the garden path, avoiding his attempt to kiss her.

Annabelle hot-footed it straight up the stairs, two at a time, and lay on Alice's bed beside her.

"You were right, Mum. The film did take me into another world, although it wasn't a happy ending. We saw the French actress, Leslie Caron in *Lili* with Mel Ferrer. I absolutely loved it. At the beginning it told us that the film was based on a true story by a man named Paul Gallico, which made it compulsive viewing for me. Can I tell you about it?"

"I'm all ears."

"Leslie Caron played the title character, Lili, a sixteen-year-old waif who becomes part of a travelling puppet act and forms a relationship with the anti-social, crippled puppeteer – Michel Peyrot. She watches the puppets perform from the front of their booth."

"Have you had enough, or shall I go on?"

"Go on, of course. I'm enjoying it, and I haven't got to pay."

"Neither did I."

"Tell me more about Matthew later. Go on with the story now."

"It really was a beautiful film. Lili performed a magical dream ballet and she sang a lovely duet, *Hi-Lili, Hi-Lo,* with Michel Peyrot. Shame about the ending though. Michel Peyrot really loves Lili, but treats her with contempt because he can only show his genuine love for her by speaking through his puppets."

Alice dabbed tears from her eyes before saying, "Now tell me how you got on with Matthew?"

"Not such a beautiful story as the film. He asked me for another date, but I didn't make one."

"Annabelle, Shame on you."

TGA: *(Annabelle was too conscientious to tell her mother about the 'illness angle', but her reply was more than plausible.)*

"But, Mum, there surely has to be an attraction there. Maybe someone other than village boys will turn up at the Insty when they have dances. Anyway, what about you? Was it love at first sight for you and Dad?"

"Oh my God yes, it definitely was. I fell in love with your dad when I was ten years old. He was sweet on my older sister Emily. On days when I was well enough, she'd take me down the High Road to window shop and if we saw him, they would chat and I'd drool."

"But, Mum, you were only...how old?" she queried, frowning.

"About ten, I suppose."

"Only a child then?"

"Well who's to say a child can't fall in love? He certainly was my idol."

439

"So you **do** know what I'm talking about."

"I do know, my love. Mr Right will turn up when you least expect it."

Annabelle did go out with another tuberculosis patient named Dennis Desmond. He dabbled in a bit of painting, so the relationship was more of a business deal than anything else for her, although they did go out for walks and chatted from time to time. She had bought some nice warm blue material from Andover market to make a dress for her mother's birthday on 18ᵗʰ June. She asked Dennis if he could paint a bouquet of anemones, her mother's favourite flower, on the left side of the front bodice. He did that and the price Annabelle paid was to be taken to his home in Hindhead, Surrey, for a weekend, where Dennis took her to a sightseer's attraction, The Devil's Punchbowl. That day she walked so much that she came home with a blister on her heel.

TGA: *(That romance didn't develop either, but it spells out to the reader, in no uncertain terms, the depth of Annabelle's feelings for her mother.)*

Alice remembered there'd been the rejection of Dave Puttock, another TB patient who was sweet on Annabelle. He was Al's snooker friend, who'd watched Annabelle decorating the crinoline lady Christmas cake she'd baked in a pudding basin. He went home to London for Christmas and never returned. News filtered through that he'd committed suicide, but the reason was unknown. Al was very shocked and upset. Annabelle hoped it had nothing to do with her rejection, but comforted herself with the fact that it would have been unfair to lead him, or anyone else come to that, on a wild goose chase.

Rehearsals for the pantomime were going well. Mr Constable had brought Dora Buck – a very talented pianist who was sister to Daisy Ewers, the farmer's wife – with him from Weyhill. Al was cast as one of the two funny men. Their scripts were amazingly comical, but astute Mr Constable didn't fail to recognise that Al was a talented entertainer. He added an item to their act whereby Al was trying to teach his counterpart, Leslie Brant, how to tap dance and the latter proved himself to be quite a contortionist.

The two young ladies that Mr Constable brought with him were singers – Daphne and Doreen Lewis. Doreen was the elder of the two and had a far stronger voice. Annabelle chatted with them because she felt certain she'd seen them before and she certainly had; they were bus conductresses.

It was obvious that Al was smitten by Daphne, the younger of the two, as he was never far from her side when there was a lull in rehearsing.

Annabelle learned her lines easily and was thoroughly enjoying the involvement. Apparently, there would be some sort of 'blinding light' to flash every time she appeared on stage. That would only be used from the dress rehearsal night onwards because of the expense involved.

When dress rehearsal night came around, Mr Constable monitored the male and female dressing rooms to check on makeup. Annabelle was already disillusioned with the plain dress she was given.

She knew her mother could have made her a much more beautiful fairy queen one with net and tulle. That disillusionment magnified enormously when Mr Constable painted black eyebrows over her blonde ones, which she knew made her look more like a witch than a fairy.

Alice accompanied her children to the dress rehearsal, so she could stay home resting on the busier nights. She tried to comfort her daughter by telling her that when one was on stage, it was necessary to be made up larger than life. While there, she met her future daughter-in-law, Daphne.

Annabelle was not comforted, but was too responsible a person to back out at this late stage.

The cast performed to three consecutive full houses, so it was obviously a success. Children from the village, including Stella Mesney, Dinah Waite, Janet Ewers and half a dozen others, performed a dance, mimicking ballet above the beanstalk, with a scenery backdrop of blue sky and some small clouds.

The pantomime received a good review in the Andover Advertiser, highlighting the hilarity of the two funny men, Al Alessandro and Leslie Brant.

Doreen Lewis was conductress on the bus when Annabelle was coming home from doing the shopping one Saturday morning. She arrived home almost in tears.

"Honestly, Mum, she was an absolute tartar. She wouldn't let three people onto the bus. She said, 'We're full up,' but they still tried to get on, so she shouted, 'Look you lot, it says no standing, and if it says no standing, it means it!' Other conductors allow a few people standing. Usually, as we get out of town, people tend to get off rather than on, so seats soon become available. She was in such a horrible mood, she had the cheek to say to me, 'I ought to charge you double for bringing that lot on the bus', because I was carrying two big full shopping bags and a 7lb bag of chicken meal under my arm."

"My God, she sounds as though she's got a chip on her shoulder. I hope her sister isn't tarred with the same brush."

"She was awful, Mum. Very mouthy with bright red lipstick that made her look common."

"I hope Al isn't going out of the frying pan into the fire. Time will tell, of course."

Tuesday 2nd June 1953 had been declared a public holiday for the Coronation of Queen Elizabeth II. Enormous crowds had gathered on the streets of London to get a glimpse of Her Majesty as the beautiful royal coach took her and her husband to Westminster Abbey for the ceremony.

Annabelle didn't want to go there. She'd never liked the chaos of London life, but was looking forward to the Queen's broadcast to the nation, and indeed the world, later on in the evening.

Alice and her two children listened intently to the Queen on this historic occasion.

(QUOTE)

When I spoke to you last, at Christmas, I asked you all, whatever your religion, to pray for me on the day of my coronation – to pray that God would give me wisdom and strength to carry out the promises that I should then be making.

Throughout this memorable day I have been uplifted and sustained by the knowledge that your thoughts and prayers were with me. I have been aware all the time that my peoples, spread far and wide throughout every continent and ocean in the world, were united to support me in the task to which I have now been dedicated with such solemnity.

Many thousands of you came to London from all parts of the Commonwealth and Empire to join in the ceremony, but I have been conscious too of the millions of others who have shared in it by means of wireless or television in their homes. All of you, near or far, have been united in one purpose. It is hard for me to find the words in which to tell you of the strength which this knowledge has given me.

The ceremonies you have seen today are ancient, and some of their origins are veiled in the mists of the past. But their spirit and their meaning shine through the ages never, perhaps, more brightly than now. I have in sincerity pledged myself to your service, as so many of you are pledged to mine. Throughout all my life and with all my heart I shall strive to be worthy of your trust.

In this resolve I have my husband to support me. He shares all my ideals and all my affection for you. Then, although my experience is so short and my task so new, I have in my parents and grandparents an example which I can follow with certainty and confidence.

There is also this. I have behind me not only the splendid traditions and the annals of more than a thousand years but the living strength and majesty of the Commonwealth and Empire; of societies old and new; of lands and races different in history and origins but all, by God's Will, united in spirit and in aim.

Therefore, I am sure that this, my Coronation, is not the symbol of a power and splendour that are gone, but a declaration of our hopes for the future, and for the years I may, by God's Grace and Mercy, be given to reign and serve you as your Queen.

I have been speaking of the vast regions and varied peoples to whom I owe my duty but there has also sprung from our island home a theme of social and political thought, which constitutes our message to the world and through the changing generations has found acceptance both within and far beyond my Realms.

Parliamentary institutions, with their free speech and respect for the rights of minorities, and the inspiration of a broad tolerance in thought and expression – all this we conceive to be a precious part of our way of life and outlook.

During recent centuries, this message has been sustained and invigorated by the immense contribution, in language, literature, and action, of the nations of our Commonwealth overseas. It gives expression, as I pray it always will, to living principles, as sacred to the Crown and Monarchy as to its many Parliaments and Peoples. I ask you now to cherish them – and practise them too; then we can go forward together in peace, seeking justice and freedom for all men.

As this day draws to its close, I know that my abiding memory of it will be, not only the solemnity and beauty of the ceremony, but the inspiration of your loyalty and affection. I thank you from a full heart. God bless you all.

(UNQUOTE)

"What a lifelong responsibility for such a young mother of two little children," said an emotional Alice.

The speech, with its steadfast declaration of lifelong loyalty to her peoples brought tears to the eyes of many, not only in No. 9 Newbury Road, Enham.

"I shall be thinking about that all day tomorrow, while I work on your bridesmaids dress for Al's wedding. You'll look lovely in mauve and mandarin neckline."

Al had not wasted any time in proposing to Daphne and they were to be married on 6th June, 1953. That date sounded ominous to Annabelle because it was Derby Day and Al, who had always loved his horse racing, usually spent the afternoon with his ear glued to the radio, hoping to discover that he'd backed a winner.

Meanwhile, Annabelle was attracting more and more boys, vying for a place in her heart, but none stirred a beat.

Her life was very full what with working all week as well as caring for her mother and the home. In addition, she enjoyed her productive hobbies, such as making her own her own clothes cheaply from material bought in Andover market, growing vegetables in the garden and playing her favourite records on the radiogram. She also tap-danced to her records to please her dad, ever since his death six years previously. Before going to bed at the end of the day, she listened regularly to Billy Ternent and his Orchestra's programme and the shorthand notebook was never far away so she could take down the words of new songs. Another thing she loved to do was go to dances in the Insty whenever one was held.

Alice took comfort from the fact that the Insty dances could give her daughter the opportunity to meet someone and fall in love. The last thing she wanted, because she'd been nurse/housemaid from when she could toddle practically, was for her beautiful daughter to grow old into a life of spinsterhood.

Al's courting days were an enigma. On meeting Daphne's father Bert, it appeared he courted him rather than Daphne. Bert was a river fisherman and was responsible for influencing Al to a hobby that lived with him for the rest of his life. To be fair, Al did ask Daphne to go fishing with them, but she always declined. She stayed at home with her mother and sister, resting on her laurels that her dad really liked Al, and that she'd beaten her older sister to finding her future husband. That unusual courtship continued until the wedding day dawned.

Before Bert got the village policeman appointment at Weyhill, he'd been the policeman at Liphook in Surrey where Daphne loved the horses and riding. Because of that, she spent her days working at the local farm earning herself a few rides, and a bonus was that she delivered milk to the big house of the famous film star, Stewart Granger.

Daphne was a nice enough girl, but a horsey type didn't seem to be a lively or quick enough personality to match Al's sparkling one. Alice found the whole affair strange. She'd expected him to choose a much daintier girl for his bride. Alright, Daphne could sing, but was by far the weaker singer of the two sisters. "Ah well," she thought to herself, "they do say 'love is blind'. Did that apply to both of them?" she then wondered.

6th June 1953, Derby Day and wedding day dawned in that order for Al. There he was in the living room with the Daily Express racing page fully spread on the table.

"You shouldn't be doing that on your wedding day," commented Annabelle, who was looking forward to being bridesmaid for the sixth time in her life.

"Why not? The wedding isn't till 2pm."

"And who are you going to marry, might I ask? Daphne or Bert?"

"Don't be so sarcastic. I can still give you a pasting, even if it is my wedding day."

"Go on then. My bridesmaid's dress will show the bruises off perfectly."

Annabelle left the room before brotherly love ignited a punch-up. "Didn't boys feel the excitement of wedding days in the same way as girls?" Annabelle asked herself.

TGA: *(As the reader may have guessed from the preamble, Al wouldn't leave home until he'd heard the result of the Derby on the radio. He'd backed the winner, Pinza, but his best man, Joe Geoghegan, wouldn't allow him to go next door and collect his winnings. "You've got a bride waiting at the church for you, mate. Come on, the wedding car is waiting."*

"But I could spend the winnings on our honeymoon."

"PRETEND YOU LOST!" shouted Joe, which made even an angel smile.)

Daphne looked daggers at him as he arrived at St. Mary's Church, Andover, grinning all over his face. Joe winked at her as they hurried to take their place in the first pew on the right side of the aisle. His imminent mother-in-law didn't just look daggers; her looks were fit to kill.

As the organist struck up Mendelssohn's *Wedding March*, Daphne slowly walked up the aisle on the arm of her father towards the waiting Vicar and groom.

"Do you, Albert Alessandro, take this woman to be your lawful wedded wife?"

"I do."

"Do you, Daphne Winnifred Lewis, take this man to be your lawful wedded husband…"

Annabelle, looking as though butter wouldn't melt in her mouth, holding the bride's bouquet for the giving of rings, was willing Daphne to say, "NO, I BLINKIN' DON'T!"

Annabelle thought, "Walk away and leave him standing there looking stupid."

TGA: *(Sisterly love? Touché!)*

449

Despite everything, the marriage ceremony went ahead and when the happy couple emerged at the top of a mountain of steps that led up to the church, Daphne looked lovely and very striking in a plain design satin wedding dress, which made the perfect backdrop for her long trailing bouquet of red roses.

Walking down all those steps on the arm of her husband, with confetti being thrown over the pair of them by all their well-wishers, had thrilled Daphne just as much as the hundreds of brides who had preceded her on those very steps.

The wedding car waiting at the bottom took them off to The Bell pub at Weyhill for their reception.

When guests started to arrive at the pub, Daphne and Al were waiting each side of the narrow doorway to welcome them. Everyone was glad to get there and started to relax as trays of sherries or glasses of beer awaited.

There was a buffet style spread with a two-tier wedding cake made by the bride's mother. Short speeches followed the food as the couple cut the cake and toasts were made. Time was running short and they needed to make a quick getaway for their honeymoon destination at Portland Bill in Dorset.

It had been quite a day for Al, but in parallel it has been quite a day for the Derby 1953 winner, Gordon Richards. He had been a flat racing jockey for nearly three decades, but on Al's wedding day he had won his first Derby race ever on Pinza, beating the Queen's Horse, Aureole, into second place.

As if that wasn't glory enough, he had received a Knighthood earlier in the week in the Coronation Honours' List.

Al and Daphne's week's honeymoon passed by in a flash and they arrived home to 9 Newbury Road on Saturday 13th June where they were going to live until they could find alternative accommodation.

The first thing Al did on the Monday morning before commencing his day's work in Enham Industries, was to put his name down for a house in the village.

The first thing Alice did, after Annabelle had left for work, was to suggest to Daphne, who had given up her bus conductress job, that she might like to do the washing, which would be a wonderful surprise for Annabelle, who wouldn't have to do it when she'd finished her day's work.

"OK," said Daphne, as she lit up a cigarette. "But you'll have to tell me what I've to do, because I don't know. My mum never let us girls do anything at home. 'Get out of the way; it's quicker for me to do it myself', she's always said."

Alice thought that was very short-sighted of their mother, considering a girl's lot in life in the main was to get married and lead a domesticated life. Nevertheless, Daphne, who was a very strong girl, was willing to learn. Her early married days were difficult, because there wasn't only washing and mangling, there was a plethora of domestic chores, including shopping, cooking and cleaning.

"Wow! Thank you Daphne," said Annabelle as she saw her mangling the washing outside the back door when she came down the back garden path at lunchtime.

"That's alright. I'm having my first lesson at married life."

"Not so good then?"

Alice told her Daphne's story, and Annabelle, who had been running a home more or less since she was eight years old, felt sorry for her.

"My God. Poor you Daphne. That must be so awful. Is there any water left in the copper?"

"Suppose so. I haven't emptied it."

"Good, then I'll do the drains before I make us some scrambled egg on toast."

Thereafter, a bit of respite followed for Annabelle, thanks to a spare pair of hands in the house.

On 18th June, Alice's birthday, all the family enjoyed a scrumptious tea of strawberries and cream, courtesy Dr MacCallum. It was his birthday too and every year for a long time he had brought Alice a huge bowl of strawberries from his walled garden with a jug of cream from Mr Ewers.

Alice looked lovely in her new blue dress and was thrilled with the colourful posy of anemones painted on it.

Sooner than expected, Al was allocated a prefab. Such a temporary home was not a disappointment at all. It had a fantastic design with all rooms branching off from the front door, which led into the circular hall. From the left, the first door was the toilet, second the bathroom, third the airing cupboard, fourth the lounge, fifth the main bedroom and sixth the smaller bedroom.

The kitchen led from the lounge and off the kitchen was a useful cupboard on the left of the back door. Opposite the cupboard was an elongated type corridor matching the short side of the lounge, big enough to store bicycles, a lawn mower and tools etc. In other words, an internal shed.

There was a total of six prefabs on the site, forming a circle, each with its own large garden. Every occupant was thrilled to be living in this type of accommodation, which had been pioneered following the destruction of many homes during WW2.

Al and Daphne were able to move in over a weekend. Friends and neighbours had been very kind giving them goods and chattels and on inspection, Alice and Annabelle thought the pair would be very cosy indeed in their temporary home in winter with its very modern, Chatelaine solid fuel burner warming the large lounge.

Life settled down very quietly for Alice and Annabelle now they were only two, but 1954 brought something that livened up their lives somewhat.

Mr Norman Cox, the accountant who worked in the next office to Annabelle, had received a letter from Andover Borough Council informing him that they were opting for a different way of choosing a carnival queen and attendants that year. They proposed that a village queen be elected from each village in the Borough, with different rounds of selection to find the 1954 Carnival Queen and two attendants. The letter continued by stating that carnival week would not be until September, because of the various rounds of selection.

Mr Cox was being asked to arrange an event whereby an Enham Alamein Queen could be chosen and her name submitted to the council. Accordingly, he put a notice on the oak tree near the Insty asking for volunteers to write their names on the poster. Two weeks passed with no takers.

Mr Cox was getting desperate and begged Annabelle one day, with hands held in prayer-like position, "Please put your name down. I bet others will follow if someone starts it off."

Feeling sorry for him, Annabelle took the plunge. The ploy worked. Ten names appeared and a dance was arranged for the voting to take place.

On dance night, Annabelle was sitting with other village girls opposite the double doors to the hall as people arrived. Just as the band started playing, a young man in a navy blue uniform with a peaked cap appeared at the door and looked straight across to her. Before she knew it, she was being swirled around the dance floor by this tall, dark and handsome stranger, now minus his cap.

They danced a lot during the evening, and he was sat next to her when the contestants were asked to go on stage.

Annabelle was shocked to learn that she had been voted winner and was presented with a bouquet of red roses. She tried to decline, asking if the person who came second could take her place, but the answer was a very positive, "Certainly not. You will represent Enham Alamein. It is the wish of the villagers."

In a daze, she went back to her seat and the young man held her hand.

"Cheer up! That was good news and I think you were the best of the bunch by far."

"I only put my name down to help Mr Cox, who was organising the competition."

"Good on Mr Cox then. You'll make a beautiful carnival queen."

At her gate, she agreed to see the young man again and he gave her a lingering kiss before cycling off to his home in Andover.

On their next date, she discovered that he was a chef in the Royal Navy and that he only had two weeks at home before sailing off again.

"Where will you be sailing to?"

"We're leaving from Portsmouth Naval Base and our first port of call will be Trondheim, Norway."

"And how long is the trip?"

"Five months, but I hope you'll see me again when we get back."

"Well, I can't answer that one. Who knows what will happen in the meantime."

"Fair enough. We've only just met, but I'll come knocking with high hopes."

Annabelle didn't really miss him. He hadn't been around long enough for that.

Alice was busy adapting a nice dress for Annabelle to wear to the next round of the carnival queen competition. In previous years, Annabelle had made herself a white dress with a pleated white skirt to wear on hot summer days. She had embroidered an arrangement of red roses and leaves on the bodice, spraying all down to the hip-line where the pleats started. Alice took off the pleated skirt and sewed on a full length billowing white net skirt.

Collecting Annabelle and her mother, Mr Betts, Dr MacCallum's chauffer said, "My goodness, you're such a striking sight in that dress; you surely must be the next Andover Carnival Queen."

He was driving them to the Drill Hall in Andover where a dance was being held in honour of all the village winners.

At the Drill Hall, all sixteen entrants had to parade in a circle around the hall with their village name band across their body, showing themselves to the spectators. Annabelle hated it. She was far from a limelight seeker. Hundreds of photographs were taken for local newspapers. That done, the date of the next round was announced when all entrants would be driven round the town in a lorry, showing off new dresses, before a final selection of three – the carnival queen with two attendants – would be made at another Drill Hall dance.

Back in the office, Annabelle said, "Blimey, I had no idea what I was letting myself in for when I did you a kindness."

"I did," replied Mr Cox with a big grin. "Mind you, you did the trick and got Enham Alamein some entrants; thank you very much."

"Well I can tell you, it was no blinkin' pleasure."

Before the next date, Annabelle was shopping as usual on a Saturday morning and had an amazing journey home on the bus. Sitting opposite her was a very good looking young man who was singing.

"Ignore him," said the conductor. "He sings everywhere he goes."

Ignoring him was easier said than done for Annabelle. He was actually looking into her eyes as he was singing *Mother Nature and Father Time*. What's more, his voice was remarkably like that of popular singer Dickie Valentine who could always be heard on the radio. No wonder Annabelle's heart turned somersaults!

Before Annabelle got off the bus he said, "If you come to the Drill Hall dance on Saturday night, I'll sing a song for you."

"I'll think about it," replied Annabelle with a smile to die for.

Alice set about making Annabelle a pale blue cap-sleeved dress with a lovely circular skirt for the lorry tour and final selection of the competition.

"The capped-sleeve style suits you perfectly," Alice remarked.

With no enthusiasm whatsoever, Annabelle said, "Just make it out of hemp, like the sacks, and that'll put an end to it."

"Don't be ridiculous, Annabelle. What mother would do a thing like that to her daughter?"

On Saturday night, Annabelle caught the bus with other village girls and went to the Drill Hall dance. She didn't say a word to the others about the verbal promise, thinking it could never happen. And it didn't happen in the way she'd imagined.

Before the young man she met on the bus sang, he jumped off the stage and danced with her. She could hear her own heart beating louder than the drummer's drums and was glad he was there to hold her up because her legs were trembling.

457

While dancing he asked how he could contact her.

"Andover 2858. That's my Auntie Dolly's phone next door, but she'll fetch me."

He took a fountain pen from his pocket and wrote the number on the palm of his hand saying, "Good, I'll be in touch," before jumping back onto the stage. He then sang to her, *Everything I have is Yours.*

Walking back to Enham that night, the girls couldn't stop going on about it.

"You'll be the next Enham girl to be married off. We've already got four weddings coming up on 14th August. There's Pat Shears, Eve Pilkington, Connie Gurr, and Les Brant, all on the same day."

"Only time will tell." she replied, cautiously.

Time did tell and Annabelle was thrilled to have a few dates with him to go to the pictures, but never Saturday nights because he was singing at the Drill Hall.

On Carnival Competition Day, Annabelle was horrified to be one of the five finalists and she then had to face the next process. Each one of the five were interviewed on stage so speaking voices could be heard. She had no problem in finding words to answer questions, but unaccustomed as she was to public speaking, her voice was not strong. Despite talking into a microphone, the audience kept calling, "Speak up!"

Eventually, officials made their selection. There was an air of excitement and tension filling the room while everyone waited to hear the name of the celebrity who would make the announcement.

That celebrity was no other than the famous film actor, Dennis Price.

Starting with the least successful, he approached Annabelle. She was overjoyed.

"Ladies and Gentleman, I have to announce that this beautiful young lady is finalist No. 5, so will not be your carnival queen nor an attendant this year."

To Annabelle, "I'm so very sorry, young lady. Carnival queens, and indeed all queens, have to be able to make speeches. I suggest you go home and do some shouting. Shout at anyone you can and strengthen that voice." There was a long pause for laughter before he said, "Better luck next year," with a shake of the hand and a kiss.

Two knocks on the chimney breast wall one night told Annabelle that there was a phone call for her.

"Hello? Oh, it's you, Danny. I'm fine, thank you."

Annabelle spent too long listening for Auntie Dolly's liking. She was anxious to hear more.

"Well, I hope your luck changes, and remember me when you're famous."

"No problem. I'll never forget you."

"OK. I'll look forward to hearing. Bye now, and good luck." She hung the phone back on the hook.

"Phew!" said Auntie Dolly, wiping her brow. "I don't know who was more excited, me or you. That was the singer, wasn't it?"

"Yes. His name's Danny Purches."

"Got another date?"

"Nope. He told me he's fed up with singing on buses and in local dance halls and never getting anywhere, so he's going to try his luck in London. He also said he'd never forget me and that he'd keep in touch."

Auntie Dolly gave her a big hug. "Stay and have a cuppa and a biscuit with me. I think I'm as excited as you are."

There had been a couple more phone calls reporting progress but in actual fact, before the last of those, Annabelle had heard a report on the BBC radio news that a young man had been singing late at night in the street outside the Leicester Square home of singing sisters, Lita Rosa and Alma Warren. The next day there was a picture in the paper of the sisters leaning out of an upstairs window waving down to Danny, definitely Danny Purches, in the lamp-lit street.

By late autumn, Tony the sailor appeared at the door of No. 9.

"I told you I'd come back hoping, didn't I," he said, with his amazingly wide smile.

Annabelle didn't invite him in. She made a date for Saturday night.

First he took her to the Drill Hall where they danced until the interval. There he surprised her by saying, "What do you say to going out for a proper drink instead of getting something in here?"

"OK," replied Annabelle, in awe of this new adventure.

He then took her to The Angel pub, at the top of the town, not too far away from the Drill Hall. It was obviously his local, because he chatted to the landlady and Annabelle discovered that his mother worked as the seamstress in Rudd's, the dress shop next door.

"What would you like to drink, Annabelle?"

"I'll have a tomato juice with ice and lots of Worcester Sauce, shaken, but not stirred please."

"That's not a drink. Have a short."

"Tomato juice is the drink I always like to have."

"OK. I'll buy you one, but I'm going to choose a 'short chaser' for you." He winked at the Landlady.

"A double rum and black for me please, and a rum and orange for Annabelle."

He took her to a seat in a corner near the lace-curtained window, where they could just see, by the light of the street lamps, occasional passers-by. With the rum and orange warming inside her, those passers-by helped keep Annabelle in the real world.

Tony was confined to Portsmouth Barracks until he was commissioned to go on another tour, so they only saw each other from time to time. When they met, they always went to The Angel pub for a drink. The pub had been an old coaching station in earlier times, which accounted for the archway by the side of it leading into a courtyard.

Meanwhile, Annabelle was listening to Danny Purches on the radio. He had been awarded a half hour slot from 10.30pm once a week for six weeks. Annabelle eagerly studied the Radio Times when it arrived, to double check when he was on. She wouldn't have missed his programme for the world and she thought every song he sang was for her.

He'd obviously made the right career move in going to London.

He phoned from time to time and when they last spoke, nearing Christmas time, he told her how he'd been booked for many well-to-do private engagements and was also going to appear in pantomime in the West End.

"I'm on the road to fame now and, like I said, you are the one who will share it with me."

Annabelle's toes curled and her heart raced. She wondered what it would be like to be a celebrity wife.

There was one more call after Christmas to say how well things were going.

"It will be impossible for me to phone for a while, what with two pantomime performances a day and private engagements on Sunday, but I'll definitely be phoning on Valentine 's Day. Tell me you'll look forward to it."

"Oh, I will. Every minute. No. Every second."

As usual, remote kisses were sent over the phone.

It was a different story with Tony. On his last weekend home before Christmas, he took Annabelle to the Drill Hall before having stiff drinks in The Angel and then ending up in the courtyard.

In that place, where horses and carriages were tethered in the days of long ago, Annabelle, at 24 years old, discovered through her clothing what was on offer. Her undercarriage had certainly been stirred!

TGA: *(Whereas Danny Purches made her heart beat too fast and gave her jelly legs, it was Tony who made her aware of how much more there was to discover. Will it be either? Or will it be neither?)*

Chapter 24

Andre Kliskey Gets Himself a Son and Heir

On 1st September 1954, Mrs Myra Kliskey, with curtain ring on her finger, gave birth.

"It's a boy!" the midwife said, as she placed the babe in her arms, which gave Myra a bigger thrill than conceiving him. Suffice to say, she'd had to work harder for this thrill.

Myra's gran was looking after her and after the midwife had left them, contented that all was well, she cooed to the baby in her arms, "Your daddy's going to be a very proud young man when he comes home and meets you."

Arriving home, Andre leapt up the stairs two at a time and found his son sucking away at his mother's breast.

"Well done Myra!" he gushed excitedly, as he kissed her forehead. "Was it very bad?"

"Not exactly a bed of roses. More like a bed of thorns, but they tell me 27 hours is quite a good birth really."

"I hated having to walk out on you this morning, but Gran said I'd be better out of the way and anyway, I didn't think I'd be able to concentrate on working in my office with your screaming going on. I went up to town and was lucky enough to get a commission."

"Andre, that's the best news ever! What a wonderful birthday present for our son. Here we are, he's stopped suckling. Do you want to meet him?"

Andre took the little bundle wrapped in Grandma's shawl.

"Hello, little Mr Kliskey. Welcome to the world. I'm very pleased you've arrived safely." Andre hugged his new son tightly and kissed his forehead. "I expected you to have auburn hair, like your mum, but you haven't got any. So, what are we going to call our little boy, Myra? What did we decide on if it was boy?"

"We both liked Christopher John."

"Chris Kliskey. Chris Kliskey. John Kliskey. Ken Kliskey. Barry Kliskey. Peter Kliskey..." Andre was thinking out loud.

"Yep, I think it's hard to beat Chris Kliskey, so we'll settle for Christopher John."

"Yes, I'm happy with that."

"OK. We're agreed, so I can go and get his birth registered tomorrow. Aren't we clever Myra? We're Mum and Dad." Andre leaned across the bed to put his arm around her shoulders, so they could have a three-way hug.

After registering the birth of his son, Andre started to concentrate on his new commission. He'd found the company concerned in Covent Garden. They were Heinemann Educational Books Ltd, London. He was required to do illustrations for a book about engineering. They'd explained what was required and even though he was qualified in engineering, he hopped on a bus to Sutton Library to look in their encyclopaedias to refresh his memory. There he made copious notes before returning to his office.

465

Anxious to get started, he was working to the sound of his baby son's crying and was relieved when he heard Gran let the district nurse in the front door.

In his lunch break he sat with Myra. "The district nurse said she doesn't think baby is getting enough milk through, so she suggested I drink plenty."

Andre cuddled his son with comforting words, "Poor little chap. Starving you are they, Christopher Kliskey?" He held his little bundle up in the air in front of him. "We'll do our best to put that right for you. I'll bring your mum up jugs of water and carry up cups of tea to save Grandma's legs. Let's hope that will settle you down."

"Hey, Myra, he just smiled at me!"

"That was wind, dafty."

Despite drinking plenty, baby Christopher still didn't settle too well, so the district nurse brought in some tins of Ostermilk and baby started to be topped up with bottles. Following her instructions, Grandma went out shopping to the chemist in Banstead to buy sterilising equipment and spare teats.

Myra was getting out of bed at regular intervals and trying to look after baby herself, but was being very cautious as she did not want to lose all her own milk.

Things were improving a few weeks later when Gran thought they would be able to manage without her, so decided to leave.

"I can't stay forever now, can I? You are coping pretty well, Myra, so I think it's right that I leave you to it."

Baby was more content with his new feeding routine and Myra was up and about and doing well. Gran had bought her the Ostermilk book of weaning from the chemist as a present.

"That'll be a good guide for you, although in my book, a mother's instinct is a good guide too. I know from experience that Farley's Rusks are a good one to start with. Just put one in his fingers. He'll know what to do with it, dear."

Taking Christopher for his first breath of fresh air in Andre's arms, the family walked Gran to the bus stop and thanked her profusely for helping them.

"That was my pleasure, dears, and don't forget, I'll babysit for you all the time I'm able. Your house or mine," she called out as the bus drove away.

Andre hadn't ceased thanking his lucky stars for his Heinemann commission when he received a letter from Tony Bach.

"Myra, Tony Bach's been paid and he wants Ted and me to go back on Monday."

"That's absolutely awful. I like you working at home."

"What the hell are you saying, Myra? It's money. We can't afford to turn it down."

"Well, it seems to me you are doing OK with Heinemann."

"I really credited you with more common sense, woman. I can't believe my getting a paid job is causing our first row. Tell me you didn't mean it."

"I'm not telling you that. I did mean it."

467

Andre went back into his office, slamming the door behind him. There he wrote back to Tony saying that he would turn up promptly on Monday. Then he went to the post office round the corner, bought a stamp and posted the letter. Returning home, he slammed the front door and sprinted up the stairs two at a time.

"You'll soon find out who the man is in this house, Madam. I have a mortgage to pay and that is my priority. Thank goodness I've managed to keep up the payments during this unemployed period," he yelled, as he slammed his office door again."

"Now you've woken the baby up," she yelled back at him.

Andre cracked on with his engineering drawings, regardless. He was the breadwinner and worked hard at that. He'd spent his life bearing the brunt of a horrible stepmother. Now he was sharing his life with a sulking wife. She wouldn't speak to him.

On Saturday he took his work up to Heinemann's place to see if it met with their approval. They described it as exemplary, which lightened his mood.

On Sunday, he tried to have it out with Myra.

"How long is this silence going to last?" he asked. "Can't we kiss and make up? It's not good for Christopher; he'll grow up dumb."

That brought a glimmer of a smile.

"Well, you're so pig-headed. I know what I want too."

"Of course you do, and I will try to get things that you want, but in order to do that I have to earn as much money as I can. Come on, give me a kiss and tell me what things you want."

She gave him the kiss and then snuggled up and said, "Well I did want you home here with me, but since I can't have that, I can see a beautiful red carpet under that oak table."

Andre laughed. "Well, I'm glad you can see it, because that's the only way you're getting it."

She punched his arm. "You old meanie."

Andre soon got back into the swing of things at Applied Optics. He'd never known any work before to give him so much satisfaction.

"How's about coming down your local pub for lunch with me, then you can wet my baby's head."

Tony declined because he needed a clear head to do his mental designing, but Ted came and so did Pamela, Tony's wife. She informed them that she was Tony's bookkeeper and apologised for the lapse in their employment.

"It's Tony's policy not to go into the red at the bank. He says, 'In business, you can never be sure where the next penny is coming from and you can't spend what you haven't got. Too risky.'"

The beef sandwiches with pickled onions were good, and they all wet Christopher's head with a cup of coffee because Andre and Ted agreed they should keep their heads clear for Tony's work too.

"Hello Myra, had a good day?" he called as he opened the front door."

"Yes, I have thank you. Baby's been settled and I've been thinking about the bar you're going to build in the L-shape of the lounge."

Eyebrows raised, "I am?"

469

"Yes, we talked about it when we first moved in."

"Look, Myra, I don't consider a bar to be an essential item. There must be hundreds of things for me to do before that."

"Well, I want a lovely home and it would be very unusual to have a bar. Not many people have one of those."

"Oh I see. Keeping one ahead of the Jones's now, are we? And where's the booze coming from?"

"We'll stock it of course. That would enable us to give Christopher a wonderful christening party."

"Myra, sit down next to me."

Andre held her hand as he said kindly, "Myra, you and I don't seem to be operating on the same wavelength. Do you think we could discuss, and both agree, before you go headlong into any more of your plans?"

"It's all very well for you; you have something to occupy your mind. I'm stuck here all day and I want a beautiful home."

"OK, OK. But I earn the money and I'll have at least an equal say in how we spend it. To start with, there'll be no booze at Christopher's christening. You'll make cakes, which will give you another occupation here and our guests will have cups of tea or squash. And while you're thinking about it, you can take Christopher for a walk in his pram to St. Peter's church in Banstead and arrange a date for it."

"So you're the boss and I have to obey you?"

"Until you can be more realistic about things, it looks like that's the way it'll have to be, although it's not the way of my choosing."

Andre began to think he'd made a terrible mistake in his life. He'd lusted after Myra without really finding out anything about her nature. Nevertheless, she was his wife, *for better or for worse*, and they had a son to bring up.

"Myra, I'll do my best to cope with your every need, but you have to remember that I'm earning the money, which leaves me very little time to be building bars, and I'm not sure I'm skilled enough to cope anyway with your hifalutin demands."

Andre was grateful to clear off to work as a distraction from his home life. The run to the office helped with that. He'd always loved his singing, but it seemed as though he had nothing to sing about and the thought of buying himself a guitar wasn't even on the horizon.

Running back home at the end of the working day, he promised himself that Myra wouldn't change his personality, so after eating his dinner of sausage, mash and baked beans, he had a cuddle with Christopher and sang him some folk songs, including *Out on the Mira,* to remind them both of better days.

"Thanks for my dinner, Myra. It's really nice to have it to come home to. You do very well on that score in our marriage. Doesn't that satisfy you?"

"Not particularly; basically it's boring, day after day after day and doing housework with our few sticks is awful. I want a nice home to look after."

471

"But Myra, a home has to be gradually collected, so every new item is a joy."

"Well, I'm not patient enough for that. I thought a husband would want to spoil his wife and make a fuss of her, especially after bearing him a son."

"Myra, a marriage is a partnership. You have your jobs and I have mine."

"Surely building a bar should be one of yours. I don't complain at having to cook your meals."

"Bloody hell. We always end up on the same tack. I haven't got time for that at the moment. Heinemann are keeping me supplied with plenty of work. As the breadwinner, I'm glad and relieved about that; and I get tired too. Better to earn it now, so when the rainy day comes we'll have something to fall back on. You have a go at building your own bar. You can use my tools and I'll look forward to seeing how you get on."

"No, thank you very much. I'll wait, however long it takes."

TGA: *(Andre was troubled. He kept asking himself if he was too hard on her. Was he forgetting that he was only a mere mortal? He was already working all the hours God sent. I could see it was not possible for him to do more.)*

To satisfy his troubled mind, Andre collected some wood on the way home from work one day, thinking he should make an attempt to please Myra. He would try to get some sort of a bar made before the christening, so she could show it off to people. Carrying the wood home from Coulsdon was challenging and forced him to walk instead of run. He put the wood in the shed at the back of the house and walked in the front door, as usual.

"You're late tonight. Where have you been?"

"Shopping."

"Whatever for?"

"Wood. I thought I'd see if I can build the bar you want so desperately, so you can show it off to everybody at Christopher's christening."

"Oh, Andre. You do love me, after all."

"Myra, you don't measure love by material things. Your yardstick is so different to mine."

"Andre, why did you marry me, I often wonder?"

"I ask myself that too. We don't get on very well together, do we?" he responded, more as a statement than a question.

Andre asked himself the question, "How fine is the line between love and lust?" He answered himself with "I am beginning to think it was all lust on my part."

He found a certain self-forgiveness in making the bar, and in actual fact enjoyed doing it. He bought fancy curved wrought iron for the sides, which provided legs for it to stand on, and a wooden back with built-in fitments to provide support for shelves etc. He sported expensive ¼ inch plate glass as a big shelf on which to pour drinks. With the wood, he was able to make a suitable cupboard with shelves to store bottles. Finally, he painted the cupboard doors glossy black and the whole thing looked decidedly classy.

"Oh, Andre! You're such a wonderful husband. Thank you."

Andre smiled to himself. "At least I know how to make her happy, and she deserves that at least."

The week before Christmas when Christopher was just over three and a half months old, all their friends gathered at St. Peter's Church, Banstead, for the afternoon christening. Andre had asked his friend Ken Pick, who was now a father himself, if he would be a godfather and he also asked his new workmate, Ted Wells. Myra's long-time friend, Kathleen, was Christopher's godmother.

It was a crisp and cold, but thankfully dry afternoon for the christening. Christopher was a model baby and amused the congregation when he sneezed as water from the 'crossing' trickled down his nose.

"That's a sign of thriving," whispered Gran.

Everyone was glad to get back to the warmth of their home where Myra had baked a good selection of cakes. Grandma was there to help and she and Kathleen willingly made the tea.

Andre watched, fascinated by the way Myra was proudly showing off the bar he'd made for her and felt compelled to say, "Sorry folks, I'm afraid it's not stocked with booze yet, so today we'll toast Christopher with a cuppa and a piece of Myra's christening cake."

After the event, Andre said, "Well, I think we pulled that off okay, didn't we? I don't think anyone suspected how difficult we are finding married life."

"You're right. Betty Wells seemed a bit of a frail woman. She obviously doted on Ted."

"I don't see anything wrong with that. Lots of wives do dote on their husbands."

474

"I see that as a weakness. They don't know their own minds, surely."

"Do you know Myra, you wondered the other day why I married you. I've been thinking about that. I married you because I'd got you in the family way. Had I got to know you and your materialistic ways sooner, I begin to doubt if I ever would have married you."

"Thanks a lot. So where does that leave me?"

"I can answer that too, if your shoulders are broad enough."

"Try me."

"The absolute truth is, I shall never leave you until Christopher is a man, or leaves home, whichever is the sooner. I want him to be brought up with his mother's love, and I know he has got that. I would not want a stepmother to get anywhere near him."

"That's assuming I can stick living with you."

"Your prerogative, of course. But I don't think you'll ever leave me. For my own conscience, if nothing else, I think it's only fair that I provide you with all the material things you desire to make up for messing up your life. I shall put a bit of money by for myself and when Christopher's age, or circumstance allows, I will leave you with the house and all your material things inside it. You'll then be free to find someone who'll enjoy sharing your material things and I'll be free to find a wife who can share love and warmth with me, even if we only have a shack to live in."

"Phew! Does that mean I can have my red carpet?"

Gran came to stay with them for Christmas 1954, which helped peace to reign in the household. It didn't mean much to baby Christopher, but they all amused themselves trying to amuse him. Andre sang him some Christmas Carols and the rest of them played quite a few games of cards.

At the New Year sales of January 1955, Andre went to Kennard's in Croydon to buy some bright red carpet to be fitted in their L-shaped room, the hall and up the stairs, but got the shock of his life. He couldn't buy such a thing, even though he had ready cash to pay for it. So, he ordered the next best thing at a bargain price, breaking into a little bit of the rainy-day money.

Over dinner that evening, Andre said to Myra, "Your 'wants' have led me on a wild goose chase in Croydon today. Where the hell did you get the idea of fitted red carpet from? You can't buy such a thing. My God, you're materialistic to the utmost degree."

"Well, I suppose I just imagined it to be luxurious, but it proves to you that I'm not just keeping up with the Jones's, if they can't buy it either."

Andre scratched his head. "Well, anyway, have you got any plans to go out on Friday 14th January?"

"Nope."

"Well, I've ordered the next best thing I could get. That's the day it will be delivered and red linoleum will be fitted. They couldn't give me a time, so I'm afraid you'll have to stay in until they've been. And I hope you'll like what comes, because it eases my conscience to think there's a way I can make you happy."

Going home after work on 14th January was exciting, even for Andre. Myra was more than happy with her red flooring. The lino was laid exactly as he'd ordered, with a huge red rug under the big table as she had visualised and one at the lounge end of the room.

"Andre, it's wonderful and will do perfectly until someone decides to make wall-to-wall carpet. And red carpet up the stairs was such a surprise. Thank you, thank you. I am really happy with it."

"Ah well," Andre thought to himself, "Half a loaf's better than none I suppose."

Sitting on the utility two-seater settee in the lounge end of their room one night, enjoying watching Christopher handling his first Farley's rusk, materialism ruined the blissful domestic scene.

"Wouldn't it be great to have a baby grand piano in our home?"

"I don't follow you, Myra. To start with, neither of us can play the piano."

"But I could learn."

"Most people learn on a second hand upright, so it's not a lot of dead money if they don't get on with it. It will always re-sell."

"How many times do I have to tell you? I will not have second hand stuff in my home."

"How quickly you forget our humble beginnings. Anyway, realistically, we'd need a bigger house to accommodate a baby grand piano."

"Okay. Wonderful; I'd really like that."

"Myra, Myra. We haven't been in this house five minutes yet and a bigger house would mean a bigger mortgage. I've told you before. I'll happily right my wrongs in the only way I can, which is buying you material things, but a grand piano that no one can play is beyond unreasonable. I'm not prepared to drop dead from exhaustion buying you such expensive things. You are just want, want, want without a breather. I am beginning to think you've got some sort of disease or phobia. Perhaps we should go together to talk to a doctor about it."

"Don't be daft. I just want a beautiful home. Surely I'm not the only woman in the world who wants that?"

TGA: *(I watch Andre daily withstanding his wife's greed. She's not going to hoodwink me. I see a lot from my vantage point. If I were a human being my heart would break in two at the loyalty of Andre to the woman with whom he made a stupid mistake in the privacy of the woods. Never a thought given to the fact that he may have been tricked. Cast your mind back. Even Gran thought he was a good catch.*

Now he's dedicating a good proportion of his young life making amends to a selfish wife and sharing the upbringing of his own son, who mustn't ever suffer at the hands of a stepmother.)

Andre decided that he must be sure to assert his influence on the home. The thought had occurred to him that Christopher could turn out to be as materialistic as his mother, and that would be devastating. Forfeiting his own young years to

478

being a father in an unhappy home mustn't be doomed from the start. He would sing to his little boy and encourage him to sing as he grew. With a bit of luck, that could lead to him becoming a choir boy where he'd be exposed to influences from outside the home. "Yes, that has to be my objective for the future," thought Andre.

With that in mind, he decided to encourage a family social life by inviting friends round at the weekends for dinner, maybe finishing with a tot of whisky from Myra's bar. She'd enjoy that too. Friends would amuse and cuddle Christopher and slowly, bit by bit, they would influence him in some way.

Feeling motivated by his strategy, Andre felt his committed future had a very worthy purpose. That resolve helped him to cope when Myra said, "Do you know what I can visualise when we get our bigger house and grand piano, Andre?"

"Nothing will surprise me. Go on, spill the beans."

"It would look so rich; I can hardly wait. Can't you just see it, a beautiful candelabra?"

Myra wasn't even aware of the silence that prevailed.

Andre's plan had only seen them through two or three weeks when another issue complicated their lives. He started having difficulty in making love to his wife, which frustrated her beyond measure.

"Take me up to the bloody woods again if that will kick start your lust," she cried angrily.

The truth of that one pierced Andre's heart; he already suspected himself of lusting after her in the

479

beginning. She was angry alright. Nothing normally reduced her to swear words.

"Myra, I truly feel for you and I wish this wasn't happening. I don't know what my problem is. Perhaps with all the work I do, earning as much as I possibly can to buy you things you want, my energy has expired at the end of the day."

"Perhaps you should go and see a doctor."

"Perhaps we should go to one together. It's a problem for the pair of us after all."

That met with a black frown.

"Waste of time going. I know what any doctor would say. 'Are there any problems in your marriage?' and we both know there are."

"Why don't we go then? Your materialistic disease or phobia will come to light and we might get help on the NHS."

"There you go again. We've been here before. I don't have a disease. I'm not ill and I'll ask you kindly to get that into your thick skull."

"Don't get bitter about it Myra. I feel I need the warmth of a woman who can love me for myself and not for the worldly goods I can provide. If that's the root cause of my problem, then maybe you'll have to make a choice between material things or sexual love."

He was looking at her with raised eyebrows wondering what her answer to that would be. "This could be the catalyst that could solve all our problems," he dared to think.

"You think this is easy for me, don't you? I love my belongings. They're not goods and chattels to me. They're treasures."

"Well, if you refuse to go to a doctor, then we're stuck with the situation. Look, putting my cards on the table, I don't want a divorce. I want my son to grow up with the love of his own mother and I want to live with him in order to have an equal part in his upbringing. I am also prepared to go on providing you with your wants, until Christopher flies the nest as I said before. But...I know as sure as eggs are eggs that you can divorce me as quickly as that," Andre snapped his fingers, "if I can't provide your conjugal rights. The ultimate choice rests with you."

Arguments ensued and tempers were frayed, but no specific choice was voiced. So their lives dragged on.

TGA: (*On many nights, neighbours could hear rows going on and I wished I could tell the two of them that neighbours were starting to titter.*)

On one occasion, after an all-night row, Andre was too tired to go to work.

"Myra, something's got to be done about this rowing, otherwise I'll be losing work and won't be able to buy you things anyway. If going to the doctor is still not an option for you, then I'll move into a separate room and I promise I'll try from time to time."

"I shall never go to the doctor. To sit while you tell him your problem would just be too embarrassing for any wife, not only me."

So that's how life ticked over for them. Not by any means ideal for either, but they both knew it wouldn't be forever. They did make a sensible pact that they would never have terrible arguments in front of Christopher, so in that way, there was less disharmony in the household.

During March 1955, their nights became disturbed for a different reason. Christopher had started teething. Myra bore the brunt of that, because she didn't have to go to work the next day. Andre tried to keep sceptical thoughts out of his head. Was she really thinking of him, or her own purchases?

It was while Andre was having his evening time with his son, singing to him while rubbing his little finger along his bottom gums, that he heard a knock at the door.

"It's OK, Myra, I'll answer it," he called out to his wife who was washing up.

Taking Christopher, he opened the door to a lady who said, "Excuse me for disturbing you..."

A strong gust of wind blew in the door so Andre invited her into the hall.

She was a middle-aged woman wearing a fawn raincoat.

"Excuse me for troubling you," she continued. "You don't know me, but I think I know your mother."

"Oh no. I'm afraid you've made a mistake. My mother's dead. She died giving birth to me."

"Are you sure about that?"

"It's what I've always been told."

"Can I ask your name please?"

"Kliskey; Andre Kliskey."

"The lady I know is Mrs Kliskey."

Chapter 25

Busy Wedding Day for Annabelle

Monday 14th February 1955 was a momentous day for Annabelle.

The postman had delivered a small parcel with a BFPO postmark. It was a Valentine's Day card in the form of a musical box. She wound the handle on the side and it started to play the tune, *Let Me Call You Sweetheart,* with all the words written on the front. She cried, despite being deliriously happy as she sang along. Goosebumps crept over her body and she was immediately back in the courtyard.

Tuesday, 15th February 1955. The previous day's promised phone call still hadn't come.

On Friday 18th Feb, with Alice in bed and Annabelle washing up, there was a knock on the front door.

"Oh my goodness, it's you! Come in, and thank you for my Valentine's card. It was lovely."

Annabelle went to give him a peck on the cheek; instead he pulled her close and they kissed like lovers.

"Look, I don't know if you realise it, but I'm very serious about you." He immediately went down on one knee and, still holding her right hand, asked, "Annabelle Alessandro, will you marry me? Please?"

"Tony, I think I am in love with you, but I'm sorry. I can't marry you. It's not fair on any young man to be expected to take on a sick mother as well as his wife and I could never leave her."

"Annabelle, I'll not take no for an answer, whatever the reason. I can help you look after your mother. I'd like to help you look after your mum. Can I meet her?"

Alice and Tony chatted easily and he ended up making a supper of what he called 'buttered egg'.

"It's very nice. I enjoyed it," said Annabelle, "but I think it's just the Royal Navy's fancy name for scrambled egg."

On their own downstairs again Annabelle said, "Look Tony, I don't care if my mum did approve. I know it's not the right way to start. If you feel that much for me, then you must go to see the vicar by yourself. Then you'll never be able to blame me if you find it too much coping with your mother-in-law as well."

The next Saturday, while being on leave for a couple of weeks, Tony's bicycle felt more like a trapeze as he flew through the air to Enham to tell his bride-to-be that they would be married on Saturday, 28th May 1955 at 2pm. After they'd kissed and cuddled, he put his hand in his pocket and brought out a little black velvet box.

"I know you admired someone's solitaire in the pub one night, so I'd like you to accept this."

Tears welled up as she held out her left hand and he slipped the ring on her finger.

Alice was thrilled for her daughter and though she was becoming more and more frail, she still managed to do her sewing with the powered treadle machine. In fact, she had a lot of work on already. She was busy making a wedding dress and bridesmaids' dresses for Pam's wedding. Now she'd discovered that there would be another wedding to sew for. The fact that she could still be of some help gave her pleasure.

Annabelle's lifelong friend Pam Angel, who had in recent years become more of a penpal, because she returned to London to live when the war ended in 1945, was going to be married on 4th June 1955. Ironically, she found her man in Enham; the boy next door. He was one of the Cox boys who lived next door to Mrs Piggin, her nan. Things worked out well for them because Malcolm had gone to Battersea to serve an apprenticeship as a train driver, so by the time he became engaged, he was qualified in his job.

Annabelle got dressed up on the night of her engagement and they went to the Drill Hall. As usual, the ballroom dancing ceased at the interval. From there, they progressed to The Angel Inn and then the courtyard. As usual, the petting began, but an engagement ring for Annabelle was not a wedding ring.

"What's wrong Annabelle? We are engaged. Don't tell me I've got to get a can opener to get inside those drawers of yours."

"That wouldn't give you what you want either. I shall remain a virgin until my wedding night. I've been horrified enough by the family stories I've heard about my Aunt Lucia in London, who dabbled before wedlock. I'll never ever put myself in that situation."

"As you wish, Miss Perfection. I can see I'll just have to tick off the days."

"Proper thing an' all."

TGA: *(I'm not enthused by this match. It is common knowledge that a sailor has a girl in every port. Sadly, I can only watch and report. Angels can't interfere. If only they could.)*

On Monday evening, surprisingly, there were two knocks on the chimney breast wall. Two knocks were Annabelle's signal, so she ran round to Auntie Dolly.

"Call for you darlin'."

"Hello?"

"Oh my goodness. It's you Danny. You're a few weeks late."

She listened patiently to his excuses while tapping her fingernails rapidly on the table.

"It's alright, Danny. It really doesn't matter. I'm engaged to marry the one who did contact me on Valentine's Day."

He gasped, but before he had a chance to respond, Annabelle continued, "Look Danny, I know you're doing well in London and that's the last place I would want to live...so I think it's time for us to say goodbye. Are you still there?"

"Yes, I am. I'm kicking myself for being so stupid, but my career does dictate living in London, so I see I have no chance with you. I hope you'll be very happy in your married life and I'll never forget you, Annabelle. I'm sorry."

Alice wasn't making all the bridesmaids' dresses for Pam's wedding because of distances for fitting the London children, but she did make Annabelle's, which was a pale green colour, as well as all the dresses for the smaller girls who were grandchildren of the Cox family in the village. Malcolm's niece – daughter of brother Desmond and Lily Cox – was one. She was a striking dark-haired five-year-old at the time.

Annabelle thought she was going to be bridesmaid for the seventh time in her life, but now with her own sudden wedding plans preceding Pam's, she would be a Matron of Honour. The plans were for her to be chief attendant, as all the others were about nine years old or younger, plus one pageboy with black shoes and big silver buckles.

It was easy to imagine Pam's wedding being pretty as a picture with all the bridesmaids' dresses being made in different pastel shades.

For her own wedding, Annabelle didn't know where to turn first. Apart from going to work and looking after her mum and the house, she had to shop for material – not only for her own wedding dress, but for all her bridesmaids. She planned to have Pam Angel as her chief bridesmaid, her London cousins, Gillian and Linda, pairing each other, and Auntie Dolly's daughter, Stella, pairing her cousin Linda from Smannell, as well as tiny Sharon Osborne and Gary Bray, children of her London cousins. They made a supreme little couple; Sharon in the palest of pink dresses and Gary in a navy blue suit with a white topped peaked cap under his arm, looking exactly like a miniature groom.

She was well aware she could have cut down on tasks by having a smaller wedding, but stuck to her guns that a bride should surely have exactly what she wanted for her once-in-a-lifetime day.

When all that shopping was done, she still had to trek to Winchester for a further day's shopping for her 'going away' outfit, as well as something for her mum to wear.

The pace of her own life had become far too fast, but the reality of a news bulletin bought her feet back firmly on the ground. Sir Winston Churchill, whose blatantly truthful speeches had helped to guide many others, as well as Annabelle, during the Second World War when she was a frightened young girl, had resigned from Cabinet. That news shocked her and it came just seven and a half weeks prior to her wedding day. To her, Winston Churchill was an institution and she had a fixation that he would be in government forever. The reason given was bad health and his successor would be Anthony Eden.

"That's life, I suppose," thought Annabelle. "The ending of an era for Sir Winston and the beginning of one for me."

Alice was far too busy for Annabelle's liking and she was praying that her mother's health would hold out for the wedding. Unbeknownst to Alice, Annabelle had a discussion with Mrs Withell, the garage owner's wife. She was another village seamstress and had undertaken to finish Annabelle's wedding sewing, if the need arose. But stoic Alice had soldiered on and her sewing work was completed with a whole week to spare.

Annabelle too had done the last of her shopping. She'd had a nice surprise earlier on when Pam Angel came down from London so Alice could fit and finish sewing her wedding dress. Annabelle then had the company of her friend on the Saturday to go to Winchester, where they were successful in finding wedding attire for Alice as well as Annabelle's going away outfit. Together, they'd so much enjoyed their last day of freedom, which turned out to be a brilliant girlie day for two, as opposed to a chore for Annabelle alone.

Friday 20th May saw Annabelle finishing her last day at work before her wedding. There was still a mountain of jobs to be done, so she'd arranged to take the week off. As the working day came to a close, Annabelle blushed scarlet at seeing so many people gathered in her office to give her the wedding present they had chosen for her from their collection. It was a dinner and tea service, together with some baking dishes, made of Pyrex. Pyrex was an ovenproof commodity, although it was see through and looked like glass.

Mr Alan C Smith, Dr MacCallum and Mr Cox made appropriate speeches, followed by one from Matron Buxton. Hers was hilarious and broke down Annabelle's tensions. She said, "I wish all you females would tell me how you catch men. I obviously haven't got the knack."

Ted Wesley retorted, "Try wearing some high heeled shoes, trim down to a tiny waist the size of Annabelle's, wear a nice flared skirt, throw away your horn-rimmed glasses and buy a nice pink lipstick. That'll do for a start."

Matron replied, "Thanks for nothing my friend. Do you really want to employ a blind as a bat matron wearing high heels on her size 8 feet, making her over six feet tall? I'd end up looking like a transvestite. No thanks. I'd prefer to remain single."

The laughter had relaxed Annabelle enough to enable her to thank everybody for their generosity, saying how pleased her husband-to-be, a chef, would be with it. She ended her little thank you speech with, "And when I can get to my dictionary, I'll look up what 'transvestite' means."

The week running up to Annabelle's wedding was a laborious countdown. She cleaned up the house to make it presentable for all the London relatives and changed all bed linen for those staying overnight, which made the weekly wash loads and the ironing pile so much bigger than usual. So many jobs, too numerous to mention.

On Wednesday 25th May, George Wiltshire, Mr Ewers' dairy farmer, came early and clicked the necks of their last four chickens. Annabelle's day was wiped out plucking, gutting and slow boiling, in order to make chicken sandwiches and mugs of soup for the London relatives when they arrived on the day.

Friday 27th May was spent washing and curling hair and a thousand and one other jobs before boiling up the copper late afternoon so she could help Alice to have a bath and then have one herself.

On her wedding day, she was up at the crack of dawn. As soon as it was time for the village stores to open, she went to buy nice fresh bread to make a mountain of chicken sandwiches to be left on the living room table, along with plates of tomatoes, two cucumbers and packets of Smith's crisps. It was a source of great relief to her to have succeeded in providing for the Londoners when they arrived after their long journey.

Next, she helped Alice to get dressed in her wedding attire and, with half an hour to spare, went to the bedroom to get herself ready.

TGA: *(The reader, along with myself, will have watched Annabelle strive throughout her entire life to get as much education as possible to compensate for her lack of schooling. Remember the piano and the French lessons, etc? Today, on her wedding day, 28ᵗʰ May 1955, she would receive the ultimate education of life; the consummation of her marriage. Her passport to natural maturity as opposed to being a mature housewife since childhood.)*

She breathed a tremendous sigh of relief when Mr Betts arrived to take her, her brother Al – who was giving her away – and Alice, to St. Mary's Church in Andover for her wedding. There was no more work to be done.

The sky was overcast and the ceremony passed in a blur. Peter Fry, the Andover photographer, had said that if it was a sunny day he would experiment with colour film for black and white price, but that was not to be. Nevertheless, people said it was such a pretty wedding that it cheered up the day.

Annabelle had chosen deep pink for her chief bridesmaid, Pam, with graduated, paler shades of pink to correspond with the reducing ages of her pairs of bridesmaids. For her bouquet, Annabelle had chosen different shades of pink roses to match the shades of her bridesmaids' dresses, together with lots of pretty green Maidenhair fern. Regrettably, that glorious display of colour could only be recorded for posterity in black and white photographs.

Back at the Landale Wilson Institute, Tony and Annabelle welcomed their guests.

"I hope you'll both be very happy, Mr and Mrs Taylor," they all said, as they looked at her wedding ring.

That sudden realisation made Annabelle feel unsteady. She hadn't had a minute to even think of that. Inside she felt very sad to have lost her Italian name of Alessandro.

There seemed to be an endless stream of guests and Annabelle was so grateful when everyone was finally seated, Grace had been said by the Reverend Machin who had married them and at last they could eat. She couldn't even remember if she'd had breakfast. Although exhausted, she concentrated hard on behaving with bride-like decorum as she knew the bride would be the focus of attention. However, an old memory saved the day, bringing bride-like smiles to Annabelle's face.

Her hunger reminded her of the day Tony had first taken her home to meet his parents. There was a fine spread on the table and shy Annabelle, so used to being the one in control, was feeling quite out of her comfort zone. Nervously she remarked, "This looks absolutely delicious. I'm ravishing."

Mr Taylor, Tony's father, a very tall, hefty and somewhat formidable Victorian type replied, "I think the word you're looking for is ravenous."

Annabelle had never felt so embarrassed before, but now, with hindsight, she could see the funny side of it.

Speeches followed the wedding breakfast, to which Annabelle listened with intent; even Al, who gave her away, was kind to her. Her very sombre father-in-law, as different as chalk from cheese to her own lighthearted father, welcomed her with open arms into his family and thought his son was the luckiest man in the world to find such a beautiful and capable bride.

In the lull before the band struck up, Annabelle was horrified to hear that her London relatives were greeted by bread and butter sandwiches, as someone had eaten the chicken out of most of them! The finger was pointed at the groom's 12-year-old brother and his friends, now being caught downing stiff drinks from the tables of the minglers.

London relatives offered comforting comments, such as, 'You can't worry about such trivialities on your wedding day. Nothing must spoil it'.

Trying to put it behind her, Annabelle had a quick chat with Aunt Lucia from London. Her two grandchildren were the pageboy and partner Sharon, who were the children of Lucia's two daughters.

"It's such a comfort to know you're going to stay with my mum while I'm away. Thank you,"

"The least I can do, Annabelle. I'm glad to be able to help you. On Thursday we can have a long chat on the train home, when you'll be going to your friend's wedding in London."

"That's right. I'll have to get dressed up all over again next Saturday."

The band was good. Annabelle loved the dancing and, to the groom's dismay, every dance

493

was an 'Excuse Me'. That meant the ladies' partners could be changed by a tap on the shoulder.

Annabelle wished she could stay there all evening, but the clock reminded her that she had to go home and get changed into her going away outfit.

Back outside the Insty dressed in her deep pink costume with pencil skirt and white accessories, it was hard saying goodbye to her mum.

"You go away and have a lovely time, my love. I'll have a good time too with Aunt Lucia."

Mr Betts drove the happy couple, still with the white ribbons on the front of the car and tin cans dangling from the back, to Andover coach station where they boarded a Royal Blue coach to take them to Dover. The peace and quiet of that journey was a blessing for Annabelle. No more jobs to be done, just uninterrupted cuddles.

She hated the disturbance at Dover because from there they had to hail a taxi to take them to their honeymoon destination of Folkestone. Dover was a regular route for Royal Blue coaches, which made booking simpler.

"Strange place to come for a honeymoon," remarked the driver, who'd spied traces of confetti.

"That was my choice," replied Annabelle. "It conjured up a picture of nice old country folk and relics of the stone age, which we studied at school."

The driver pulled a face as if to say, "Where has this bride been all her life?"

It was late by the time they arrived at the guesthouse and for some unknown reason there was a firework display. After a long lovers' kiss,

Tony went to the window and opened the nets for a better view.

"What a welcome. Fireworks outside and fireworks inside. How's about that for a honeymoon!"

"I'm just going to the toilet."

Secretly, Annabelle took her nightie to the bathroom and got undressed there, glad to flop into bed without delay and end this long exhaustive week.

By the time Tony got into bed, she was almost asleep. A wandering hand disturbed her.

"Not tonight, Tony. I'm tired." She turned over.

"Good God Almighty. My mates'll never believe me when I tell them I felt like an old married man on my wedding night! Ah well. Folkestone doesn't know it, and neither does Annabelle...yet, but there'll be all day fireworks here tomorrow."

Chapter 26

Andre Finds Mother; a Tainted Miracle

Mrs Sullivan, still wearing her fawn raincoat, called for Andre on Saturday morning. She was taking him to her place of work where he could talk to the staff about their patient, Mrs Kliskey.

First, they took the bus to Banstead and then one to Sutton where Andre received the shock of his life. They alighted before getting to Sutton and Mrs Sullivan was leading him to the Belmont Lunatic Asylum.

There he was greeted by a Mrs Fricker, who looked up records that revealed that their Mrs Kliskey had been admitted on 13th May 1930, two weeks after giving birth to a baby boy.

"My God. This is too much to take in. Jesus. Do your records say who committed her to this life?"

"They do. It was a Mr Eugene Kliskey."

"The bloody bastard!" Andre stared at the floor for a long time. "That's my father. I'm sorry. It's just that I was brought up by a horrible stepmother and my childhood into teenage years was indescribably miserable. I'd go as far as to say she hated me."

"Mr Kliskey, this is a lot for you to take in. Would you like a cup of tea before you have a peep at the lady who I am sure is your mother. You are the image of her."

"Yes please. This is so shocking. My mother coming back from the dead; it's eerie. How does one cope?"

"If you'll excuse me, I'll love and leave you now, dear. I must get on with my work."

"Of course, and thank you Mrs Sullivan for putting me in touch with my mother."

Drinking his tea, Andre asked, "So is my mother a lunatic? And what on earth do you call her? Is she an inmate? Does she have a prison number? I'm on very strange ground here."

"We call your mother Mrs Kliskey, and we think of her as a patient. She sits in a nice lounge with the quiet ones. There is another room, of course, for those who need it."

"Would you like to have a peep at her now, through our window where we keep an eye on everyone?"

"Yes I would, please."

"Good God. It's uncanny." He paused for a while, grappling with reality. "As you say, I am the image of her. It's tragic. She's been locked in here for twenty-five years!"

"That's correct. She was admitted two weeks after you were born."

He detected that the lady might have had golden hair in younger days, although very greyish now. She was wearing a white blouse with a cherry red cardigan, but the armchair in which she was sitting restricted his view of her skirt and feet.

"She's sitting very straight. Is she an upright lady and can she walk?"

"Oh yes. She's very nimble and she often stretches her legs by having a walk around the room and looking out of the windows. She's only allowed into the garden with a chaperone for fear she might try to run away. She has nowhere to go, of course."

"The more I learn, the worse it gets. It seems she's had a rougher deal than I have. Can she hold a conversation?"

"Oh yes. She's very literate. She listens to the radio and as we take in daily papers, she always chooses to read The Times. In fact, she completes The Times' crossword every day."

"My God, what the hell do I say to her? Shall I tell her I think she's my mother?"

"Hard to say really. This is a first time experience for us too, but my instinct tells me to advise that honesty is the best policy."

When he'd finished his tea, Mrs Fricker asked, "Are you ready?"

"As ready as I'll ever be."

"Mrs Kliskey, you have a visitor."

"Really? Is it someone to take me home?"

Avoiding the question, she said, "It seems your son has discovered where you are."

She looked up in amazement. "But I haven't got a son. I had a baby boy once, but he must have died and that's why they put me in here."

"I'll leave the two of you to have a chat about it."

"Do you mind if I hold your hand?" asked Andre.

"I don't think that's a decent thing to do with a stranger, but you can shake it," Mrs Kliskey replied.

"How do you do, Mrs Kliskey. It's such a pleasure to meet you. Do you want any help with that crossword?"

"No, thank you. I usually manage to complete it by myself and it passes the time, too."

Andre found it difficult to know what to talk about and didn't want to outstay his welcome anyway, so after about fifteen minutes he said goodbye with another shake of the hand.

"I'll visit you again next Saturday. Would you like me to bring anything in for you?"

"No, thank you, I have all I need here."

"Cheerio for now then. I'll see you next week."

Andre explained to Mrs Fricker why he didn't stay very long.

"She seemed to have difficulty in accepting that I was her son. I can see I'll have to be patient. I so wanted to hug her and call her 'Mum', but it wasn't an option. I'll come again next Saturday."

"That's right. Gradually she'll get to know you and feel more confident with you."

TGA: *(Andre was seething as he ran home from the asylum. He wanted to kill his evil and wicked father, but decided he must be patient about that too. He would look after his mother first.)*

Myra asked how things went and he was grateful for that. However, things soon reverted.

"I've seen something in Banstead I want to buy for the hall. You'll be very pleased with me

499

because it's actually second hand. There was a notice in the bookshop window, so I went in. It's a magnificent grandfather clock. They are giving me first refusal. Will you buy it for us, Andre?"

"Myra, I'll buy it for you. Material things don't interest me at all. Right now I'm going up the corner shop and buy something for myself."

"Whatever's that?"

"I'm going to buy myself a packet of cigarettes. Finding your own mother back from the dead is a bit mind blowing."

Andre was out of his depth in the shop. They had shelves of different cigarettes and he had no idea which to choose. He eventually settled for a packet of 20 Players Navy Cut and a box of Bryant and May's safety matches.

"That'll be 22d. (pence) please, sir."

Back at home, Andre spent time with his baby son.

"Do you know, Christopher, you've got another Grandma?"

Christopher smiled.

"Good boy; it is good news, isn't it? She's my mum and I look like her. I wonder if you'll look like us when you grow up? She's Mrs Kliskey and do you know, I don't even know her Christian name. I must remember to ask next week."

It wasn't long before Andre came face-to-face with a grandfather clock in the hall when he arrived home from work one night. In his opinion, it was far too big for their little home and he had to remind himself that it was the price he was paying to keep his wife happy. Before going to bed at the end of the day, he went into the back garden to get some fresh air.

"Dear God," he said, looking up to the starry sky, "give me the strength to honour my commitment to Myra. It's harder than I ever realised."

He studied the clear night sky and recognised Orion's belt, which was a commonly known constellation. He also recognised one or two others and decided he'd like to learn more. On a clear night, they were free for anyone to study. The next time he went to Sutton Library he borrowed a book on astronomy and gradually got very interested in the subject. "Might come in useful one day if I ever have to illustrate a book about the heavens," he thought.

On Saturday he was greeted by Mrs Fricker.

"Mrs Fricker, I don't even know my mother's Christian name. "Can you tell me?"

"Yes, of course. She is Amy. Just Amy. She did have a sister, Susie, who visited often in the early days. Susie was desperate to get her out of here, but as she wasn't the one who committed her, her hands were tied. Susie's husband died of consumption and a few years later she married a Scotsman and they went to live on one of the Orkney Islands. She corresponded with Amy for a time, but over the years that has dwindled."

"Seems my mother's had no luck at all in this world. Has she spoken about me at all since last week?"

"Yes, she has. I had a chat with her and explained that you are her son. She's fascinated by that, although had difficulty in connecting you with the baby she lost."

"I would like to take her home for a day soon, so we can gradually build our relationship. Would you allow that?"

"I don't see why not. Not wise to take her on a public bus though. I think a taxi to take her door-to-door would be advisable."

"Splendid. Thank you. I'll go and see her now."

"Hello, Mrs Kliskey. How are you today?"

"I'm well, thank you. I've been looking forward to your visit. Mrs Fricker told me you are my son."

"That's true. I am and we do look very alike."

"Oh dear. How strange. You're a man and I didn't have one of those; I had a baby boy. I've always understood he died."

A few weeks later Andre took his mother home. When they got out of the taxi at his gate, Mrs Kliskey began to tremble.

"Whatever's all that going up and down the road?"

"It's only cars. They won't hurt you."

"They're frightening me. I want to go back home."

Pointing he said, "There's my door. You're going to spend today with us," and got her indoors as quickly as he could.

Myra greeted them at the door. For his mother's benefit, Andre closed the front door quickly as she had obviously become institutionalised. She had spent decades behind closed doors, protected from the modernisation of traffic.

"Mrs Kliskey, I would like you to meet my wife, Myra."

"Thank you for having me, dear."

"Hello, Mrs Kliskey; come in the lounge and sit down. Dinner won't be long."

"It smells very nice, thank you."

As she entered the lounge end of the room she drew breath. "This is very, very posh. You must be rich."

TGA: *(She couldn't have said anything better for Myra, who had a fixed gaze on Andre as if to say, "I told you so. Even your mother approves.")*

Andre sat with his mother while Myra served up the dinner.

"With any luck we'll be able to eat before Christopher wakes up."

Mrs Kliskey couldn't really do justice to the roast beef dinner. It appeared she had a very small appetite, but she got on better with the tinned peaches and tinned Nestlé cream.

Christopher's crying interrupted the clearing of the dishes. Myra was the one to run upstairs to collect him.

As Myra was proudly showing him off, Mrs Kliskey senior said joyously, "Oh my dear, how wonderful. Bless your heart." Tears were streaming down her face and her arms were outstretched. "Thank you for finding my baby."

A chill swept over both Andre and his wife. They had not been prepared for this. Andre took Christopher in his arms and placed him on his

503

mother's lap. Mrs Kliskey held him tightly to her bosom.

It was heartbreaking to watch her crying her eyes out as she rocked backwards and forwards and said, "Thank you, Lord. I didn't think I'd ever see him again. Thank you, thank you!"

Christopher started to cry and Andre struggled to get his baby back from his mother. He then gave Christopher back to Myra who took him out of the room.

"Mrs Kliskey screamed at the top of her voice, "Please don't take my baby away from me again! You mustn't. I'd rather die." She continued to sob. I hate you, I hate you," repeating the same three words over and over.

Carrying the baby, Myra went up the road to the telephone kiosk and phoned for the taxi.

Mrs Kliskey put up a big fight as they tried to get her out of the door. "I won't go without my baby," she screeched. She was very angry and behaved like a vicious animal. "I'm not going to lose him again!"

"Sorry about this," Andre said to the driver.

"That's OK, mate. I can see why she's in the asylum." He screwed his finger to his forehead.

That hurt Andre. It would have been better directed at his father.

"Come with us, Myra, and bring the baby too. We'll get my mother back to her secure home."

Mrs Fricker, who was just about to go off duty, was appalled to see them back so soon.

"I'm afraid she's very upset," said Andre. "She thought our baby was hers."

"Oh my goodness. Come on my dear," she soothed, putting her arm around Mrs Kliskey. "Let's get you to your bed. You two please wait. We'll talk about it when I've got Mrs Kliskey settled. I'll call a doctor to give her a sedative. I'm sorry you've been so upset, Mrs Kliskey.

"That's better. I discussed the situation with the doctor and he's going to keep her sedated for a couple of days. After that, who knows, perhaps we can work the oracle by telling her she must have been dreaming."

She took the three of them into a private room where they could all be seated.

"I'm sorry for your traumatic time Mr and Mrs Kliskey. It's not something anyone could have foreseen. It appears as if time in here has just stood still for her."

"Well I feel it's all my fault for wanting to take her home in the first place. If only I'd been satisfied with visits."

"You mustn't reproach yourself, Mr Kliskey. You were trying to make amends to her for past events. However, the doctor advises that you stop visiting your mother."

"That will be hard to swallow, but I understand she was quite contented here before I found her. Perhaps I can call in from time to time just to look through the window and have a peep at her, hoping to see her get back to where she was before I came in on the scene?"

"Of course you can. Now go home and enjoy your baby. You weren't the only one involved in this sad episode."

Andre went to look at his mother twice more only. The first Saturday Mrs Sullivan was on duty.

"Mr Kliskey, I do apologise for the traumatic saga I inflicted upon you. I really wish I could put the clock back."

"Please don't fret yourself, Mrs Sullivan. I'm very glad you knocked on my door and I found out that my mother was alive, even though it's better for her that I no longer visit. You have absolutely nothing to reproach yourself for."

The following Saturday, Andre told Mrs Fricker that he would not visit his mother any more, even for a peep.

"It's as though I'm returning her to the dead woman that's always been in my life, and that truly is worse than torture. However, I will always keep you informed of my address and telephone number if ever I'm rich enough to own one, so you can contact me if her health starts to fail. I would like to pay for a decent funeral for her and send her off with at least one family member in attendance."

"How touching, Mr Kliskey. I'm so sorry. I appreciate this has been a heartbreaking experience for you and I'll certainly write your wishes in bold letters on her file." They shook hands as she said, "My very best wishes to you."

As he was leaving, Andre turned and asked, "I wonder whatever happened to my mother when I was born to lead her into this terrible isolation?"

"That one I can answer, Mr Kliskey. If the same thing happened today, your mother could be treated. It's a medical condition known as Post Natal Depression, but that condition was unknown in the days when you were born."

506

"So what my mother really needed was a doctor and certainly not a lunatic asylum."

"That's absolutely correct, with hindsight of course."

After delivering a completed job to Heinemann's, Andre seized the opportunity to go to the National and the Tate Galleries to look at some paintings as a distraction from recent miseries. He saw many beautiful paintings, but the one that left a lasting impression was *The Avalanche*, painted by Philip James de Loutherbourg. It matched his mood.

Travelling home, he thought what a wonderfully satisfying hobby that must have been and resolved that by the time he was 40 years old, he would start to paint. Furthermore, he decided there and then that his first attempt would be a watercolour of St. Paul's Cathedral, a most distinctive London building that he had admired for a long time.

TGA: *(Andre was currently absorbed in his studies of astronomy and often went into the garden on clear nights to find the stars and constellations about which he'd been learning. His new ambition to become an artist appeared to me to be satisfying an inner rebellion against the materialism he'd had to endure through married life.)*

The next Saturday, Andre travelled in a totally different direction. East Croydon was his destination. He had a few scores to settle with his father.

"I've come to pick a few bones with you, Mr Eugene Kliskey."

They were in the scullery and Andre could see a deep collared overcoat hanging on one of the pegs. "Put that coat on."

"Are we going out?"

"No. Just do as I say."

Andre had noticed the coat was double-breasted. "Now do all the buttons up."

Andre was a bigger, taller man than his father and he was strong.

TGA: *(I watched in awe as Andre picked his father up as though he were a child and hung him on the peg. To my utter amazement, the deep collar, together with the support of the double-breasted coat under his armpits, held him there. I can share with you the fact that I was looking forward to the next bit. In my view, Mr Kliskey deserved whatever was coming to him.)*

Andre shouted, "I am a very angry man today and I want answers. Where is my mother?"

"She's dead."

"Where is my mother?" He shouted more loudly.

"She's dead."

Shaking his fist in front of his father's face, he growled, "Look, I don't have to listen to this shit. My mother is alive today and she's a very clever lady. I know because I've seen her. In fact, I look very much like her and she is the mother I've been deprived of all my life. I repeat, for your thick skull; my mother is far from dead. I found her in a

lunatic asylum, where she was committed by a Mr
Eugene Kliskey, two weeks after my birth. So, let
me ask the question again. Where is my mother?"

Mr Eugene Kliskey looked as though he was
about to cry, or maybe die.

"You're right. She went loopy after you were
born."

"I want to hear you speak the truth. Tell me
what you did, just as I've told it to you."

"I committed my wife to Belmont Lunatic
Asylum after you were born."

"Thank you. Did you think to call a doctor
before taking such drastic action?"

"No."

"No? What was the reason for that?"

"I can't remember."

"Don't bullshit me again. I'm beginning to get
the measure of you. It probably suited your
purpose.

He spat in his father's face as he hissed, "Scum
of the Earth!"

Andre couldn't be more livid. Everything was
becoming clear. It was as though he knew all the
answers without being told.

"When did you meet my stepmother?"

Silence was his answer.

Andre put his hands up and clasped them round
his father's throat.

"I'm prepared to swing for you. I don't want
any more fuckin' lies. You've been caught red-
handed. If you've any common sense at all, you'll
come clean now or suffer the final sacrifice."

Quietly, to the point of inaudibility, he replied,
"I met her before you were born."

"Say it louder. For God's sake, be a man for once in your life!"

Louder this time, he repeated, "I met her before you were born,"

"So it did suit you to have my mother locked up for life?"

"I'm sorry."

"No you're not fuckin' sorry. How did your new woman feel about having a baby dumped on her?"

"She didn't mind."

Andre punched his father on the jaw.

"How DARE you lie to me when I know first-hand how she hated me. Try again, scumbag!"

"She wanted me, but she didn't want you."

"At last. At last. Straight from the devil's mouth. Now I'm free to get on with the rest of my life without murder on my hands. As for you...I hope you rot in hell."

"It's small reward, but there is great comfort for me to leave you here shitting yourself daily, wondering when the police are going to catch up with you, YOU PATHETIC BIGAMIST!"

Addendum

I have watched over these two young humans through thick and thin and it has been my earnest desire that they should meet each other and fall in love. What a miracle in the whole scheme of things that would have been. Life has been tough for them both and what very considerate, understanding and grateful partners they would have made for each other, with the giving and receiving of respect as well as love. It would have been the perfect adult life for them.

Instead, they have made their own beds and married other people. Annabelle still cares for her ailing mother, but now has a husband who says he'll help with that. Andre has his own roof so is free of his stepmother. My job is done.

Thank you readers for your interest in my account of their lives. Goodbye and God bless you all.

The Guardian Angel

P.S. Nearly forgot to tell you that I can see into the distant future, so you may be as pleased as I was to see what it holds.

My Annabelle,

Today is Monday, the second day of yet another week in a lifetime of Mondays.

Our Sunday, my Annabelle, was good; for a while we were together and though there were people, they were but passing shadows of the day, for within my heart there was only you, and today in my allotted one hour for lunch I think and dream, hold you close to me and give you my thoughts, for at this moment in time this is all I want from life. Together in my mind we are completely isolated and walk only along the paths and valleys where dreams are made. So read my words and head softly with me, my Annabelle, thro the valleys and glades where, because we love, we may wander; there shall be no snares or pitfalls, or people to impose their wills upon us, for our kindred spirits are as one and our love for eternity.

Let us then walk together, my Annabelle, hand-in-hand thro those valleys that are within my mind, that you shall share so completely with me. Let us start from the sunset on a warm summer evening and walk into the night; the night of soft dark velvet that shall enshroud us and then into the dawn of another day. Close your eyes my sweet one and together we shall step into those realms.

The winds of time caress us as we drift into the galaxies of the night for here, with peace and silence so complete that the beating of two hearts are as one, shall we float together into the beautiful 'bridal veil of Cygnus', the veil of light and matter that flows out into the Universe, further back than life itself, twisting, turning and

*undulating into the long ago, so far back in time
that the fairy story words, 'Once upon a Time', no
longer have meaning. Into this 'veil' shall we
lightly tread and into your golden hair shall I
weave the 'veil', for you are at the centre of all
things; but how may I bear to look at you standing
thus amid a backcloth of eternity. Sweet Annabelle,
my soul cries out in its love for you. Hold fast to my
hand lest I lose you.*

*From Cygnus on this night shall we travel to
Andromeda. Andromeda who was rescued from
'Hydra' by the mighty hunter 'Orion' on the swift
feet of 'Pegasus', into the vastness that is
Andromeda, into her heart that is the 'Great Spiral
Nebula', of the Universe where worlds are in the
making and being destroyed within the blink of an
eye. Let us stand together to witness this creation;
but together my Annabelle, we are strong and the
creation is but the beating of our hearts and the
awe that we feel, and is of the love and tenderness
that is between us.*

*Float then my Annabelle with me, enshrouded in
your veil of time, for the haunting beauty I hold
within my mind of you steers us among the stars
and the beauty of creation that surrounds us.*

*I hold you close and tightly my Annabelle; in my
embrace you are serene and happy. It must always
be this way for in our love there is magic; a love
story that has no end, as timeless as the paths that
we tread in my mind.*

*Soon must our journey thro the night end, for
somewhere another day calls to us, but yet we shall
not part for in the closing of an eye the winds of the
night shall again embrace us.*

513

So, my Annabelle, are we not at the very beginning of a fairy story? And thro my pen will flow the words that write the chapters, for there is a 'Once upon a Time' for us – and – 'they lived happy ever after.' We must make that come true.

Time, as ever, is against me and soon I must end, though truly my mind will not cease to think and dream. I saw you last evening and tho for no time at all, it is now another memory.

Sweet Annabelle, I know not how many words I must write to you. I know only that in the writing there is peace within me; a peace that is not always there when I wish to be with you and circumstances will not allow. I think that things may be hard for us, but always we must rise above and know that we love and that one day we shall be together.

Andre Kliskey

Song Title Acknowledgements

WEE WILLIE WINKIE, poem written by William Miller, 1810 – 1872. First published date, 1841. Public Domain.

TWINKLE, TWINKLE, LITTLE STAR. Public Domain.

MY GRANDFATHER CLOCK. Written 1876. Words and Music by Henry Clay Work; 1832 – 1884.

GLAD THAT I LIVE AM I. School Hymn. *A Little Song of Life* by Lizette Woodworth Reese. American Poet; 1856 -1935. Public Domain.

MY LITTLE DOLLY IS VERY SICK. Anonymous.

WON'T YA' BILL. Anonymous.

MELODY and *MARCH.* Both by Lea Thorne. From music book *WRIGHT'S PIANOFORTE TUTOR* by Albert H Oswold.

GOD SAVE OUR GRACIOUS KING (The National Anthem). Lyrics by Henry Carey; music by Thomas Arne.

RULE BRITANNIA. Lyrics by James Thomson; music by Thomas Arne.

RUN RABBIT RUN. Lyrics by Noel Gay and Ralph Butler; music by Noel Gay.

WITH A SONG IN MY HEART. Lyrics by June Hershey; music by Don Swander.

I KNOW WHY (AND SO DO YOU). Lyrics by Mack Gordon; music by Harold Warren and Mack Gordon.

LITTLE MISTER BAGGY BREECHES. Lyrics by RP Weston; music by Herman Darewski.

SMALL FRY. Hoagy Carmichael.

SOMETHING ABOUT A SOLDIER. Noel Gay

THE LAUGHING POLICEMAN. Lyrics by Billie Grey; music by George W Johnson.

WE'RE GONNA HANG OUT THE WASHING ON THE SIEGFRIED LINE. Jimmy Kennedy.

STROLLING. Bud Flanagan and Joseph McCarthy.

THERE'LL ALWAYS BE AN ENGLAND. Ross Parker and Hughie Charles.

ALWAYS. Irving Berlin.

WANDERING VAGABOND. Unable to establish.

THE ROSE OF TRALEE. Lyrics by Edward Mordaunt Spencer; music by Charles William Glover.

THE KNIGHTSBRIDGE MARCH Signature tune of Radio Show 'In Town Tonight'. Eric Coates

KISS ME GOODNIGHT SERGEANT MAJOR. Art Noel and Don Pelosi.

YOU ARE MY SUNSHINE. Paul Rice, Jimmie Davis and Charles Mitchell.

ROLL OUT THE BARREL (BEER BARREL POLKA). Lew Brown and Jaromír Vejvoda.

I TAUT I TAW A PUDDY TAT. Billy May and Warren Foster.

HAVE A GO JOE. Signature tune, start and end of radio show *HAVE A GO.* Jack Jordan. My endeavours to establish with BBC Radio whether there is a copyright issue with the signature tunes have been unsuccessful. If that situation remains when ready to go to print, I hope it can come under the heading of 'Fair Use'.

JEZEBEL. Wayne Shanklin.

OUT ON THE MIRA. Allister MacGillivray.

HI-LILI, HI-LO. Lyrics by Helen Deutsch; music by Bronislau Kaper.

WEDDING MARCH. Mendelssohn.

MOTHER NATURE AND FATHER TIME. Words and music by Kay Twomey, Fred Wise and Ben Weisman.

EVERYTHING I HAVE IS YOURS. Lyrics by Harold Adamson; music by Burton Lane.

LET ME CALL YOU SWEETHEART. Lyrics by Beth Slater Whitson; music by Leo Friedman.

CHRISTMAS CAROL ACKNOWLEDGEMENTS

HARK THE HERALD ANGELS SING. Charles Wesley, 1739.

WE THREE KINGS. John Henry Hopkins, 1857.

NURSERY RHYME ACKNOWLEDGEMENTS

RING-A-RING O' ROSES. First published 1881 in England. Traditional.

LONDON BRIDGE IS FALLING DOWN. First published in 1744 in England. Traditional.

PRAYER ACKNOWLEDGEMENT

THE LORD'S PRAYER

Postscripts

Typo gaffs, which I found before publishing:

The Shite House for The White House

Pubic Domain for Public Domain

Additional Information:

Lady Louise Mountbatten, sister of Lord Louis, was a great fundraiser for Enham.

Winston Churchill was demoted from 1st Lord of the Admiralty after Dardanelles and Gallipoli.

The Landale Wilson Institute in Enham Village Centre became popularly known as The Insty for the children of WW1 settlers.

THE FOURTH FORM AT ST. MICHAELS - THE NEW BOY, which was performed by young boys in the Insty in Enham and surrounding villages, was one of three Will Hay sketches recorded by Columbia. Despite popular perception that the schoolboys on these records were Moore Marriot and Graham Moffitt, Will's film stooges, they were not yet part of his team. Will and his Fourth Form at St. Michaels' sketch were chosen to appear in the Royal Command Performance at the Alhambra Theatre, Leicester Square, on 12 February 1925 before King George V and Queen Mary.

Papworth Hospital, which was founded by Sir Pendrill Varrier-Jones' pioneering work in 1917, became famous many years later for heart transplant surgery.

Song Title Acknowledgements: I understand, from various sources, that song titles are in the public domain. I have written words of songs in full where I have established they are already in the public domain, or are anonymous.

Because Annabelle's story is a sequel to my first book, *World War 1 and Workhouse Hill*, which used fictitious names, I have had to continue to use the name of Alessandro (Aless) in this book. I would like it written in black and white for posterity that we were actually the Enham family known as Mr and Mrs Marchi (Alberto and Annie), Peter and Pauline.

The era of this book takes place before decimal currency was introduced in the UK on 15 February 1971.

Photo Gallery

Enham British Legion

This picture relates to the 'Preface for Annabelle's Story', where Mr Cotton is referred to as one of the four men considered 'temperamentally unfit for village life'.

Enham Christmas Party

Enham children's annual Christmas party;
inadvertently not mentioned in book, but very
worthy of mention. Alice is on stage, sixth from
left, with bow fronted jumper. Annabelle is in
front of Alice on her left and Al is on
Annabelle's left.

Alberto in open-necked shirt with settlers

Alberto on LWI verandah with settlers. He is
wearing an open-necked shirt because he can't
do up a tie with only one arm. Dr Stockdale is
centre front with Rev. Webb, front right.

Mr F Cox with Mr Arthur Cotton and Desmond, Mr Cox's Eldest Son

Mr Arthur Cotton, a permanent lodger with the Cox family during all his Enham life (picture 1, Enham British Legion and *Preface for Annabelle's Story* also refer) and Desmond, Mr Cox's eldest son.

Success Cookery Book; Walnut Ketchup

Walnut Ketchup. A labour of love!

Mr and Mrs Cleverley

ANDOVER ADVERTISER

[Photo] [Press Fay]
Mr. and Mrs. E. H. Cleverley, of 8 Anton Lane, Enham-Alamein, who celebrated their golden wedding on 16th June. All the people in the Centre were present at the reception, held in the Landale Wilson Institute.

Mr Cleverley was the village baker for many years. His bakery was in the building across the lane from 9 Newbury Road, Enham. (The back of the Charity shop in 2016.) His son Fred, known as Sunna, assisted his father. His bread, lardy cakes and doughnuts, sold themselves as the delicious aroma wafted over the village.

Mr and Mrs Cleverley had 9 children: George, Reg and Sunna, Daisy, Dora, Elsie, Hilda, Marjory and Violet.

Mr F Cox displaying cup

Mr Freddie Cox displaying his veggies and
the cup he won at the Enham Horticultural
Show.

Enham Civil Defence etc., WW2

Standing: FG Moody, AEG Coxhill, F
Dukes, JW Chambers, JB Edwards.
Seated: W Baker, FC Cox (Senior Warden),
R Charlton, MBE, JP (Chief Warden), W
Holley (Head Warden), J Beaven (Deputy
Chief Warden), Mrs PA Chambers, JJ
Stewart.

Annabelle on left with Pam Angel

Bandy and knock-kneed

The Mikado in the Insty

Standing from left: Mr Geoghegan,
Mr Tempero, Mr Marchi (Alberto Aless),
Unknown, Mrs Tempero, Frances Taft,
Ada Guest (leading lady), Mr Moody,
Mrs Chambers, Mrs Peacock,
Mr Pilkington, Mrs Johnstone,
Mrs Moody.

Sitting from left: Christine Sutton,
Joyce Withell, Nora Geoghegan,
Alice Piggin, Peggy Brooks,
Evelyn Dickens.

Enham Glamour Girls

ENHAM

Help from the "Glamour Girls."—
A small party of married women
living in the village, who syle themselves the "Enham Glamour Girls,"
have been very successful in their
efforts to raise money for national and
charitable causes during the past
three years; their initiative is worthy
of emulation in other places. They
have given £15 for a rubber dinghy,
£10 for the Merchant Navy, £5 for
Wings for Victory, £10 for Hampshire prisoners of war, £10 for the
Red Cross and St. John Joint
Prisoners of War Fund, and recently
(by means of a dance) £20 for the
Merchant Navy Comforts Fund; a
total of £70.

The £70 raised by The Glamour Girls in WW2
would equate to approximately £3000 today.

Enham Youth Club, 1945

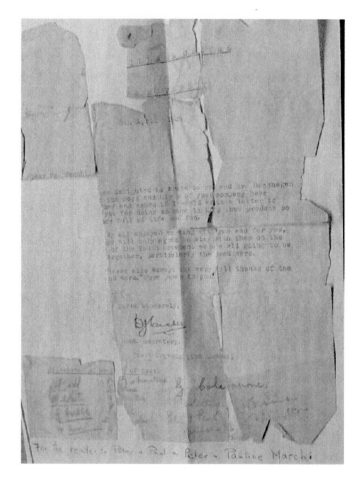

As WW2 was coming to an end, the British Government made it a priority to promote youth clubs to get young people out and mixing again.

Wonderful neighbour, Auntie Dolly on right, Alice on left

Auntie Dolly, a wonderful neighbour and second mother to Annabelle. Leaning against the wall is evidence that she has some log sawing waiting to be done.

Ann Cox, 3rd prize, Enham Horticultural Society Annual Show

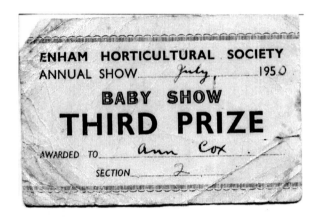

Baby Ann wins 3rd prize in a baby show at one of Enham's Horticultural Society Shows.

Official Opening Ceremony of Alamein Housing by Field Marshal Viscount Montgomery

From left, ignoring children in front: Mrs Tarrant,
Mrs G Withell, Mrs Dowling, Mrs Moody,
Hazel Wood, Mrs Rose, Mrs Marchi (Aless), Mrs Ewers,
Field Marshal Viscount Montgomery of Alamein,
Rita Rose, Mrs Mesney with Stella in front, Mrs Wood,
Olive Cronin, man behind unknown, Maureen Broughton,
Dinah Waite.

Enham Alamein Souvenir

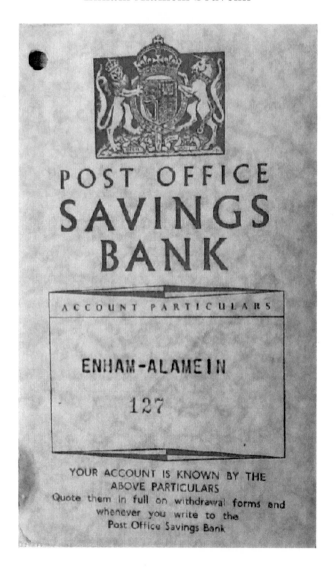

Annabelle's Post Office savings book. A
souvenir of the unusual village name.

Annabelle with her mother at the Carnival Queen Competition, Andover Drill Hall

Annabelle with her mother, Alice, at Drill Hall dance for a meeting of all the village queens in the Carnival Queen Competition.

Village Carnival Queens on Lorry

Annabelle, Miss Enham Alamein, top row, second
from left.

Enham WW1 Settlers Buried in the Churchyard of St Michael's and All Angels, Knight's Enham
(Not everyone had headstones)

Barrett, Albert	Gurr, Edwin
Blackburn, Edward	Hallin, Albert
Bland, Joe	Highfield, James
Brooks, Arthur	Johnson, Sam
Browning, George	Livermore, George
Chambers, John	Loffler, Sidney
Close, William	Marchi, Alberto
Coombs, Edgar	Mesney, Phillip
Cotton, Arthur	Mulligan, James
Cox, Freddie	Murphy, Paddy
Cox, Norman	Parsons, Charley
Coxhill, Arthur	Piggin, Robert
Crabbe, Jack	Rodrigues, Christopher
Crannis, Jesse	Rose, Jack
Davies, William	Saunders, Walter
Dawkes, Albert	Shergold, Stanley
Dixon, Geordie	Skippings, Len
Dowling, Percy	Smith, John
Edwards, Cocker	Soper, Sydney
Ewers, Ted	Spratt, Herbert
Geoghegan, Joe	Tempero, James
Greener, John	Weeks, Steve
Guest, George	Wood, Joe

Enham WW1 Settlers Buried in the
Churchyard of Christ Church, Smannell
(Not everyone had headstones)

Armes, Eddie	Evans, Tom
Baker, Walter	Gamblin, William
Barrs, Arthur	Haggar, Frank
Basting	Hayes, Sidney
Betts, Frank	Holley, William
Bird, Albert	Howland, Arthur
Brant, George	Johnstone, Fred
Bright, Herbert	Lowman, Victor
Broughton, William	Pilkington, Charles
Budd, George	Robson
Canning, James	Roll, Alfred
Chant, William	Rutter
Cooper, Henry	Spencer, Charles
Davis, Alfred	Tarrant, Joseph
Dickens, Albert	Truman, George

A few WW1 settler names that should be mentioned in the context of living out their disabled lives in Enham, although they were not buried in either of the two churchyards mentioned above, are:

Arnold, Joseph	Shears, Allan
Cronin, William	Stuart, Jack
Hall, Fred	Withell, Charles
Moody, George	

Lightning Source UK Ltd.
Milton Keynes UK
UKOW01f0416220816

281204UK00002B/31/P